Schooling the Freed People

D1546136

THE UNIVERSITY OF NORTH CAROLINA
Chapel Hill

Schooling

the FREED PEOPLE

Teaching, Learning,
and the Struggle for
Black Freedom,
1861–1876

RONALD E. BUTCHART

© 2010 The University of North Carolina Press

All rights reserved

Designed by Jacquline Johnson

Set in Walbaum MT

by Keystone Typesetting, Inc.

Manufactured in the United States of America

The paper in this book meets the guidelines for permanence
and durability of the Committee on Production Guidelines for Book
Longevity of the Council on Library Resources.

The University of North Carolina Press has been a member of the
Green Press Initiative since 2003.

Library of Congress Cataloging-in-Publication Data

Butchart, Ronald E.

Schooling the freed people : teaching, learning, and the struggle
for black freedom, 1861–1876 / Ronald E. Butchart.

p. cm.

Includes bibliographical references and index.

ISBN 978-0-8078-3420-6 (cloth : alk. paper)

ISBN 978-1-4696-0729-0 (pbk. : alk. paper)

1. Freedmen—Education—Southern States. 2. Education—Southern States—
History—19th century. 3. African American teachers—Southern States—
History—19th century. 4. Reconstruction (U.S. history, 1865–1877) I. Title.

LC2802.S9B874 2010

371.829'960730750934—dc22

2010011936

cloth 14 13 12 11 10   5 4 3 2 1

paper 17 16 15 14 13   5 4 3 2 1

Contents

Illustrations and Tables

Illustrations

Tables

Preface

If there is one constant in historical writing, it is revision. Each generation of writers brings its own perspectives and troubles to bear on the past, finds new material, and reinterprets old sources. The result is new understandings of old stories, new images and portraits, revised pictures of the past. Reconstruction's history bears dramatic evidence of that process. Attentive readers of that history have moved the earlier images of the actors and processes of Reconstruction to dusty mental storage rooms, replacing them with new, often starkly different images. Reviled villains have been redrawn as tragic victims; heroic causes have been revealed as ignoble, murderous treachery.

Yet in one corner of Reconstruction historiography, the history of the schooling of the freed people, interpretations have shifted, but the portraits of the primary actors have been only lightly retouched after a century of historical study. Whether their history was captured by W. E. B. Du Bois, by historians in the Dunning tradition, or by revisionists of the last three decades, the foreground of that picture has remained remarkably unchanged. While each historiographic tradition has intended something different by the exact shadings and details of the portrait it rendered, the main figures in the portrait have been largely untouched in the process.

W. E. B. Du Bois sketched the most enduring elements of the educators' image. Describing what he called "the crusade of the New England schoolma'am," he wrote, "Behind the mists of ruin and rapine waved the calico dresses of women who dared. Rich and poor they were, serious and curious. Bereaved now of a father, now of a brother, now of more than these, they came seeking a life work in planting New England schoolhouses among the white and black of the South."[1] Several of the salient elements of the teachers' enduring portrait were etched deep in that poetic description: the teachers were New England schoolmarms, a description that implied that they were young, white, single, female, well educated; they were endowed with particular regional character traits of New Englanders whose interpretation shifted depending on the standpoint of the viewer.

Meanwhile, southern historians associated with the Dunning school of interpretation, contemporaries of Du Bois, began work on the same portrait. They painted a darker, more sinister background against which to set the teachers and filled in a middle ground that suggested that these New England schoolmarms were naive, foolish, or despicable. Summarizing much of his own scholarship and that of other southern historians, Edgar W. Knight described the teachers as part of a " 'messianic' invasion of the South" whose blind zealotry resulted in "much insane intolerance" in the region.[2] Henry Lee Swint, author of the most exhaustive study of the freedmen's teachers published before 1980, characterized the teachers as predominantly from New England and, as a necessary consequence, abolitionist fanatics and impractical visionaries when not simply incompetents, frauds, and malingerers.[3]

In the Dunning rendition, the mood, tone, texture, and quality of the portrait shifted dramatically from that produced by Du Bois, yet the foreground figures remained largely unchanged. The teachers were young, single, white women from New England, of evangelical Protestant roots and abolitionist convictions. Since the teachers gave months or years to the freed people, the early writers imagined that they were from privileged homes. While Du Bois rendered them selfless and noble, southern historians portrayed them as fanatical meddlers at worst, foolish idealists at best.[4] They were drawn south to find husbands, to enjoy a respite from harsh New England winters, or because they were too incompetent to teach in northern schools. Wilbur Cash added an ad hominem flourish to the picture, describing the teachers as "horsefaced, bespectacled, and spare of frame."[5]

A subsequent generation of historians dissented sharply from those writing within the tradition of William A. Dunning. The revisionists painted out the dark, foreboding background and redrew the middle ground. Gone were images of fanaticism, zealotry, and retribution. Though one revisionist perspective portrayed teachers who were engaged in a slightly suspect "domestication of the South,"[6] the dominant portrayals by the revisionists were positive, if often cast in martial metaphors—the teachers were "soldiers of light and love," "gentle invaders," an "army of civilization."[7] More often, they were the champions of black literacy, if too often racist.[8]

But the foreground, the image of the teachers themselves, shifted only

marginally. Revisionists more clearly delineated the teachers' privileged
middle-class background, affirmed their New England roots, and established their competence. James McPherson, for example, argued that the
teachers were predominantly of New England stock, either by birth or by
the birth of their parents, and reasoned from that claim that they carried to
the South a Puritan and abolitionist ethos.[9] Jacqueline Jones, working from
a sample of over 350 teachers, found that the typical freedmen's teacher
was "white, in her late twenties . . . Congregational. . . . She came from a
relatively comfortable small-town or rural 'Yankee' home. Her father
[was] a native New Englander," and three-fifths of the teachers were
themselves from New England. Building on that portrait, Linda Perkins
claimed the teachers were "upper or middle class" New England women
who "saw teaching in the South primarily as an escape from their idle and
unfulfilled lives."[10]

After a century of work, then, historians have revised their interpretations of the teachers' motivations and the deeper meaning of their service,
but the characteristics of the teachers, the foreground of the collective
portrait, has remained largely unchanged. Gazing from the canvas are
teachers who were youthful, white, single women from New England.
They professed a northern variant of evangelical Protestant faith, subscribed to abolitionist perspectives, and gained social advantages from
relatively privileged homes.

It is time to start anew with a clean canvas. Working from a broader
range of sources and a database of thousands of the teachers, *Schooling in
the Struggle for Black Freedom* reveals that the foreground figures in the
enduring image represent only a minority of the teachers, and even their
portrayal is inaccurate. Because the portrait has been incomplete and inadequate, it has distorted our understanding of the first generation of teachers in southern black schools and our evaluation of early southern black
education. The corps of teachers who actually taught in the freed people's
schools bears little resemblance to the reigning image. A more accurate
foreground will have important implications for the ways the next generations of historians are able to paint the middle ground and the background
—the contexts and interpretations of the work of these "soldiers of light
and love."

The new portrait offered here requires a more varied palette than employed by earlier writers, for the teachers were far more interracial than
historians have realized.[11] One of every six northern teachers was African
American at a time when blacks constituted a bit over 1 percent of the

northern population. Effectively, then, northern African Americans participated in the education of their race at a rate twelve to fifteen times greater than northern whites. The color of the teachers is even more striking when the entire teaching force, northern and southern, is considered. More than one-third of all the teachers in the southern black schools between 1861 and 1876 were African Americans. The constant reference to the freed people's teachers as white paints out thousands of the teachers.

When historians have spoken of the teachers as "New England school-marms," it is likely that they understood that not all of the teachers technically came from the six states that constitute New England. Some historians may have used New England or "Yankee" as a proxy for a broader geographical indicator, but one that suggests specifically the presumed mentality of New England—politically and racially more liberal than much of the nation, prone to reformist action, well educated, self-righteous, and entrepreneurial. Still, the impression remains that New England dominated the educational movement in the South.

In fact, New England as a region was not the dominant source of the teachers. It contributed not more than one-fifth of all the teachers. Over one-half of the teachers were southerners. White southerners, almost entirely ignored in earlier histories, accounted for nearly one-quarter of all teachers who can be positively identified in the southern black schools before the end of Reconstruction, and doubtlessly far more than that.

Historians of every stripe have argued that the teachers were abolitionists. For the earlier generation of historians, that was an epithet. To be abolitionist, in their view, was to be irrational, naive, utopian, spiteful, and motivated by an abiding hatred for the South and all of its traditions. Abolitionism brought on an unnecessary civil war, bankrupted the South for a century, and sowed the seeds of racial antipathy. Abolitionist teachers, in turn, imported abolitionism's messianic zealotry into the heart of the South to turn a contented but gullible people against their natural friends and defenders. Revisionist historians, immersed in the scholarship of the 1960s and 1970s that traced the roots of the modern civil rights movement back to the abolitionists, reversed the formula. Abolitionists stood on the moral high ground, developed a cogent critique of slavery and oppression, and worked with African Americans to improve northern black life. Abolitionist agitation gave moral direction and backbone to the eventual outcome of the Civil War. Revisionists assumed that abolitionism pervaded the freedmen's education movement, providing a vision of an interracial society to guide educational activities. Some revisionists found the movement insufficiently abolitionist, however, noting its many compromises with racist actions and policies and its teachers' lack of empathy with or understanding of the aspirations and demands of the freed people. Yet the predominant image of the teachers within more recent scholarship retains a strong abolitionist cast.[12]

It is no longer possible to cling to that image, however. First, as argued in chapter 4, few of the teachers self-identified as abolitionists in their letters of application for teaching jobs, though they were often writing to leaders of the prewar abolitionist movement, and few can be found in abolitionist organizations in the years before the war. Further, those few who clearly did identify themselves as prewar abolitionists, or who can be so identified in other ways, followed dramatically different trajectories in their work in the South when compared to the great majority of the teachers. The occasional abolitionist teacher spent many more years— often the remaining decades of his or her life—in service to the freedmen, while teachers with no clear evidence of abolitionist leanings did well to muster two years of work in the South. The leadership of the northern effort to assist the freed people traced its origins to one or another of abolitionism's streams, but the teaching force itself was not, overall, particularly abolitionist.

Second, prewar abolitionism itself was no guarantee of a commitment to postwar black advancement in American society. Abolitionism was about ending slavery, but opposition to slavery could be rooted in many concerns unrelated to the victim of slavery. There was no necessary relationship between embracing the abolition of slavery and working affirmatively to assure that legal emancipation would be followed by political and economic emancipation. Indeed, the northern state that made the greatest strides toward a presumably abolitionist stance in the late 1850s and 1860s contributed the least to the education of the freedmen. Iowa, with perhaps the strongest antiblack laws and practices in the 1850s, had become, by the end of the 1860s, one of the nation's most racially liberal states, yet mustered the lowest proportion of its population to serve the freed people.[13]

The small group of women and men who spoke clearly of their abolitionism when they went into the South and who went on to devote entire lifetimes to the freed people, then, were not merely abolitionists. They were race radicals. Abolition was not the end of their commitment. Their work among the freedmen was motivated by a dedication to black freedom, and they lived that dedication. This study explores that motivation, but attends as well to the dominant motivation among the majority of the teachers, finding that black freedom was virtually absent in their thinking and acting.

In the final analysis, abolitionism's legacy is too ambiguous to carry much weight in understanding the trajectory of education for the freed people. Abolition was as much about antebellum economics and politic as about black America. After slavery's end, the issue for America was the reconstruction of the South—and the North—to create greater equality, greater opportunity, greater community, a goal that continues to elude the nation in the twenty-first century. The portrait of the teachers must reveal the remarkable minority of teachers who strove to add their mite to that reconstruction, yet it must at the same time portray accurately the majority, who had no interest in social reconstruction. For them, the social panacea was the spiritual and moral regeneration of the freed people; the problem was the freed people themselves, not the society in which they had to construct their freedom. All the teachers were courageous, doubtless, but not all courage is equally effective in moving history out of its timeworn paths.

For traditional historians, the emplotment of the teacher as youthful reinforced their rendering of these teachers as frivolous, immature, and misguided. For revisionists, the same youthful image suggested idealism and energy. It may have reflected their own political roots in the youth movement of the 1960s and early 1970s. In either case, however, the image was inaccurate. The mean age of white teachers in their first year of work in the South was thirty.[14] If youthful idealism had not yet ebbed for these teachers, it likely had been well tempered by the time most of them opened their school doors. If a few were frivolous, the vast majority were mature women and men with a decade or more of adult work behind them. Paint them mature, for surely they were.

The portrayal of the teachers as female is one of the more curious foreground details, for certainly no historian who has studied the teachers believes that women were the only teachers. Yet most descriptions speak of schoolmarms, not schoolmen, and almost uniformly apply a female pronoun to descriptions of the teachers. Jones claimed that the corps of teachers in Georgia was 80 percent female; McPherson claimed the national movement was 75 percent female.[15] The gender composition was, in fact, a good deal more complex than that. Across all groups of teachers, women and men taught the freed people in almost equal numbers. There were, however, sharp and telling differences in gender participation within racial and regional groups, as detailed in the chapters that follow.

Preface

What, then, of the social class background of the teachers? Relative social class status is always a difficult issue historically. It consists of measures of impermanent occupational status, relative wealth, changes over time, and, above all, complex social, economic, and political relationships among people. It has no clear rules or definitions. It exists; yet describing it seldom yields satisfactory insight into its meaning. Gathering comparable social class evidence on individuals from a variety of regions in the nineteenth century is daunting; amassing sufficient evidence regarding enough individuals to make empirical claims about them as a group multiplies the challenge. Nonetheless, evidence drawn from the manuscript censuses for thousands of teachers is suggestive. It troubles the notion that the teachers were relatively affluent. Indeed, what may be most interesting about the teachers is the numbers that were from relatively poor or declining families. Many of the single women had been boarding with families to whom they were not related well before their service in the South and appear not to have had families of their own they could rely upon, a sure marker of economic marginality; some were widows; some were desperate to find work as teachers in the South, for they could no longer compete on equal terms for positions in northern schools with young teachers willing to work for low wages while living at home. Much work remains to be done on this question, but it appears that as many of the teachers came from the lower tiers of a genteel but declining middling class as came from lives of prosperous leisure. Certainly very few can accurately be portrayed as yawning through "idle and unfulfilled lives."

Historians' stock-in-trade is the art of creating compelling images, painterly portraits, intricate mosaics, to hang in the public galleries of our collective memory. The historical images change as new historians take up the image-making media. This study offers a more complex, but hopefully more accurate, portrait of these fascinating women and men, black and white. All contributed to black literacy, though, as the diversity within their ranks suggest, some mustered great courage and commitment to serve the ends of emancipation while others can only be said to have contributed.

THIS STUDY IS NOT ONLY ABOUT THE FREED PEOPLE'S TEACHERS, THOUGH teachers should loom large in any study of education. The study seeks, rather, to sketch a broader picture that captures as much as possible about the educational effort of the freed people to become a free people. It examines the essential work of the freed people themselves seeking to become authors of their own narratives. It studies the teachers in relationship to the freed people's goals and particularly in relationship to how the work of teaching contributed to, contradicted, or was simply irrelevant to, the efforts of the freed people to construct their own freedom and secure the fruits of emancipation. It studies the classrooms, seeking to understand and interpret the curriculum and pedagogy embedded in early black education and whether the pedagogy, particularly, and the curriculum, secondarily, bore any relationship to the ends to which the freed people sought to bend their education. Throughout, the study considers the first generation of black schools and those who worked in them in the context of an abortive Reconstruction.

The book begins with a meditation on the freed people, literacy, and the response to emancipation, holding that there is no historical precedent to the African American demand for access to knowledge or historical equivalent to the black effort to assure that access. It then devotes a chapter each to three distinct groups of teachers who worked with and against black aspirations. Chapters 2 and 3 examine the teachers that have been most fully ignored by previous scholarship, the black teachers and the southern white teachers. Chapter 4 reexamines the northern teacher. To add texture and color to those chapters, each begins and concludes with brief biographical sketches of individual teachers who exemplified themes explored in the chapter. Chapter 5 is a history of the black classroom in the first generation of southern black freedom. While the curriculum of early black schools has received some attention, and the curricular issue of industrial education is central to many debates about black education in the second and third generation after freedom, historians have ignored the pedagogy practiced in the first generation of schools. This chapter attempts to bring the teaching, not just the teachers, into focus. Finally, the study ends with a very different sort of meditation than the one that launches the study. African Americans responded to freedom with an unprecedented expectation to gain literacy and proved unequivocally that they could master an alien curriculum under teachers applying an uncompromising pedagogy. Deployed in opposition to their aspirations, however, was the overwhelming power of white supremacy. The white South expressed that power forcibly to blunt black aspirations. In the course of Reconstruction, white supremacy gained legitimacy as the North sought reunion on southern terms. Such power as education might convey had little efficacy against the brutish power of resurgent white nationhood.

Preface

each of which merits some explanation. First, much of the narrative is based on traditional archival sources. I have sought to reach into a far greater range of archives than previous studies of the teachers of the freed people, however, in part to overcome the overreliance on American Missionary Association (AMA) teachers and archives that mark most work to date. Freedmen's education was not merely the AMA writ large, thought it has largely been interpreted as though it were. Uncritical uses of AMA sources have masked much that was going on in southern black schools and among the teachers. The reason for the heavy use of the AMA papers is not difficult to fathom. The AMA archives are large, wonderfully organized, and accessible, while others are smaller, scattered, and more difficult to access. Yet accessing the latter is essential to an effort to fully comprehend the first generation of postslavery black education.

Second, many of the study's specific claims about the corps of teachers are based on the findings of a large-scale database, the Freedmen's Teacher Project. I launched the project many years ago to answer many of the questions I had about the teachers after I completed *Northern Schools, Southern Blacks, and Reconstruction.* The project attempted to positively identify as many as possible of the women and men who taught in southern black schools between 1861 and 1876. The resulting database currently includes more than 11,600 individuals representing upwards of two-thirds of all the teachers who actually worked in black schools over the fifteen years of the study (most of the remaining teachers are probably unrecoverable). To be included in the database the project required, at minimum, a last name, the state in which the individual taught, and the years she or he taught. For most of the teachers, however, the database includes far more information. Among other things, the project sought prosopographic information on each individual, including race, gender, birth year (from which to calculate a teacher's age when she or he began teaching), birth state, home prior to teaching, all years in which the individual taught, supporting organizations if any, parents' occupation, parents' birth state, family wealth, the teacher's occupation both before and after teaching the freed people, all locations where the individual taught, religious affiliation, familial relations among teachers, evidence of prewar abolitionist leanings, education attained by the teacher, and, when appropriate, higher educational institutions attended.

To gain that information, the project mined all missionary society and freedmen's aid society publications and combed archival resources, including the archives of the aid societies and missionary organizations; state archives; the records of the Freedmen's Bureau, the Freedmen's Bank, and the Southern Claims Commission; military and pension records; college alumni catalogues and archives; and manuscript census returns, including slave schedules, city directories, and similar resources. The project also sought biographical and autobiographical accounts of the teachers, narrative accounts of the schools, and secondary studies of the teachers, the schools, and other accounts that would provide further data.

It is likely that the project has identified nearly every teacher who taught from the establishment of the major aid societies until the late 1860s. However, as southern states began staffing the schools, and after the withdrawal of the bureau and many of the aid societies, the data becomes less complete. A few states, notably Texas, Alabama, and South Carolina, preserved remarkable records for the very earliest years of state support for black schools (only two or three years of records in each state); Louisiana and North Carolina have partial records for the period; and the teachers in the District of Columbia can be identified with great accuracy through printed sources. For most of the rest of the South, however, the picture after 1870 is incomplete, though highly suggestive.

The Freedmen's Teacher Project database forms the foundation for this book. The study that follows is not a quantitative study in the normal sense of the word, however. It relies on findings from the database for many of its conclusions, and many of its stories could not have been constructed without it, but the narrative presents rounded frequencies and percentages rather than precise numbers, complex calculations, and the other mechanics of quantitative history. The data is not the sort that lends itself to sophisticated quantitative analysis, in the first place. More saliently, however, I have attempted to breathe life into the data, to capture voices where they still exist, to tell the actors' stories even when the voices have died, and to provide relevant data when it enriches the archival material or reveals patterns and tendencies that cannot be known from archival sources alone. The database and the findings that derive from it will be published in the future, including more precise calculations not generally provided here. My intention is to publish the database in a form that will allow users to locate individuals and groups as well as to perform their own calculations. Claims made in the narrative that are based on evidence in the database are indicated in the endnotes as having been drawn from the Freedmen's Teacher Project.

Preface

schools and their teachers. The earliest generation of historians condemned the schools and the teachers because they were, those writers held, political, designed to indoctrinate gullible black citizens into Republican views. Subsequent historians, myself included, were inclined to see the teachers, and by extension, the schools, as insufficiently political or politically timid. The leaders of the northern aid effort, for their part, frequently denied any political intentions and joined with the Freedmen's Bureau in warning teachers against bringing politics into their classrooms.[16]

All such debates, denials, and directives, however, ignore the central truth about education. Education is always, everywhere, and inevitably political. It cannot be otherwise, for no form of education can be conceived that does not carry within it an intended outcome; that outcome will inevitably spring from one or another vision of human possibility and will intend to have an influence on its recipients' future and thus on the distribution of justice, goods, and resources. Since politics is ultimately about the distribution of justice, goods, and resources, education is political. Thus, if the northern teachers had, in fact, been abolitionists and carried their abolitionist dreams into classrooms, the effort surely would have been political. To that extent, the traditional historians were right. By the same token, however, had northern teachers abdicated the work to white supremacist southerners, the efforts of the latter would also have been political. The two poles of political intent would have been worlds apart. Those two poles did not define the range of possible political intentions, of course. Further, those who declared themselves apolitical could not, in the end, be apolitical; their work, too, would have political effects, though probably political effects that were not conducive to extending the reach of emancipation.

The task of the historian, then, is not to judge whether the freed people's schools and teachers had political intent or political effects—it could not have been otherwise. The task, rather, is to identify the competing and overlapping politics enacted in the variety of classrooms these teachers created for this emancipated people, and to seek relentlessly to understand which of the many possible politics of education, or politics of emancipation, held the greatest potential for realizing the fullest freedom for the freed people.

That is the difficult burden this volume attempts to carry. It concludes that not many of the teachers taught toward, or even gave much thought to, an expansion of black emancipation and freedom. Some taught to curb and deflect black freedom. Yet at the same time, the pedagogy and curriculum practiced in many classrooms carried their own political logic, a logic that occasionally promoted black intellectual emancipation beyond teachers' intentions.

A NOTE ON QUOTATIONS: TO REDUCE THE INTRUSIVENESS OF THE EDITORIAL voice in quotations, I have, as far as possible, abandoned the tradition of noting misspellings and grammatical infelicities within quotations with the ubiquitous and usually unnecessary *sic*. I have moved *sic* to the endnotes when an error was in the original. In a very few cases, where a misspelling reads like a jarring typographical error, I have retained the bracketed in-text *sic*. I have likewise reduced other editorial conventions to a minimum, expanding abbreviations or an author's shorthand only when the meaning might not be clear from the context.

Acknowledgments

A scholarly project that has spent as many years in gestation as this one owes far more intellectual debts than its author can ever fully acknowledge. To the many colleagues, friends, and institutions that I cannot enumerate here, you have my deepest gratitude.

Portions of the research for this book were supported by grants from many organizations. Cortland College, the University of Washington, Tacoma, and the University of Georgia provided travel grants and research grants. Grants, stipends, and research fellowships from the National Endowment for the Humanities, the Iowa Historical Society, the Virginia Historical Society, the Radcliffe Institute for Advanced Study at Harvard University, and the New York African American Institute added substantially to my ability to explore important archival collections. Finally, a major three-year grant from the Spencer Foundation was crucial in completing the work, allowing me and my assistants to spend months working in dozens of collections from Texas to Maine. The material support of these organizations is gratefully acknowledged. However, they bear no responsibility for any views expressed here.

Literally hundreds of librarians and archivists across the country, from small, local history collections to large state libraries and university archives, graciously answered questions, located fugitive files, delivered trolley loads of manuscripts, and offered invaluable suggestions. Most must remain unnamed here, but I particularly offer my thanks to Roland M. Baumann, archivist at Oberlin College, who welcomed me each time I visited the college and patiently answered dozens of subsequent letters. Donaly Brice of the Texas State Archives located crucial material that had never been catalogued. A special thanks, too, to Gwen Henderson, archivist, Guilford College; Patricia J. Albright, archivist, Mount Holyoke College Library; Emory S. Campbell and Veronica Gerald of Penn Community Center; Catherine Schlichting, curator, Ohio Wesleyan University Historical Collection; and Patricia and Lloyd Paterson of the Iowa Yearly Meeting of Friends. The Patersons not only made previously unexamined records available but also transcribed one important document for me before I arrived and provided coffee and congeniality during my stay.

I was the fortunate recipient of unsolicited information and historical documents from strangers who heard of the Freedmen's Teacher Project. Among others, Judith Hillman Paterson and Barbara Sellers Darden sent photographs and documents from ancestors who had worked with the freed people. Frances Karttunen and Barbara White offered primary source documents and the results of their own research to enrich my understanding of teachers from Nantucket. Perhaps most extraordinary were the offers from Linda Breaks and Elizabeth P. Marlowe, descendants of Ellen Murray, to visit their homes and examine rare family papers and photographs of Murray's fifty-plus years of teaching at St. Helena, South Carolina.

Many colleagues from around the country added their wisdom and grace to this effort. Ann Duffy, Susan M. Yohn, Polly Welts Kaufman, Carleton Mabee, Kathy Kerns, and Afua Cooper shared material from their own research. Sandra Boyden O'Neal spent hours organizing the first iteration of the database that became the Freedmen's Teacher Project. Russell Irvine gave me access to his remarkable collection of material on early black college graduates. Derrick Alridge, Elliott Barkan, Paul McBride, Margaret Nash, Judkin Browning, and John Inscoe read portions of chapters and offered invaluable advice. In the final four years of the project, an unrivaled group of undergraduate and graduate research assistants— Rebecca Lane, Regina Barnett, Mary Ella Engel, Christina Davis, Melanie Pavich, Drew Swanson, and Michele Lansdown—gave hundreds of hours of dedicated work, but more importantly gave their enthusiasm and ideas to the project. It owes its current form to them. My thanks, too, to my many colleagues who, over the years, have patiently listened to conference papers, offered criticisms, and encouraged me as I struggled to rethink this project and locate new material, among them Ann Short Chirhart, James D. Anderson, Wayne Urban, Daniel Perlstein, Valinda Littlefield, Barbara Finkelstein, Stephen Kneeshaw, Richard J. Altenbaugh, William J. Reese, Rob Levin, and Linda Eisenmann.

The last thing one says in any communication is usually the most important. That is particularly true in this case. This book may never have been completed if it were not for my most loyal but unsparing critic, Amy Rolleri. Ferocious organizer, chief research assistant, unfailing muse, and best friend: you are my inspiration.

Acknowledgments

Chapter One

At the Dawn of Freedom

The long, long years of *law* against slaves learning to read,
has created in them a deep determination to master all the
difficulties that lie in the way of gaining knowledge now
that a way is opened.

National Freedmen's Relief Association, 1863

I never saw people more anxious nor Schollars
labor harder to learn.

*Robert Lindsey, former slave owner and
Confederate veteran, 1869*

Their steady eagerness to learn is just something amazing.
To be deprived of a lesson is a severe punishment. "I got no
reading to-day," or no writing, or no sums, is cause for bitter
tears. This race is going to rise. It is biding its time.

Laura Towne, 1877

At the very dawn of freedom, well before the nation moved grudg-
ingly toward formal emancipation, southern black slaves began to
forge their own destiny. From the first days of freedom, through
the displacements of war, and into Reconstruction, they pursued many
strategies calculated to assure their self-emancipation. During the war,
they fled plantations to reach Union lines. They reconstituted families,
built their own churches, negotiated contracts. And they demanded access
to literacy. They raised teachers from the literate among themselves, welcomed teachers from afar, even urged former slave owners to teach them,
and filled schoolhouses to overflowing. Out of their great poverty they
raised funds to buy land for their schools, supplied the labor to build the
schools, supported teachers as best they could, and maintained such an

effective network of schools across the South after the Civil War that W. E. B. Du Bois could argue that the postwar system of southern public education arose from the foundation laid by the freed people.[1]

Slavery's great failure lay in its inability to crush the black longing to read and write. The dream of literacy would not die despite two and a half centuries of bondage and enforced illiteracy. Many of the slave states made it a crime to teach slaves to read and write. Where black literacy was not banned by law, it was effectively banned by custom. Many slaveholders meted out fearsome punishment to slaves who were caught with reading or writing materials. Literacy opened the possibility of encountering ideas opposed to human bondage and carried the potential of written communication between black conspirators. More important ideologically, keeping the masses of African Americans illiterate contributed to the myth of racial inferiority, a conveniently circular logic: blacks were intellectually incapable of mastering the skills of literacy; illiterate blacks were proof of black intellectual incapacity. Though some slaves succeeded in stealing their literacy and an occasional slaveholder taught a favored slave to read and write, it is likely that by the time of the American Civil War, not more than one in ten southern blacks were literate. Yet the black desire for literacy burned bright to the very end of slavery.[2]

African Americans acted on the possibilities of freedom with an overwhelming surge toward the schoolhouse door. As W. E. B. Du Bois observed, African Americans responded to their flight from slavery differently than any other largely illiterate people freed from bondage. Most former serfs and slaves have assumed that ignorance was their natural lot, or they have embraced their folk wisdom as superior to formal learning. "American Negroes never acted thus," Du Bois wrote. "The very feeling of inferiority which slavery forced upon them fathered an intense desire to rise out of their condition by means of education."[3] Seventy years earlier, as the freed people's response to emancipation was first manifesting itself, John W. Alvord, superintendent of freedmen's education within the Freedmen's Bureau, made the same observation. "This is a wonderful state of things," he wrote in his January 1866 report. "We have just emerged from a terrific war; peace is not yet declared. There is scarcely the beginning of reorganized society at the south; and yet here is a people long imbruted by slavery, and the most despised of any on earth, whose chains are no sooner broken than they spring to their feet and start up an exceeding great army, clothing themselves with intelligence. What other people on earth have ever shown, while in their ignorance, such a passion for education?"[4]

At the Dawn of Freedom

The education of the freed people was, first and foremost, an education by African Americans, the work of the freed people themselves and of black Americans from the northern states. The freed people welcomed the help of northern white teachers and northern aid organizations, though they resented the paternalism and arrogance of the white efforts. In the end, however, the black community gave much more toward their own educational emancipation than did the far wealthier and far more numerous people that surrounded them. Indeed, the efforts of whites in black schools from the dawn of freedom and into Reconstruction were often equivocal and contradictory to the best interests of a truly free people. But to understand that story, it is necessary first to explore the unprecedented response of African Americans to freedom and the freedom to learn.

The freed people's demand for literacy overawed all efforts to accommodate it. In the first decade of freedom, teachers often taught in classrooms numbering one hundred students or more. Harriet Buss, teaching alone on an isolated island plantation in South Carolina in 1863, had 118 students in her school.[5] Fannie J. Scott taught over 200 students with her sister in Vicksburg in 1864 and delighted in her students' great "zeal to learn."[6] A graduate of Mount Holyoke established the first black school in Sumter, South Carolina, in the summer of 1865, and immediately attracted over one hundred students. She gave that school to two other teachers and ventured further into the interior, establishing a second school in Dover Depot that quickly had one hundred students.[7] In 1866, Trinity School in Augusta, Georgia, "one of the smallest schools in the city," had over 160 students on its rolls and over one hundred in daily attendance studying under a single teacher.[8] In 1869, a black teacher working on the coast of Georgia reported that she had to close her school to new students when enrollment "increased to 125 and they kept coming."[9] In 1872, Sallie B. Gove had 130 students a day, "all crowded together in a small house that has neither door nor window." Two months later she had gained an assistant, but her school had increased to over 200.[10] As more teachers were recruited, classroom crowding eased, though students continued to number fifty or more per class in the cities before the 1870s.[11]

Nor did the black demand for schools fade after its initial flowering in the springtime of emancipation. Despite predictions that black schooling was a passing fancy of a childlike people, despite the precipitous decline in northern support by the end of the 1860s, and despite rising violence against black education in the course of Reconstruction, the freed people were determined to educate their children, even as poverty drove the adults back to fields and shops. More than a decade after emancipation, Elizabeth Hyde Botume reported that her students at Beaufort, South Carolina, continued to protest having to take recess and were reluctant to "put up their work when the bell rings for the closing of the school."[12] Caroline Alfred, who taught in the black Claflin School in Columbus, Georgia, beginning in 1867 and observed the Deep South's descent into terrorist violence in the 1870s, could still report in 1875 that "the interest in the school among the colored people seems greater than I have ever known it."[13] "It rained one day last week," Laura Towne wrote in her diary in 1877, "but through the pelting showers came nearly every blessed child. Some of them walk six miles and back, besides doing their task of cotton-picking. Their steady eagerness to learn is just something amazing."[14] In the course of a single decade, black school attendance quintupled from less than 2 percent of all African Americans on the eve of the American Civil War, virtually all in the northern states, to nearly 10 percent by 1870, held down not by lack of desire but by lack of teachers and funds. In the following decade, it tripled again, to nearly one-third of black children of school age.[15] The initial burst of black schooling was not confined to elementary literacy; a mere decade after emancipation, the southern freed people and their supporters had established well over one hundred secondary and postsecondary schools, most of which continued to serve black students far into the twentieth century.[16]

The first teachers to respond to this fierce will to know were themselves African Americans. Months before northern missionary societies and freedmen's aid groups organized their work, black teachers who for years had shared the forbidden codes of literacy in the shadow of slavery threw off their veil of secrecy. In Washington and Baltimore, where free black children and an occasional favored enslaved child had quietly attended private black schools before the war, black teachers opened their schools to all black children. Around Norfolk and Alexandria, Virginia, and on the Sea Islands of South Carolina, where Union forces gained their first toeholds in the Confederacy, other black teachers opened the first "free" schools.[17]

By the end of 1861, at least forty southern black teachers had expanded their schools or established new schools to accommodate the swelling masses of eager students. Six months later, those forty southern black teachers constituted nearly half of all teachers working in the freed people's schools. Fifty more were teaching by the summer of 1863, including nearly a dozen northern black teachers. By the time the war ended two years later, over 280 African Americans, most of them literate southern blacks, were answering the urgent call of their people. African Americans constituted one-eighth of the nation in 1860; literate African Americans could not have accounted for one-fiftieth of the nation.[18] Yet here in 1865, at the dawn of freedom, well over one-quarter of the freed people's first tutors were their own people. Some of those early black instructors taught briefly, until more capable teachers could be found, but most taught much longer than their northern white counterparts.[19]

The freed people did not wait for experienced teachers to begin the literacy work. So eager were they for schools that black settlements organized themselves into learning communities or created schools and pressed their literate members into sharing their knowledge. Slaves fleeing into Kansas in the first confusion of the war immediately started a school in Lawrence with one hundred students. Within days of the Union occupation of New Orleans, black schools sprang up and literate free blacks were urged into service as teachers. The black community pressured commanding general Nathaniel Banks to organize the black schools of New Orleans into a public system. When the federal government suspended the schools in November 1865, black New Orleans immediately opened private schools across the city staffed with black teachers.[20] In 1864, an agent of the National Freedmen's Relief Association went into the rural parishes of Louisiana to establish schools but reported that "the colored people themselves were ahead of us," with flourishing schools in operation supported by a tuition system that exempted orphans and students with fathers in the military.[21] When Mary S. Osborne, a northern white teacher, went to Church Creek, Maryland, in 1865 to establish a school, she found that the people had already organized one "immediately on their emancipation, and for nearly a year those who had been able by any means to gain a knowledge of letters have been imparting it to others."[22]

In Georgia the freed people, "assisted by a few white friends," created the Georgia Education Association in January 1866, a sophisticated organization with county-level affiliates, each with its own officers. The task of county affiliates was to create schools, "provide the schoolhouses, employ and pay the teachers," with expenses to be borne by "the scholars and their parents."[23] Even earlier, the freed people of Marietta, Georgia, had created the Marietta Freedmen's Association, possibly the model for the later statewide organization.[24] One year after the war ended, thirty of the thirty-five black schools in Missouri were "sustained almost entirely by the struggles of the colored people." Thirty-three black teachers taught in those thirty schools.[25] The spontaneous movement of southern African Americans to launch their own schools and support their own teachers prompted one Freedmen's Bureau agent to contrast their work with southern whites. In Wilmington, North Carolina, he wrote, "the Freedmen have started a school of their own, and employ at their own expense a colored teacher. A similar movement is commencing among the Freedmen in several other places, evincing a thirst for knowledge and a desire for improvement that finds *no parallel* among that numerous and degraded class, the 'poor whites.' "[26]

The military witnessed equivalent educational enterprise among black troops and black civilian laborers. Those black adult learners bought spellers and primers, cajoled literate white soldiers to tutor them or chaplains to set up classes for them, and subscribed funds to pay teachers for their services. One black regiment raised $700 in four months for its own education and donated another $60 to maintain a school for the black children of a nearby town.[27] Black laborers working in one white regiment prevailed upon the regimental chaplain to open a school for them in their few leisure hours.[28] The 7th U.S. Colored Infantry established a literacy education program for the black noncommissioned officers. Those men in turn and on their own initiative created classes for their privates, teaching the soldiers what they had learned in their own lessons.[29]

Southern African Americans emerged from bondage penniless, often with little more than the clothing on their backs. Their stupendous poverty was rendered more grinding in the years immediately following the Civil War. Their embittered former owners attempted to do without their labor or routinely defrauded African Americans when they did hire them. Extraordinary crop failures due to floods, droughts, and insects in the later 1860s made matters worse for whites and blacks. Yet in spite of their poverty, the freed people found ways to purchase land for school purposes, lumber for the schoolhouse, and schoolbooks for themselves and their children. Their unpaid labor built the schoolhouses. They paid tuition to teachers and often boarded the teachers as well. They supplied fuel for heat in cold weather. In Georgia, for example, by late 1866 the freed people were fully supporting fifty-six of the state's one hundred black schools and half their 113 teachers. The black Georgia Education Association asserted, "This result has been accomplished by patient but organized effort, carried on through great difficulties."[30] As the Freedmen's Bureau closed its books in 1870, a wealthy nation had, through the bureau, expended roughly five and a quarter million dollars to assist southern black education. By 1870, all of the northern freedmen's aid societies combined, drawing on the philanthropy and benevolence of the wealthy North, had raised and spent about eight million dollars. The freed people, landless, impoverished, surrounded by bitter, angry southern whites, raised and expended another two to four million dollars, counting only the expenditures for the schools that the bureau tracked. They may well have doubled that amount if we consider the value of the donated labor of those who built and maintained schoolhouses, the value of board for teachers and fuel to heat the buildings, the value of the labor of underpaid black teachers, and the other intangible costs they bore to assure access to literacy.[31]

Learners of all ages attended the earliest schools, "from the gray-headed old man with his spectacles, down to the child of six years." By the mid-1860s, adults increasingly had to attend night school so that they could work during the daytime, and the black day school began to look more like traditional schools, filled with school-age children. As the adults sacrificed for their children's education, the children manifested the same dogged commitment to education as their parents. Older students whose labor was needed in the fields worked early and showed up at the schoolhouse door after midday despite many hours of work. In many southern cities, black children attended with greater regularity and in greater numbers than white students until well into Reconstruction when Redeemer governments cut funding and reduced the school year. Black students routinely begged teachers to skip recess, to hold classes through traditional holidays, and to continue teaching through the summer vacation.[32] When teachers did cease teaching for vacation or to escape the southern summer heat, students and parents looked for others to carry the school through vacation. "That schools should be kept open through all the warmth of a summer vacation, with a full and voluntary attendance of the pupils, seems rather incredible," William R. Hooper wrote in *Lippincott's Magazine* in 1869.

> That they should be kept open nearly under the Tropics, in all the heat of a Southern summer, seems more incredible. But that they should be kept open in summer, under a tropical climate, at the request of the boys and girls themselves, and partly at their expense, seems altogether incredible: it is not juvenile human nature. And yet it is the fact. So desirous of learning are the dark-hued scholars of our Southern States that their schools, when closed for the three months of summer, that their Northern teachers may return home to recuperate, have been reopened and their old teachers either engaged to remain or new ones been employed of their own color.[33]

At the Dawn of Freedom

8 AN OCCASIONAL WHITE TEACHER IN THE EARLY BLACK SCHOOLS WAS
certain that the freed people did not understand the meaning of schooling
or have "any deep and intelligent conviction of the true value of education,
though delighted with the novelty of it."[34] Most of the teachers had a more
positive, though often vague, sense of what the freedmen thought of
schooling. Still, it is the former view that dominated the thinking about
the freed people's education for most of a century of historical writing.
Walter L. Fleming, writing in 1905, claimed that, as a result of their
inherently childlike nature, the freed people flocked to schools to imitate
white masters and enjoy forbidden privileges. Fifty years later, a leading
historian of the Freedmen's Bureau could only understand the longing for
literacy as a nearly religious faith. "In learning to read," George R. Bentley
wrote, "he was eating of the fruit so long forbidden to him, and he was
entering a Mystery which seemed almost holy."[35] In an essay that in other
regards has revisionist overtones, Edgar B. Wesley suggested that the freed
people "caught the vision of education as the magic carpet on which to
float onto social prestige, economic security, political power, and general
superiority. They were eager to possess this talisman that elevated its
owner and insured a life of dignity and ease."[36]

Nothing in the words or actions of the freed people sustains such claims.
Rather, the claims reflect the historians' response to the sheer effrontery of
an enslaved people demanding, as free women and men, the rights jeal-
ously reserved for those who enslaved them. Their actions, from adults
who had to " 'fight long' with their lessons," to children "whose eagerness
to learn surpasses any thing I ever knew before among men," bespoke a
people inured to hard struggle, a people who knew that there were no
magic carpets.[37] But they also knew that formal learning had value, no
matter the struggle required to gain it. They had spent more than two
centuries observing the powerful with formal learning, as well as the poor
largely without it, and knew that the codes of power that lay in literacy
were essential to a people who were to continue to live among whites, both
the powerful and the powerless. Some of them had observed the labor
required to master literacy: they had watched privileged white children at
their study. A Quaker group apprehended the central issue: "Great indeed
is the mental darkness of that part of our land, and these people feel and
know it, and eagerly do they embrace the opportunity, and earnest are
their desires to qualify themselves to fill their new relations in society."[38]

What exactly did this unprecedented demand for education mean?
What did the freed people see as the purpose of literacy? How did they

At the Dawn of Freedom

Students from the Capitol Hill School, Washington, D.C., c. 1868. Courtesy of the Trustees of the Boston Public Library/ Rare Books.

understand "their new relations in society" and the role of literacy in filling those relationships?

People in conditions analogous to the conditions of the freed people in the 1860s do not commonly leave philosophical reflections describing their expectations of processes and skills such as literacy. Nonetheless, by attending carefully to their words, and the words of those observing them, we can gain valuable glimpses into the freed people's understanding of literacy. A number of themes emerge, though all fall under one overarching purpose for literacy.

The theme most commonly reported by teachers was a desire on the part of the freed people to be able to read the Bible. Two teachers in Yorktown, Virginia, taught a large class in the daytime, and a night school of 190 students. The night school comprised "mostly grown people, who after toiling all day, come eager to learn to read, some quite old men and

At the Dawn of Freedom

women, who, as one said to me the other night—'jes wants to larn a little Missus soes I ken read my Bible.' "[39] Lucinda Humphry wrote to the American Missionary Association from Memphis, Tennessee, in 1863, that the adult freed people with whom she worked "were pious, and I found them so anxious to learn from the Bible, that I adopted the word method of teaching, which with oral exercises, proved a success, inasmuch as I left them with their minds richly stored with some precious promises which they could read, and they could read every word contained in them."[40] Martha Johnson said of her students, "to be able to read the Bible is their great desire"; and another teacher wrote, "to be able to read the Bible for themselves, is the greatest inducement one could offer them for effort."[41]

It is not surprising that northern teachers and other northern observers reported so frequently that Bible reading was the goal of black literacy. Most thought of themselves self-consciously as missionaries first rather than teachers. Further, they were writing to northern missionary societies and their financial supporters who wanted confirmation that the freed people were amenable to northern religious influences. Yet for the freed people, Bible literacy was not simply an end in itself, nor merely an expression of black piety. It was, rather, a means to a symbolic end. To be able to read the Bible for oneself was to declare one's emancipation from white churches and from decades—centuries—of being told by white preachers what to believe. It was another aspect of the impulse that led southern blacks to abandon en masse the southern white churches they had attended all their lives in favor of black denominations: it was religious emancipation.[42]

Further, literacy as a means to read the Bible was often linked explicitly in the freed people's minds with other, more specifically political, ends. Southern African Americans knew there was much more at stake than access to sacred text. Literacy had political meaning for the freed people. Anna Kidder, working with over 200 night students, described "old gray-headed men and women coming every night to learn to read so they can 'read the Bible' they say, and sending their children day-times so they can be 'right smart' and not a bit below 'white folks.' "[43] A northern white observer, commenting on the freed people's extraordinary sacrifices for their children's education despite their astounding poverty, noted the link that the freed people made between emancipation, literacy, and equality. "The people are keen for education," he said, "which they see to be necessary to their children in the future of equal rights."[44]

Some freed people apparently associated political literacy with a relatively narrow sense of citizenship training. After his first year of teaching the freedmen in Texas, for instance, Richard Sloan wrote, "I find them very teachable and all they want is to know what our Government requires for them to do, and they will be obedient to the Lincon Government as they call it."[45] Others imagined a more critical political literacy. A black teacher in North Carolina found that the patrons of his school expected their children's education to prepare them as "fit objects of all the rights and privileges heretofore so cruelly infringed upon," and observers remarked on the role of the freed people's schools to prepare them for the franchise.[46]

Learners occasionally spoke bluntly about the political ends of literacy. While visiting a black teacher's school in Virginia, Jacob Vining, an official with a Quaker aid organization, asked the children why they came to school: " 'To learn and to mind teacher.' 'And why should you learn?' One said he knew but could not express it. A girl spoke up—'To learn to count money.' Another, 'So we can read our Bible and love God.' Then a boy,—'So we may know when people lie to us.' 'Why, how, what do you mean?' 'We can read the papers and see if what they tell us is true. They told us the Yankees had horns, and if we had read the papers we would have found it was not so before.' "[47]

Some understood the political importance of literacy to their effective use of the franchise and were aware of the nation's betrayal of their trust when, by 1870, the government had abandoned its halfhearted support of their interests and protection.[48] Ralza M. Manly, long active in support of freedmen's education in Virginia, reported in 1870, "They feel and say that the Government, having given them freedom and franchise, should not leave them in ignorance."[49]

For the freed people, in other words, emancipation meant more than the mere end of slavery, and literacy meant more than just reading the Bible. If emancipation was to be meaningful, if it was not to end in a form of freedom not far removed from slavery, it must also be political. It must promote equality, protect autonomy, and provide access to information. Literacy, the freed people hoped, would provide the means to that sort of emancipation.

Literacy also had very practical dimensions, though even the most practical reasons for literacy carried important political overtones. The freed people understood that if the full promise of emancipation was to be realized, they needed the skills to engage in a variety of enterprises and needed information to protect themselves against fraud. Literacy was one such skill, and an important means to self-protection. Jacob Vining's young respondent's comment, "To learn to count money," was one expression of that understanding, echoed by former slaves in Virginia who sought literacy to detect cheating and counterfeit money.[50] Likewise, in 1868 a freed man in North Carolina expressed both his vision of one possible future and his understanding of the barriers to that future without literacy: "I don't know much, but one thing I do know: I want edication, and we, as a people, want edication. We must learn to keep books and do our own business, for already the white man is marking and thinking how cheap he can hire us, and how easily he can cheat us out of our pay."[51] More pointed was the comment of a former slave woman in Florida. When asked why she was so determined to learn to read, she replied simply, "So that the Rebs can't cheat me."[52]

The idea of literacy to protect against fraud and to advance economically carried with it implicitly, and often explicitly, another of the freed people's goals of emancipation and of literacy—a sense of agency and autonomy, often expressed in gendered language as a sense of manhood. Frederick Douglass expressed that goal succinctly at the dedication of the Douglass Institute in Baltimore, Maryland: "The mission of the Institution and that of the colored race are identical. It is to teach [the race] the true idea of manly independence and self-respect."[53] A black sergeant, writing to one of his commanding officers to request more educational opportunities for the black troops, said much the same thing, if less eloquently: "We Wish to have some benefit of education To make of ourselves capable of business In the future. We wish to become a People capable of self support as we are Capable of being soldiers."[54]

Overall, the freed people understood literacy as one means to extend their emancipation beyond the minimal legal termination of bondage. Access to sacred texts would contribute to emancipating them from slaveholders' distortion of Christianity; access to privileged knowledge would strengthen black claims to equality and make them better informed voters; a literate people could better protect themselves against fraud and could enjoy broader economic prospects. Above all, literacy and the other benefits of formal education were deeply symbolic and political. They symbolized freedom from white control, and freedom to think for oneself was deeply and inevitably political. All of those benefits of literacy, the freedmen believed, would contribute to self-respect and independence. All would bolster and fortify their emancipation. Literacy and schooling were central to the freed people's emancipation project.[55]

At the Dawn of Freedom

The reach and power of literacy are never uncontested, however. They are constantly mediated and circumscribed, their trajectory deflected, their velocity impeded. The freed people had purposes and visions for their literacy linked to their hopes for emancipation, but their teachers also had purposes and visions for the uses of literacy linked just as clearly to the teachers' expectations of emancipation in Reconstruction America. One group of teachers shared the freed people's expectations of literacy, another group may have shared some of them. The first group included the thousands of black teachers who taught in the first generation of southern black schools, many from the North, the rest former slaves or southern free blacks.[56] The second was a small group of northern white teachers who, from the outset, spoke the language of black freedom and black rights in a reconstructed southern social order.[57]

Arrayed against those teachers were the majority of teachers who held less expansive views of the ends of black literacy. For many northern white teachers, the point of literacy instruction began and ended with otherworldly concerns, or those that, though of this world, embraced primarily the task of securing the freed people to one or another northern denomination. Frequently, the teachers' expressed purpose for teaching in the South was primarily rooted in concern for their own souls, seeking, as Mary Bowers wrote, to be "useful in my Masters Vineyard" in order to gain "stars in my crown of rejoicing."[58] Such teachers were silent regarding the secular and political needs and demands of an emancipated people.

Even more problematic, however, were the thousands of southern white teachers. They accounted for more than half of all teachers in the freedmen's schools by the end of Reconstruction. Poverty and desperation drove most of the early southern white teachers to the distasteful work of teaching black students. A few may have understood black education as a chance to authentically cooperate in the reconstruction of a prostrate society. Others taught to ensure that emancipation was held within bounds acceptable to an unreconstructed white supremacy. For the latter, and doubtlessly for many of those who taught for purely monetary ends, the culture of slavery and white supremacy led, consciously in some cases, unconsciously in many cases, to teaching in ways that would assure the perpetuation of southern white mores and values. In some cases, southern white teachers' senses of the possibilities of literacy were simply irrelevant to the hopes and expectations of the freed people, though even the most benign would inevitably teach in ways that would fail to realize the fullest potential of an emancipatory literacy. In many more cases, however, those teachers' visions of literacy were in direct and hostile contradiction to the sorts of literacy any free people must have.[59]

Henry Lee Swint wrote in 1941 that, for the freedmen, "The school had all the glamour of the new and the strange, and the printed word that particular attraction which is characteristic of all forbidden fruit."[60] There can be no doubt that the school was new and strange to many of the freed people, though there is little to suggest they saw any particular "glamour" to it. It is also true that literacy had been "forbidden fruit," though Swint was unwilling to talk about the moral and political reasons that white southerners had feared and forbidden black literacy. Nothing in the historical record, however, sustains the implication that the freed people saw literacy as an easy road to wealth and position. They did hope, perhaps too naively, that literacy would be emancipatory, or that "knowledge is power," as the black delegates to the Zion Church Colored People's Convention in Charleston, South Carolina, resolved in November 1865.[61] Historically, the actual formula may be the reverse: Power trumps knowledge, though clearly it remains preferable to have knowledge than not. In the case of southern African Americans, however, absent a broad national commitment to changing the power relations of the South, literacy would certainly prove better than illiteracy; but by itself literacy could only shore up the margins of emancipation. It was symbolically vital, but symbols alone would not change the reality on the ground.

Ultimately, neither the freedmen's vision of literacy nor the visions carried by teachers and curriculum would determine how fully emancipatory black literacy might be. Some freedmen doubtlessly mobilized their private literacy to advance their individual position, though even the most literate among them would experience the humility of disenfranchisement and segregation within half a century of formal emancipation. African Americans as a group, however, despite improving their literacy rate by well over 400 percent between the end of the war and 1900, found themselves at the nadir of their history at the century's end.[62] What literacy could not change was the distribution of power or the logic of race in the American South, no matter who the teachers were or what vision of an emancipatory literacy was dominant.

BEFORE THE AMERICAN CIVIL WAR, FORMAL EDUCATION STOOD SENTINEL AT two distinct social boundaries in the southern slaveholding states. One was the immutable and heavily fortified boundary between the sorts of education allowed to white learners and to black learners. The other was a more

porous but still distinct boundary between the educations gained by different white social classes. The former boundary was inscribed in legislation
outlawing literacy training for slaves and, in many states, even for free
blacks; it was policed aggressively by both literate and illiterate whites.
The latter was maintained by custom and a general southern indifference
to public, universal education.[63]

The carefully policed educational boundary between whites and blacks
bespoke a deep fear among members of the dominant race of the potential
power of literacy. Southern states enacted legislation barring black literacy
when slave unrest seemed to wax. Thus, South Carolina and Georgia
proscribed formal schooling for their African American population in
1740, after the Stono Rebellion, and much of the rest of the South passed
similar laws in the 1830s, following publication of David Walker's *Appeal
to the Coloured Citizens of the World* and Nat Turner's insurrection.[64]

For many southern whites, opposition to black literacy betrayed an
uneasiness about white racial superiority as the bedrock of slavery: Literate
African Americans in a society that imagined formal education as an
accomplishment reserved for elite whites inevitably troubled the easy assumptions of the righteousness of white dominion and of slavery itself.
Thus illiterate poor whites entered as enthusiastically into enforcing laws
and customs regarding black literacy as did their social superiors. Nighttime slave patrols, often manned predominantly by poor whites, roamed
the rural roads between plantations and scoured the back streets of the
South's towns and cities, watching for signs of clandestine schools or other
black literacy activity. Slaves caught reading might face whipping. Those
found writing might suffer the loss of a thumb to make it difficult to hold a
pen. Anyone caught teaching an African American to read risked impris-
onment, fines, and corporal punishment.[65]

Slavery as an institution engraved social boundaries deeply into the
South's cultural map. Emancipation as a historical moment and process
threatened to obliterate that map. As slavery collapsed during the American Civil War, southern African Americans forcefully challenged the
meaning of formal education as a social boundary. Despite the hardship
and poverty of their new and contested status, they demanded access to
literacy, built schoolhouses, recruited teachers, and attended schools, old
and young, in overwhelming numbers. They expected nothing less than to
remap southern social and racial boundaries. They intended to make the
schoolhouse a fortress of freedom, set deep into territory long claimed by
their oppressors. Where formal schooling had once symbolized elite white

privilege, the freed people redefined it as symbolic of emancipation and independence from white control.[66] Their efforts did not, of course, go unanswered. Their southern white opponents fought ferociously to reinforce and barricade old borders and defend traditional territories.[67]

The teachers in the freed people's schools mediated that struggle. They participated in the efforts to redraw social and cultural maps, though they often did not fully share the freed people's goals and therefore surveyed educational boundaries well short of the frontiers intended by the freed people. Further, the teachers were frequently engaged in boundary keeping and border transgressions in their own worlds, quite independent of the educational and political needs framed by emancipation. Thus, while the teachers did not initiate the South's black literacy project, they inevitably were implicated in its outcomes, through the intentions of their work, the limitations of their imaginations, and the distractions of their own struggles. We turn now to their stories.

Chapter Two

To Serve My Own People

Black Teachers in the Southern Black Schools

I believe *we* best can instruct our own people, knowing our own
peculiarities—needs—necessities. Further—I believe, we, that are
competent owe it to *our people* to teach them as our *specialty*.

Hezekiah Hunter, 1865

And now I think it my duty to fight for my race against the great
foe of ignorance wielding with my willing right hand, the pen &
from my mouth speak forth words for their elevation & education.

George W. Bryant, 1867

I myself am a Colored woman, bound to that ignorant, degraded,
long enslaved race, by ties of love and consanguinity: they are
socially and politically "my people."

Sarah G. Stanley, 1864

Richard H. Wells was born enslaved in Virginia but was sold to a
Florida slave owner at some point before the Civil War. He was in
his thirties when he and nearly 170 other slaves on James Kirksey's properties were freed. Kirksey was a wealthy merchant in Tallahassee, though, given the size of his slave holdings, he doubtlessly was also a planter. It is possible that Wells gained his literacy from Kirksey while enslaved, or, like many literate slaves, he may have appropriated his learning on his own. By whatever means he had learned to read, he established a black school in Tallahassee within a year of the end of the war. Two years later, he won election as a delegate to the 1868 Florida constitutional convention and represented Leon County in the state House of Represen-

tatives from 1868 to 1872. He taught in his Tallahassee school for two decades or more.[1]

Samuel H. Smothers was also born in Virginia, within two or three years of Wells, though his early years could hardly have been more different from the other man's. Where Wells was born enslaved and taken to Florida, Smothers was apparently born free. At some point before 1860, he moved from Virginia to Indiana, graduated from the interracial Union Literary Institute of Randolph County, Indiana, began teaching in the Quaker community of New Garden, Indiana, and married a young black woman. After serving in the U.S. Colored Troops during the war, he was discharged in Texas. Three years later, he moved his family to Louisiana to open a school for the freed people in Shreveport. He subsequently moved to Texas, where he continued teaching the children and grandchildren of the freed people for more than three decades.[2]

Before Smothers had established his family in Indiana, Beverly Harris, a black cook and carpenter in Monroe, Michigan, decided to relocate to Oberlin, Ohio, in order to give his children the advantages of an education at the nation's leading interracial college. His oldest daughter, Blanche Harris, graduated from Oberlin's literary program in 1860; the next younger, Elizabeth E. Harris—Lizzie—attended Oberlin but did not graduate; the youngest, Emmerett, who went by Frankie Emma, graduated from Oberlin in 1870. All three worked in southern black schools. Blanche began in 1863 in Virginia. Lizzie followed two years later for one year in Mississippi before returning to her studies, then going to North Carolina and Virginia with Blanche in the late 1860s and 1870s. Frankie Emma taught with her older sisters for one year before she graduated, then went with Blanche to Knoxville, where both sisters became principals; Blanche taught there to 1890. Lizzie began teaching again in 1878 in North Carolina, where she continued to 1908. Frankie Emma left Knoxville in 1874 to teach in Mississippi, North Carolina, Missouri, and Kansas, including two faculty assignments in black colleges. All three women married in the 1870s but continued to teach. Together, the Harris women gave a total of more than one hundred years to southern black education, Frankie Emma accounting for fifty-four years herself.[3]

THE LANGUAGE THAT SCHOLARS EMPLOY TO DESCRIBE SOUTHERN BLACK schooling in the 1860s and 1870s—freedmen's education—often implies a passive process, something done to and for the freed people. The implied actors are northern white teachers and the benevolent organizations that

supported them. In most accounts, the role of the freed people often appears to have been limited to gratefully accepting the gift of literacy
provided by others.[4] For scholars writing in the last few decades there
usually was no intention of diminishing African Americans, and some
writers attempted to document the contributions of blacks to freedmen's
education, though none grasped the size of the black teaching corps in the
first generation of freedom.[5] The impression left by the current body of
scholarship is that freedmen's education was of and for the freed people
but provided by others.

Freed people's education was, on the contrary, emphatically a work
performed by African Americans for their own emancipation. Whites assisted, surely, in some cases generously. But the authors were the freed
people and others of their race. As the stories of Wells, Smothers, and the
Harris sisters suggest, black educators played a leading role in assuring
that the freed people's struggle for literacy began and continued as an
expression of black aspirations and intentions. Seldom acknowledged in
most historical narratives, black teachers were by any measure the most
important of those who entered the black classrooms. The metaphors
historians use to describe the teachers—the "Yankee schoolmarms," the
"soldiers of light and love," the "gentle invaders"—conjure up images of
the freedmen's teachers as white New England women.[6] Many narratives
have reified those images by speaking almost exclusively of the teachers as
northern white women and limiting their research to that population.

In fact, between 1861 and 1876, black teachers outnumbered northern
white teachers four to three.[7] When all white teachers, northern and
southern, are included, black teachers still accounted for more than one-
third of all teachers in the freed people's schools.[8] The participation of
black teachers is even more striking when one recalls that African Americans were only one-eighth, or 12 percent, of the population of the nation in
1870; northern African Americans were less than 2 percent of the northern
population. Measured conservatively, northern African Americans were
twelve times more likely than northern whites to engage in teaching in a
southern black school as a proportion of the northern population, assuming that blacks and whites had equal access to the education and experience needed to become a teacher.[9]

Those factors were not equal, however. Northern blacks had far less
access to education than did northern whites. They were barred from
public schools in many northern states and received an inferior education
where they could attend. By 1870, northern black illiteracy ran three to six

TABLE 1. **Teachers of the Freed People by Race and Region of Origin**
(Total teachers currently identified, 1861–1876: 11,672)

Race of All Teachers	n	% of Race Known	% of Total
Black	4,140	46.8	35.5
White	4,702	53.2	40.3
Native American	1		
Unknown	2,829		24.2
Race by Region of Origin	n	% of Race Known	% of Total
Northern teachers			
Black	773	18.6	14.1
White	3,203	81.4	61.7
Native American	1		
Unknown	1,255		24.2
Southern teachers			
Black	3,408	67.6	51.9
White	1,639	32.4	24.9
Unknown	1,535		23.2

Source: Freedmen's Teacher Project, 2009

times the northern white illiteracy rate, varying greatly by state. Thus, it would be more accurate to say that northern blacks were fifteen times more likely to have taught in the freed peoples' schools than were northern whites.[10] Finally, African Americans spent more years as teachers to the freed people compared to white teachers, despite the fact that many of them taught only briefly, sharing their knowledge until someone better prepared could replace them. Throughout the 1860s, northern black teachers taught, on average, more than a year longer than northern white teachers, and more than two years longer than southern white teachers; southern black teachers taught a few months longer than northern white teachers and more than a full year longer than southern white teachers.[11] Five black teachers had uninterrupted teaching careers from 1861 or 1862 to the end of Reconstruction and beyond; only five white teachers had similar records, all beginning in 1862.[12]

African Americans were the first teachers to open schools for their people. They organized schools or threw open the doors of their existing, often clandestine, schools months before the first northern white teachers could reach the South. Among longtime black educators in Washington, D.C., who welcomed the first refugees from slavery were Elizabeth Smith,

To Serve My Own People

James and Joseph Ambush, Isabella Briscoe, Annie Washington, Eliza Ann
Cook, Charlotte Gordon Carroll, and George F. T. Cook, later the city's first
superintendent of colored schools. Seven other black teachers opened
schools in the city before the end of the 1861–62 school year. All but two of
those fifteen teachers taught to the middle of the decade, and most taught
to 1870; four of them were still teaching by 1880.[13] Across the river in
Alexandria, Anna Bell Davis, Mary Chase, and Jane Crouch were teaching
refugees as soon as federal forces secured the city immediately after secession began. Clement Robinson, a former slave who had gained an education at Pennsylvania's black Ashmun Institute, returned to his native Alexandria to open the South's first black secondary school a year later.[14] From
the outset of the war, Baltimore's schools for free blacks were opened to
escaping slaves by the teachers, the Berry sisters, Martha and Mary, and
William Fleetwood. Lewis Fortie opened a new school for the freed people
a few weeks later; Fortie and Fleetwood continued teaching in Baltimore
through the 1860s.[15] In Louisville, Henry Adams had established a school
in 1841 for both free blacks and such enslaved children as could avail
themselves of an education. William H. Gibson began teaching with
Adams in 1847. Their school was the first in Louisville available to the
freed people; Adams, sixty years of age when the war began, appears to
have taught until 1865, but Gibson continued in the school until 1874.[16]

Black educators repeated that pattern throughout the war years: many
who had taught secretly before 1861 continued and expanded their work,
while others seized the opportunities created by the arrival of self-
emancipated African Americans to establish new schools. Many of those
teachers continued to serve their people for many years. On the Norfolk
peninsula, for instance, William Davis, Lucinda Spivery, and Emma J. Williams opened schools and continued them through the war and into Reconstruction.[17] From 1862, three years before Richmond fell to Union
forces, Lydia Judah conducted secret classes for black students; she continued her Richmond school openly to at least 1867.[18] In Charleston, Mary
Weston, Edward Beard, Helena J. Stromer, and Simeon Beaird had been
teaching before their white neighbors conspired to fire on Fort Sumter;
Stromer's school dated to 1820. They continued teaching into the late
1860s.[19] In Savannah, Lucinda Jackson's and Jane Ann Deveaux's schools
had been operating secretly for many years before the war, Deveaux's since
the 1830s. They finally retired when the city organized public black education after 1868. Within weeks of Savannah's surrender, James Porter, who
had taught secretly in Charleston in the 1850s, opened another school for

the city's freed people along with Lewis B. Toomer, employing an all-black staff. Porter continued to teach in the black public schools of Savannah to the end of Reconstruction and to administer black schools elsewhere in the South into the 1880s.[20]

With the collapse of the Confederacy in 1865, black teachers accelerated the pace of school creation across the South, opening no fewer than 400 new schools from North Carolina to Texas, Missouri to Florida, in one year. Ariadne Woodliffe opened a school in her native Macon, Georgia, where she would teach for nearly a quarter of a century. Elijah P. Marrs opened the first school in Shelbyville, Kentucky, in January of 1866 and continued to teach in the state for nearly two decades. Henry D. Smith began teaching in Natchez, Mississippi, in 1864 and was still teaching there a decade later. Sarah and Robert Wren established an independent school in Galveston, Texas, in 1865. Sarah Wren moved to Brazos County, Texas, after Robert Wren's death and continued teaching into the 1870s. Woodliffe, Marrs, Smith, and the Wrens were representative of hundreds of black educators.[21]

One out of five of the black teachers who taught between 1861 and 1876 were from the North (see table 1).[22] Some of the northern black teachers were returning to a land from which they or their parents had fled years earlier. They must have crossed the Mason-Dixon Line with dark anxieties as well as bright hopes. Harriet Jacobs, author of *Incidents in the Life of a Slave Girl, Written by Herself*, had escaped from slavery in the 1850s. She taught briefly in Alexandria during the war then worked as an agent for a northern aid society, while her daughter Louisa taught for several years in Alexandria and Savannah.[23] The parents of Walter and Moses Williams had fled from Virginia to Canada in the 1830s. The Williams brothers returned south in 1867, traveling on their own initiative to Louisiana. They established a school in rural Lafayette Parish where they remained as teachers, Moses into the 1880s, Walter until the 1900s.[24] Hardy and Susan Mobley, born, reared, and married in Georgia, purchased their and their children's freedom for $3,000 and moved to the North in the 1850s. Hardy Mobley was among the first northern teachers to enter Georgia after Savannah surrendered, where he taught for three years. In 1869, he returned to the South with his family. He, his wife, and three daughters taught in Missouri and Louisiana for many years; two daughters and a grandson were still teaching in New Iberia, Louisiana's, black schools in 1900.[25]

Robert and Cicero Harris were born free in North Carolina. They moved with their family to Ohio in 1850. They returned to North Carolina in 1866

To Serve My Own People

to establish what would become North Carolina Colored Normal School.
Robert taught until his death in 1879, Cicero until 1888.[26] Charles W.
Harris had somewhat less direct roots in the South. His parents were from
Virginia and Kentucky, though he was born in Indiana, grew up in
Madison, Indiana, and attended Eleutherian College, an antebellum inter-
racial school in Lancaster, Indiana. Beginning in 1869, he taught one year
each in Kentucky and Mississippi before taking a school in Liberty County,
Texas, where he taught into the 1910s.[27] About one-third of the northern
black teachers had roots more or less directly in the South, either by
southern birth or the southern birth of their parents.

The great majority of the black teachers, however, were the freed people's own neighbors and family members. They were southern African
Americans, many of whom had been enslaved not long before they entered
black classrooms as instructors in literacy and numeracy; others were free
born. Probably more of the southern black teachers had been enslaved
than free, though that is not yet certain.[28] Their surviving letters and
reports seldom speak about the sources of their literacy skills, though some
wrote with flawless grammar and spelling and deployed what the nineteenth century called a "fine hand"—the careful, almost elegant script that
clerks and amanuenses mastered for formal documents and business letters.[29] Others were only slightly less practiced. Not surprisingly, many
wrote awkwardly, as did many southern white teachers.

Among northern black teachers, men and women taught in nearly
equal numbers and for nearly equal amounts of time. Among other groups
of teachers, however, gender was a salient factor in determining who
became a teacher. Among southern teachers, white as well as black, men
were more likely to teach, but women tended to teach somewhat longer
than men.[30] In contrast, northern white women outnumbered northern
white men by more than two to one, and taught, on average, a few more
months than men (see table 3 and Appendix A). Overall, black teachers
were significantly younger than white teachers when they first entered the
southern black classrooms.[31] Nearly one-third of the black women teachers
were married or widowed when they began their teaching careers.[32]

The northern white teachers who traveled into the South to work in the
freed people's schools were not usually wealthy, but their families' reported wealth put most of them solidly in the comfortable northern middle
class.[33] Northern black teachers seldom had equivalent advantages. They
and their families typically owned little real estate and held little other
tangible wealth to offset the costs of travel, board, and room. Northern

Isabella Gibbons, enslaved before the Civil War, opened the first black school in Charlottesville, Virginia, in early 1865. When Anna Gardner, a Quaker teacher from Nantucket, Massachusetts, opened a second school a few months later, Gibbons closed hers and enrolled in Gardner's school. Within weeks, Gardner hired Gibbons to teach in Gardner's school while Gibbons continued her own studies. Gibbons continued teaching in Charlottesville for two decades or more. Courtesy of the Trustees of the Boston Public Library/Rare Books.

African Americans who became teachers fell well below the 1860 national average family wealth of $1,500; half of the households of the northern black teachers held less than $500 in wealth that year.[34] Mary Cornish and William A. Jones were typical. Cornish, daughter of a black sail maker, taught in Maryland for two years before returning to her home in Philadelphia to continue teaching to support her widowed mother. Her family estimated its total worth at $50 in 1860, $300 by 1870.[35] In 1867, at eighteen years of age, Jones traveled from Elmira, New York, to Mississippi, unaided, and taught for fifteen months, then taught in Georgia and Texas for four more years with partial support from the American Missionary Association. He may have taught in southern public schools for a few more years. By 1880, however, he had returned to Elmira and taken a job as a laborer to support his mother. Before he began his work with the freed people, his father, a laborer in Elmira, was worth $750, including $600 in real estate.[36]

Southern black teachers were, of course, even more impoverished. By 1870, few had been able to amass any property at all. George Angelo Hall, for example, was born enslaved in 1851. By 1870, at age nineteen, he was raising his orphaned siblings. He was worth $100 that year. He began teaching in Mobile, Alabama, in 1873, where he continued to teach and serve as school principal until his death more than three decades later.[37] Francis P. Johnson opened a school in Augusta, Georgia, in 1867. He owned no real estate and had no other form of wealth three years later. In 1872 he was able to open a savings account, which he doubtlessly lost two years later with the collapse of the Freedmen's Savings and Trust Company. He continued to teach at least into the 1880s.[38] Lucretia Evans's father, a free black laborer in Warren County, North Carolina, had no wealth to report in 1850, $100 in 1860; by 1870, Lucretia was "keeping school" in Littleton, North Carolina, reporting no wealth.[39]

There were exceptions. Mosko Bartee, an African American fresco painter from New Jersey who taught for one term in Baltimore, was worth a remarkable $23,000.[40] Martha and Mary Jarvis had both attended the preparatory school at Oberlin College and subsequently taught in the Deep South for a combined nine years. Their father was a prosperous black Ohio farmer with a net worth in 1860 of over $16,000; by 1870, he had doubled his wealth to over $33,000.[41] Alfred Jones owned a successful feed store in the District of Columbia from before the war until his death in the 1870s. He was worth an estimated $40,000 in 1870. Three of his daughters taught for many years, though they did not stray far from home to do so—

all three taught in the black schools of Washington.[42] A handful of exceptions aside, however, the black teachers among the freed people faced enormous personal financial hardships before they even launched their efforts to extend their people's literacy. Parsimonious teachers' salaries provided no cushion against continuing hardship.

Despite African Americans' limited access to education in the antebellum North, many of the northern black teachers had attained impressive credentials by the time they began their work with the freed people. Of those whose education has been established, nearly one hundred had attended or graduated from college, while nearly one hundred more had attended a normal school or preparatory school such as Oberlin Academy or Philadelphia's Institute for Colored Youth. Many of the southern black teachers began their careers in the late 1860s and 1870s after having attended such newly established schools as Fisk, Howard, Shaw, and Atlanta Universities, Talladega, Roger Williams, and Central Tennessee Colleges, teacher training schools such as Biddle and Hampton Institutes, and the scores of black normal schools and normal classes that sprang up across the South to meet black demand. Yet before southern black institutions could begin to send out their graduates, college- and university-educated African Americans were teaching throughout the South, hailing from black colleges such as Wilberforce and Lincoln and white colleges including Dartmouth, Harvard, Iberia, Knox, and, most famously, Oberlin.[43] Among northern higher education institutions, Lincoln produced the most black teachers for the first generation of southern schools, at least seventy, while Oberlin prepared forty-six. At the academy level, Philadelphia's Quaker-supported Institute for Colored Youth sent at least sixty-five black teachers to southern black schools, while Oberlin Academy sent thirty-eight.[44]

While a small but remarkable group of the black teachers had attained secondary or higher education, most had the rough equivalent of a common school education or, often, much less. The southern critics of the freed people's schools have often been contemptuous of the poorly educated teachers in the earliest schools, and subsequent writers have delighted in mocking the schools and their teachers. They missed the point. The black community wanted knowledge. Anyone who had skills that others lacked could at least share that much and move the community ahead. The critics also forget that most teachers in contemporaneous northern common schools also had no training beyond the common school.

The black teachers often understood their limitations as well as their potential. A northern white teacher met one such teacher in 1864, a black woman who had initiated a small school on a plantation near Helena, Arkansas. She could only teach reading, and that imperfectly. He remarked to her that she would soon need to turn her students over to a better-trained teacher. She readily agreed, but replied, "I kin cair 'em a heap farther'n they is."[45] A thousand miles away on the South Carolina coast, a freedwoman teaching at St. Helena employed similar imagery when she brought some of her students to a neighboring school, telling the teachers at that school "that she could carry them no further."[46] Ruth A. Grimes, a freedwoman who established a school in Union Point, Georgia, explained the motivation of hundreds of poorly educated southern black teachers like herself: "my Education is feeble compared to the people North but sir the little I know I am willing to impart with my fellow people."[47] Felix Smith may have been representative of many others. He was teaching in Green Ridge, Virginia, in 1869, at the urging of his neighbors. He had a "limited education," according to the local Freedmen's Bureau agent, and was "ready at any time to give up to a more competent Teacher."[48]

Since virtually all of the southern black teachers lacked formal education, the education project pioneered by the freed people emphasized teacher education from the earliest years. The first black normal school in the former slaveholding region was Beulah Normal and Theological School in Alexandria, Virginia, founded and led by a former bondsman, Clement Robinson, in 1862. Within five years, a half dozen normal schools were preparing black teachers, and by the end of the decade, across the South nearly ninety high schools, normal schools, and higher education institutions established for and by the freed people were educating teachers for the expanding network of public and private black schools.[49]

At least six of the early black normal schools were established by African Americans.[50] A seventh, Lincoln Institute in Jefferson City, Missouri, was initially funded through pledges by the black troops of the 62nd Regiment, U.S. Colored Infantry.[51] Not surprisingly, however, given the poverty of the southern black community, most permanent secondary, professional, and higher education institutions established in the first decade of freedom were built by northern whites. Black education activists anticipated the need for northern assistance. The Georgia Educational Association, for example, explained in 1866 that "the Northern Associations propose to establish first-class schools at important points. The colored people, being poor as well as ignorant, will at first establish schools that are extremely rude; but, in time, as they gain knowledge and wealth they will establish better schools. The schools established by Northern Societies, will educate teachers who will be employed by the colored people."[52]

By the end of Reconstruction, the freed people and their northern allies had built and filled 125 schools in the South intended for professional training and other higher learning, and they would continue to add to that number in subsequent years. It is doubtful whether any other people, similarly situated, have approximated that explosive growth in educational institutions. The rapid expansion of teacher training among the freed people in the first generation of freedom reflected the demand from the freed people themselves for the opportunity to educate their own people.[53]

That demand for teachers was met not only in specialized, permanent institutions. More often, for the earliest southern black teachers, local schools promoted teacher training in what were known in the nineteenth century as "normal classes," their name derived from the same root as normal schools. Normal classes were made up of the most advanced students in larger black schools. The earliest normal class may have been one created a mere two years after the first school appeared on the Sea Islands of South Carolina. The National Freedmen's Relief Association explained in 1864 that its teachers had "selected sixty of the most promising pupils and placed them in a school by themselves with a view of fitting them for teachers." The writer added, "many of them are really enthusiastic at the prospect of becoming instructors of their own race."[54] The American Freedmen's Union Commission established normal classes in its Nashville, Murfreesboro, and Huntsville schools in 1865. It established normal classes in two more schools the following year. The commission's superintendent explained that the normal-class students practiced their skills in the lower classes of the schools they were attending, then were "employed in *our schools* as Assistants one year then sent out to found schools of their own, & a new selection made to take their places."[55] In 1867, the Quakers decided "to institute Normal classes" in all their larger schools, "that from among the colored people themselves teachers may be supplied."[56] The American Missionary Association disliked the idea of normal classes, claiming that the moral disorganization of southern black homes required that future teachers attend boarding schools where they would only experience "influences, social and domestic, alike favorable." Nonetheless, in 1867 it reported normal classes in seven of its schools, in addition to the normal departments at Fisk University and the Storrs School in Atlanta, and planned teacher training for the following year at Hampton and Avery Institutes.[57] The association appears to have discontinued normal classes the next year.

Oscar M. Waring, a northern black teacher writing from Florence, Alabama, in 1868, summarized the importance of this less formal, less expensive, and less centralized form of teacher education: "From these Normal classes we have not only been able to supply the primary departments of our schools with good teachers, but also to send teachers into the country to open small schools of their own, which are generally self-supporting. So it will be seen that every central school is, to a great extent, a Normal school, and, properly conducted, is able to do much toward supplying the surrounding country with teachers."[58]

Normal classes were not confined to large schools with multiple teachers. Single-teacher schools such as the one Jane Briggs Smith was teaching in Sumter, South Carolina, also included teacher training in their curriculum. In 1868, Smith wrote that she had five classes to teach. The top class, "my Normal Class, which occupies an hour," drilled on arithmetic, grammar, and geography, along with lessons on teaching. The class members were all intent on becoming teachers.[59] Finally, some future teachers received their pedagogical training not in classes but in one-on-one tutoring in what amounted to in-service training. Adam H. Erwin, a Quaker teacher in North Carolina, asked the Freedmen's Bureau to support a teacher in an adjoining village for a few months in spring and summer. "The teacher is a young man now under my care," he noted. He wrote again a month later on behalf of freedman Monroe Fullenwider, a teacher in another school, explaining, "He receives weekly lessons from me & I think will make a diligent teacher."[60] Erwin never identified the first teacher, but Fullenwider continued to work as a school teacher after his informal training with Erwin.[61] Similarly, J. L. Evans and William P. Hays were students of Abby Winsor, a white teacher from Connecticut working in North Carolina; they both received tutoring from Winsor to become teachers. They taught in rural schools not far from Winsor.[62]

Black teachers with but little schooling themselves accepted teaching positions hesitantly, no doubt. Their reports reveal their concern and uncertainty. A teacher in Jones County, Georgia, reporting in 1869, asked the recipient of her report to "excuse ignorance. I know you can see it in every line. I have attend school but a little myself. and I don't know [much?] so I trust you will look over all mistakes." Another Georgia teacher appended a note to his report: "Sir, I never [had] any dealing with this work of teaching school before, and it is real awkward, to me." Anna Bond, previously enslaved in Tennessee, wrote in 1867, "I hope you will excuse all mistakes in my letter and also the [monthly teacher's] report it is the first one I ever filled in my life. A year ago I could not make a letter." A year later, still teaching, and writing in a clear hand, Bond was still apologizing for her writing, concluding, "Indeed Sir 3 years ago I had neither the privilige nor the ability to use the pen."[63] Many of the less well-prepared teachers doubtlessly failed, just as many whites failed as teachers—we know the names of hundreds of southern black teachers who taught a term, then disappeared from the records, or appeared in the next census as farmers, housekeepers, or laborers. They probably never intended to make teaching an occupation but only entered the classroom at the insistence of students and parents. But thousands persevered.

BEFORE THE SOUTHERN STATES BEGAN TO CREATE SYSTEMS OF PUBLIC BLACK schools in the last years of the 1860s, most of the schools taught by black teachers, particularly southern black teachers, were independent, private ventures, established by individual teachers at the request of neighbors in small settlements and villages, on plantations, and in larger cities. They were supported by a monthly tuition, usually running from twenty-five cents to a dollar per child. Constantine C. Singleton's explanation of his situation in Augusta, Georgia, was common to many: "I am not teaching under the auspices of any Society or Church having commenced some what on my own expences," he wrote in 1869. "I have not got nor do not expect to get anything for teaching besides my regular tuition fee."[64] Laura Holt, a young black woman teaching in Clinton, Georgia, in 1869, left a more detailed account of establishing and teaching in a tuition school:

> I have a school consisting of 60 pupils—a class of boys and girls that spell quite well—read a little—from (12) to (18) years of age. The building in which I teach is owned by the white people of this settlement. The colored people tried to purchase it but they would not consent to part with or dispose of it. The colored people are putting up a building for that purpose and I expect to commence my school there some time next week. I teach from (8) o'clock in the morning till (5) in the afternoon. Pupils have from (4) to (10) miles a day to walk. There are no schools near here white or colored. I have some few slates in my school—not half of my pupils have them, are not able to get them just now as their

crops are not layed by. I have not received anything for teaching yet on
that account I expect to receive it at the close of the month. I charge (40)
cents per month for each pupil.[65]

Given the poverty of the freed people, black teachers in private schools
frequently worked for months for little more than their living costs. For
instance, James B. Deveaux, sent by the Freedmen's Bureau to various
locations in Georgia to establish schools that could then be given to less
experienced teachers, started one of those schools in Jones County, Georgia, in 1869. After four months, he reported, "my people here are very poor
indeed should my school fail it would be a very severe blow to them and
without some pecuniary aid it will be next to impossible for a teacher to
thrive here. I am now in debt for my board &c."[66] A black teacher in
Tennessee had received only nineteen dollars after teaching six months.
"We are very poor here and try to do all in our power," he wrote, adding, we
"find our arms are to[o] short."[67] Yet despite the poverty of students and
teachers, private black schools proliferated in the mid- to late-1860s. In the
1870s, southern Democrats regained control of state governments and
slashed state support for public schools, providing only enough for three or
four months of schooling per year. In response, many black communities
returned to the practice of paying tuition to the teacher to extend the
school year and assure their children as much schooling as they could
manage.

In addition to tuition-supported private education, some black teachers
received at least partial support for their schools through the Freedmen's
Bureau or gained placement in a school through the assistance of bureau
agents. The bureau attempted to coordinate the work of hundreds of
schools and dozens of competing agencies. Its assistance was often uneven
and unreliable, however. Regulations from Washington changed, turnover
among bureau officials was high, and congressional funding was invariably
inadequate throughout the agency's brief half-decade of operation. Its
education work was limited to providing transportation for teachers sent by
the northern aid societies, advising the freed people about organizing their
schools, providing funds to repair school buildings, helping the schools find
teachers, and gathering data through burdensome monthly reports. It
received far more requests for assistance than its resources could allow,
including perennial pleas for more teachers than it could find.[68]

The bureau's ability to pay salaries was circumscribed. In its first two
years of operation, it was limited to sending teachers to communities that

could assure a small salary and arrange for board. In 1867 and later, when deepening poverty made local support increasingly difficult for the freed people, the bureau developed a creative way to support some teachers and stretch the budgets of northern agencies—it paid rent on schools owned by the freed people or the aid societies. The rent, usually ten to twenty dollars a month, could then be paid to the teacher.[69] Yet scores of black schools suffered the fate of Lucy Browns's in North Carolina. She wrote to the Freedmen's Bureau in March 1868 begging for assistance for her school. The freedmen were desperately poor, she reported. A widow, she was renting both a schoolhouse and her living quarters from her former master and was deeply in debt. Without bureau aid she would lose her school and her livelihood, the only support for herself and her family. F. A. Fiske, the North Carolina bureau superintendent of education, replied that the bureau was unable to extend any assistance, its fund having been expended. Brown held on for six more months but finally closed the school "on account of her family she being unable to support it by her present employment," as a correspondent explained to Fiske.[70]

Working with the bureau could be a trying experience for black teachers. Bureau agents made promises they could not honor or broke promises when it seemed expedient. Bureau agent W. H. H. Peck reported in the spring of 1866 that Allen A. Williams, a black teacher, had been teaching for a year in Tuscaloosa, Alabama. Williams had built, at his own expense, a log house to accommodate his students. Peck recommended that the bureau compensate him for the cost of the building, in part as a means to encourage him to continue with his work. A few months later, however, Charles Arms, Peck's successor, removed Williams from his own school, replacing him with John A. Hart, a white teacher from Ohio. Williams protested, pointing out that the bureau superintendent had hired him for the year, and refused to turn over his school to Hart. Arms accused him of being "self-conceited, ignorant, crafty, and I believe dishonest," yet also recommended that the superintendent find a rural school for him: "he makes a *good pioneer* and I hope you have use for him in that capacity," he wrote. Williams was forced out of Tuscaloosa but continued to teach, though he never again reported to the Freedmen's Bureau.[71]

The bureau treated Solomon Derry more contemptuously than it did Williams. Derry, enslaved before the war, was one of the first black teachers in Montgomery, Alabama. The bureau superintendent for Alabama, R. D. Harper, had personally encouraged Derry to organize a school in

Union Springs, Alabama. He promised Derry that if he could average at least forty-five students, the bureau would pay twelve dollars in rent, or twenty dollars if his school averaged eighty students. Derry went to work raising money to buy land, renting a house in the meantime for the school, and arranging for school furniture.[72] Harper, meanwhile, sent Horace C. Atwater, a white Yale graduate, to take over the work. Derry protested, reminding Harper, "you said we must have Teachers of our own color," and reiterating Harper's promises of aid and encouragement for his work. Harper shot back:

> I am surprised to find that you sh'd seem to insist upon the occupancy of the house & school, where a competent teacher had been provided & sent to the work. I certainly understood you to say that it was the interests of the colored people and not your own personal interests that you wished to subserve. I hope I have not been mistaken in my impressions. My desire is to educate the freed people of this state. The arrangement of occupying Union Springs as contemplated, would have secured this object much more successfully than it is possible for you to do, for I presume you do not consider yourself competent to the great work of education.

Then, transforming Derry's desire to educate his people into a desire for personal advancement, Harper concluded, "I desire your cooperation in this work but I shall never consent to sacrifice the interests of a whole community for the personal welfare or comfort of a single individual." Harper doubtlessly thought that would silence Derry.[73]

Derry responded immediately to Harper's claims and misrepresentations. Regarding his ability to teach, Derry wrote, "So far as my competency are concern, I feel competent of teaching the branches I told you I could." He repeated Harper's original promises, adding that Atwater was free to organize a second school, but added, "I am not willing for him to drive me out of my house. I have rented it according to your orders & have gone to the trouble & bought Seats & put in it & made up the number of Scholars you required & promised to pay rent for."[74]

Harper turned over to his clerk the task of responding to Derry. H. M. Bush continued Harper's attack on Derry's character, heaping insult on him and on the freed people of Union Springs in the process. "When you were encouraged to commence school at Union Springs, you represented your fitness for the work and stated that you could teach," Bush wrote. "Your conduct since shows your total unfitness for the duties."

You call yourself a teacher and claim pay from your colored brethren for such work when it would have been far better were you paying some one for teaching you. When Dr. Harper told you that the colored people must depend upon those of their own color for teachers, he meant those who had attended school and become competent to teach. The ignorant man cannot teach what he does not know himself, and I would advise you to turn over your school to the 1st competent teacher that offers, for we cannot pay rent for any building as totally unfit as you appear to be. When you ask assistance you must be willing to accept it when tendered, and the colored people must not ask any assistance further from the Bureau for Union Springs until they show sense enough to prefer a competent for an incompetent man as teacher.

How much better for you and for your colored brethren had they welcomed Mr. Atwater and said to him We are glad to have a competent man come among us. Be our guide! But no Solomon Derry must be our guide, an ignorant selfish man wholly unfit for the work. We prefer him not because he is good and educated but because he is black and a minister.[75]

The black community at Union Springs, Alabama, heeded Bush's words, never again asking the bureau for assistance and never again reporting the Union Springs school to the Freedmen's Bureau. Solomon Derry continued teaching in Union Springs for six years in the school he had built, attracting 150 students each year, then building another school in nearby Tuskegee that reputedly became the foundation for Booker T. Washington's later work. He continued teaching elsewhere in the state for many more years. Horace C. Atwater, meanwhile, had the good grace to leave the Union Springs school in Derry's capable hands. He returned to Montgomery to teach for the remainder of the year, then became the principal of a black school in North Carolina.[76]

Other Freedmen's Bureau officials were supportive of black teachers, however, even when they recognized that a particular teacher did not have all the teaching skills they might desire. In recommending an African American whose attainments were "not very encouraging," an agent in Tennessee wrote to his superior, "It is better that [the freed people] should be gathered together and learn a little than to be left without instruction when they so greatly desire to obtain [it]."[77]

The northern freedmen's aid societies—the New England Freedmen's Aid Society, the Pennsylvania Freedmen's Relief Association, the Friends

Joshua E. Wilson moved from Charleston, South Carolina, to Florence, South Carolina,
to establish the city's first black school. He taught there for three years, 1868–1871,
and then became a Methodist minister. He subsequently served as the county
superintendent of public schools for eight years. A school in Florence still bears
his name in memory of his role in establishing education for the freed people
in the city. Photo taken c. 1868. Courtesy of the Trustees of the
Boston Public Library/Rare Books.

Freedmen's Association, the Methodist Episcopal Freedmen's Aid Society, and upward of four dozen other secular agencies and missionary societies—contributed significantly to southern African American education. The aid societies were not, however, a major factor in the lives and work of most of the black teachers. Fully three-quarters of the first generation of black teachers found their way into the schools of the freed people with no assistance from the northern aid societies or from the Freedmen's Bureau.[78]

Many of the southern black teachers opened schools in their own neighborhoods, but others taught in schools in distant communities. Meanwhile, northern black teachers who were not affiliated with the aid societies traveled hundreds of miles from their homes to open schools. After their schools were operating, these teachers might appeal to the bureau for assistance, and some gained a commission from a northern aid organization after teaching for a few years. George LeVere, O. L. C. Hughes, and Mrs. H. G. Jones, all northern blacks, sought bureau aid only after they had established schools in Knoxville, Tennessee, and labored in them for several months.[79] Sarah S. Jackson and her husband, William A. Jackson, from Middleboro, Massachusetts, taught for a year in Berryville, Virginia, unaided, before the American Missionary Association assisted William; Sarah received a partial salary from the association for only one of the five years she taught there, although she was the principal of the school.[80] Junius B. Jones, born in North Carolina but educated in Ohio, traveled to Jefferson County, Tennessee, and taught there unaided for two years. The American Missionary Association paid him the following year, when he moved to Lebanon, Tennessee. He taught in Lebanon for many years thereafter with no further northern aid.[81]

Such exceptions aside, most southern black teachers never received bureau or northern benevolent aid. Similarly, some northern black teachers traveled to the South, established schools, and made long careers in southern black education, yet remained independent of the bureau and the major aid societies. Susan L. Waterman, for example, grew up in New Jersey, where she gained a common school education, taught briefly in a public school, and then continued her education at the Institute for Colored Youth in Philadelphia. She applied to a northern aid society for a teaching position in the South but was turned down. Undeterred, she left for Florida in 1866 without aid. She was one of the first teachers in Lake City, Florida, where she remained as teacher and principal until her death in 1884.[82] Frank McKeel found his way unaided from New York City to rural Alabama in 1869 where he taught for two years before gaining a position in a public school. He later taught in Georgia through at least 1880, then became principal of the West End Public School in Shreveport, Louisiana, where he remained into the 1910s.[83]

While most black teachers began their work without aid from the major northern societies, and many were never associated with the aid agencies, a few hundred were supported by those groups for much or all of their southern careers. Northern blacks were somewhat more likely to gain aid society sponsorship than southern black teachers. When black teachers were commissioned by a northern aid society, they were usually employed by the northern groups for only a few of the years they taught, commonly for only one or two years, yet they continued teaching long after assistance was withdrawn. Abram Bryant, for example, taught in self-supporting schools for three years in North Carolina, was aided a fourth year by the American Missionary Association, then began teaching in public schools. The American Missionary Association supported William J. Moore's school in 1864; he continued to teach in North Carolina for two more years before the association again aided him for a year, then left him once more to teach as best he could until the state began paying his salary in the 1870s. The Methodist Church, North, supported Alexander Swanson for one year, 1868; Swanson went on to teach for many years in Georgia with no further northern aid.[84]

Very few northern white teachers followed similar paths; most gained and retained aid-society support throughout their southern work. Only a few black teachers had the luxury of support from northern aid societies for extended periods. The Presbyterian Committee on Home Missions to the Freedmen sustained Georgians Mary Bomar and her mother in Dalton, Georgia, for six years and Pennsylvanians James and Mary Chresfield in North Carolina for more than a decade. The New England Freedmen's Aid Society supported Mary Billings's Charleston school into the 1870s as an alternative to the city's black schools with their all-white southern faculty. The American Missionary Association employed Hattie Miller as one of its Avery Institute staff for eight or more years, and William W. Mallory from Massachusetts for more than a decade in Memphis.[85]

Sallie Daffin, Amanda Thompson, Louisa L. Alexander, and Mary Emma Miles, among other black teachers, gained support from several different organizations during their first years of long southern careers. Philadelphian Daffin received aid from Quaker organizations, the American Missionary Association, and the Presbyterians over an eight-year period before going into the public schools of Washington, D.C. Amanda

Thompson of Alexandria established her own school and taught there for four years before winning support from the National Freedmen's Relief Association, the Pennsylvania Freedmen's Relief Association, and the New England Freedmen's Aid Society for one or more years each. Oberlin College graduate Louisa L. Alexander had an on-and-off relationship with the American Missionary Association, gaining its support for two of her first six years while she established schools in Georgia, South Carolina, and Kentucky. She subsequently taught in cooperation with a Quaker group in Alabama for one year, then started schools with state support throughout the South for the next three decades. Mary Emma Miles, an African American widow from Philadelphia, started a school independently in Virginia in 1865. The Protestant Episcopal Freedmen's Commission took note of her work the next year, sustaining her school for two years. When the Episcopal group dropped her from its rolls, the Philadelphia Quakers offered their assistance, supporting her for several more years as she established schools in Kentucky, Virginia, and North Carolina.[86] It appears that these and other experienced teachers moved frequently with the intention of starting new schools that young black teachers could take over, but it remains unclear why their sponsorship shifted so often, and whether the changes were the result of the black teachers' initiatives or the decisions of the aid societies.

While nearly all the northern groups appear to have hired black teachers for their southern schools, the groups varied greatly in their policies toward black teachers. Some hired very few black teachers, even as they trained black teachers in their normal schools and normal classes. Only 10 percent of the teachers supported by the United Presbyterian Church were African Americans, but closer to one-fifth of the teachers assisted by the Methodist missionary society were black. Other groups were more eager to support black teachers and promote black independence. Forty percent of the teachers supported by the American Baptist Home Mission Society were black, for example.[87]

Northern aid societies also differed in their deployment of black teachers. Some, holding that it was safer for black teachers than white teachers to teach in the countryside, habitually assigned black teachers to areas outside the larger towns and cities, usually in small, one-teacher schools. The American Missionary Association, for instance, argued that black teachers "can go where white ladies cannot, on the plantations, into the interior of the country, living in the negro cabins, and 'roughing it' in the most primitive way."[88] Likewise, a bureau agent in Florida was certain that

James H. Bowser was born free in Smithfield, Virginia. In 1867, at seventeen years of age, he began teaching in Richmond, Virginia, for the New England Freedmen's Aid Society. In 1869, the Presbyterian Board of Missions to the Freedmen supported his teaching; the following year the Richmond school board hired him. He became a postal clerk later in the decade; his wife, Rosa Dixon Bowser, began teaching in Richmond in 1872 and continued for many years. Courtesy of the Trustees of the Boston Public Library/Rare Books.

if black teachers were assigned to rural areas, they would "be allowed to engage in their vocation unmolested, when white teachers would be liable to abuse and insult."[89] The result was that black teachers had the more difficult work. In the larger population centers where white teachers were more frequently assigned, such pioneering as had to be done was accomplished quickly. Schools were organized and graded as soon as the aid societies could reach them; virtually every population center in the South had one or more school founded by freedmen's aid organizations by the autumn of 1866. White teachers sent south after that could expect to work in a well-organized school and to live in a teachers' home, often with a matron to look after housekeeping and meals.

For those that the aid societies sent into the interior, usually black teachers, the work was far more challenging. They were expected to navigate local customs as a stranger, locate a vacant building, arrange for school furniture to be built, find lodging and board, gather the children, establish and collect tuition (required by all aid societies as their funds began to dwindle in the later 1860s), and manage all of the other details required in establishing and teaching a school in a small community. The few black teachers who were assigned to established schools in larger towns and cities usually had to find their own board and room; their white co-laborers often refused to board with black teachers in the teachers' homes, and some of the societies feared that interracial mingling in the teachers' quarters would stir up hostilities among southerners who were already suspicious of their work.[90]

An occasional northern society put leadership in the hands of black teachers and sponsored schools with all-black faculties, but others exhibited a good deal less faith in their black educators. The American Missionary Association staffed a school in Norfolk with an all-black staff, an experiment that, while apparently quite successful, was abandoned after only one year; it would be decades before the American Missionary Association would again allow black professionals to run its institutions.[91] Yet all-black faculties, supervised by black principals, were not unusual in other organizations. The largest black school in Alexandria in the spring of 1864, sponsored by a Quaker aid society, was administered and taught by two northern black women, Marianna Lawton and Louisa Jacobs. The Old School Presbyterian Church's Committee on Freedmen supported the Zion School in Charleston from 1865 into the 1870s; for several years it boasted of fourteen black teachers and a black principal. Fannie B. Waring, also supported by the Presbyterian Church, supervised two other black teachers in Winchester, Virginia, in 1869. The Pennsylvania Freedmen's Relief Association sustained a school in Norfolk in 1867 presided over by Mary E. Miles and four black teachers. Beulah Normal and Theological School had an all-black staff from its beginnings in 1862. The Sumner and Phillips Schools in Fayetteville, North Carolina, were both staffed entirely with northern black teachers. The first postwar school in Savannah, Georgia, had a staff of eight black teachers. Sarah Jane Woodson was the principal of a school in Hillsboro, North Carolina, from 1867 to 1870, with a number of black teachers working under her, including two men. She and her faculty were supported by Philadelphia Quakers.[92] More unusual was a school supported by the radical abolitionist group the American Baptist Free Mission Society in South Carolina. From 1863 to 1865, its black principal, Jane Lynch, from New Jersey, supervised the work of Elizabeth Howard, a white teacher from Campville, New York. The American Baptist Free Mission Society turned its work over to the National Freedmen's Relief Association in 1865, and NFRA continued to support Lynch to 1870, in schools from South Carolina to Maryland and Virginia, when she became a public school teacher, first in South Carolina and then in Mississippi.[93]

Finally, nearly thirty black teachers worked part or all of their southern Reconstruction-era careers in southern black colleges or universities. They represented about one in every seven faculty members identified to date in the Reconstruction-era black institutions of higher education. More than half of them taught at Howard, including such notable black leaders as John Bunyan Reeve, John Mercer Langston, and Alexander T. Augusta; Langston was acting president of Howard from 1873 to 1875. Amanda M. Perkins first taught at Leland University and then at Straight University; Charles Henry Thompson and Pelleman M. Williams also taught at Straight. Hiram Revels and Charles Thompson both served as president of Alcorn Agricultural College before the end of Reconstruction. Others held positions at Atlanta, Claflin, and Shaw Universities, and Berea and Talladega Colleges.[94]

NORTHERN BLACK VETERANS MADE UP AN IMPORTANT GROUP OF AFRICAN American teachers that have been ignored in prior studies of the freed people's schools. Perhaps as many as 400 of the black male teachers were veterans, though positive identification is difficult for most of them.[95] Of the teachers who can be positively identified as veterans, nearly 250 men, one-quarter were northern blacks and three-quarters were from the South. Many of the southern black veterans gained their literacy while in the military. Like the other black teachers, some of the veterans taught only briefly then turned to other pursuits. Yet three-quarters of the veterans taught for two terms or more, and more than one-quarter taught from the mid- to late-1860s through Reconstruction and beyond. Military service may have been the means by which some northern black veterans found their way into the South; some, like Steven A. Swails and Reuben P. Clark, began teaching near where they were mustered out of the service in 1865 and 1866, and Jacob Nocho returned to teach in Greensboro, North Carolina, remembering it as a pleasant city through which he drove teams of horses during the war.[96]

The black veterans served their country as warriors before they took up the book as teachers to their people. One black woman served the same cause as a Union spy, and thus was a veteran in fact if never in name, before becoming a teacher in the freed people's school. Mary J. R. Richards, born into slavery in Virginia, had been educated in New Jersey by her owner in preparation for missionary labor in Liberia. She spent four unhappy years in Africa, returning to Virginia in 1860. Her owner, an unwilling slaveholder and ardent Unionist, managed to gain a place for Richards in Jefferson Davis's household where, as servant in the dining room, she overheard the dinnertime conversations of Davis and his military advisors and generals. She relayed the conversations to her owner, who passed them on to Union contacts in the White House. In that way, Mary J. R. Richards served as one of the major conduits for Elizabeth Van Lew, one of the Union's most important and most daring spies. Richards went on to teach in Richmond after its surrender, then in Manchester and Norfolk, Virginia; St. Marys, Georgia; and Jacksonville, Florida. Referring to both her educational advantages and, apparently, her familial relationship to the Van Lew family, she explained her decision to teach in 1867: "I felt that I had the Advantage over the most of my Race both in Blood and Intelligence, and that it was my duty if possible to work where I was most needed."[97]

In addition to their work as teachers, more than 130 of the black male teachers held political offices, often while continuing to teach. They served their people and their states as legislators, delegates to constitutional conventions, trial justices, justices of the peace, mayors, local and county superintendents of education, and county commissioners, and in other offices. Hiram Revels and George Washington Murray served in Congress after stints as teachers. James D. Lynch, Joseph C. Corbin, and Jonathan C. Gibbs served as state superintendents of education, Lynch and Gibbs after three or four years as teachers in the freed people's schools, Corbin before accepting a position at Lincoln Institute for two years and then founding Arkansas's Branch Normal College. Gibbs also served as the Florida secretary of state. Scores of the male teachers became ministers as well as teachers, combining the inadequate salaries of both positions to be able to continue to teach and lead their communities.[98]

As southern cities and states began to take up the work of public black education, black teachers increasingly used the new state systems to gain positions in free schools. The earliest system to broadly employ black teachers was in the nation's capital where, by 1870, forty black teachers were working in schools administered by black principals and a black superintendent. Black schools in Baltimore, New Orleans, and other cities had mixed-race faculties, usually under white principals. Cities such as Petersburg and Charleston, on the other hand, would only hire white teachers in their black public schools, leaving black teachers no option but to open private black schools or to find work in the state schools in smaller cities, towns, and rural villages.[99]

"MORE THAN I DESIRE MY OWN LIFE I DESIRE TO ELEVATE THESE, MY people," George C. Booth wrote in 1863.[100] His words captured the two themes that ring through nearly every black teacher's application to teach or plea for assistance: racial solidarity and racial uplift and elevation. Black Union veteran from Ohio and teacher in Louisiana George W. Bryant, in urging bureau aid for his school, wrote that he was "endeavoring to elevate my down-trodden race."[101] Robert Harris reported that he and his brother were doing "all in our power for the elevation of our long oppressed race."[102] Christopher McKinney applied to teach in Charleston "to labor for the intellectual advancement of my people."[103] "It is not my purpose to be South for mere selfish motives to satisfy a romantic, roaming, poetic sentiment," John Wesley Cromwell wrote, alluding to the motivation of many northern white teachers, "but to assist in the elevation of my *own* down-trodden, unfortunate, illiterate, yet not God-forsaken people."[104] Southern black teachers employed the same language as their northern counterparts. Although her neighbors could not pay their children's small tuition, Mary A. Best struggled to sustain her school. "I felt it my duty to try to elevate the mindes of my color," she explained in a letter to North Carolina governor W. W. Holden. Her hope was, she wrote, "to elevate the poor colord children so they would not always be troden underfoot."[105] Robert P.

Martin, an ex-slave teaching in Roxboro, North Carolina, wrote to the bureau requesting aid, "for without help we can't begin to be elevated and prepared for the duties that seem to await us."[106]

Although some black teachers applied to northern evangelical societies for aid, very few spoke of their teaching in moral or religious terms. Their language of elevation occasionally carried political connotations, as heard in Robert Martin's expectation that education would prepare the freed people "for the duties that seem to await us," or in Robert Harris's sense that teaching the freed people "promises so much for the elevation of our race and the good of the State."[107] Edmonia G. Highgate's "desire to be a pioneer in trying to raise [the freedmen] up to the stature of manhood and womanhood in 'Christ Jesus'" did reflect a religious impetus, yet in the racial shorthand of the nineteenth century, black manhood and womanhood also carried political freight, and Highgate herself would later speak of her work as "hastening the equalization of political and social recognition of manhood irrespective of color."[108] At its heart, the teachers' expectation of racial elevation through education implied moving their race toward equality, raising them to a higher social and economic plane, and inscribing them within boundaries previously denied to them.[109]

As will be seen, there was a sharp difference in perspective, expectation, and vision between black teachers and most white teachers, whether southern or northern. Only the most politically astute northern white teachers spoke with the same clarity as black teachers about the goals of the freed people's emancipation project. The nineteenth-century language of elevation and uplift bespoke a sense of a people being moved, through education, toward a new relationship with the rest of the society. The goal was greater equality. Only rarely did black teachers fret about their race's spiritual condition. For the black teachers, education was intended to extend and secure emancipation.

A commitment to the emancipation of their people made the black teachers by far the most important of the teachers in the first generation of postbellum black education. They were many times more likely to take up the task of education than either southern whites or the northern whites who have long been lauded for their work. Further, their dedication to the work manifested itself in their longevity in the southern classrooms. While most northern teachers can be tracked back to their northern homes, and their careers in southern black education can be fairly accurately mapped, the paucity of southern school records in the later years of Reconstruction and the institutional racism of the census, which frequently failed to note

the professional occupations of African Americans, makes it far more difficult to track many of the southern black teachers. Further, black male
teachers frequently became ministers but continued to teach for most of
their lives, yet primary and secondary sources note their ministerial occupations but fail to document their simultaneous careers as teachers. It is
likely, though it cannot be documented at this point, that the longevity of
black teachers was far higher than this study can report.

NO SINGLE BIOGRAPHY CAN CAPTURE THE RICHNESS AND DEPTH OF THE
experiences of the thousands of black women and men who were the freed
people's first teachers. Still, the story of one family of northern black
teachers amplifies and illustrates many of the themes and patterns that
run through the black teachers' collective biography.

Charles and Hannah Francis Highgate raised six children in Syracuse,
New York, in the 1840s and 1850s. Hannah Francis Highgate had been
born in Virginia, Charles in Pennsylvania. Charles Highgate, a barber,
owned no real estate in 1860 and had no other wealth. Yet he attended to
the education of his children. His oldest daughter, Edmonia, was one of the
first six students to graduate from Syracuse High School and apparently
the only African American in her class. She graduated with honors. Both
Edmonia and her sister Caroline followed the high school "normal course"
to prepare themselves as teachers. Edmonia taught in northern Pennsylvania for one year, then became principal of a black school in Binghamton,
New York, in 1861. Her father died that year.[110]

In January 1864 Edmonia wrote to the American Missionary Association asking to be sent south as a teacher. "I have felt an intense interest in
the education of my freed brethren South," she explained.[111] A month
later, she left her position in Binghamton, spent four weeks raising funds
for the National Freedmen's Relief Association of New York, then left for
Norfolk, Virginia. In Norfolk, she taught with three other black women,
two of them graduates of Oberlin College. In early 1865 she organized
a school on Maryland's Eastern Shore; by summer, she had moved her
mother, Hannah Francis, and her youngest sister, Willella, to Darlington,
Maryland, to assume control of her school. Once assured that they were
capable of carrying the school forward, Edmonia left for New Orleans.[112]

No longer an employee of a northern aid organization, Edmonia threw
herself into organizing schools and teaching. "We have a flourishing school
in the Creole district, called after our eloquent champion, Frederick Douglass," she wrote in early 1866, adding, "your *amie de plume* is principal,

assisted by an able corps of educated colored teachers." Her sister, Caroline V. Highgate, joined her in New Orleans, assuming the principalship of another freedmen's school named after General Baird. They assisted in organizing the Louisiana Educational Relief Association that spring. It was a primarily black organization intended to raise money to support schooling for indigent black children.[113]

Never one to mince words with northerners who fancied themselves friends of the freedmen, Edmonia remarked in July 1866,

> I only wish that our northern radical spoken friends, who are now at their fashionable summer resorts, while we teachers are laboring on a salary, only what our certificate calls for and less by a third what our expenses are, would feel it their duty to enclose some substantial evidence of their interest in this work, in a cheerful letter to us. We dare not send away twenty or thirty children from our schools, because they cannot pay their tuition fee. Their fathers may have been of the Port Hudson heroes. Yet we expend our strength teaching them, and have not wherewith to supply ourselves with more than one meal a day, or money for a car-ride, but must foot two or three miles of weary distance beneath a tropical sun. Think of these things, theorists, and withhold your aid if you can.[114]

July 1866 was not a good month to be a northern African American in postwar New Orleans, however. On 30 July, policemen shot into a peaceful assembly of black and white Republicans, killing dozens and injuring over one hundred. That incident touched off two days of rioting by white southerners, venting their wrath on African Americans especially, and northerners in general.[115]

The Highgate sisters nursed the wounded in hospitals while continuing their schools, but by autumn they felt it best to leave the city. Caroline returned to the North, taking charge of a black school in Woodbury, New Jersey. Edmonia moved to Lafayette Parish, well to the west of New Orleans, where she taught day, night, and Sabbath schools. Her new location did not remove her from racial and political tensions, however. "There has been much opposition to the school," she wrote in December 1866. "Twice I have been shot at in my room. My night scholars have been shot, but none killed. The rebels here threatened to burn down the school and house in which I board." Edmonia's absence from New Orleans lasted only a few months. By March 1867 she had returned and opened another school, where she taught 125 indigent students supported by the Louisiana Educational Relief Association.[116]

The New Orleans riot of 1866 chastened most of the city's black teachers and principals. When a committee from the Orleans Parish School Board interviewed all of the black school principals in August and September 1867 to ascertain their and, presumably, the black community's attitudes regarding integrated versus segregated schools, all but Edmonia spoke circumspectly, careful not to offend the segregationist leanings of the board. Edmonia, on the other hand, spoke as forthrightly to southern men as she had to her northern supporters. She offered no apologies for her position "that there should be no distinction made in the schools" between white and black students. She did concede that, given the temper of the time, "mixing the races now may create difficulties and injure the cause of education for the time being," but in the long run, equality of access was essential. Her interviewers remarked to the board, "Miss Highgate is a very intelligent, and apparently highly educated lady."[117]

Meanwhile, James R. Highgate, just a year older than Caroline, was teaching in Rapides Parish, Louisiana. Caroline resigned from her New Jersey school in the autumn of 1867, despite pleas from students and community, and established a school in Jackson, Mississippi. She taught there independent of any northern association except for one year, 1868–69, when the Pennsylvania Freedmen's Relief Association paid a portion of her salary.[118] Edmonia moved to Mississippi in January 1868, establishing a school in Enterprise, eighty miles east of Caroline's school in Jackson. Their mother and youngest sister, Willella, also moved to Mississippi to establish a school in Canton, twenty miles north of Jackson. By 1869 their two surviving brothers, James and William, had joined the rest of the family as teachers in Mississippi—the oldest brother, Charles Highgate Jr., two years younger than Edmonia, had died of wounds suffered at the Battle of Petersburg in April 1865.[119] Six of the eight Highgates—the entire surviving family—were in the freed people's school in Mississippi before the end of the decade. Edmonia had gone from an honor graduate of a fledgling high school in New York State to a pioneer teacher in the dark interior of a slave kingdom whose body was broken but whose spirit was alive and virulent. Her learning was always evident: she spoke effectively before churches, conventions, and a venerable abolitionist organization to admonish, cajole support, and offer analyses. She wrote, even while teaching seventy to one hundred students a day, becoming a frequent contributor to the African

Methodist Episcopal Church's notable national newspaper, the *Christian Recorder*, and her letters appeared in the *American Freedman*, the *National Anti-Slavery Standard*, and the *American Missionary*.

Edmonia Highgate took a part of 1870 to return to the North to raise money for her school. In February 1870 she spoke before the Massachusetts Anti-Slavery Society, observing ominously that the work of abolitionists was "not yet half done; and if it is not now thoroughly done, it will have to be done over again."[120] While Edmonia was away, Caroline Highgate met A. T. Morgan, a white former Union officer from Wisconsin who had bought a plantation and gained a seat in the Mississippi legislature. The two fell in love and were married in August 1870, after Morgan had prevailed on his fellow legislators to rescind the state's antimiscegenation laws.[121] They left immediately for McGrawville, New York, home in the 1850s to the interracial New York Central College, for their honeymoon. Edmonia met them there. Twenty-six years old, homesick for family, watching the happy couple, she, too, fell in love with a white man. She was preparing to return to Mississippi to work in the normal school at Tougaloo College and had written some weeks earlier, "I have no other expectation and much prefer to devote the remainder of my years to that branch of the work," teacher training.[122] But that was not to be. Edmonia G. Highgate died in a failed abortion two months later. Her train tickets to Tougaloo were found in her trunk. Her paramour, John Henry Vosburg, betrayed her, abandoning her to the abortionist's blade to return to the wife he had never revealed to her.[123]

Caroline Highgate Morgan did not return to teaching, but Hannah Francis, Willella, James, and William Highgate continued to teach in Mississippi after Edmonia's death. William, the youngest of the Highgate family, taught the children and grandchildren of the freed people the longest. He served as president of Mississippi State Normal School in Holly Springs for thirteen years, and taught elsewhere in the South to at least 1912.[124]

The Highgates are symbolic of the many northern black teachers who flooded into the South even before Appomattox "to do something for my people who have been less fortunate than myself," as Hannah Francis Highgate wrote in 1865.[125] Their northern white counterparts have long been celebrated or, by traditional southern historians, vilified, yet it was black teachers who served in disproportionate numbers in the schools for the freed people, who taught longer, and who labored in more dangerous and less prestigious places. Like the Highgates, black teachers were much more likely than white teachers to go fearlessly into the urban and rural South to establish schools independent of the northern aid societies, confident that "the keen relish which [the freedmen] have for knowledge," in Edmonia's words, would sustain them.[126]

BY THE END OF THE 1860S, THE WORK OF EDUCATION AMONG THE FREED people was established. The important initial work performed by literate southern black farmers, laborers, and seamstresses, working alongside experienced black teachers, had laid deep foundations not just for black education, but for southern public education for all. Many of those who had lent a hand in the early years returned to their fields and hearths. Others, perhaps never intending initially to become teachers, continued teaching, having found a calling among their people.

Black teachers, northern and southern, were committed to a new South free of traditional educational boundaries. Southern black teachers, whether recruited by their black neighbors for a few months to share the knowledge they had acquired or organizing classrooms that they would occupy throughout Reconstruction and beyond, and northern black teachers, both those who would spend a lifetime in the South and those with only a year or two to spend, explored frontiers deep into the interior of traditional southern white prerogatives. Together, they built and staffed primary schools, secondary schools, normal schools, and seminaries. Within the new boundaries that these teachers surveyed, universal education was born in the American South.[127]

Through their work, black teachers crossed many borders. Their very self-creation as the second group of southern black professionals, after the long-established black ministry, was a momentous transgression across long-forbidden racial and class boundaries. That collective act established a profoundly symbolic survey marker in a remapped South. Even more than the northern black teachers, southern black teachers crossed symbolic economic, social, and political borders as well. Rejecting their racial "place" in the South, they engaged in paid labor, largely free of white dictation, unavailable to the plantation economy. In contrast to their work for the prior two and a half centuries, they engaged in labor requiring independent thought and action, labor connected to high ethical norms, labor with political implications for their people. Likewise, the hundreds of black women who took up teaching violated traditional southern gender boundaries, like their white southern counterparts, but with the added

Massachusetts native Mrs. Ida S. Marshall taught in Rhode Island briefly before traveling to Maryland in 1865 to begin teaching among the freed people. The New England Freedmen's Aid Society supported her from 1867 to 1871. She continued teaching in Maryland and South Carolina to at least 1875, apparently with state support. Courtesy of the Trustees of the Boston Public Library/Rare Books.

transgression of violating expected racial norms. Northern black teachers, meanwhile, crossed another border with both emotional and political freight, the geopolitical border between the North and the South. They labored in territory long closed to northern free blacks, lands of terror and despair, in order to "assist in the elevation of my race," in the words of Ida S. Marshall.[128]

Chapter Three

It Will Result in a
Better Understanding of Their Duties

*Southern White Teachers and the
Limits of Emancipation*

My hands are anxious to improve their minds; in which they
evince a spirit I am desirous to encourage; for I think it will result
in a better understanding of their duties, as well as be a benefit
to society and the country.

W. H. Sharp, 1866

I live among a people greatly prejudiced against the education of
Freedmen, and down on me with a double vengeance and would not
loan me a mess of meal if I were starving (a few honorable exceptions).

Thomas Collins, 1867

We need the money here and are as capable of teaching them
as Northern men and really feel more interest in them
than people at the North.

Sarah A. Payne, 1871

In the spring of 1868, Josephine Stell applied to the Freedmen's Bureau in Texas for a teaching position. To make her case, she explained, "I feel interested in the education of the freed people,—the more intelligent they become, the less trouble they will give to our country, and they will be better, happier, and more useful." When her application did not immediately prevail, she wrote to the provisional governor of Texas. She was, she informed him, "a young lady" who had attended "a fashionable boarding school" and was thus "competent to teach any of the English branches, the Latin, and Music too. I am an Orphan," she continued, "have no friends in the State, and but few acquaintances. In my homeless, friend-less, and penniless condition, I know not to whom to apply for assistance but your self. What I ask of you Gov. is this—give me a colored school—any where that I can make a support." She was recommended by a Texan who was certain that for "a lady of her position in society to volunteer to teach Freedmen School would I think, have a good effect." Neither Stell nor her reference mentioned that she was the daughter of slaveholders. She taught for a year but was dismissed after the freed people expressed dissatisfaction with her for whipping the children.[1]

John Hollis Caldwell had also held slaves. Directly after the Civil War, he, his wife, and his son taught together in a black school in LaGrange, Georgia, for a collective fourteen years. Caldwell, a southerner by birth and a Methodist minister in Newnan, Georgia, by 1860, had delivered a ser-mon toward the end of the Civil War in which he declared that there was a divine message to the South in the scourge of the war: "We have sinned and God has smitten us." Such language, critical of slavery and of the Confed-erate cause, was intolerable to his congregation and others in Newnan who drove him from his church. He was reassigned to a rural circuit but chose instead to take his family to the North. In 1866, they returned to Georgia, settled in LaGrange, and began teaching with support from the northern Methodist Episcopal Freedmen's Aid Commission. John and Elizabeth T. Caldwell taught until 1872, their son William from 1867 to 1869.[2]

Austin Groner had never had the luxury of affording slaves. Just before the war, he was attempting to establish himself as a grocer, though the 1860 census gave his total wealth as $300 to support himself, his wife, Sophia, and an infant daughter. He spent a portion of the war in the 4th North Carolina Cavalry. Immediately after the war, the Mercantile Agency, which had commented in 1861 that he had little capital and was operating a small retail shop, noted simply, "Quit—broke." By 1870, Groner was working for the railroad and worth $150, half what he held in 1860. To assist the family fi-nancially, Sophia Groner opened a school for the freed people in 1868. A bureau agent reported, "The freedmen of the County appear well pleased with her efforts, and desire that she be encouraged as far as the Bureau can assist her. She is the only Southern woman of proper respect & character I have met, who would take a school, and from all I can learn she does very well for a School of young children such as she has." She taught for two years.[3]

THOSE WHO HAVE WRITTEN ABOUT FREEDMEN'S EDUCATION STRONGLY imply that the early black schools were taught almost exclusively by north-

It Will Result in a Better Understanding

ern teachers.[4] Some early historians went so far as to claim that the northern schoolmarms' domination of the black schools was the root of the "insane intolerance" and "xenophobia" of the postwar South.[5] Yet from the earliest days of the freed people's schools, southern whites such as Sophia Groner, the Caldwells, and Josephine Stell were at work as teachers. Before the first decade of black education had run its course, southern white teachers dominated the teaching force. Many came to the work for the same reasons as Stell and Groner—necessity—though, like Stell, they also occasionally indicated a concern to school the freedmen to assure against "trouble." Like the teachers profiled above, southern white teachers had been slave owners, Confederate soldiers, shopkeepers, farmers, and housekeepers. Some had once been wealthy; others had always been relatively poor though sufficiently educated to be able to teach the skills of literacy.

In 1865, fewer than 200 southern whites were teaching in black schools. From 1866 onward, the number of southern white teachers in the freed people's schools began to rise steeply; by 1870, and perhaps as early as 1867, more southern whites than northern whites were teaching in the southern black schools. In South Carolina in the 1868–69 school year, for example, twice as many southern whites were teaching in black schools as northern whites, roughly 160 southerners to 80 northerners. Forty-four southern blacks and six northern blacks rounded out the state's teaching force in black schools that year. Three years later, over 600 southern whites, nearly 500 southern black teachers, but only 75 northern teachers (22 of them northern black teachers) taught in the state's black schools. By the end of Reconstruction, the number of southern white teachers in South Carolina's black schools had declined by half as a result of an impressive increase in black teachers to over 900. Only forty-two northern white teachers remained in the state's black schools in the last year of Reconstruction.[6] In Louisiana, southern white teachers outnumbered northern teachers by four to one before 1865 and nearly six to one from 1865 to 1870. In Texas during that same half-decade, more southern whites than northern whites taught in black schools, by a small margin; but black teachers were more than twice as likely to become a teacher in Texas as northern and southern whites combined.[7]

The Freedmen's Teacher Project has documented a total of over 1,600 southern white teachers, with no more than about 740 in any one year. Data from a few states, such as those noted above, however, suggest that far more southern white teachers worked in black schools than can currently be fully identified for inclusion in the project. Conservatively, it is

TABLE 2. Participation Rates of Teachers by
Race and Region of Origin, 1861–1876

| Years | Northern White Teachers[a] | African American Teachers | | | Southern White Teachers[c] |
		Northern[b]	Southern[c]	Total	
1861–62	61	2	45	47	1
1862–63	219	70	17	87	4
1863–64	664	42	94	136	7
1864–65	1,036	76	152	228	187
1865–66	1,293	178	385	563	381
1866–67	1,212	207	613	819	460
1867–68	1,176	253	738	991	506
1868–69	1,090	319	1,080	1,399	660
1869–70	1,039	358	1,392	1,750	680
1870–71[d]	667	264	1,035	1,299	739
1871–72	626	211	883	1,094	466
1872–73	510	188	771	959	371
1873–74	407	171	747	918	198
1874–75	369	160	734	894	157
1875–76	234	131	627	758	89

Source: Freedmen's Teacher Project, 2009

[a]Includes foreign-born white teachers, except those known to have lived in the South prior to 1860.

[b]Includes foreign-born black teachers, such as those who migrated from Canada, the West Indies, or Africa to teach.

[c]Given the nature of the sources, these totals for southern teachers are far too low. Southern whites probably numbered closer to 6,000 by 1872; southern black teachers probably numbered 3,400 in that same year, and double that by 1876. See Appendix B for estimates of the actual number of black and white southern teachers, and the method of reaching those estimates. Given their speculative nature, I have decided to confine the estimates to the appendix rather than reporting them here alongside firm, documentable numbers.

[d]The Freedmen's Bureau discontinued its work in 1870, and several of the northern voluntary aid associations had withdrawn by or before 1870. After 1870, numbers for northern white teachers, primarily identifiable through manuscript sources and published reports of northern agencies, are probably close to actual participation rates; numbers for southern teachers, black and white, are definitely well below actual participation rates due to a lack of manuscript or printed sources in most states. Identifiable southern teachers decline sharply after about 1871 when southern states ceased collecting records on individual teachers.

likely that throughout the South more than 3,000 southern white teachers were in the black schools by 1869, rising to nearly 6,000 two years later.[8] Overall, in the first generation of southern black schooling, 1861 to 1876, the majority of the teachers in the black schools were southern whites. Table 2 reports only the teachers who have been positively identified.

It Will Result in a Better Understanding

Southern white freed people's teachers were more likely to be men than women, in sharp contrast to northern white teachers.[9] They were also the oldest of the teachers. Southern white men were, on average, over thirty-eight years old when they began teaching; southern white women were over thirty years of age.[10] Of the southern white women who taught, single women outnumbered married or widowed women by a slim margin; one out of seven was a widow.[11]

Prior to the Civil War, most southern white women did not work in paid labor. With few exceptions, those women who did work for pay "did so out of necessity, and their labor carried with it a stigma of debased status and an aura of vague disreputability," as Drew Gilpin Faust has observed.[12] It comes as no surprise, then, to learn that most of the southern white women who taught the freed people had little experience beyond housework prior to their teaching. They were, then, crossing a double boundary when they entered black schoolhouses, the boundary between traditional women's domestic work and paid labor, on the one hand, and the boundary limiting interracial contact, particularly contact that would promote black intellectual reach. Of the southern white women teachers whose prewar occupations have thus far been identified through censuses, letters, or diaries, fewer than eighty indicated any sort of paid labor, almost exclusively as teachers. The great majority are found in the census with no occupation designated or noted as simply "keeping house," "at home," or, rarely, "attending school." The southern white men who taught the freedmen, on the other hand, had worked in virtually all occupational categories except domestic or service work. More had been simply "farm laborers" than had been clerks; eighty had pursued professional occupations, including thirty-five ministers. Despite the claim of one northern observer that the southern white men seeking teaching positions were primarily "broken down school masters," less than one-fifth of southern men in the black schools had been teachers before the war. Two-fifths of the men had been planters and farmers, the largest occupational category.[13]

Most of the southern white teachers remained in the freed people's schools very briefly. More than half taught no more than one term. As a group, they averaged just over a year and a half of teaching, with men remaining in the classrooms a few months fewer than their wives, sisters, and daughters.[14] The brief amount of time that southern whites spent in schools that were, in nearly all cases, in the teachers' neighborhoods, suggests that most of the southern white teachers had little commitment to

It Will Result in a Better Understanding

black education. Teaching was a task of convenience or a work of necessity. In other words, where northern teachers, black and white, had to travel great distances to work in a hostile region, often alone, and thus carried to their work a measure of commitment, a dose of courage, and some vision of the ends toward which they taught, southern white teachers were working in familiar surroundings, often with freed people they had long known and occasionally had owned. Their work required little if any commitment, though, as we shall see, remaining in the work occasionally did require some courage. They very seldom articulated their expectations for the freed people or for their teaching, but their occasional words and, more forcefully, their profile and behavior betray expectations of different ends for emancipation than those aimed at by the freed people.

BEFORE THE SOUTHERN STATES ESTABLISHED THEIR SYSTEMS OF PUBLIC education in the very late 1860s, southern white teachers found their ways into black schools through a variety of paths. Like many of the southern black teachers, some southern white teachers began offering instruction at the urging of the freed people themselves. One former slave owner reported that he began teaching in response to his former slaves' desire for instruction in reading and writing. "My hands are anxious to improve their minds," he wrote. Others started independent schools, hoping to raise sufficient tuition from the freed people to make a living, or turned to the Freedmen's Bureau to apply for a teaching position or to ask the bureau to support a school already in operation. Julia A. Wilson, for example, a widowed white native of Talbotton, Georgia, opened a school near her home right after the war, gaining partial support from the New England Freedmen's Aid Society for her first two years but expecting to be fully supported by her students after 1867. A year later she was asking the bureau to assist. "The Freedmen is not abell to pay," she wrote in 1868; "I cannot continue the school without pay much long[er]. I hope you will do somthing for the colored Peopel."[15]

As in the case of Wilson, the northern aid societies often welcomed southern white teachers, certain that the growth of a corps of southern teachers working with the freed people was a sign of social and political change in the South. The American Freedmen's Union Commission declared publicly, "The more Southerners we can take into our schools with us, the better," and proceeded to hire a score or more. Nearly one-fifth of the Presbyterians' white teachers were native southerners. In Louisiana,

It Will Result in a Better Understanding

more than one hundred southern white teachers found employment in the black schools organized by the military government in New Orleans in the early 1860s. On the other hand, to extend greater southern white control over the freed people, some black schools established by southern whites would employ only southern white teachers in the later years of the decade, including the school created by Episcopal minister A. Toomer Porter in Charleston and the city schools in Petersburg and Charleston.[16]

To understand the full significance of southern whites teaching in the first southern black schools, it is essential to recall that the very idea of black literacy had long been anathema to most southern whites. Southern opposition toward black intellectual attainments did not melt away in the heat of civil war. Rather, like iron forged in fire, racial attitudes hardened among many southerners during and after the war. Postwar black schools stood as an affront to white beliefs in black inferiority and symbolized all that was wrong in the aftermath of rebellion and defeat. While an occasional southern white teacher reported that their neighbors' attitudes were favorable toward the freed people's schools, more reported local sentiment toward the schools as "indignant" and described southerners as "very *bitter* in their opposition."[17] Southern white teachers faced the same violent opposition to their work in black schools as did northern white teachers.

Despite deep-seated opposition to black literacy, revulsion toward anything tending to move African Americans toward equality with whites, and consequent threats from neighbors, several thousand southern whites nevertheless chose to teach in the new southern black schools. We can discover the names of many of them and can identify which black schools they taught in. Understanding the decisions of southern whites to teach the freed people is more difficult than for other teachers, however. They apparently left no diaries and far fewer letters than black or northern white teachers. Having been a teacher in a black school appears not to have been a point of pride among these teachers, in contrast to their black and northern white peers. Thus they wrote no memoirs or retrospectives of their work. Many never reported their schools to the Freedmen's Bureau or to the northern aid societies. The statements of those who did report must be read with care—they were often dependent upon the bureau or northern groups for their small salaries and doubtless chose their language carefully. Still, what we can learn about them as a group, or as identifiable groups within the larger universe of southern whites, supplemented with their own words when they can be found, fleshes out an unexpected story.

One group of the southern white teachers had northern antecedents and

thus might have viewed black education less negatively than other southerners. Some of that group of southern teachers had been born in the North
but had lived for many years, married, and had children in the South, while
others were the children or spouses of northerners.[18] It is certainly possible
that their direct or proxy northern antecedents explains their inclination to
go against the southern grain, an assumption strengthened by the fact that
there was some tendency among them to remain in black education longer
than the average among southern white teachers. Among them was Mary
A. Neely, who was born in Ohio in 1836, married a North Carolinian in the
1850s, and began teaching the freed people in 1866. She taught for at least
three years. Edmund Grover, a native of Vermont, moved to the South in
the late 1830s or early 1840s and married a woman from South Carolina.
They lived in Georgia and Alabama and raised a family on a bookkeeper's
salary. He and his Georgia-born daughter taught in Calhoun, Alabama, for
at least five years. Mary J. and Charles A. Gilbert migrated from New
England to Alabama in the early 1840s. Charles Gilbert became a wealthy
merchant worth over $140,000 in 1860, including five slaves. He fought for
the Confederacy in the 1st Regiment, Mobile Volunteers. Mary Gilbert
taught two years at the end of the 1860s, by then a widow.[19]

Foreign immigrants who had lived most or all of their lives in the South
after immigrating, along with the children of foreign immigrants to the
South, also occasionally became freed people's teachers. They, too, may
have had less aversion to teaching African Americans than their white
southern neighbors, though the traditional immigrant hostility to African
Americans militates against that presumption. Like those with northern
antecedents, immigrants tended to teach somewhat longer than native
southern white teachers. For example, George Mutch, born in Ireland, was
a Confederate veteran who, with his wife May (a native southern white
woman), taught for two years in Alabama immediately after the war.[20]
Thomas Hart, also born in Ireland but living in Texas since the early 1840s,
lost a son in the Civil War fighting for the Union. Hart taught a black school
for three or more years in Nacogdoches, Texas.[21] Sidney S. and Mary Murkland were both born in Scotland and immigrated to the Americas in the
1830s and to the South in 1851. They began teaching in North Carolina in
1866, dedicating the rest of their lives to establishing schools and churches
among the freed people.[22]

Teachers with roots outside the South were exceptions, however,
amounting to not more than one in forty of the southern white freed
people's teachers throughout the period. The great majority of the south-

ern whites found in the freed people's schools were born in the South, most, not surprisingly, in the state in which they were teaching. The freed people's southern white teachers were overwhelmingly native-born, yet, as observers noted at the time, "Southern whites will not, as a rule, teach negroes."[23] Something more than immigration to the South was at work, then, that brought these teachers to the black schoolhouse door.

Historian Robert Morris suggested one factor. He argued that "a major portion of the Southern teachers considered themselves Unionists" and posited loyalty to the Union as a factor in the decisions of southern whites to engage in teaching the freed people.[24] While a very few Unionists can be shown to have taught the freed people, the claim that "a major portion" of southern white teachers of black children were Unionists cannot be sustained. In the thousands of letters and reports in the Freedmen's Bureau papers and in the archives of northern aid societies, not more than a dozen teachers are identified as Unionists by bureau agents or other observers. Even fewer southern white teachers self-identified as Unionists in their letters or reports, despite the fact that they were applying to, and often desperately appealing to, men who they would have known would be susceptible to appeals to loyalty.

A counterexample is heuristic: When governmental control of New Orleans was returned to civil authorities after the war, the city's white school system promptly fired nearly twenty experienced southern white teachers on the grounds of their wartime Unionist stance, yet only two of those Unionist teachers sought to continue teaching by taking positions in the black schools operated by the freedmen's bureau. Neither of those two teachers remained in black education beyond one year.[25]

Even more striking is evidence from the files of the Southern Claims Commission. The commission considered compensation claims for wartime losses suffered by southerners who had remained loyal to the Union during the war. More than 22,000 southerners asserted their Unionism before the commission; an insignificant handful of those self-proclaimed Unionists—fourteen—can be found among the thousands of southern white freedmen's teachers.[26] There was, in other words, nothing inherent in loyalty to the Union that translated into a propensity to teach in the freedmen's schools. Loyalty to the Union explains little if anything about southern white decisions to engage in work with the freed people.

Disloyalty, in fact, predicted who among southern whites would spend a term or more in the black schools more frequently than loyalty. Hundreds of the southern white male teachers were Confederate veterans, men who

It Will Result in a Better Understanding

had risked their lives in defense of racial slavery, willingly or not.[27] Like
other southern whites, Confederate veterans tended to teach only briefly.
T. Alonzo Harris, for example, taught for one year in a black school in
Lexington, Georgia. A native of South Carolina, a slaveholder, and a student at Wofford College before the war, he served the Confederacy as a
private and chaplain in the 1st South Carolina Infantry and became a
teacher in white schools after his term in Lexington, Georgia's black
school.[28] Likewise, William B. McKell fought with the 14th Mississippi
Infantry. Five years after Appomattox, he taught for a term in a black
school in Starkville, Mississippi.[29] Less typical was James Lazenby, a lieutenant with the 11th Virginia Infantry who taught in Emmaus, Virginia,
for four years beginning in 1866.[30] Very few began teaching as early as
Lazenby—most entered the schools after 1868 or 1869—and few taught as
long as he. Confederate military service did not inherently predispose
veterans to participate in the freed people's education project any more
than Unionism did. Southern Unionists and Confederate veterans may
well have taught in roughly equivalent proportions. On the other hand,
wearing the Confederate gray into black classrooms, even if only symbolically, doubtlessly spoke volumes to black children about their teachers'
commitment to black liberty and emancipation.

Along with Confederate veterans, former slave owners or the wives and
children of slave owners also became teachers for the freed people. Some
taught informally, holding classes on their postwar plantations on Sundays
or during slack times in the agricultural cycle. A bureau agent's report in
1867 that "a good many colored children in my Dist. are taught by members of the Planters['] family" was echoed by other observers.[31] Some
former slave owners such as R. P. Taylor constructed schoolhouses on their
property and conducted classes on a more formal basis. A North Carolina
planter, Taylor was worth over $40,000, including seventeen slaves, in
1860. He was "much reduced" in wealth as a result of the war, but had
"built at his own expense and on his own land a handsome large schoolhouse for the Colored Children," in which he was teaching in 1868.[32] Mary
E. R. Boyd's northern-born husband held six slaves as part of his $12,000 in
wealth in 1860; by 1868, she was teaching African Americans on her
plantation near Natchez, Mississippi.[33] Other former slave owners found
themselves teaching in public village and city schools or in private, tuition-
dependent schools throughout the postwar period.

The slaveholders-turned-teachers were not drawn from the ranks of the
South's elite slave owners—most owned between three and fifty slaves as

It Will Result in a Better Understanding

62 opposed to the hundreds held by the wealthiest southern families[34]—but they all had a direct economic stake in the slave system prior to the war. Most of the male slaveholders who taught the freed people had served in the Confederate military. They each had a major part of their prewar personal wealth invested in slaves. For example, George A. Goodman was the adult son of a moderately wealthy planter in Louisa County, Virginia, before he became a colonel in the 13th Virginia Infantry. His father owned twenty-five slaves, while Goodman, a teacher in 1860, owned five. Together, they were worth over $50,000 in 1860, including the value of the thirty African Americans they owned. By 1870, their collective wealth was $15,000. Goodman farmed for a few years after the war but returned to teaching in the 1870s, becoming the principal of the black school in Louisa, a position he held from 1872 to 1878, at least.[35] At the other end of the scale, Francis Flake from Anson County, North Carolina, had fewer advantages. He owned no land of his own, though he had managed to purchase four slaves to help him work on land he rented in 1860. Those he enslaved made up most of his reported net worth in 1860 of a bit over $2,600. He enlisted in the 43rd North Carolina Infantry in 1862, was promoted to lieutenant, and was among the Confederate troops who witnessed the surrender at Appomattox in 1865. By 1870, he owned no land and could report no net worth. In 1868, he had taught a term in a local black school, probably while continuing to farm, the occupation he continued to pursue thereafter.[36]

Former slaveholders appear to have taught a month or two longer than most of the southern white teachers, though the sample from which that conclusion is drawn is small. The 103 known slaveholders, or wives and children of slaveholders, who taught the freed people spent collectively nearly 200 years in black schools before 1876, and a half-dozen continued to teach after the end of Reconstruction. Benton C. Rain had held thirty-two African Americans in bondage before the war and served in the 15th Alabama Cavalry. He became the principal of a black school in Mobile in 1871, a position he retained for several years.[37] Ezra Hixon taught in a public black school in rural Butler County, Alabama, from 1868 into the 1880s. A grocer before the war and owner of a single male slave, he had served in the 59th Alabama Infantry.[38] Jay McCondichie had been worth over $30,000 in 1860, including his twenty slaves. He fought for the Confederacy in the 44th Alabama Infantry. He began teaching the freed people in Snow Hill, Alabama, in 1867, and continued teaching to at least 1874.[39]

Religion played a surprisingly minor role in motivating southern white teachers to teach the former bondspeople, to judge from their words and actions. The Protestant Episcopal Church, the only major denomination to avoid a schism over slavery in the decades before the Civil War, was also the only major denomination in the South to engage in postwar black education. Its Protestant Episcopal Freedmen's Commission supported nearly two dozen southern black schools by 1868, but interest waned swiftly; the next year it could sustain only seven schools, and it continued to decline thereafter, apparently closing its work in 1877. The Episcopal effort began and largely remained an inadequately funded initiative of a small group of northern Episcopal ministers and lay people with the cooperation of a handful of southern Episcopal divines.[40]

Otherwise, southern denominations made declarations of their "paternal care" for "the colored people within our bounds," and a few spoke of supporting black education as a part of that paternalism. The white laity and most of the ministers of the southern churches, however, refused to rally behind those declarations. A Baptist minister in Virginia found that members of his denomination considered it degrading to teach a degraded race and thought black education a waste of time. Even white clergymen who had ministered to black congregations before the war failed to engage in their erstwhile parishioners' education. Robert Ryland, for example, who had been the white pastor to a large black Richmond, Virginia, church for twenty years and was a slaveholder himself, taught for a single year in a new black seminary in Richmond, then went on to ministerial duties with white congregations elsewhere. White southerners' racial views, along with the freed people's wholesale abandonment of southern white churches in favor of their own denominations, resulted in a failure of the major southern denominations to engage in any sustained educational effort for the freed people before the end of Reconstruction, leaving the organized work almost entirely in the hands of northern missionary societies.[41]

Southern Quakers were the sole exception. Southern Quakerism was limited primarily to central North Carolina and parts of southern Virginia by the 1860s, having been largely driven out of the South over the previous century because of the Quaker witness against slavery. North Carolina Quakers, particularly, made a sustained effort to support southern African Americans in their education project. Like northern Quakers, they had a long history of opposition to slavery and sympathy for African Americans and their education. They had refused to participate in the rebellion and, as a result, suffered persecution at the hands of Confederates. Meanwhile, their pacifism provided no protection from the physical and economic

It Will Result in a Better Understanding

devastation of war. Despite their own straightened condition, southern Quakers taught in black schools in Guilford and surrounding counties in North Carolina, from the end of the war to the end of Reconstruction and beyond, with financial assistance from Quakers in Maryland and Pennsylvania. Although the sect was a tiny minority of white North Carolinians, less than 2 percent of the state's church membership, they made up more than one-fifth of all the state's white teachers in black schools between 1865 and 1876.[42]

Most of the southern Quaker teachers taught for one or two years, though some, such as Judith Mendenhall and William C. Welborn, taught for ten years or more, Welborn through 1880 at least. The mean number of years that southern Quakers spent in the freed people's schools was 2.75. Five members of the extended Mendenhall family spent seventeen years teaching the freed people. Noting her long history of support for African Americans, one observer remarked of Mendenhall, "She and her family have been for years the friends of the colored people running much risk both before and since the war on their account."[43] Edward Payson Hall and Amanda Hall are typical of the Quaker work, though unusual in the fact that he was the son of a slaveholder who became convinced that slavery was unjust and converted to the Quaker faith during the Civil War. They established two black schools in North Carolina in 1866, each teaching in one. After two years, Edward set up other schools and put his more advanced students in charge of them, then spent part of each week traveling between schools to supervise and provide further instruction to the teachers. He and Amanda Hall gave the freed people near his home an acre of land for a schoolhouse and gave them enough logs from their woods to build a large schoolhouse. The efforts of the freed people and the Halls to construct the school were, however, rebuffed by their neighbors at every opportunity. "Surrounded as we are by a white community opposed to our plans, we can expect no assistance," Hall wrote. "Extortionate demands for horses & wagons would be made, in the neighborhood. The mills would not *saw* for us." Hall and the freed people completed the schoolhouse themselves with a small appropriation from the Freedmen's Bureau. The Halls continued to teach and supervise their black schools until the autumn of 1870, when white opposition became so threatening that they had to flee for their lives.[44]

While religious obligations failed to move most southern churches and congregations to take up black education, religion did figure in the motivations of a few individual white southerners. Mary Bowers remarked on the financial and social sacrifice she was making as a result of teaching the freed people near Chapel Hill, North Carolina, but added, "I feel that I am *doing good* and therefore I am willing to bear having my feelings hurt or any thing else for I know I am useful in my Masters Vineyard." A teacher in Louisiana also referred to the social costs of teaching the freed people, but, like Bowers, trusted that her faith would sustain her. "It is a kind of Missionary spirit that prompts me to the work," she wrote in 1865, "and that spirit will uphold me through all the odium and scorn that the slaveholder may please to throw on all who engage in the glorious work."[45]

What is most striking about the testimony of those teachers, however, is that virtually no other southern whites spoke in such terms in relation to teaching the freed people. Northern whites almost always appealed to religious motivations when describing their work or applying for a position, hoping that they might mobilize the schoolroom for the salvation of their charges or of themselves. In contrast, while the evangelical South had long defended its paternalistic role in Christianizing African Americans, southern white teachers were silent on religious motivations for their work in black schools.[46]

While southern white teachers seldom mentioned religious motivations or spiritual ends for their work in black schools, an occasional southern white teacher indicated a desire to do well by her black neighbors and to move the South toward more progressive racial and sectional politics. For instance, Sarah J. Percival, a lifelong resident of Winchester, Virginia, explained that she had taught the city's freed people "without hope of recompense except the desire to see the people educated."[47] Esther Christian acknowledged that her poverty necessitated that she find work, but added, "thinking of no object more worthy, I commenced the teaching of a school for the Freedmen" despite deep antipathy from her white neighbors.[48] James E. Rhodes, an agent of the Friends Freedmen's Association, noted an unnamed southern woman, a native of Richmond, Virginia, who was "conscious of the social sacrifice she makes" in teaching the freed people but had "entered upon the work from real interest in it." And Chapel Hill, North Carolina, native Mary Bowers echoed his observation when she wrote simply, "I feel a great interest in the improvement of the colored people."[49] Such teachers were among those southerners that suggest to some historians that there was a brief moment after the Civil War when things might have been different, when interracialism might have flourished, when the South might have experienced a genuine reconstruction not unlike postwar Germany or Japan eight decades later. Yet like

It Will Result in a Better Understanding

expressions of religious interests in black education, these sorts of progressive political and social expressions from southern white teachers were rare. They are also as progressive as one can find from southern teachers. Ultimately, they are also ambiguous, never speaking clearly about the writers' racial or social visions.

The names southern white teachers gave to their schools occasionally appear to have reflected high expectations for the results of the teachers' labors. The schools were sometimes called academies, a term implying an expectation of outcomes higher than would be achieved in a primary school. For example, Elizabeth S. Thompson called her school in Columbiana, Alabama, Oak Grove Academy. Jennie Carswell's school was New World Academy; Rev. H. W. Lawley named his school Vernon Academy; R. H. Westmoreland taught in Lightfoot Academy. More remarkable was Mrs. S. S. Dupress's school, the H. W. Beecher Academy, named after antislavery leader and northern theologian, Henry Ward Beecher. Dupress was a white southern native of Opelika, Alabama.[50]

Southern white teachers' left few comments on their students' achievements, but those that have survived are often as positive as any made by northern white teachers. Jacob M. Jennings, a Confederate veteran teaching in Alabama in the spring of 1867, reported that he was "highly gratified at the regret manifested by the pupils" when he closed the school at the end of the term. He believed that "as much has been accomplished in the time in which this school has been operating, as ever has been in the time and with similar material." He did not reopen his school, however, despite his apparent success.[51] "I have been teaching school more or less for thirty years," North Carolinian Isaiah Bodenhamer wrote in his second year of teaching the freed people; "my pupils in this school are learning faster than any white pupils I ever had in school."[52] A South Carolinian teaching a black school in northwestern Georgia in 1867 expressed his dismay at having to close his school because the pay was too low: "I regret it the progress of the children was very incouraging to both the Parents & myself."[53] The bureau superintendent of education for Alabama found southern white teachers' enthusiasm for black learners ubiquitous. "Whenever a Southern man becomes a teacher of colored schools," he wrote to a northern minister, "I have noticed that he thereby becomes practically a radical and becomes more lavish of praise for his pupils than even Northern teachers."[54]

Historians must, of course, deal with such testimony with a measure of care. Many of the white teachers were desperate for wage labor, and were doubtlessly sufficiently sophisticated to recognize their audience and to speak to its concerns. Even the names given to schools may reflect something other than positive southern white teachers' attitudes and expectations. We do not know, for example, whether the teachers or the black community named the schools; we do not know whether white teachers referring to their school with such elevated titles as "academy" intended to convey pride in their students' potential or meant to mock their students' naïveté. We do not even know if Dupress's celebration of Beecher was a reference to Beecher's antislavery activism or his postwar betrayal of African Americans and wholehearted embrace of Confederates.[55]

The great majority of southern white teachers left no record of their feelings toward the freed people or their attitudes regarding the future of southern African Americans. Susan W. Hubard, daughter of a very wealthy slave owner in Virginia, provides an apt example. She taught a black school for one year, 1868. Many of the letters she wrote that year, filled with news, gossip, and opinions, have survived. Never once did she mention her school or her students in her letters to friends and family. The only correspondent who knew of her work was a Union officer to whom she wrote asking for books for her school.[56] Likewise, of the applicants for positions in the black schools established in New Orleans in the early 1860s by the Department of the Gulf, only two of more than one hundred spoke directly in their letters of application about the students who would populate their classrooms. All of the others simply described their experience or educational attainment, and, quite often, spoke of their own desperate need for employment.[57] Many southern white teachers appear to have approached their duties in a manner similar to that of a southern white woman that Cornelia Hancock hired to teach at what became Laing School in South Carolina: "She does her duty in school but takes no interest in the scholars further than that," Hancock observed.[58] It is telling, too, that the southern white teachers who spoke glowingly of their students' academic prowess remained in black classrooms no longer than other southern teachers, one to two years.

While very few southern whites spoke of religious ends, or philanthropic intentions, or social or political visions for their work, many of them, very many, did voice their immediate reasons for engaging in the black schools. Others did not say it, but their circumstances spoke as loudly as words. Their reason was simple. They were poor to the point of desperation. In less than a decade, the South had lived the manmade destruction of war and the nature-wrought devastation of flood, drought, and insects. The result was, for many white southerners, a poverty so great that even

It Will Result in a Better Understanding

prejudice had to be set aside. They were, in the words of a Virginia school superintendent, "persons already sufficiently humbled to be willing to earn their necessary bread by teaching colored children."[59] Like an echo, a teacher from the other end of the former Confederacy remarked, "I am not ashamed to teach a Freedmen's school if it pays me," though a bureau agent said of her, "Only hunger compels her to teach."[60] A former slave mistress spoke for hundreds: "I am a poor widow with 8 little children," Stacy Mayfield wrote in 1869. "I have been trying to make my living for the last 14 months teaching Freedmen."[61]

Most of the southern white women who taught the freed people were very poor, and their poverty goes far toward explaining their willingness to cross the double southern boundaries of race and gender roles—teaching the freed people, in the first instance, and taking up paid labor, in the second. The households of three-quarters of the southern white women teachers located to date in the 1870 census declared total wealth of $500 or less; most of that group had no wealth at all.[62] Like Stacy Mayfield, some spoke openly of their poverty in their applications for positions in black schools. Maria Cochrane, for example, applying in 1864 to teach in the freedmen's schools of New Orleans, wrote, "I am in very indigent circumstances, having no one to help me, and finding it very hard to support myself." This graduate of New Orleans' Girls High School taught in black schools for six years.[63] Letters of recommendation revealed the indigence of others. A writer disclosed that Mary A. J. Ryan was a poor white Catholic woman supporting a widowed mother by teaching the freed people in Tuscaloosa, Alabama.[64] M. E. Golden, who would teach for at least five years in black schools in rural Louisiana parishes, was described as "an *Orphan* and being poor not having been blessed with wealth, and being thrown upon the resources of her own industry to obtain an honest livelyhood.[65]

Many of the poor white women teachers were widows. Some, like Harriet Hart and Anne E. Setzer, had been widowed by the war. Sarah Bowman, a poor widow with one child, taught in Livingston, Alabama's black school in 1867–68; three years later, at thirty years of age, she was still teaching, though apparently in a white school. Sarah T. Bullock, thirty-five, widowed, with four children, and equally as poor, taught in a black school in Dennards Bluff, Alabama, for at least three years, beginning in 1870. Mrs. E. P. Elam supported herself and two daughters as the principal of a black school in Petersburg, Virginia, from 1868 into the 1880s.[66] Esther A. Christian, at the start of what would be at least five years in the freedmen's school that she established in Americus, Georgia, explained, "my

It Will Result in a Better Understanding

condition in life,—being widowed, very poor, and having two daughters to support—rendered it necessary for me to enter into some arrangement whereby I could gain an honest livelihood."[67] Similarly, widow Georgia A. Grimes wrote of her Tennessee freedmen's school, "this is my dependence for a support for myself and two children."[68] None of those widows had any wealth to report in the 1870 census. Savilla Edge, a widow in Randolph County, Alabama, conducted school in her home until opponents of black education burned her house down; by 1870 she listed herself as a farmer with $160 worth of real estate and no other wealth.[69]

More married women than widows taught, and most of them also lived in impoverished situations when they began teaching the freed people.[70] Not surprisingly, most of their husbands were farmers—Mary Davis's husband, for example, worth $500 in 1870; Elizabeth Welch's husband, worth $300; or Eudoxey S. Winn's husband, who owned no land of his own and reported only $250 in personal wealth.[71] Wives' wages from teaching also supplemented income from nonfarm occupations among the husbands of poorer white women teachers, including a bookkeeper, wagon maker, turpentine worker, laborer, and carpenter, none with family wealth of more than $125.[72] Anna H. Wigg's husband, a judge, doubtlessly had social status but claimed no wealth in 1870. Rhoda Faggard taught a freedmen's school alongside her teacher husband. In their fifties, the Faggards had no wealth to claim in 1870.[73] Daughters also taught to ease family hardship. Typical cases include Emily Adams, daughter of a drayman worth $200; Mary Henderson, forty-year-old daughter of a penurious teacher; and Jennie D. Freeman, twenty-seven-year-old daughter of a farmer with no wealth. Single southern white freedmen's teachers living alone or boarding almost invariably reported no wealth.[74]

Although more southern white men found their way into the black schools than southern white women, the women as a group, at 42 percent of the southern white teachers, were a significant part of the work, and their experiences speak to issues of southern white womanhood in the period. Prior to the Civil War, southern white women were less likely to engage in paid labor than northern women, though prewar wage earning was not as uncommon for southern women as historians once argued, and even the most privileged women worked as unpaid labor. The war and its aftermath inexorably changed women's work in the South, moving increasing numbers of them into paid labor, not least of all into teaching. The feminization of teaching, largely realized in the North by mid-century, accelerated rapidly in the South beginning in the late 1860s.[75]

It Will Result in a Better Understanding

Still, during Reconstruction the majority of southern teachers continued to be male. There is little evidence that different motives animated the southern white men. Poverty and the mounting hardships arising from postwar southern agricultural disasters drove many of them, even Confederate veterans, into classrooms to which they had little commitment. Among many examples, Sam Adams had been a successful newspaper publisher in Troy, Alabama, in the 1850s. He was a lieutenant in the 9th Alabama Infantry. By 1867, a northern credit agency considered him an honest but impoverished man. In 1870, he taught a freedmen's school for one term.[76] As an Alabama planter, Robert A. Burnett was somewhat more typical: a young slave owner and a partner in a dry goods store before the war, with $6,000 worth of land and $20,000 in personal estate, including fourteen slaves, Burnett enlisted as a lieutenant in the 38th Alabama Infantry. The war, emancipation, and a dishonest partner ruined him. In 1870, when he took up teaching black children for a year, he had no landholdings and little else of value.[77] William McKeown lacked the advantages of Adams and Burnett but ended up in the same predicament. He was a blacksmith who owned about $300 in property and had nearly as much in personal estate in 1860. He spent the war as a private in a South Carolina infantry regiment. In 1869, impoverished, he taught for a single term. The following year he reported that he was propertyless with a total worth of less than $200. All three of these men, and nearly all of the rest of the Confederate veterans who taught, were in serious financial distress when they became teachers. Teaching paid poorly and uncertainly, suggesting how serious were the hardship these teachers faced.[78]

Nonveterans in the black schools were in no better financial condition. James G. Carstarphen was a Methodist minister who, along with his family, lived with his slaveholding father in Missouri. He and his father were worth over $31,000 in 1860. By 1870, he was living in Tennessee, having been teaching the freed people for three years at fifteen dollars per month to support his family; he could report no wealth of any sort.[79] James G. Billingsley had been a nonslaveholding farmer near Austin, Texas, before the war, holding $5,000 worth of land. A decade later, he was listed as a farm laborer with no wealth. Described as "a very competent teacher, but somewhat old & feeble," he taught a black school from 1867 to 1870.[80] Not all began with wealth, of course, though some, such as Green B. Bush, had other sorts of stakes in the prewar southern society. He had been an overseer on a Richland County, South Carolina, plantation. He owned neither real estate nor personal estate in 1860; by 1870, the year he taught a black school, he still had no real or personal estate.[81]

Being poor in the postwar South did not mean that southern white teachers were necessarily from the South's antebellum lower classes, as the cases above indicate. Like Burnett and Carstarphen, many had been slave-holders before the war. Louiza Simmons and her husband had owned forty slaves before emancipation; in the late 1860s they were preparing their freed bondspeople to become teachers in Troy, North Carolina.[82] Mary A. Chambers of Pekin, North Carolina, had also been a slaveholder and claimed to have taught her servants to read before the war. Explaining her decision to start a school for the neighboring freed people, she wrote, "we have always had a plenty but the War has ruined us."[83] Fanny Harvey's slaveholding family had been wealthy until the late 1840s when her father "managed badly and got into debt." She became a freedmen's teacher in 1865 in Lynchburg, Virginia, and continued in that city's black schools through Reconstruction and possibly longer.[84] Collins D. Elliot, who taught in Nashville's black schools for at least a year along with his wife, was the former principal of an elite women's school and owner of ten enslaved people. He was worth $175,000 in 1860, but was reduced to relative penury by 1870.[85]

Not all of the southern teachers were driven into the classroom with the lash of poverty, of course. Jennie Carswell, the Georgia teacher who called her school the New World Academy and taught in it for two years, was married to a farmer who had $5,300 in total wealth in 1870, quite comfort-able at more than double the national median wealth of the era. Sarah Ann Steer taught for at least five years in a freed people's school in Loudon County, Virginia, though her father, a tax assessor, was worth $11,000 in 1870. John H. Webster, a farmer in Perry County, Alabama, taught in a black school in 1872, though he was worth more than $8,000 in 1870, only a minor decline from the $10,000 he was worth in 1860.[86] Remarkably few of the southern white teachers were financially solvent by 1870, however, and a teacher with the resources of Webster was extremely rare.

FOUR TEACHERS—TWO INDIVIDUALS AND ONE MARRIED COUPLE— encapsulate several of the characteristics and possible motives of southern white men and women who taught the freed people. Their biographies provide further glimpses into what it meant that, before a decade of eman-cipation had passed, southern whites had become the majority of the teachers of the people just emancipated from bondage to southern whites. While no four people could be considered fully typical of the thousands of southern white teachers, these four come close, with three caveats. First, both of the men were Confederate veterans, whereas probably fewer than half of the southern white male teachers were veterans. Second, three of the four had northern antecedents, contrasted with a small percentage of all of the southern white teachers. Third, all of them had been slaveholders, whereas it is likely that only a minority of the entire corps of southern white teachers had owned slaves.

On the ruins of her plantation in the coastal plain of Georgia, Harriet A. Hart gathered her former slaves and the freed people from neighboring plantations and began teaching them in late 1867. She had lost everything in the war. Sherman's army had destroyed the plantation's livestock and much else of value; her husband had died shortly thereafter; her stepchildren had inherited much of the land except for the lot her house stood on and some woodland; and little else of value remained. She had gone from being the mistress of a modest plantation worth over $9,000, including twelve slaves, to poverty. "I have called the colored people together, & given them permission to get lumber off my place, & put up a schoolhouse on my lawn in front of my house free of charge, & told them I would open a day school for the children, and a night school for adults," she wrote to the Freedmen's Bureau. "I could do no more. For those who know how to read I charge a dollar a month, for those commencing, 75 cts. They are to pay me in poultry & eggs & moss, or anything that they can, at market prices."[87]

The daughter of missionaries to India and born in Bombay, Hart had been educated in Geneva, New York. She made her way into the South in the early 1840s as a teacher and tutor in white families, first in Tennessee and then in Georgia. About 1851, she met Smith S. Hart, a widowed planter several years her senior, and became stepmother to three teenaged children and mother to three more, one of whom she lost in infancy. After her husband's death, she went north briefly to leave her daughter with friends, then returned with her ten-year-old son "to my desolate home, for no other purpose but to add my mite of efforts, towards bettering the condition of the blacks in an educational point." She saw her work as a continuation of efforts she had made before emancipation: "While slaves I taught all who came to me, on the sly at the risk of a heavy fine." In her postwar school, she taught twelve hours a day, her eighty students coming for their lessons in groups, the most advanced students coming last. She later wrote of her hopes for the freed people—"I want to encourage them

It Will Result in a Better Understanding

in their efforts to rise from their present condition"—but also spoke of the hostility with which her efforts were met: "I am sorry to say that public opinion with regard to their education is very much against them. My neighbors have been heard to say I ought to be drove out of the county for teaching the 'black dogs.' "[88]

Hart taught, assisted by her son, from 1868 into the 1880s. She spent a part of 1871 in a futile attempt to gain compensation for her wartime losses. The Southern Claims Commission found, seven years later, that while her husband did not actively support the Confederacy, neither was he a Unionist. Her own convictions were irrelevant to the commission, since the property belonged to him, not to her. Her appeal of the commissioners' findings speaks both to her continuing poverty and the continuing attitude of southern whites to black education in 1878:

> I was left a widow with young children, and only some land, & no means to cultivate it. It has been touch & go with me these past 12 yrs, I have been teaching the colored people since 1869 with no remuneration, as they poor souls, are not able, save for three months in the year. I get a small salary from the County School Board. For this act of benevolence, I am ostracized by all white neighbors, not a soul comes near me, in sickness or health. My young son is just come of age, & commenced farming, & needs means to give him a start. I need means to buy a horse, wagon, harness, farming utensils, cows, hogs, & sheep. I am living in a little log house, with but two rooms, my own dwelling having tumbled down, for want of means to repair it.[89]

Her appeal failed.

MARY STEWART TRAVELED FROM NEW JERSEY TO LAGRANGE, GEORGIA, IN the 1840s and started a millinery business. She was sufficiently successful to allow her to purchase "a fancy negro woman for $1,000" in the early 1850s while still in her late twenties. John D. Witham, a native of Maine, also left the North for Georgia in the 1840s, working with a stagecoach line in Meriwether County for a few years, then moving on to LaGrange about 1851 as an agent of the line with responsibilities for its livery stable. Stewart and Witham met in LaGrange, both in their thirties, and were married by 1853. Despite the marriage, however, Mary Witham managed to keep her finances distinct from John's, a wise move since he proved an improvident businessman. By 1859, Mary Witham owned her business, city property, and three slaves. A correspondent for the Mercantile Agency estimated her wealth at $6,000 but noted that John Witham "is seeking to avail himself of the Insolvent Debtor's Oath." The following year, however, the agency found that she had become a poor credit risk and had fallen into debt. The war ruined any chance she had to rebuild her credit. Her first postwar credit report indicated that her store was closed. "She is here & now teaching Negroes, do not regard her as w[orth] anything," an agent reported. The following year, John Witham joined his wife in the black school, but after four months both of them left black education to pursue other opportunities. John became a tax collector; Mary returned to millinery, despite declaring bankruptcy in 1869. The Mercantile Agency's final notes on her read, in the agency's gossipy shorthand, "A Bkpt & sorter rascally," and cautioned merchants, "Look out. Poor chance. Better sell for cash." Between them, the Withams taught for a total of three short terms.[90]

TWELVE HANDPICKED YOUNG CONFEDERATE OFFICERS SERVED AS THE inner circle of aides to General Robert E. Lee. Giles Buckner Cooke was one of the twelve. Born to relative affluence—his father was a miller who owned fifteen slaves in 1850—Cooke had an excellent education. He attended two private grammar schools, two academies to prepare himself for military school, and the prestigious Virginia Military Institute, from which he graduated in 1859. He taught school for a term after VMI then began to study law in Petersburg. He entered the service of the Confederacy within days of Virginia's declaration of secession, a commissioned officer on the strength of his military education. In the course of the war, he attained the rank of captain.[91]

Although Cooke's family was not among the elite of Virginia's slaveholders, it was firmly on the second tier, more on the strength of family connections and education than land or slave holdings. His educational advantages compensated handsomely for his status and his military experience, while serving as aide to the revered general of the Army of Virginia crowned his ascendancy. Cooke had imbibed and defended in battle the culture and worldview of southern slaveholders, particularly their strong sense of hierarchy and of paternalism toward African Americans.[92] After the war, Cooke returned to Petersburg. He dallied briefly with a private school, but felt compelled to teach the freed people as a means to salvage as much of southern racial paternalism and racial distinction as possible in the unsettled years of Reconstruction. He began teaching in a black public school in 1867, then accepted a position as principal of Petersburg's black public high school in 1868, a position he held for four years while qualify-

It Will Result in a Better Understanding

ing himself for the Episcopal priesthood. After a falling-out with the
Petersburg school board for refusing to submit to a required qualifying
examination (arguing that a diploma from VMI should provide all the
necessary evidence of his qualifications), Cooke left the public school to
start a private Episcopal normal school for black students.[93]

When Cooke left the public school, he reportedly took "the larger number of his upper class from the Colored High School, whose parents were
well to do. The free negroes, who in Petersburg were very numerous and
respectable before the war, are very much attached to Mr. C." Cooke became an ordained Episcopal priest in 1874, ministering primarily to black
Episcopalians in Petersburg while expanding the "Major Cooke School"
with the addition of a theology department. He taught the Petersburg
black students who could afford to pay tuition until 1885. The theology
department of his school became the Bishop Payne Divinity School, the
Episcopal Church's only theological seminary for black priests until well
into the twentieth century.[94]

The reported preference of the Petersburg free black community to
retain a distance between themselves and the freed people—"to worship
separately, and to be separately educated," according to *Spirit of Missions*,
the Episcopal missionary organ—fit well with Cooke's conservative views.
In an interview late in his life, he told his interrogator "that his real
contribution to history and to humanity was the work he initiated in the
dark days of Reconstruction." That work was inspired by the examples of
Robert E. Lee and "Stonewall" Jackson, who both reputedly taught their
slaves before the Civil War as a means of training them to servitude. "Giles
Buckner Cooke was the pioneer in the 'New Deal' for liberated Negroes in
the matter of education," his interviewer enthused. "He realized that the
welfare of both white and black depended on proper training of the latter."
An earlier observer wrote that Cooke turned to black education after the
Civil War in the conviction "that the freedmen must be given wisely-
fashioned education" to wean them from northern ideas and influences,
echoing another southern Episcopal divine's dictate that southerners had
to control the education of the freed people in order "to keep them as
friends" and preclude northern influence among them.[95]

Hierarchical distinctions, the "proper training" of subordinate peoples
—such was the stuff of paternalistic education. Cooke sought to fashion a
schooling free of the overtones of social equality that he associated with
carpetbaggers and scalawags, a schooling that would retain as much of
antebellum hierarchical race relations as possible. Yet even a quintessen-

It Will Result in a Better Understanding

tial southern white teacher of black youth faced stern opposition from other southerners. In an unpublished biography, a descendant of Cooke wrote that his decision to take a teaching position in black schools "cut him off from many of his friends and made many of his old associates turn their backs upon him. It meant social ostracism for any Southerner in 1868, to openly associate himself with the negro cause."[96]

WHILE MANY WHITE SOUTHERNERS LOATHED THE IDEA OF BLACK SCHOOLS, the southern white teachers, by the very act of transgressing the boundary separating whites and blacks educationally, acknowledged that, at least in the arena of literacy, the world had changed. Few embraced the fullest measure of emancipation through education, however; few expected their labor to further the changes in their world any more than necessary. Most entered the black schoolhouse reluctantly, forced by destitution to accept wages for work for which they must have felt a great ambivalence, if not revulsion, remaining in the school for a brief term or two. Their language very seldom betrayed any vision of the sort of world for which they sought to prepare their charges. The brevity of their tenure in the schools doubtlessly communicated negative expectations to wary black learners. For every Harriet Hart who taught for many years in the expectation that her work was "bettering the condition of the blacks" or promoting "their efforts to rise from their present condition," hundreds of Withams taught briefly with, at best, a mild solicitude for their students but, so far as the evidence can demonstrate, no expectation that education could or should raise African Americans to any degree of equality within the social order. Many may, like Giles Cooke, have intended to use education to foreclose the possibilities of an open and equal society, to limit emancipation and preserve racial hierarchy and white privilege. African American teachers spoke consistently the language of uplift, of raising the freed people to a new social and political plane. A rare Harriet Hart excepted, southern white teachers never spoke such language. By the rare hints they give us directly, and more frequently in their behavior and the racial expectations they carried with them, it appears that they expected that the schooling they provided would prepare the freed people to remain on the plane they had always occupied, though now at least moderately literate.

Freedmen's Bureau agent Ralza M. Manly was right, at least in part, when he said of the increasing numbers of southern white teachers taking up black schools in the 1860s, "While such teachers are not the best, they are better than none for children who are as yet entirely untaught."[97]

It Will Result in a Better Understanding

Literacy is better than illiteracy, no matter by whom it is facilitated. Yet intentions, vision, and expectations matter in the serious business of teaching and learning. The intentions, visions, and expectations brought to black classrooms by former slaveholders, Confederate veterans, and desperately poor southern white teachers, few able to fully emancipate themselves from the legacy of racial slavery, hierarchical social relations, and paternalism, were likely to establish educational boundaries far short of those staked out by black teachers and demanded by the freed people for their emancipation.

Chapter Four

A Desire to Labor
in the Missionary Cause

Northern White Teachers and the
Ambiguities of Emancipation

My object is to do good, and improve my health and
knowledge of the conditions of the South.

George C. Carpenter, 1866

I have resolved to give myself to the work of evangelizing
the Freedmen, if you have need of me.

Cornelia L. Lloyd, 1869

Then *social* justice will follow *in time*: not soon, perhaps
not for generations, but *in time*. That secure, every exertion
must be made to educate the people; to give them not
book-knowledge only, but knowledge of moral & social duties.
I am appalled at the hugeness of this work. What is one, what
am I, before such an Herculean task! I tremble, & shrink, &
want to run away. And it *must* be done, or the consequences
will be terrible beyond conception.

Jane Briggs Smith, 1865

W hen the American Civil War began, Mary J. Mead was living
alone in the quiet college town of Hillsdale, Michigan. In the
previous decade she had been widowed by the death of her
attorney husband and had lost her daughter, Ella. Her husband had left her
with investments sufficient to keep her comfortable—indeed, sufficient
enough that the census taker in 1860 had given her the honorific of "lady"
as her occupation to indicate that she did not need to work for a living. In

1864, at forty-two years of age, she accepted an invitation from the Michigan Freedmen's Aid Society to teach for a year in a school for former slaves who had fled to Kansas. Thus began a seven-year career of teaching among the freed people. Mead went from Kansas to Virginia, North Carolina, and Tennessee, ending with three years in Selma, Alabama, working for three different aid organizations over those seven years.[1]

As Mead made her way to Kansas to begin her work, Private Walter McDonald lay in a hospital in Fortress Monroe, Virginia, recovering from wounds received in battle. He had enlisted with the 7th New Hampshire Volunteers only four months after the war began, a thirty-nine-year-old immigrant from Scotland. When McDonald finally mustered out in Florida in 1865, he remained in the South, purchasing property in Bainbridge, Georgia. As business began to falter in 1868, however, he turned his building into a schoolhouse for the freed people. He taught there for two years.[2]

Six months after the war ended, the National Freedmen's Relief Association sent Julia E. Benedict to teach in its school in Alexandria, Virginia. When she returned to her home in Woodbury, Connecticut, in 1866, her schoolmate, Eliza Ann Summers, was entranced by her stories. The two friends applied to the American Missionary Association for teaching positions and in January 1867 they were posted to the Sea Islands of South Carolina. Benedict was twenty-one, Summers was twenty-two. Summers, an experienced teacher, observed that her black students learned as fast as the northern white students she had taught in the past and wrote of the freed people, "I would much rather teach them and cannot bear to think of ever teaching up North again." Despite that declaration, Eliza Summers only taught in the South for six months. Her many letters say little about the freed people or teaching but much about "sociables" and outings with other northern workers. She returned to Woodbury and was married two years later. Benedict did not return south immediately, but in 1869 she went to Fisk University, where she taught for two more years.[3]

TAKEN TOGETHER, MEAD AND MCDONALD, SUMMERS AND BENEDICT, exemplify particular aspects of the corps of northern white teachers who taught in the freed people's schools between the opening guns of the Civil War and the end of Reconstruction. Though their sobriquet, the "Yankee teachers," suggests homes in New England, they were more likely to come from the middle and western states than the Northeast. Most were women, by a ratio of more than two to one.[4] Among both men and women, more than twice as many were single as married or widowed. Some, like Mary Mead,

A Desire to Labor in the Missionary Cause

were comfortably situated, but others, including Julia Benedict, must have struggled—Benedict was the orphaned daughter of a dyer who had been worth only $1,500 in 1850.[5] Some were deeply committed to the work, though they defined the work in a variety of ways, while others appear superficial. A few—about 250 in all—taught as long or longer than Mead's seven years; most taught one-third that long.[6] Writers have delighted in speaking of the northern white teachers in military terms—an "army of civilization," the "soldiers of light and love," perpetrators of a " 'messianic' invasion," or "gentle invaders." Yet at fewer than 4,500 women and men, spread over fifteen years, the northern white teachers could scarcely have mounted the formidable assault on the South that such language portends.[7]

Northern white teachers never numbered as many as 1,300 in any one year. Indeed, the movement of northern white teachers into the South expended itself early. The school year immediately following the war, 1865–66, was the peak year of northern white teachers' participation, with 1,293 of them working in the southern black schools. Even in that year, northern white teachers constituted less than three-fifths of the entire teaching force; thereafter, they never constituted even half of the total number of teachers for the freed people. Their numbers began to dwindle after 1866, slowly at first, then more rapidly. By 1870, the number had fallen by half to 667 northern white teachers. By the end of Reconstruction, roughly 230 northern white teachers remained in the southern black schools (see table 3).[8]

When the notion of the Yankee teacher is extended beyond the usual image of northern whites, however—when the portrait includes black Yankees—the profile of the northern teacher in the South and the meaning of the work changes dramatically. The number of northern black teachers did not peak until 1870. In 1868, the number of black teachers (northern and southern) exceeded the number of northern white teachers. In that latter year, there were more black teachers working in the freed people's schools—nearly 1,400—than the northern white teachers had managed in their best year, 1865. The following year, there were more than 1,700 black teachers at work, compared to 1,000 northern whites. Thereafter, as the Freedmen's Bureau closed, northern aid societies retrenched or withdrew, and overall northern benevolent contributions to freedmen's education plummeted, the total number of northern teachers fell to nearly one-quarter of its peak, while northern black teachers continued to constitute a quarter or more of the northern contingent.

Gender played out differently among northern white teachers than

	Males			Females		
	n	Percent	Years Teaching	n	Percent	Years Teaching
Northern black teachers	365	50.0	3.66	364	50.0	3.59
Northern white teachers	1,047	33.1	2.17	2,115	66.9	2.61
Southern black teachers	2,081	62.4	2.70	1,251	37.6	2.83
Southern white teachers	926	57.9	1.50	674	42.1	1.66

Source: Freedmen's Teacher Project, 2009

among the other groups of teachers. As we have seen, southern men, whether white or black, were more likely to teach the freed people than southern women; northern black men and women served in virtually equal numbers. Among northern white teachers, on the other hand, men were less likely to teach than women. Only one of every three northern white teachers was male. Further, northern white women taught longer than northern white men, though only by a matter of months on average. Although most of the northern white women were single, a significant one-quarter of the northern women were married or widowed. Predictably, most of the married women were in the South with husbands who were also teaching or engaged in other work, though an occasional woman went to the South alone, leaving a husband to fend for himself. Mary H. Stoutenburg, for example, left her husband, Abram, to care for their farm in New York while she and her daughter taught in Fredericksburg, Virginia, for several months each year from 1865 to 1868.[9]

One-fifth of the northern white teachers went into the South in some form of family group. Over 400 went as husbands and wives and another one hundred couples taught with one or more children. Sisters frequently went together; brothers accompanied sisters less frequently; and brothers went together relatively rarely.[10]

As a group, the northern white teachers were well educated. Of the nearly 800 whose educational attainments have been established, over 580 had attended some form of advanced secondary or higher education; nearly three-fifths of those had graduated from college. Thus, the northern white teachers as a group had probably attained more schooling than the average middle-class adult of their era. They had attended a broad array of institutions, more than eighty different schools in all, ranging from elite colleges

A Desire to Labor in the Missionary Cause

Between 1861 and 1876, scores of teachers, black and white, died or were killed while in the South or immediately after returning from the South. Mrs. Eunice Leland from Neposett, Massachusetts, forty-eight years old, and Miss Ellen S. Kempton from New Bedford, Massachusetts, twenty-six years old, were among those who died in the work. Courtesy of the Trustees of the Boston Public Library/Rare Books.

and graduate-level theological seminaries through the antebellum period's most transitory colleges and academies. Many more had attended normal schools.[11] Harvard, Yale, Dartmouth, and Brown were represented by nearly sixty teachers; ten had attended Andover, Chicago, Union, Western, and other theological seminaries; Ohio Wesleyan Female Seminary and Ohio Wesleyan University had graduated two dozen, Amherst College twenty, and Williams College a dozen. Two schools, however, accounted for over one-third of all the teachers. Oberlin College, interracial and coeducational from its founding in the 1830s, led with 131 white students who became teachers for the freed people (when the black Oberlin College students mentioned in chapter 2 are included, Oberlin's total comes to 177); thirty more had attended Oberlin Academy, the college's preparatory school. Mount Holyoke Female Seminary, as academically rigorous as any men's college of its day, sent eighty-eight teachers to the South.[12]

While an occasional northern white teacher was as young as Julia Benedict and Eliza Summers, not long out of school themselves, more of them were closer to or into their middle years, about thirty years of age in their first year of teaching the freed people.[13] They were for the most part, then, mature women and men with a decade or more of adult life and work behind them, in sharp contrast to the assumption frequently repeated that the northern white teachers were primarily young women. The women who had engaged in paid labor before their southern work were, overwhelmingly, experienced teachers. Of the more than 600 northern white women whose occupations prior to teaching in the South are known, only about 80 had engaged in other sorts of work, primarily as dressmakers, milliners, factory operatives, and clerks.[14] Not surprisingly, the northern white men had a broader range of occupational experiences before they taught in the South. Some had been skilled workers—carpenters, painters, blacksmiths, shoemakers, bakers, even an iron fence builder. More had been ministers, teachers, farmers, professionals, and clerical workers, in that order. It is likely that many were like Massachusetts native Luke Bemis, who had "usually worked, as a mechanic" but also had experience as a teacher, or like New Yorker Harvey S. Beals, who was listed as a master pail maker with five journeymen pail makers boarding with his family in 1855 and a lumberman by 1860, but could claim seventeen years of teaching experience when he applied to the American Missionary Association.[15]

As their occupations suggest, the northern white teachers were drawn from a broad swath of the middle class. A few came from wealthy families. Anna Caroline Woodbury, for example, was the daughter of a Michigan

A Desire to Labor in the Missionary Cause

banker who was worth a total of $100,000 in 1860. Cordelia Curtis's father
was a Connecticut manufacturer worth over $91,000. Both taught in Virginia for one year in the mid-1860s. Even more remarkable was the father of Helen and Kate Ireson. He was a Lynn, Massachusetts, merchant whose wealth grew from $3,500 in 1850 to $61,000 in 1860, then nearly tripled to $170,000 a decade later. The sisters taught in the South for a total of three years.[16]

Yet for every teacher from a wealthy family, another was from apparently genteel poverty. Thomas Putnam Fenner, his wife, and his eighteen-year-old daughter taught at Hampton Normal Institute for a combined eight years in the early 1870s. He was a musician with no wealth to report in 1860, and a modest $600 by 1870. Maine native Melissa R. Whitehouse taught in a black school in Richmond, Virginia, in 1869 and was principal of another black school in Wilmington, North Carolina, from 1870 to at least 1873. Her father, a carpenter and day laborer with a wife and five children to support, had no real estate in 1860 and estimated his personal estate at $125; in 1870, he reported no wealth at all.[17] Overall, the modal wealth of the northern white teachers in 1870 was $1,000 in an era in which the median family wealth in the northern states ranged between $1,000 and $3,000, but the range of the teachers' wealth is striking—fully one-third of all the northern white teachers came from homes with no landholdings at all and total wealth of $200 or less.[18]

A number of the northern white male teachers were Union veterans, perhaps as many as 600.[19] A few taught in the early years of the war before they enlisted, a handful taught while still in uniform, but most became teachers to the freed people after they were discharged. Some of those who taught first and then enlisted, such as Samuel S. Higginson, George N. Carruthers, Abner D. Olds, Oscar E. Doolittle, and Thomas Calahan, became officers in black regiments.[20] A minority of the veterans began teaching immediately upon discharge; most began later, either returning to the South after a few years or turning to black education after trying their hand at other work in the South. Union veterans taught the freed people longer than northern white men who had not been veterans, averaging a bit over two and a half years each.

The teachers were overwhelmingly a religious group. They grew up, after all, in what historian Jon Butler has called the American "antebellum spiritual hothouse," an era marked by widespread spiritual belief and religious pluralism but rising Christianization.[21] The ascendancy of Christian denominations and institutionalized church extension after midcen-

Joshua Stuart Banfield, a Union veteran and graduate of Dartmouth College, was a superintendent of New England Freedmen's Aid Society schools in Virginia and Georgia for four years, 1863–1867. Courtesy of the Trustees of the Boston Public Library/Rare Books.

tury was reflected in the organizations that dominated the northern benevolent effort in support of educating the former slaves. More than two dozen denominations mobilized their mission societies or organized new freedmen's aid societies to send teachers and books to the freed people. The American Baptist Home Mission Society and American Advent Mission Society, along with the American Missionary Association, putatively interdenominational but largely Congregationalist, simply expanded mission work they had long pursued, diverting resources to southern blacks. The Protestant Episcopal Freedmen's Commission, the Presbyterian Committee of Missions for Freedmen, and the Methodist Episcopal Freedmen's Aid Society, among others, were new missionary organizations that their denominations built from scratch, segregated from the rest of their missionary activity. Most of the denominational societies preferred to send

A Desire to Labor in the Missionary Cause

only teachers who were members of their own faith, though they made exceptions, and all were careful to eliminate any applicant who did not present unblemished evangelical credentials. They all made clear that the first priority was to extend their particular denomination into the South by winning black souls away from southern denominations and from each other—even the American Missionary Association worried about extending the Congregational Church, almost exclusively northern at midcentury, to the South. The evangelical coloring that the denominational agencies gave to the educational work was deepened by leadership within the Freedmen's Bureau that had strong ties to the American Missionary Association and other evangelical societies.[22]

Only one religious group working with the freed people, the Quakers, abjured a proselytizing or church extension mission in its work. The Quakers saw their work as the logical continuation of their long effort to end slavery and to aid and educate African Americans. Their century-old antislavery witness had made them pariahs in the South, placed many of them in the forefront of the abolitionist movement, and eventuated in Quaker leadership in support of northern black education from the late 1700s to the eve of the Civil War. Although most of the teachers they supported in the freed people's schools were Quakers, none of the Quaker organizations —primarily committees of the various Yearly Meetings—declared any denominational criteria for supporting individual teachers.[23]

In addition to the various Quaker groups, other agencies that supported teachers rejected the militantly evangelical and proselytizing thrust of the denominational work. A score of secular, voluntaristic organizations sprang up during the war representing northern states or regions—the New England Freedmen's Aid Society, the Pennsylvania Freedmen's Relief Association, and others. Until 1866, the secular agencies raised more funds and sent more teachers to the South than did the denominational societies. Thereafter, however, the missionary societies, led by the American Missionary Association, began a systematic raid on the smaller secular groups while vilifying the larger groups. Thereafter, the fortunes of the secular option in freedmen's education declined quickly. By the end of the decade, every secular society save one had disappeared; only the New England Freedmen's Aid Society managed to continue supporting a few schools through the end of Reconstruction.[24] Some teachers who began their southern work with groups such as the American Freedmen's Union Commission or the National Freedmen's Relief Association turned to denominational societies as their original sponsors fell behind in charitable receipts,

A Desire to Labor in the Missionary Cause

but many would never have been commissioned by the denominational groups. It appears that no Unitarians were ever supported by any denominational society and not more than 6 out of nearly 400 northern Quaker teachers were acceptable to groups such as the American Missionary Association. Liberal Protestants, agnostics, and other nonevangelical northern white teachers such as Jane Briggs Smith found it increasingly difficult to find support for southern work by the late 1860s as the northern secular societies closed up shop. Smith, a staunch abolitionist and a free thinker who rejected church membership, taught for six years under the New England Freedmen's Aid Society, and a seventh in a southern black public school.[25]

Thus there are several objections to the oft-cited claim by James M. McPherson that the teachers' Puritan and evangelical heritage accounted for their motivation and for their long service. "Without this Puritan-evangelical sense of mission, many teachers could not have stayed on the job in the face of southern white hostility, discouragement with the slow progress of the freed slaves, harsh physical conditions, and poverty-level salaries," McPherson wrote. "Their faith gave them a staying power unmatched by other educators or civil rights workers in that era or in our own."[26] What is obscured in that claim is that the deck was stacked against teachers from other faith, or nonfaith, communities. Unless they could support themselves as southern teachers without a northern sponsoring agency, gain sponsorship from a Quaker group, or make the transition from a secular society to a southern state public school, those from non-Puritan, nonevangelical heritages had little chance of demonstrating that they were "moral athletes" of equal courage with those whom McPherson lionized.

The Puritan-evangelical staying-power thesis becomes even more untenable, however, in the face of those who in fact did stay in black education for many years. On a proportional basis, they were not those with Puritan-evangelical roots, remarkably enough. Of the 250 northern white women and men who taught for seven years or more during the 1861–1876 period, more than one-tenth were Quaker, yet Quakers constituted a tiny fraction of the religious groups in the United States at midcentury, less than 1.5 percent of all churchgoers. In other words, nonevangelical Quakers were many times more likely to continue teaching through hostility, discouragement, and difficult conditions than teachers with Puritan-evangelical antecedents. The longevity of nonevangelicals becomes more striking as the length of service increases. Quakers and Unitarians alone constituted one-fifth of the teachers who had taught at least ten years by

1876, but those two communities together did not make up even 2 percent of the religiously inclined.[27] Finally, and most remarkably, of the women who displayed the greatest fortitude and commitment, those women who established secondary schools, normal schools, and institutes and spent many years, often the rest of their lives, in dedicated service to the freed people, more than half were Quaker or Unitarian, or held to another nonevangelical faith.[28]

Gender loomed large in the southern careers of the northern white teachers. Many of the men moved into prestigious positions as presidents and faculty members in the new southern black colleges and universities such as Fisk, Atlanta, Central Tennessee, or Shaw, where they tended to remain longer than those who taught in the lower schools. For example, Joseph T. Johnson, Eliphalet Whittlesey, Gideon S. Palmer, William Bascom, and Albert G. Riddle taught at Howard University for seven or more years before the end of Reconstruction; none taught in any other black schools before becoming founding Howard faculty members. Stephen Mattoon was president of Biddle Institute from 1869 to 1884; Henry M. Tupper founded Shaw University in 1866 and served as its president to 1893; John W. Braden was instrumental in founding Central Tennessee College, where he served as president from 1869 to 1900.[29] Altogether, nearly 120 of the northern white men taught primarily or exclusively in black higher education.[30] Few men who failed to land a position in black higher education continued to work with the freed people for more than one to two years; virtually none remained more than a decade except those few who became presidents of black colleges or universities.

The men were not alone in teaching at upper levels of the freed people's new system of schools, however. More than sixty northern white women also taught in southern black colleges and universities during Reconstruction.[31] Julia Alvord, daughter of John W. Alvord, the Freedmen's Bureau superintendent of education, taught at Howard University, along with Emma L. Crane, Emily and Sarah M. Robinson, Matilda Nichols, Lillia Camp, and Dr. Isabella C. Barrows. Before 1876, at least twelve northern white women taught at Fisk University, and eight taught at Atlanta University, including Mrs. Lucy E. Case, who remained at the school for thirty-seven years. Two of the first three teachers at Knoxville College were women, Jennie McCahon and Agnes Wallace. Elnora Plotner taught mathematics to black students at three different institutions, Central Tennessee College, Rust University, and New Orleans University, between 1873 and 1887.[32] Women held faculty rank at Shaw, Talladega, Tougaloo, Berea, and

A Desire to Labor in the Missionary Cause

Claflin. Scores more taught in black normal schools and institutes, all of which were staffed primarily or entirely by women.

Northern white women also founded higher schools for the freed people —secondary schools, normal schools, academies, and female seminaries. The female school founders did not establish colleges, a prerogative of northern men, with one notable exception: Alida Clark was, for twenty-two years, the driving force behind the creation of Southland College. She was also the only northern white female school founder who was married.[33] The others seldom had any masculine assistance. The women who founded southern black schools made it women's work; most also made it their life's work. Caroline F. Putnam established the Holley School in Virginia in 1868 and continued as its principal and teacher for the remaining forty-seven years of her life; her life companion, Sally Holley, taught at the school irregularly for her last twenty-three years.[34] Laura Towne and Ellen Murray founded the Penn School on St. Helena Island, South Carolina, in 1863. In less than ten years, they grew it into a normal school. Between them, they prepared black teachers for the South Carolina Low Country for over eighty years.[35] Martha Schofield created the Schofield Normal and Industrial School in Aiken, South Carolina, in 1866, administering and teaching in the school until 1912, forty-six years later. She died on the school grounds in 1916.[36] Philadelphian Emily L. Austin taught for a year in Greenville, South Carolina, then began teaching in Knoxville, Tennessee, in 1870; she raised the funds to build Knoxville's first black high school (later named for her) and founded the Slater Training School in 1885 for teacher education. She died in 1897, still engaged in teaching African Americans.[37] Sarah A. Dickey taught the freed people for eight years before founding Mount Hermon Seminary, patterned after her alma mater, Mount Holyoke Seminary, in 1875. She remained in charge of the black women's school in Mississippi until her death in 1904, after thirty-seven years in black education.[38] Rachel Crane Mather founded the Mather School in Beaufort, South Carolina, in 1868 and taught there until her death thirty-six years later.[39]

Others among the women school founders did not devote their entire lives to their schools but still left powerful legacies. In 1865, Cornelia Hancock established a school at Mount Pleasant, South Carolina, that would become the Laing School; she remained at the school until 1875, when Abby Munro took the helm. Munro devoted a total of thirty-seven years to southern black schools.[40] Sisters Lucelia and Philomela Williams were central to the initial work of establishing Hampton Institute, carrying much of the initial load of institution building while Samuel Chapman Armstrong busied himself with political matters. When he discovered that they had been teaching Latin and algebra to one of the Hampton students, a breach of the racial etiquette he intended to establish and a violation of his gradualist racial ideology, he peremptorily fired them. They subsequently founded a teacher education school in Jacksonville, Florida, naming it after Lincoln's secretary of war, Edwin Stanton. Stanton Normal School was the first and, for many years the only, black secondary and normal school in Florida.[41] And while Elizabeth Hyde Botume did not establish a higher school—her Whitney School in Beaufort, South Carolina, remained an elementary school throughout its long existence—she belongs with this group of women for having taught in Beaufort from 1862 to 1902; she died two years later.[42]

Northern women had been creating notable educational institutions since early in the nineteenth century. Emma Willard built Troy Female Seminary into a nationally renowned institution starting in 1821, though she actually established her first school in 1814. In 1823, Catherine Beecher founded the school that became Hartford Female Seminary, then, nine years later, laid the intellectual foundations for the Western Female Institute in Cincinnati. Zilpah Grant established Ipswich Female Seminary in 1828. Mary Lyon opened Mount Holyoke Seminary in 1834. Other women followed their lead to extend women's schools across the northeast. Thus the work of these women in southern black schools was not unprecedented. As daunting as the antebellum female work of northern school founding was, however, it paled in comparison to the work facing Dickey and Austin, Mather and Clark, Schofield, Putnam, Towne, or Hancock. Northern women's schools were aimed at students who, though often not affluent, and possibly even in straightened conditions, had the benefit of several years of common school. Further, the students grew up in a social milieu that at least tolerated, and often supported, the education of middle-class women. Northern schools created by women were established in periods of market growth when funds could be raised from affluent benefactors. They were built in communities that welcomed the potential economic and prestige benefits of a school in their midst. Finally, the curriculum of these schools tapped into, and often defined, the emerging cult of domesticity.[43]

By contrast, the women who established black normal schools, seminaries, boarding schools, and other institutions for black learners faced vast challenges. Their potential students were desperately poor. The schools would have to provide the elementary foundation as well as the higher studies, since the students and their families had, for generations, been denied access to any literacy. Although southern states established public education systems during Reconstruction, public education for African Americans rapidly fell far behind that provided for white students, and some states stopped providing any sort of secondary education for their black citizens in the last decades of the century. The women were building schools in communities that were at best deeply indifferent to the education of black children, and more commonly openly hostile to that goal. The schools were being established at the beginning of the South's long post-bellum economic descent, fueled by debt, destruction, and a dogged determination to retain an agricultural society rooted in cotton; the schools were arising in communities that did not embrace the northern ethos of local boosterism and institution building and that found no prestige at all in hosting an institution devoted to the cultural and intellectual refinement of those they thought only fit for fieldwork.[44] Finally, the curriculum of these schools did not fit easily into local dominant discourses, as did the northern schools' domesticity. Rather, their curriculum envisioned autonomous black activity, intellectual ability, and black access to middle-class occupations and status, when much of the white South instead envisioned a subservient, docile black future.[45]

Thus the work of school founding required skills, commitments, and grit rare enough in men, but almost never encouraged and nurtured in nineteenth-century women, whether black or white. Where the national culture continued to define proper womanhood in terms of domesticity, with grudging acceptance of extending domesticity into the public sphere, the school founders in the South had to be executives, fundraisers, diplomats when possible, and quiet revolutionaries when necessary. They had to be educators, accountants, recruiters, administrators, janitors, counselors, and, since most of their schools had multiple teachers, they also had to be personnel officers, supervisors, and principals. They had to hone the unfamiliar skills of bargaining, pleading, demanding, and leading. And they had to do that while coping with the South's summer heat, insects, and diseases.

Some added to those tasks by taking on public roles in their southern homes. For example, Laura Towne's neighbors elected her to the position of public school trustee in the early 1870s, a position to which she was continually reelected until well into the 1880s, when South Carolina amended its constitution to bar women from holding public office. Caroline F. Putnam became the postmistress in Lottsburg, Virginia, and located the village post office in her schoolhouse, both as a means to supplement her school's income and to bring her white neighbors into the school to accustom them to the idea of black education. Though abused for her early efforts in Aiken, South Carolina, Martha Schofield gained sufficient respect from the community for her work that by the turn of the century she was appointed a vice president of the Aiken Improvement Society.[46]

Further, school founders and other female teachers with long tenure in southern black education had to face organized terrorism, death threats, and the enervating grind of daily verbal intimidation. White students from the University of Virginia continually broke schoolhouse windows and cursed Philena Carkin and Anna Gardner while they taught at Charlottesville, and the Klan made dark threats against them. After a decade of harassing Sarah M. Barnes, a white mob sacked her Barnes Institute in Texas in 1875, prompting her to leave the South. Martha Schofield faced down a Klan-led mob intent on lynching a black couple she was protecting in her house and on chasing her from Aiken, South Carolina. Sarah Dickey attempted to make light of the threats she faced while teaching in Clinton, Mississippi. "Some things are a little annoying sometimes it is true," she wrote to her Mount Holyoke classmates in 1872, "such as having a pistol fired in at ones front door, after the lamps are lit, to receive a Ku Klux warning to get out of the place within ten days, and if you are not gon at the expiration of that time, you may expect to visit your school throught bullets and brickbats, and rest under the same treatment at night, to be whooped and yelled at on the street by college boys."[47]

The northern white men who established southern black institutions faced many of the same problems as women, but with three major differences. First, of course, much of men's formal training, and nearly all of their informal acculturation, prepared them for mastery, leadership, and autonomy. Decision making, entrepreneurship, and administration were masculine prerogatives and the explicitly intended outcome of their education. The northern women school founders, on the other hand, might have wrung from their formal education the skills, ways of being, and habits of mastery, leadership, and autonomy, though few women's schools intended such an outcome, most certainly not mastery. Further, their informal acculturation would seldom have resulted in a bent for entrepreneurship. It is doubtless significant, then, that of the eighteen women school founders discussed above, eight were raised in Quaker or Unitarian faiths, where a measure of gender equality, a commitment to black education, and political radicalism were more likely to be found than among other faiths. The informal acculturation of those eight women may have prepared them better for this sort of work than the acculturation of most women of their era.[48]

Second, virtually all of the schools that northern men created had the backing of major northern churches, missionary agencies, or other sources of funds, organizational assistance, and prestige. To be affiliated with such organizations lent gravity to the work of southern college building, though even the wealthiest churches consistently underfunded their black schools. When women established schools, by contrast, they were largely on their own. Southland College, Penn School, and Laing School received some aid from regional Quaker Yearly Meetings, though the Quakers were not in the business of building Quaker schools the way other denominations built schools to hold converts and proselytize others. Stanton Normal School was apparently the only school founded during Reconstruction by a woman that received aid from the American Missionary Association. The other female-initiated schools had to rely entirely on the ingenuity, determination, and hard work of their founders.

Third, nearly every northern man, black or white, who established a southern black college or secondary school had a wife. Without giving it a thought, they delegated to wives the domestic duties of cooking, cleaning, washing, ironing, provisioning, and all the other miscellany of everyday life. Doubtless, in most cases the wives were also expected to take on many of the symbolic duties of their husband's station—hosting receptions, boarding guests, being part of the public face of the institution. And many of those wives were also part of the school staff, either officially as faculty member or matron, or unofficially as unpaid but crucial labor in support of the school, always available to counsel students, assist with janitorial duties, and assume the other tasks that fall to the wives of principals or presidents of small schools.

The northern women who founded schools, on the other hand, did not have wives. The everyday tasks fell to them, on top of their leadership roles; the symbolic tasks were theirs alone; if teaching or counseling or matroning was to be done, it would be done by the principal, or she would pay to have it done. It is probably not coincidental, then, that some of the women who remained longest in the South, whether in a school they founded and named, or as principal of a long-standing public school, were with a daughter, a sister, or a life partner—Philomela and Lucelia Williams, Elizabeth and Hannah Hunn, Anna and Elizabeth Haley, Laura

A Desire to Labor in the Missionary Cause

Towne and Ellen Murray, Caroline Putnam and Sally Holley, Anna C.
Harwood and Carrie Segur, Elizabeth Barnes and Sarah A. G. Stevens,
Mary Jane Doxey and Rachel G. C. Patton. Family members and partners
did not take on the roles of wives; rather, they shared roles, shared tasks,
and provided shared comfort and support. The bonds between them made
the work easier.

ALTHOUGH IT WAS COMMON FOR NORTHERN BLACK TEACHERS TO GO INTO
the South without northern sponsorship in search of a place to establish a
school, it was uncommon for northern white teachers to do so. Nearly all
northern white teachers relied on the northern aid agencies for employment in a southern black school. Of the few who began their southern
teaching without an aid society, some were veterans who tarried in the
South to teach for a year or two. James A. Goodwin was discharged from
the Union forces in Texas where he taught for two years, on his own for the
first year and with Freedmen's Bureau aid the following. Nelson G. Gill
had fought with the 33rd Illinois Infantry. He brought his wife to Holly
Springs, Mississippi, right after the war, and the two of them began teaching in a black school without northern aid. At the urging of the bureau, the
American Missionary Association paid part of their salary the following
year. He became the Holly Springs postmaster after two years of teaching,
though his wife continued teaching for several more years. Other veterans
taught longer without support, probably none longer than William L.
Webb. He served in Connecticut infantry regiments throughout the entire
war, was mustered out in South Carolina in August 1865, and immediately
began teaching the freed people in Georgetown. He remained there with
no northern support, serving the freed people for the rest of his life, for a
total of twenty-three years of teaching.[49]

Northern white women also plunged into the South to start schools
without the aid of a northern benevolent group, though not nearly as often
as northern black women. One of the earliest was Eliza Chappel Porter,
who established a school in Memphis in 1862, teaching the freed people
when her duties with the Sanitary Commission allowed; three years later
she established another independent school for the freed people of Browns-
ville, Texas, and taught there from 1868 to 1870, the last year with partial
support from the American Missionary Association. Samantha Neil went
south in 1864 in search of her husband's body after the Battle of Shiloh; at
the urging of the freed people of Amelia Court House, Virginia, she opened
a school there that gained the support of the Presbyterian freedmen's aid

A Desire to Labor in the Missionary Cause

group the following year. She continued teaching in Amelia County and Jetersville until her death in 1909.[50]

Some of the northern white teachers who began their southern work with an aid society were assisted subsequently by the Freedmen's Bureau or began to receive part or all of their salaries from southern state school systems. Fannie Campbell was initially sent by the American Missionary Association to Louisiana in 1864 but was almost immediately hired by the Board of Education of the Army's Department of the Gulf. In January 1866, she went from Baton Rouge to Austin, Texas, to teach in a self-sustaining school overseen by the bureau; in 1867, she went to Williamson County, Texas, to start a new bureau-supported school. She left Texas when opponents of black education burned down her school in 1868. Carrie H. Loomis taught in Charleston and Columbia, South Carolina, for the National Freedmen's Relief Association from 1865 to 1869, after which the public school system paid her salary until 1874, when the state paid her as a member of the faculty of the South Carolina Normal School. Elijah C. Branch combined a number of options in his fifteen years of teaching the freed people. A Union veteran who was twice a prisoner of war, he was discharged in late 1862 for disabilities resulting from his escape after the first capture. In 1863 he opened a black school in Memphis under the American Baptist Home Mission Society. In 1864 he taught in New Orleans, supported by the Northwestern Freedmen's Aid Commission, then went to Mobile for two years, assisted for one year by the American Missionary Association. In 1867 he started a school in Jacksonport, Arkansas, with bureau support for two or three years until he was employed by the public school system in Jacksonport, where he remained until 1877.[51]

Still, northern white teachers working without support or with only partial support from a northern aid society were the exception. Most spent their years in the South working for one or another, and sometimes two or more, aid societies. The competing groups followed different policies on issues such as school administration, salaries, and teacher placement. The result was different experiences and opportunities for the teachers and, more important, different experiences in classrooms for learners. In school administration, for example, the American Missionary Association was much less willing to appoint women as principals than other groups. Still, nearly 200 northern white women served as principals in the freed people's schools, compared to only 130 men; at least 20 women were appointed as superintendents, though 127 male superintendents dominated that category of leadership. Further, it was not unusual for a female principal to

have charge of male teachers. Mary E. F. Smith superintended a school in
Wilmington, North Carolina, with a male assistant, for instance, and Rev.
George W. Jackson was the assistant teacher in a school in the District of
Columbia led by Miss Mary L. Smith.[52] The more progressive aid societies
paid women and men principals equally.[53]

Women were superintendents of schools under some benevolent societies but never under others. Beginning in 1865, Laura Towne superintended all of the schools operated by the Pennsylvania Freedmen's Relief
Association on the coast of South Carolina. By 1870, Lucy Case and Sarah
M. Wells superintended schools in Milledgeville and Albany, Georgia, for
the American Missionary Association, and Caroline Alfred superintended
four schools in Columbus, Georgia, for the New England Freedmen's Aid
Association. In 1865, Abby and Richard Battey were co-superintendents of
the freedmen's school sponsored by the New England Yearly Meeting of
Friends in Washington, D.C. They were followed by Hannah Gove, who
served as superintendent from 1867 to 1872. Ada W. Smith had charge of
the Episcopal freedmen's schools in Norfolk from 1867 to 1870.[54] There
was, in short, no lack of female leadership in the southern black schools,
contrary to recent claims, though the deployment of women in administration differed between agencies.[55]

Salaries were low for work in the freed people's schools. The aid societies
paid half or less of what a teacher could earn in a northern school; the
denominational societies generally paid less than the secular societies. Low
pay forced some teachers to withdraw from the work. Mary E. Clark, for
example, informed the American Missionary Association that her father
opposed her returning to the South because of "my inability to support
myself on the salary that I receive—that I have been an expense to him
during my stay south—so I must stay and try to do somthing that will bring
me more money."[56]

The secular societies and the Quakers equalized salaries between men
and women by 1866, attracting a number of women teachers as a result.[57]
The American Missionary Association changed its salary policy a year or
two later, largely as a means to neutralize the advantage the secular groups
had gained. It then began an unseemly raid on the teachers of the secular
agencies, with an inevitable disruption of schools as teachers were taken
from one school and assigned to another. Elizabeth P. Breck, for example,
chose to work for the New England Freedmen's Aid Society because "she
was paid a larger salary than A.M.A. was paying at the time." The American Missionary Association worked to win her over after it equalized sal-

A Desire to Labor in the Missionary Cause

Betsey L. Canedy, an 1842 graduate of Framingham Normal School, was
forty-six years old when she began her career in southern black schools,
"the most blessed ten years of my life as a teacher," she later wrote.
She opened the first black school in North Carolina in 1863; for most of her
decade of work she was principal of a black normal school in Richmond, Virginia.
Courtesy of the Trustees of the Boston Public Library/Rare Books.

aries, then removed her from her school in South Carolina to send her to
Virginia.[58] In its effort to dominate the northern effort, the American
Missionary Association overextended itself and had to cut the 1867–68
school year by two months to save money, again disrupting schools and
diminishing the teachers' incomes.[59] Low salaries allowed the aid societies
to send more teachers to the South but probably also contributed to the
high turnover among the teachers.

More than salaries were at stake when it came to the sponsoring agencies. The aid societies also followed contrasting policies regarding the
placement of their teachers. The Presbyterians, Baptists, Quakers, and
Episcopalians and the Pennsylvania Freedmen's Relief Association tended
to assign teachers to a single locality and sustain them there for many years.
The American Missionary Association, particularly, and the National
Freedmen's Relief Association and the New England Freedmen's Aid Society to a lesser extent, moved teachers frequently. Those who taught for
the American Missionary Association for seven years or more, for example,
were twice as likely to teach in three or more locations as to have stayed in one
or, at the most, two different schools for the entire time they taught. The
National Freedmen's Relief Association and the New England Freedmen's
Aid Society moved teachers half as often. The rest of the societies preferred to
keep their teachers in one or two locations for an extended period—those
teaching for the Quakers and Presbyterians were six times more likely to
remain in a single place as to be sent to multiple assignments, while the
Pennsylvania Freedmen's Relief Association, Methodists, Baptists, and Episcopalians almost never moved their teachers more than once. The same
patterns are clear when analyzing teachers who taught for as few as four
years or as many as ten.[60] While some of that geographical mobility may have
been at the request of the teachers (though there is little extant evidence of
that), the high correlation of mobility with sponsoring society suggests that it
was most often a result of decisions made by the organizations.

The divergent policies of the aid societies affected the teachers' work
and the quality of the schooling the freed people received. Societies that
paid poorly in order to increase the number of teachers they could send,
such as the American Missionary Association, lost teachers at a higher rate
than those who paid better, such as the United Presbyterians. Students in
schools supported by agencies that moved their teachers arbitrarily and
frequently did not experience the depth of relationship and care enjoyed
by students who worked with the same teacher year after year. Aid societies that worried more about extending their church to the South than

about the sort of education most needed by a recently emancipated people were more likely to be thinking strategically about fruitful locations for churches rather than about pedagogical content. Organizations that expected an evangelical, missionary spirit to make up for discriminatory pay lost good teachers who could not afford the sacrifices demanded of them or who were uncomfortable with the demands laid on them to be missionaries rather than teachers.

In other words, it probably mattered to the young minds at Wilmington, North Carolina, for example, that Cornelia A. Drake spent only one year with them before being sent to Savannah (the second of four American Missionary Association schools to which she was assigned in her seven years of teaching), that Abbie B. Clark came to them the next year from Norfolk for two years before being sent to Bainbridge, Georgia (as the third of six of her American Missionary Association assignments in ten years of teaching), to be replaced by Sarah E. Cargill for one year (en route to four more American Missionary Association schools in five years), followed by Cynthia Anthony for one year (who would teach elsewhere in North Carolina for a decade under another organization). The students in Albany, Georgia, studied under thirteen different American Missionary Association teachers between 1866 and 1872, most of whom stayed only one year, with only one staying longer than two, and all but one of whom taught in two to six other schools over the course of their time in the freedmen schools.[61] Conversely, it doubtless mattered quite differently to the learners at Statesville, North Carolina, that the Presbyterians sustained Emily H. Billingsley from 1868 through the end of Reconstruction; to the students at Danville, Virginia, that the Friends Freedmen's Association made it possible for Alfred H. Jones, his wife, and his two adult children to teach in Danville for a combined thirty-four years; to the young people in Columbus, Georgia, that the New England Freedmen's Aid Society thought it important to maintain Caroline Alfred in their school for eight years.[62] We catch just a glimpse of the heightened influence that might come from a teaching relationship that extended over several years in a letter that Alfred received from a young freedman just before the "redemption" of Georgia drove her back to the North. "I could not tell were I to try how often I think of you," Henry J. T. Hudson wrote to Alfred in 1875, "and when I think of you my mind is ever reflected to hours I have spent under your care and instruction and the great good you have done me."[63] While it was doubtless better that some sympathetic teacher taught than no one, the sponsors' policies affected the quality and depth of the teaching avail- able in those classrooms.

AS WITH BLACK AND SOUTHERN WHITE TEACHERS, THE PROFILE OF THE northern white teachers provides some initial clues to their decisions to take up the task of contributing to the literacy project of the freed people. The fact that the corps of northern white teachers was predominantly female reflects the very different life experiences and conditions of northern and southern white women and men in the 1860s and 1870s. Northern middle-class women were more attuned to public life than southern white women, whether working in wage labor or engaging in philanthropic and religious work. A burgeoning consumer market had reduced home production within much of the northern middle class, resulting in less need for young women's domestic labor; at the same time, age at marriage was rising, as was the frequency of "blessed singleness." There was not yet, however, a parallel increase in respectable paid work for northern middle-class women except in teaching, and there were not enough teaching jobs to absorb the potential labor market of young women. Southern women's labor, by contrast, continued to be defined by traditional domestic production.[64]

Thus, at one level, the very existence of a large pool of underemployed women, and a scarcity of underemployed men, explains some of the gender dynamics within the northern contingent of teachers. Another portion is explained by the sorts of northern gender ideologies that emerged in the nineteenth century. Northern Protestant gender theology sanctified women's increasing role in missions and other forms of evangelizing, while southern religious thought continued to stress women's subservient and domestic roles. At the same time, an industrializing northern marketplace ideology implicitly excused men from traditional religious and cultural obligations in the family and community, expecting instead that men's work was in the competitive marketplace. But as the center of production moved out of the household and northern men increasingly embraced the marketplace, the center of reproduction remained in the household and in extensions of the household such as schools. The task of nurturing the next generation and assuring the intergenerational transmission of culture became women's work, then, justified by evolving gender ideologies that, rejecting centuries of Christian teaching, pronounced women the more pious and pure of the genders and hence the logical ones to nurture children and husbands, to look after the family's religious interests, and to

A Desire to Labor in the Missionary Cause

teach, while men looked after economic interests. Yet if those emerging gender identities tended to suggest separate spheres of influence for each gender, women mobilized the gendered rhetoric to extend their sphere well beyond the household and into the public arena, creating and justifying women's increasing roles in teaching and missions. Southern manhood, on the other hand, like southern womanhood, tended to remain more traditional through midcentury, though the war and its aftermath would accelerate changes in southern gender roles and expectations.[65]

At the same time, greater affluence and the processes of class formation resulted in expanded educational opportunities for women in both the North and the South, though the impact was more widespread in the North. The combination of social and economic transformations led to dramatic changes in the life course of northern middle-class women. As the intellectual ferment of the Enlightenment, reactions to the Enlightenment, and scientific advances filtered into women's schools and as the market of books and magazines by and for women burgeoned, women's self-concept began to change. "Women began to think of themselves as individuals with their own identities, goals, rights, and callings separate from those of kin, church, or community and defined by personal need and desires, not the prescriptions of gender," as Lee Virginia Chambers-Schiller has observed. "Women began to express the very human desire to grow, to accomplish, to succeed. They wanted to make their own choices, to be responsible for their own achievements and failures, to establish their own priorities, and to enact them." The South, on the other hand, was moving in a different direction. While educated women in both sections were more willing to accept a life of "single blessedness" than previous generations, southern gender ideology prescribed devotion to service to others, but particularly to family, rather than movement into public spheres.[66] Given those ideological contexts, it is not surprising that women outnumbered men among northern white teachers but not among black or southern white teachers.

Gender dynamics and gender ideology provides a partial explanation of the patterns of participation of northern white men and women in southern black education, but other factors were at work as well. It is significant, for example, that most taught relatively briefly, two to three years; further, as a group their participation peaked early, in the year right after the war and before northern benevolent support began to turn sour. They were largely from an educated middling class, yet many came from relatively poor homes. To better understand the motivations, expectations, and

A Desire to Labor in the Missionary Cause

length of service of northern white teachers, then, it is necessary to listen to their own explanations. As opposed to other groups of teachers, these teachers left a rich record of their thinking, mostly in their own voices.

For some, teaching in the southern black schools was a work of convenience, something available that paid a wage. These were the northerners who were already in the South for some other purpose and turned to teaching in a local black school, sometimes at the urging of the freed people. For instance, Harriet Round, Louisa Hyslop, and Sarah Fullenwider, among others, had gone to southern locations during the war to be near their husbands' military posts. Each taught for a few months before moving on with their husbands or returning to the North.[67]

Likewise, some Union veterans taught in a black school briefly before returning to their northern homes, as noted previously; other veterans taught while establishing themselves more or less permanently in the South in nonteaching occupations. John Conant, for example, moved his family to the coast of South Carolina as soon as he was discharged from the Union army in 1863. He taught for a single year then became a planter and business man in Port Royal, where he remained for the rest of his life. His daughter, Lucy Ann Conant, took over her father's school for one year; five years later, she consented to teach for another year.[68]

Nonveterans also went south seeking a new life and became involved in southern black education almost incidentally. William P. and Susan A. Austin fit this pattern. After the war they had migrated to Virginia, where William purchased land, began farming, and became involved in local politics, including serving as state senator. Susan Austin took up teaching soon after their arrival and taught for at least six years.[69] Frances H. Bartlett, a northern teacher with long experience, accepted a school in New Orleans sponsored by the American Missionary Association in 1863. The following year she petitioned military authorities for a principalship in one of their schools. "My pecuniary circumstances are such that until there is an opening for me of the kind I should be happy to accept almost any position if you should wish my services," she explained. She was apparently in a situation not unlike that faced by a teacher from Muscatine, Iowa, who was stranded in Louisiana.[70] Carrie Baker did not explain why she wanted to teach the freed people beyond writing plaintively, "I am here without money or friends." Bartlett taught for two more years, Baker for one.[71]

Others were not yet in the South but, like Baker, Bartlett, the Austins, and others, they appear to have been drawn to the work out of purely

A Desire to Labor in the Missionary Cause

personal circumstances disconnected from larger considerations and motivations. William C. Gannett, who would go on to a notable career as a Unitarian minister and leader in the women's suffrage movement, confessed to an aunt that, at twenty-two years of age, he had not yet struck upon a career choice that suited him and thought that "practical experience of negro life & character is probably the most useful way of spending the unsettled yrs. of the war." He taught on the Sea Islands of South Carolina for four years. Another teacher who would spend several years with the freed people applied to the American Missionary Association because she faced "a crisis when a change in my sphere of labor must be contemplated." She felt that her attention had been directed to teaching the freed people "providentially" in response to her personal problem. Others merely applied "to obtain a situation as teacher in some of the southern states," in Lucy M. Doolittle's words, often with no particular reference to who might benefit from their work. Most of those simply looking for work remained in southern black schools for only one year.[72] In general, then, when teaching the freed people was simply something to engage in because it was convenient and paid a wage, it frequently did not keep the teacher engaged.

The surge of teachers from the North into the South in the autumn of 1865 may also provide insight into another set of reasons northern whites engaged in the work. In part, that sudden increase was simply a result of access to the South that accompanied the end of warfare. But it may have had as much to do with a spasm of patriotism and emotional release at war's end as with careful thought about contributing to the freed people's emancipation project. Hundreds flooded into new black schools in that school year; most flowed back out nearly as quickly, a wave of emotion that crested on the southern shore, then ebbed as quickly as it had come.[73] A few of the northern white women spoke of the war's effect on their decisions about teaching. Reminiscing about her two years' work with the freed people of Abbeville, South Carolina, four decades after the fact, one teacher remarked, "I had in a way pledged myself to this work while still the Civil War was being waged. I reasoned that as women could not fight for the freedom of the slaves they could have the privilege of teaching the Freedmen how to use the blessing of liberty."[74] Likewise, during the war Melvina A. Babcock explained her decision to apply for a position: "All of my brothers are in our Army & I have wished it were in my power to contribute my mite in some way."[75]

When Babcock wrote again a few months later, however, she professed a judging from language many of them used. "My reason for wishing to engage in this work," she wrote in 1864, "has been from a desire to do some good in this cause."[76] Another wrote that her application to become a teacher to the freed people was "prompted only by duty and a desire to do good," an echo of Henry H. Griffin's wish "to find *permanent* business where I can teach and *do good*."[77] Amelia J. Twitchell explained that she wanted to go to the South "because I think that in so doing, I can do more good—more for God and my country than in any other way."[78]

Even more frequent, and used synonymously with "doing good," was the language of "being useful," which peppers the applications and letters of the teachers. When Emily and Eunice Knapp were asked why they wanted to teach the freed people, Emily wrote, "I can conscientiously say, a desire to do good, to be of some use in the world"; and Eunice responded, "I have contemplated it for some time & hope and pray I may be of *some* use amoungst them."[79] Caroline H. Merrick made the connection between "doing good" and "being useful" explicit when she explained to a friend that she was not "doing much good" at home. "A life that is not useful seems to me no life at all. I want to spend my time and strength to some good purpose." Within three years, Merrick's "good purpose" was teaching the freed people of Georgia.[80]

Frequently the language of doing good and being useful lacked any mention of the freed people or their needs, however, even when the language was employed to seek work among the freed people. Doing good and being useful were self-referential needs, longings that had to be met within the writer; the object for which good might be done was not as important as the doing. John C. Tucker explained that he was applying from a desire "to do all the good I can while I live so that as I advance in years I may be able to look back upon a life well spent to feel that I have been the means of doing some good to my fellow men around me." Eliza H. Twitchell applied to the American Missionary Association, explaining, "I desire to make myself useful and at the same time receive some compensation for my labors." Two weeks later she added that, should the American Missionary Association not have a vacancy for her in the South, "I would accept of any situation you saw fit to give me." Another northern teacher who, with his wife, taught for the American Missionary Association for one year, wrote, "My object is to do good, and improve my health and knowledge of the conditions of the South." Mary J. Kimball's "strong desire to donate a portion of my life in trying to do what I can for the poor colored or

A Desire to Labor in the Missionary Cause

white of the South" was somewhat more explicit about the object of her work, though it mattered little to her whether she worked with the freed people or southern white people.[81]

The northern teachers' ubiquitous emphasis on good works and usefulness was frequently linked explicitly, and almost always implicitly, to another major theme, a strong religious motivation. M. Jerusha Rice employed language similar to many others when she explained that her "reason for wishing to engage in this work is that I might be useful to my fellow man, the desire to win souls for Christ."[82] Matilda M. Atkinson began with a simple assertion, "Reason for engaging in this work—Benevolence," but went on to elaborate on what benevolence meant to her: "the longing, absorbing aspiration of my soul is to be useful in the cause of my Redeemer."[83] Like Rice, Atkinson, and many others, Sarah S. Smith made no reference to the freed people when she applied to the American Missionary Association, declaring simply, "I believe I am prompted by a sincere desire to serve Him more entirely in my works."[84] Likewise, Harriet Hoffman wrote, "My reason for seeking to engage in this work, is a desire to labor for Christ, and the good of mankind." Their desire to win souls and assure their own salvation was sufficient to sustain each of those teachers for a single year in the schools for the learners they would not name.[85]

The religious motivation of the northern teachers was often expressed in terms of mission, missionary work, and evangelism. War-widowed Mary J. Conkling explained her application for a teaching position simply: "My object in seeking this life is from a desire to labor in the missionary cause."[86] Twenty-year-old Maggie Webster explained in more detail: "From childhood I have looked forward to the time when I might engage in missionary labors believing that when I became old enough a door would be opened that I might enter in to work," she explained. "That time has come. I can no longer be content to stand and wait even though it be not idly. I am eager, impatient to begin a service to which, if God will, I solemnly, joyfully consecrate my life."[87] Conkling and Webster taught two years each.

Northern women had begun appropriating the language of mission and moving into mission fields, both domestic and foreign, for two or three decades before the freed people became a mission field for them.[88] The applications that posited mission as the primary motivation referred to missions in the abstract, "a desire to labor in the missionary cause," rather than speaking about the concrete needs of those to whom they might minister, including the freed people. Jesse L. Paterson, who would serve missionaries to India. As a result of her experiences on the mission field, she had from childhood gained "a love of Missionary Work, and sincere interest in the progress of the cause universally," the only consideration she offered in order to gain an appointment.[89] Others mentioned the freed people almost in passing while continuing to privilege their desire for missionary labor. Louisa Hylsop, for instance, indicated her desire "to go South as Teacher to the blacks," but explained that desire in terms of a larger consideration: "Have many times during my life felt that I would like to contribute my little aid in the work of a mission and assist in spreading the triumphs of the cross."[90] Hyslop's mission lasted one year.

The link that the teachers made between benevolence, usefulness, good works, and mission came easily and probably unconsciously to them. They were drawing on a discourse that had begun to emerge in the antebellum years and gained ascendancy rapidly, fueled in great part by the revivals that swept much of the North in the second quarter of the century. In the space created by evangelicalism's rejection of Calvinism in favor of an Armenianism that stressed free will and presumed that men had the "moral capacity to work out" their own salvation, revivalists such as Charles G. Finney constructed a theology of disinterested benevolence. Salvation was not the end of the religious journey but simply the beginning, according to Finney; the essence of the Christian experience lay in the rejection of one's own interests and its replacement by benevolence, usefulness, and good works for the benefit of humanity and for the promotion of God's kingdom. As John R. McKivigan emphasizes, Finney preached that converts "should set out with a determination to aim *at being useful in the highest degree possible*."[91] Within the theological tradition that Finney and others constructed, the target of benevolence, the object of mission, was of little moment. What was important for one's spiritual life, perhaps even for one's own salvation, was to be in mission, to find outlets for usefulness, to engage in good works. Thus Rachael S. Walk would write of her wish "to do good in the world, and aid all in my power to hasten the Redeemer's Kingdom," and Charles S. Strong would refer to his desire "to be engaged in some way for the benefit of the coloured unfortunate race now thrown upon the hands of phylantropists & Christians."[92] Between them, Walk and Strong taught three years. Thus, too, scores of the teachers, possibly one hundred or more, moved easily from missions to the freed people to foreign and other missions.[93] For them and many other teachers, the work was not about black emancipation but about being a missionary somewhere, anywhere.

A Desire to Labor in the Missionary Cause

The discourse of usefulness and mission appealed to many of the sponsoring agencies, particularly the evangelical societies, but the teachers' need for mission and usefulness was easily met after a year or two, and the teachers moved on to other fields of benevolence and service. After Strong's single year in the South, he moved on to other missions—serving as a clergyman to a rural New York church, a chaplain at Sing Sing prison, the founder of the Western New York Home for Homeless and Dependent Children. Walk married; her brother John, who had taught with her in Washington, D.C., found his next outlet for mission as a staff member in the Philadelphia House of Refuge. For many of the teachers, the work was not about the freed people; it was about themselves.[94]

Others, however, did speak of the freed people. Some used language reminiscent of the black teachers, invoking the imagery of "elevating" the freed people. Some were vague about the end toward which they might be elevated, speaking generally of wanting "to do something personally for their instruction and elevation," or wanting "to enlighten and elevate that class of human beings" who had been "kept in ignorance and degradation."[95] Others, though, understood the expectation that education might move the freed people toward more equal social and political relationships. After serving in the Union forces for more than four years, William Treadwell wrote, "I now desire to elevate these people to enjoy the rights to which they are inalienably entitled."[96] Mary H. Seymour asked for a role "in the glorious work of endeavoring to elevate those degraded blacks and fit them for the place they ought to fill as men and women of the purified South."[97]

Such language suggests a commitment to the future of the freed people, a perspective on the nation and race that might trace to antebellum abolitionism. Indeed, abolitionism has long been urged as the primary explanation for the invasion of the South by the northern schoolmarm. Yet the assumption that abolitionism was central in the thinking of the teachers or in the structure and intent of the northern-sponsored schools has seldom been accompanied by evidence from the teachers themselves or from the schools and their curriculum. For traditional historians, hostile to the teachers for their effrontery in teaching in the South, the very fact that the teachers were northerners who would teach African Americans was evidence enough of abolitionism. For other writers, the domination of the education movement, at least after 1867, by the antislavery American Missionary Association was also taken as evidence that abolitionism and a corollary belief in racial equality was at work in the teachers' thinking when they went to the South.[98]

Some teachers did speak of their abolitionist roots when applying to teach. Yet, given the fact that the teachers were writing to men and women in the aid associations who were known to have been abolitionists, it is remarkable how few applicants appear to have thought it important to indicate their like-mindedness. Eunice Browne's proclamation, "I am a thorough Emancipationist," and Walter L. Clift's description of being bullied as a youth for his abolitionism, were relatively rare statements of antislavery sentiments from those who applied to become teachers.[99] Others claimed a longstanding concern for the slaves—"I have prayed to God for the liberation of the slaves," in George F. Mosher's words—that may have implied abolitionism.[100] Letters of recommendation written on behalf of applicants were, infrequently, more forthright in claiming the mantle of abolition for an applicant than the applicants' own letters. George Grinell, for instance, noted that Alma Baker "has allways been thoroughly Antislavery in her views," though all Baker said for herself was that her "feelings and sympathies have ever been with the African race."[101]

Beyond a few relatively clear declarations of abolitionist leanings, however, most applicants employed ambiguous language regarding their prewar beliefs about slavery or about the future of postslavery African Americans. Did an inclination to "lend a helping hand toward undoing our country's great wrong" reflect a longstanding abolitionism or a recent conversion to the rhetoric of antislavery?[102] Was one who was "specially interested in the welfare of the colored people" an abolitionist or simply benevolent?[103] Was one whose purpose was "to do good and if possible benefit those too long oppressed and denied the blessings of Education" expressing abolitionist commitments or employing the language of evangelical mission?[104] Did references to "this *downtrodden* and *oppressed* people" and a hope "to alleviate their sufferings" arise from prior work in opposition to slavery and in favor of black freedom, or did it belie a commitment to shouldering the white man's burden?[105]

If abolitionism is to have meaning as a motivation for teaching and as a potential influence on the direction and force of southern black education, it must, arguably, mean something distinct from the nineteenth-century North's generic antislavery stance. Much of the North had begun to oppose slavery, or at least the extension of slavery, by midcentury, but opposition to slavery often had little to do with those who were enslaved. In fact, areas of the country that were most opposed to slavery were often the states that enacted the harshest laws against African Americans. Abolitionism was not necessary egalitarian; abolitionists were often racially insensitive; and not a few abolitionists abandoned African Americans before the century was out. Still, by the nature of its critique of slavery and its recognition of the humanity of the slave, abolitionism had the potential of prompting greater solidarity with the intentions of the freed people to construct their own freedom.[106]

There is, in fact, a marked difference between the language employed by the great majority of those who were eventually sent to the South and the language of those whose abolitionism can be confirmed independently of their association with the freed people's schools. Abolitionist Laura Towne, deeply critical of the northern evangelicals around her in South Carolina, was blunt about her intentions: "We have come to do antislavery work, and we think it noble work and we mean to do it earnestly." She and her life companion, Ellen Murray, would spend the next four decades teaching the freed people, and the grandchildren of the freed people, always understanding that the work was about reversing the impact of slavery and preparing African Americans for full participation in society.[107] Similarly, Martha O. Quaiffe made note of her twenty years of abolitionist work in arguing that, though the enslaved had been freed, "my labor for them ought to be continued." She and her daughter gave seven years to continue their abolitionist work before she died of cholera in Texas in 1866.[108] Hundreds of others went to do religious work and spent a year or two teaching the freed people, with apparently little sense of what their work should accomplish for the future of African Americans in American society.

On just about any measure, remarkably few of the northern white teachers can be demonstrated to have been abolitionists before the war began. Yet the evidence is quite powerful that those who were abolitionists carried with them into the South a greater commitment to the freed people than those who took up the work of black education out of other motivations. Abolitionists remained in black education far longer than those who did not have a clear abolitionist tradition behind them. Using a relatively rigorous standard, considering a teacher an abolitionist only on clear evidence, abolitionist teachers remained in black education over twice as long as teachers for whom there is no clear evidence of abolitionism.[109]

The American Missionary Association's role in southern black education has contributed to the confusion over the relationship between abolitionism and freedmen's education. The association was, from its origins, a strongly antislavery body, identified with, and to a large extent defining, the evangelical, anti-Garrisonian wing of abolitionism. Yet its evangelical strain of abolitionism had consequences for its postwar work. As contrasted with the far more militantly abolitionist American Baptist Free Mission Society, for example, which sought from its first work in the South to put control of its schools and churches in the hands of the freed people, the American Missionary Association followed a distinctly conservative, paternalistic path, one that has been largely obscured by the fact that by the end of Reconstruction, if not before, more radical options had been eclipsed.[110] Without detracting from the association's long and firm support of southern black education from the 1860s until the middle of the twentieth century, it is essential to recall that the association and its teachers were not exponents of a postwar interracial or egalitarian agenda. The American Missionary Association was, first and foremost, a missionary association bent on evangelizing, preferring to ignore the fact that the former slaves had been thoroughly Christianized in their centuries of bondage. The goal of converting the freed people had consequences for the association's educational work, putting proselytizing above the political needs of the freed people.

Thus it is instructive to examine the applicants to the American Missionary Association who were not commissioned as well as those who were. A remarkable group of applicants for teaching positions failed to win the approval of the association, a collection of aspirants that arguably, to judge from their applications, were more clearly abolitionist and egalitarian than those who were sent to the South. They are worth hearing in the effort to clarify the place of abolitionist-inspired thinking among the teachers. Among those who applied but were not commissioned was Elvira Leland, a thirty-three-year-old woman with extensive teaching experience. After expressing her desire to be sent to work with the freed people, she asserted her belief "that these people may by education become a self-sustaining and independent people, and that their incapacity be no longer urged as a plea for their enslavement."[111] Others not commissioned made clear declarations of their commitment to abolitionist ideals. Rhodelle Miller felt that her roots in abolitionist beliefs prepared her for working with the freed people: "My Parents early instilled antiSlavery principles into my youthful mind which have 'grown with my growth' and 'strengthened with my strength' until my sympathies are fully enlisted particularly for the poor oppressed slaves of the South"; while another applicant made a point to say,

"I was born and reared among ultra Antislavery people my father always holding slavery in abhorrence since my earliest recollections, so that I have often remarked, that 'I was born and raised an abolitionist.' "[112] Several of those rejected by the association spoke more clearly about the fate of the freed people than many of those whom the association chose. Mary J. Lane wrote of her wish "to assist more directly than I have been able in the great work of elevating mentally and spiritually this long oppressed race," while George F. Mosher alluded to his abolitionist hopes, asserted his conviction "that freedom will prove an injury instead of a benefit to [the freed people], if left as they are," and offered his services "to help them all I can."[113] Despite these candidates' abolitionist credentials and their demonstration of a clear sense of what they might be teaching toward, the American Missionary Association selected none of them.

It is worth noting the association's requirements for teachers. Its published guidelines did not require that its teachers have antislavery credentials, be free of prejudice, or have a commitment to the freed people. Indeed, its list of six qualifications did not mention the freed people at all. The first requirement was "missionary spirit," followed by good health, energy, common sense, an absence of "marked singularities and idiosyncrasies," and experience as a teacher.[114] Significantly, all of the teachers above, whose applications indicated an abolitionist bent and an interest in the secular future of the freed people, made a point of noting their stamina, strong constitution, evangelical credentials, and extensive teaching experience. Yet the American Missionary Association failed to commission them, while it readily filled its classrooms with relatively immature young women such as Mary S. Williams, who admitted that her health was not robust, she had never taught, she had only a common school education, and, although twenty years old, she had never been away from home.[115] Others were commissioned despite poor health. Kate A. Dunning had to cut her first year short because of sickness yet was recommissioned for a second year, only to have to again abandon her school because of ill health.[116] Gorham Greely was commissioned despite the association's understanding that he was in "feeble health & may not be able to preach much but may do well as a teacher."[117]

The American Missionary Association's first criterion, "missionary spirit," was apparently the only, or at least the most relevant, criterion, a likelihood made more certain by the little evidence that remains of what transpired in the association's interviews with candidates. One applicant wrote to an American Missionary Association secretary after her interview

A Desire to Labor in the Missionary Cause

to say that she felt she had not made her case "half as earnestly, as I should have done." To strengthen her application, she repeated a query posed to her, very likely a query posed to all applicants, and, it appears, one whose response carried much weight in determining who would be the teachers to assist the freed people in their secular emancipation: "You asked if I would make it 'a special object to lead them to the Saviour'?" She assured the association that such a goal would be her primary work.[118]

Such an emphasis meant that the American Missionary Association and other denominational societies appointed applicants who professed a deep love of missionary work but betrayed no particular interest in the freedmen. One teacher looking back retrospectively on her work in the very last year of Reconstruction admitted as much. "Taking the year as a whole, it was a profitable one to me, it gave me experiences that were wholly new to me, *and an interest in the people that I had never had before,*" she wrote. "I acknowledge that when I entered the Miss. field that my interest wasn't very strong. Missions always have had a place in my heart, and I have sometimes had a longing to enter the work. In our own country it did not seem like Miss. work, till I entered into it myself."[119]

GIVEN THE CONSTELLATION OF MOTIVATIONS AND INTENTIONS THAT THE teachers revealed, the average length of tenure in the South begins to take on meaning. There should, in fairness, be no doubt that some simply failed as teachers or as teachers of black learners and withdrew from their classrooms. Others left their schools out of genuine fear for their lives. Some could not afford the sacrifice of more than one or two years, particularly those from poorer homes, though there is no significant correlation between wealth and length of time teaching in southern black schools. Beyond those reasons for leaving the work early, however, it is likely that for many of the northern white teachers, the fundamental considerations that spurred their interest were insufficiently compelling to keep them involved. Having gone south with no clear objective relative to black freedom, they had nothing against which to gauge their work except their desire for mission or usefulness. They had served in the vineyard; they had achieved their announced objectives; little more could be expected of them.

On the other hand, those northern white teachers who did go with an objective rooted in service to an emancipated people often found a vocation. Given the worsening conditions in the South, the collapse of some of the aid societies and retrenchment of the others, and the withdrawal of the Freedmen's Bureau, most eventually had to curtail their work, yet they managed to give a significant part of their lives to the freed people, sufficient in many cases to assure that a full generation of freed people would gain a solid academic footing to move forward as teachers, ministers, businesspeople, and farmers.

THREE OF THE TEACHERS EXEMPLIFY CENTRAL ASPECTS OF THE STORY OF the northern white teachers. All three were in their middle years, as half of the northern teachers were; all three were women, as were two-thirds of the northern white teachers; one was strongly abolitionist, another generally antislavery, while the third never revealed any particular interest in the enslaved before beginning to teach. They are atypical primarily in the fact that all were from Massachusetts, when, in fact, the teachers hailed from across the northern states. The relationship between the degree of awareness of the political and social position of the freed people and commitment to the work is clear in their stories.

Esther A. Terry was an experienced teacher in her forties when the Civil War began. To judge from the quality of her writing, she was well educated. She and her widowed mother owned enough property in Sutton, Massachusetts, about $2,500, to consider them middle class, though they boarded another family to provide some income. Following the example of many patriotic northern women, Terry went to Baltimore in 1864 to work in a military hospital.[120] While still engaged in nursing she wrote her brother, "Though no plan is definite I sometimes think I will go to Washington and see what I can do in the way of teaching the Contrabands." She went on to explain, "there is nothing to be done in Sutton and I feel this is part of the vineyard where God calls me to labor. I hope I shall be found faithful."[121] She went to Washington, though still as a nurse rather than teacher, in the autumn of 1864. She finally applied to the American Missionary Association for a teaching position in February 1866 and was almost immediately sent to Virginia. She described her work as aimed primarily at evangelizing, reporting approvingly that there was "some religious interest here among the scholars. Several are indulging hopes that they have become Christians in the different schools."[122]

Terry taught in Virginia for four months in the spring of 1866, then went to Macon, Georgia, in December 1866 to work as matron of a hospital for dependent women and children through the spring of 1867. By autumn she had applied to the American Tract Society to go to Florida—"as a teacher of the whites."[123] She did not go to Florida, for reasons she did not reveal in her letters, but returned to Sutton to supervise the construction of

A Desire to Labor in the Missionary Cause

straw hats. Two years later, she took a position in New York "to labor amongst the Jews—that being the field of my choice." "Our Heavenly Father has kindly provided something for me to do in His Vineyard," she wrote a couple months later.[124] Jewish immigrants in New York, whites in Florida, freed people in Georgia and Virginia—all were mission fields; none had any particularly compelling hold, so long as northern women like Esther Terry could be at work in the vineyard.

HARRIET BUSS WAS ONLY A FEW YEARS YOUNGER THAN TERRY, IN HER MID-thirties when she began working in a southern black school. Her father, a farmer, was worth a modest $1,500 in 1860. Nonetheless, she received a strong academy education, reveling in the luxury of study. When she was twenty-four she had declared, "if I were only rich, I would not do anything but study then. I shall study my lifetime; something or nothing is yet my motto, I will have no halfway grounds." She also took a firm feminist stance, intending to make her mark: "If life and health are continued, the *world* shall know that I live in it," she informed her parents, "and in *future ages* it shall know that I have lived in it, for I will have mine impress deeply traced upon it."[125] Her feminism included an intention to remain independent. Remarking on marriage when she turned thirty-four, she wrote, "I don't want to obey one of creation's lords. Never could I be told to go or stay, do this or that, and surely never could I ask. I submit to no human being as my master or dictator."[126]

Buss was also outspoken in her antislavery views, though hers was a political antislavery stance. She never spoke of abolishing bondage but spoke stridently against slavery as a political issue. In January 1860, she railed against the "contemptible and unprincipled men we have" in Congress who would not stand up to southern demands regarding slavery.[127] Less than a month later, responding to the resolutions that Jefferson Davis introduced in the Senate intended to extend the protection of slavery, Buss exploded. She raged to her parents against the proposals, concluding with a feminist twist: "Even if he could stop the men's tongues, he would find another job after that, he must silence the women's too, and that is more than he can do. Why we would shut him up in a cell so dark and deep he would never get out again." While Buss spoke bitterly about slavery as a political force and a national evil, she never mentioned the enslaved.[128]

Buss taught throughout the 1850s, eventually taking a position in a tiny town in Illinois. "I would not be surprised if I should teach here a good while yet," she informed her parents in 1859; "I am first on the ground,

A Desire to Labor in the Missionary Cause

and the field will be mine." She spoke of her work in Freedom, Illinois, much as one might expect a northern teacher in the South to speak a decade later: "You might say, let others come here," she wrote to her family, "but those that we think might most easily repair to the distant and difficult fields are not always the ones who are ready to make sacrifices. A teacher who loves ease and wishes to be as genteel and as aristocratic as possible will stay East, but one who teaches to bless the world, to make it better, and help save his country from ruin, must be willing to work in hard fields, and far from home too, perhaps." Being "first on the ground" was not enough to assure her of her position, however. She lost her teaching position in Freedom, apparently to a younger teacher, and a year later was back in Massachusetts, deeply discouraged.[129]

It was in that context that she turned to the National Freedmen's Relief Association for a position in the South. The association sent her to Beaufort, South Carolina, in March 1863, then to Hilton Head Island in November. Though she found the students "mischievous," she concluded, "I find I can train them without much trouble, and I like the work, if it is up-hill work; I enjoy myself very much both at home here, and in school."[130] By the spring of 1864, the association awarded her the principal position in her school, yet she did not return in the fall, deciding instead to teach again in the North. She judged her school in South Gardner, Massachusetts, "the hardest school I ever had."[131] After three years in New England schools, however, she was complaining of the weather in Massachusetts and wishing to be in the South once more. She applied again, this time to the American Missionary Association, though insisting to her parents, "I shall not go out unless I can have a voice in the matter where I will go."[132] By October of that year, she was teaching the freed people in Norfolk, Virginia. The following year she accepted a position at the Raleigh Institute, the American Baptist Home Mission Society school that would become Shaw University, where she remained until 1871.[133]

Buss never spoke of her need for mission nor spoke of herself as a missionary. She never commented on how her work affected the freed people or the nation, though a decade earlier she had been certain that her work in the West was linked to saving the "country from ruin." Her attitude toward her students did seem to soften over time, however. She thought her students in South Carolina, whom she referred to frequently as "darkey children," did not learn as quickly as northern children, but wrote from Virginia of the pleasure she took in talking with her students after class and of gently teasing them when they begged her not to give them a Christmas vacation—"I tell them I suppose they love their teacher so much they don't know how to have her away a few days; yes, they say it is so."[134] A combination of her antislavery political stance and a feminist determination to blaze her own path in life contributed to her five years of work in the South and, at the same time, to the inconsistent trajectory of that work. She was as much engaged in her own emancipation project as in the freed people's emancipation project.

JANE BRIGGS SMITH WAS THIRTY YEARS OLD WHEN SHE BEGAN TEACHING the freed people around Washington, D.C., in 1864. She was the daughter of a relatively prosperous farmer, worth about $3,500 in 1850; her widowed mother was worth closer to $4,000 by 1870. Smith appears to have had a solid education, given the quality of her writing and her frequent literary allusions. Judging from the way she talked about her teaching in the South, it is likely that she taught extensively before beginning her work with the freed people. She taught for the New England Freedmen's Aid Society for six years and in a black public school for a seventh, in Washington and South Carolina. She taught in Sumter, South Carolina, from 1866 to 1870, yielding her place only after the South Carolina public school system was well established and her sponsor had to cut its teaching force due to declining revenues.[135]

Smith was an unsentimental Garrisonian abolitionist who wrote about as clearly as any teacher could have regarding what was at stake for the freed people and the uncertainty of the work before them and their supporters. "It is true that this great problem, What shall we do with the black man! is at last solving itself, & is sure to come out right in time," she wrote in one of her earliest letters from South Carolina. "I hope it will be in our generation but I don't know."[136] Only two months after the war ended at Appomattox, Smith was asserting the right of the freed people to full citizenship, including the franchise. They were more qualified than immigrants, she argued: "This is their native land, they have by their labor done their share toward making it productive; what right of native born Americans is there to which they are not entitled?" She asserted the imperative need for "*legal* justice" and "*social* justice" for the freed people.[137] It was that work, the work of social justice, that took Jane Briggs Smith into the South and kept her working for seven years. "My duty is there; my inclination leads me there; a great noble work is there which I am fitted to help do; my heart is in it;—why should I turn away?" she asked. Then, as if offering a gentle critique of those who were devoted to mission, not to the

A Desire to Labor in the Missionary Cause

Jane Briggs Smith was the principal of the freed people's school in Sumter, South Carolina. One of the few northern white teachers who spoke clearly about her hopes for the freed people from an abolitionist perspective, she taught in the District of Columbia and in South Carolina for seven years. Courtesy of the Trustees of the Boston Public Library/Rare Books.

freed people, she added, "I never like to talk about my devotion to other people, because it sounds so silly; but if I know myself, I do love the work with my whole heart." Jane Briggs Smith was devoted to the freed people and their future. That kept her working on their behalf more than twice as long as the average northern white teacher.[138]

LIKE THE AFRICAN AMERICAN AND SOUTHERN WHITE TEACHERS, NORTHERN white teachers also crossed racial, gender, and class borders in their work in the freed people's schools. Their border crossings were often more tentative and ambivalent than the boundary transgressions of black teachers, yet they pressed new educational borders further into territories being colonized by the freed people than did southern white teachers. A few joined the freed people in declaring new borders that asserted radically altered racial, gender, and class relationships. Most of the northern white teachers,

A Desire to Labor in the Missionary Cause

however, spoke of the education of a freed people in terms that betrayed little sense of the political, economic, and ideological struggle southern blacks faced. For them, teaching the freed people was "a field of Christian labor" or an agency of usefulness "in the cause of my Redeemer."[139] The freed people emerged from slavery to confront a darkening and bloody South controlled by a bitter, angry, violent people, yet too many of their teachers imagined the work as simply "guiding this poor & oppressed people up from the depths of degragation [*sic*] & sorrow into the pure & radiant atmosphere of an intelligent & refined christianity."[140]

A schooling that took that task as its objective, absent any notion of the social and political context of the postslavery South, was unlikely to take the freed people seriously as the authors of their own destinies, or to design a curriculum that made race, society, and power the central subjects of legitimate and sustained inquiry and action. On the contrary, such a schooling was more likely to result in racial accommodation, class differentiation, and curricula that stressed a "discourse of respectability."[141] The educational boundaries that such teachers built around their schools offered a moderately more expansive field of thought and action than those defended by southern white teachers, but they fell short of those imagined by black teachers and the freed people and blunted the liberatory potential of education.

Chapter Five

You Will, of Course,
Wish to Know All about Our School

Learning and Teaching in the Freed People's Schools

A few evenings since I read Abraham Lincoln's Proclamation
of Emancipation aloud in the night school; they had never
heard it before—never were a more attentive set of men than they
as I read and explained it, and the conversation that followed was
pithy; every one wanted to express his opinion.

Elizabeth Pennock, May 1869

Their aptitude is quite wonderful. I have had considerable experience
in teaching, but never saw their like for learning to read quickly.

Eunice Congdon, July 1864

The colored student does not come to us bred in the atmosphere of
a Christian home and community; but too often with the inheritance
of a debased nature, and with all his wrong tendencies unchecked
either by innate moral sense or by good domestic influence.
The later it is ours to supply.

Samuel Chapman Armstrong, 1872

Those who worked with the freed people in their schools came from
far more diverse backgrounds and carried far more divergent aims
than writers have previous imagined. But what should we make of
that? At one level of analysis, it should not have mattered whether the
teachers of black learners were white or black, northerners or southerners,
teaching in Union blue, Confederate gray, or Quaker black. Freed students
in Liberty, Mississippi, in 1869 may have become as proficient in arithmetic under John Gummer, a Confederate veteran, as freed students in Lib-

erty, Virginia, in 1867, learning arithmetic with the assistance of Frank Forrest, a northern white male; black learners in Liberty County, Georgia, in 1867 probably became every bit as literate with Mrs. Harriet Golding, a local black teacher, as the black learners in the same year in Liberty County, Texas, learning to read with Mary Young, a white Yankee teacher.[1] Slavery systematically denied literacy to those black learners; after emancipation, Gummer, Forrest, Golding, Young, and several thousand other teachers provided systematic access to literacy to those learners. No matter the teacher, with skill and patience each could introduce conscientious learners to the skills of reading and calculating. It is doubtlessly true, ultimately, that any teacher with a modicum of competence is better than no teacher.

A recent study of Reconstruction and its aftermath argues that a central value of the freed people's schools was their students' experience with interracialism.[2] Logically, of course, that lesson could be gained from southern white teachers, including former slaveholders, slave mistresses, and impoverished southern neighbors of the freed people just as well as from northern white teachers. Further, that argument could suggest that southern white teachers were more valuable than the thousands of black teachers who taught and administered schools from the earliest days of black freedom—the black teachers did not provide that sort of window into interracial possibilities. Presumably, southern whites had the added virtue of crossing a long-established boundary to assist in black literacy.

Yet surely it did matter who taught and toward what vision of the educated individual they applied their craft. If it was important that the freed people had positive interracial experiences from the first days of freedom, it was also important that those experiences were with women and men who had fought for black freedom rather than for continued enslavement. If it was important that the freed people had object lessons in black intellectual achievement and political courage, it was also important that they had teachers such as the Highgates or the black union veterans or the other thousands of black teachers. All sorts of teachers could contribute to their literacy and engage them in the elementary sciences, yet each sort would have conveyed quite different lessons about compassion, commitment, race, democracy, justice, and human possibility. If those intangible lessons are the lessons that have the deepest imprint on the spirit, well beyond the academic ends of memorizing the major rivers of the European continent and naming the parts of speech, then it mattered to the freed people that some of their teachers saw education as part of the struggle for an expansive emancipation while others intended only to be useful, and still others intended to extend subordination. It mattered that a disproportionate number were women and men of their own race. It mattered, though differently, that some aid groups moved their teachers frequently, breaking bonds of trust and commitment between teacher and student. It mattered that most white teachers, both northern and southern, only committed themselves to a year or two of teaching; it mattered that some teachers cared only about the temporal advantages of teaching recently emancipated learners. It mattered that some teachers intended to use their schools to reimpose white paternalistic control.

It is not enough, then, to simply celebrate indiscriminately all who were involved in the schools for freed people, or even to limit the celebration to the "Yankee" teachers, or to treat the many aid societies as simply variations on an inevitably progressive theme.[3] Elizabeth Hyde Botume was being kind, but historically myopic, when she wrote, still teaching in the school she had established forty years earlier, "A common cause made all friends."[4] The cause was never common, particularly on the South Carolina Sea Islands where Botume began her work. It was riven with denominational jealousies and ideological discord from its origins at Port Royal, South Carolina.[5] Most important, those laboring in the cause never shared a common vision of the future of African Americans in the nation.

Many African Americans recalled with great respect and fondness the first teachers they encountered in their schools, many of them Yankee teachers. A critical stance toward the aid movement and its teachers does not sully those memories or disrespect the gratitude for the teachers' work and sacrifice. Nor should that stance be read to fault the work of the northern race radicals who, in the face of rising racism after Reconstruction, fought alongside African Americans to sustain the fragile but vital system of black secondary and higher schools across the South.[6] It is to argue, however, that African American religious leaders were right to criticize the white missionaries for attempting to wean southern blacks away from black churches for the sake of increasing membership in white churches; it is to argue that policies and choices made by the aid societies brought them more teachers bent on evangelism than teachers committed to liberation; it is to argue that teachers' intentions and perceptions are important even though students may make something very different out of their education than teachers expected.

WHO THE TEACHERS WERE, THEN, WAS SIGNIFICANT. SIGNIFICANT, TOO, was what the teachers taught and how they taught it. Predictably, tradi-

tional historians were critical of the original curriculum in the schools the
freed people built. It was, they said, irrelevant to a peasant people. It
caused the freed people to put on airs, fed their vanity, and educated them
away from their natural destiny. Worst of all, according to Walter L. Fleming, in teaching the freed people "not to be servile," the schools taught
them "to be insolent."[7] Such critics of the first generation of black schools
argued that it was worse than a waste of time to give the freed people the
same curriculum that was given to white students, it was almost criminal.
Racially incapable of authentically benefiting from such learning, they
could only wear their learning foolishly rather than truly benefit from it.
As one of the best known of the northern white freedmen's teachers,
Samuel Chapman Armstrong, argued at the time, "the differentia of races
go deeper than the skin." Given what he saw as the insuperable racial
deficiencies of the freed people, their education needed "less of mathematics, but more manhood," which, he was certain, would be gained by scaling
back academics and adding manual labor and even more religion than
nineteenth-century education already stressed.[8] Armstrong's insistence on
black inferiority and cultural barbarism fundamentally shaped the black
school that would make him famous, Hampton Normal and Industrial
Institute.

Armstrong was as concerned with *how* blacks were taught as with *what*
they were taught. "The spirit and method of study is of more consequence
than what is studied," he asserted before the National Education Association in 1872. In fact, however, Hampton Normal and Industrial School
made its mark on the curriculum—*what* was taught—rather than the
pedagogy—*how* it was taught—of black schools.[9] Historians, meanwhile,
have until recently almost universally ignored the pedagogy in the early
black schools. In an argument that in some unfortunate ways harkens back
to Armstrong and in other uncomfortable ways anticipates recent scholarship calling for "culturally relevant" curriculum and pedagogy, Bertram
Wyatt-Brown criticized the schools for employing a pedagogy that "was
totally unsuited to the rural and penurious character of black life." The
schools that the northern teachers imported into the South ignored the
fact that "abstract concepts required a special concentration for which the
rural setting and black styles of thought were uncongenial," he continued.
"No wonder black pupils preferred group learning, not individual reflec-
tion; concrete experience, not cogitation; copying, not composition; para-
ble, anecdote, and story, not categories, formulas and abstract rules." After
arguing that the problem of a culturally inappropriate pedagogy was par-

ticularly apparent in the schools' inability to teach arithmetic to the freed people, he summarized his criticism by arguing that what had been needed was the ability "to bend pedagogy to meet the needs of a basically peasant society with a strong heritage of nonliterate ways of thinking."[10] That bending did not happen, he claimed, much to the detriment of the freed people.

Two issues, then, frame an investigation of the teaching performed by the teachers. First, what, in fact, was taught—what was the curriculum of the freed people's schools? Second, how did the teachers teach—what was the pedagogy employed? From that analysis we can gain insight into the question of the appropriateness and meaning of the teaching.

TO FULLY APPRECIATE THE CONTENT OF THE INSTRUCTION IN THE FREED people's schools, two aspects of the curriculum deserve analysis. They include curricular materials (the textbooks and other resources used in the schools) and the content of the intentional curriculum (the subjects studied). The implicit curriculum—the attitudes, ways of being, habits of mind, and sense of self, among other traits, that are encouraged or nurtured by teachers' attitudes, classroom practices, and other aspects of the teaching and learning setting, whether designed intentionally or appearing incidentally—is also important but nearly impossible to document historically, though it was, in many ways, the aspect of the school most feared by many southern whites.

Two sorts of curricular materials were available for use in the freed people's schools: textbooks written specifically for the freed people, on the one hand, and the broad market of midcentury common school textbooks and other resources published for all learners, on the other. The former focused specifically on the needs of recently freed black learners, at least as those needs were defined by some of their educators; the latter gave no thought to those needs. Consider first the former sort. Within a matter of months after the first teachers began teaching in the earliest black schools, the American Tract Society recognized an opportunity to create special textbooks and primers aimed at the emerging market of black students. Following good business practices, the society established its own black school in Washington, D.C., in 1863, "precisely for the purpose of determining what kinds of books were needed to teach the freedmen," as historian Samuel L. Horst discovered. It used the school as something of a pilot study for its *Freedmen's Library*, then, after one year, transferred control of into publishing its new series.[11]

The *Freedmen's Library* included a spelling book, two primers, three graded readers, a monthly four-page, single-sheet paper reminiscent of contemporaneous Sunday School papers, and several didactic books written as advice manuals or, in a couple of cases, as admonitory stories. There were fifteen titles in all. They were inexpensively produced and often available free to southern black schools. All of the material in the *Freedmen's Library* was written expressly for the freed people, in a level of prose and diction—fictional black conversation was invariably rendered in mock vernacular—and with images and ideas that the authors presumed would be familiar to southern African Americans. It was curriculum that was "culturally appropriate" with a vengeance. It was, simultaneously, unrelievedly offensive. In its engravings, stories, sketches, and illustrations, the society's publications portrayed the freed people as an ignorant, docile, apolitical southern black mass passively looking to godly white teachers and ministers for advice and direction, speaking a stereotyped ungrammatical patois, striving pathetically to mimic their white superiors. Its engravings provided contrasting images of impossibly noble, serious, well-clad Victorian white children and heedless, slovenly black children and adults. While the *Freedman*, the monthly paper, occasionally included news of freed people establishing and running their own schools and churches, it and most of the rest of the society's curricular materials constructed their readers as dependent and improvident. Both in tone and in much of the didactic advice, the tract society publications encouraged southern blacks to accept their place as field hands and domestic servants in a postwar agricultural economy dominated by southern whites. Ideas of black strength, autonomy, equality, and pride found no place in the society's many publications.[12]

Among curricular material designed specifically for the freed people, there were only two alternatives to the *Freedmen's Library*. In 1865, abolitionist writer Lydia Maria Child published, at her own expense, *The Freedmen's Book*. The contrast with the American Tract Society material could hardly have been more dramatic, from the language employed to the images of black life evoked. Child never stooped to writing in dialect and avoided the driveling sentimentality that larded the American Tract Society textbooks. Anticipating curricular strictures a full century after her time, Child sought to build racial pride through biographies of courageous, strong black leaders, from the revolutionary Toussaint L'Ouverture to Frederick Douglass. Her hope was that the freed people might "derive fresh strength and courage from this true record of what colored men have accomplished under great disadvantages," as she explained in the book's preface.[13]

Similarly, the African Civilization Society, a northern black organization, sought to compete with the American Tract Society's monthly school paper. The *Freedmen's Torchlight* followed the same four-page format as the tract society's *Freedman*, but its content diverged sharply. Like Child's book, the *Freedmen's Torchlight* openly advocated black pride and black control of freedmen's education. Where the *Freedman* invariably spoke of the freedmen's teachers as white, the *Freedman's Torchlight* argued that African Americans were best able to educate the freed people; where much of the American Tract Society material held up northern middle-class white cultural standards for black emulation and drew negative caricatures of black life and living standards, the *Freedmen's Torchlight* portrayed the freed people as intelligent, independent, and capable of defining their own cultural standards.[14]

An analysis of textbooks intended for the freed people may reveal much about the intentions of the writers, but it indicates a good deal less about what transpired in classrooms, for the simple reason that these sorts of resources seldom reached the students themselves. The American Civilization Society was apparently unable to raise the funds to publish more than a few issues of the *Freedmen's Torchlight*. Child's book was used in the black schools in New Berne, North Carolina, at least, but there is no evidence that it gained wide use in southern black schools. The Freedmen's Bureau, with close ties to the American Tract Society, sent free supplies of the *Freedmen's Library* to some teachers, though the teachers rarely refer to using them, more frequently employing them in Sunday Schools than in their weekday schools.[15] It is, in short, unlikely that more than a small number of black students had an opportunity to read Child or the *Torchlight*, while a somewhat larger group may have been exposed to the tract society's more conservative textbooks.

Rather than these special texts, the schoolbooks found most frequently in the freed people's schools were exactly the same schoolbooks with which students across the country, but particularly in the North, were familiar. They included many of the major schoolbook series, such as Webster's speller, Greenleaf's or Eaton's texts on arithmetic, Mitchell's or Monteith's geography, and McGuffey's or Willson's readers. In 1865, the leading aid

To Know All about Our School

societies met to determine whether they should agree upon a uniform set of schoolbooks, "thereby securing efficiency & economy" in the education effort. They decided, however, that since there were many series of equal merit, "it would be hardly just treatment of publishers, should we adopt any one series." The minutes from that meeting made no mention of the special freedmen's text series published by the tract society.[16] One of the teachers, reminiscing five decades after her work in Charlottesville, Virginia, listed many textbooks used in her school, concluding, "In short we were not confined to special text books, but read and taught from what seemed to offer the best instruction."[17]

Likewise, the subjects studied in the freed people's schools were no different from the subjects studied in elementary and grammar schools throughout the country. The curriculum of the black schools reached far beyond the hoary reading, writing, and arithmetic. Black students in the rough equivalent of the fourth grade in Charleston, South Carolina, studied "Guyot's Intermediate Geography, Child's Book of Nature, Felter's Intellectual Arithmetic, and are about half way through Payson & Dunton's Writing Book, No 3. They write Compositions, and have oral lessons in Grammar. They have already had a thorough training in the four rules in Arithmetic, thus following out a simple course in Fractions and Denominate Numbers."[18] Three years after her students began their studies on St. Helena Island, South Carolina, Laura Towne wrote in her diary, "The children have read through a history of the United States and an easy physiology, and they know all the parts of speech, and can make sentences, being told to use a predicate, verb, and adverb, for instance. Ellen's class is writing compositions. We are going to have a grand school exhibition before we close, with dialogues, exercises in mathematics, in grammar, geography, spelling, reading, etc., etc."[19] A teacher in Murfreesboro, Tennessee, reported in 1868, "In the morning, we have writing, geography, and written arithmetic. This study is varied every other day by mental arithmetic. In the afternoon we have Willson's Third and Fourth Readers, grammar, and spelling. We have also paid some attention to physiology and the History of the United States. In spelling they are very ambitious to have perfect lessons."[20] Calisthenic exercises filled a portion of the school day in some larger schools. A freedmen's teacher in North Carolina closed school each day with "a few questions on Familiar Science." Her students could "explain the causes of rain, lightning, expansion and contraction by heat and cold, and other simple matters."[21] Jane Briggs Smith taught what would today be called civics, after which "the children could tell you every principle which our representatives were bound to uphold." She also taught the rudiments of geometry.[22] The thousands of monthly tabular reports submitted to the Freedmen's Bureau from teachers all tell the same tale: after the basics of literacy and numeracy had been learned, usually within a year or two, the curriculum broadened to embrace all of what nineteenth-century educators called the common branches.[23]

Further, the curriculum continued to expand as students progressed. After only six years of access to schools, the African American students in Petersburg, Virginia's, public "colored" school passed a three-hour "examination in French, Latin, Algebra, Arithmetic, Geography, &c."[24] The first principal of the South Carolina Normal School reported that his corps of prospective African American teachers had studied "Arithmetic, Geography, Grammar, Geometry, Reading, Writing, History, Drawing, Spelling, Map-Drawing, Latin, Algebra, Botany, Mineralogy, Physiology, Object Lessons, and Theory and Practice of Teaching, Constitution of South Carolina."[25] From across the South, teachers consistently reported teaching languages, mathematics, sciences, geography, history, and other traditional subjects.

Of course, to attend to a curriculum does not assure that one masters the curriculum. Armstrong and others claimed that black learners were "capable of acquiring knowledge to any degree, and, to a certain age, at least, with about the same facility as white children; but [they lack] the power to assimilate or digest it." Armstrong went on to argue, "The negro matures sooner than the white man, but has not his steady development of mental strength up to advanced years. His mechanical faculty works quickly and outstrips his understanding. He will read a passage wonderfully well, but not be able to state the 'gist' of it in his own language."[26]

Yet tens of thousands of black students in hundreds of southern schools throughout Reconstruction gave the lie to such racial theorizing. They succeeded in public examinations in which visitors as well as teachers posed the questions. Those posing questions did not accept simple rote recall but demanded explanations of answers. A visitor to a school in Virginia remarked in a private letter, "the examination in Arithmetic, and especially in fractions was the most interesting. It surprised me; and I think I never heard a class of the same age, who gave so clearly & understandingly the rules, and the reasons for them, by which fractions are changed in adding, subtracting, multiplying & reducing them."[27] In South Carolina, students only three years out of slavery were examined in U.S. history, physiology, geography, civics, grammar, composition, spelling "in

Three children in Mary A. Upton's class in Charleston, South Carolina, about 1868. The children may have been chosen to emphasize the range of racial characteristics among the freed children. Courtesy of the Trustees of the Boston Public Library/Rare Books.

words of four syllables," and other traditional subjects. One examination problem in arithmetic required the students to calculate "on the blackboard the price of two bales of cotton sold here at the market price per pound, and then [if they] took two bales to New York, deducting expenses, commissions, &c., and selling it at the market price there, to find the advantage or disadvantage of the two plans."[28] Scores of further examples could be provided. Nor can these testimonies be dismissed as the predictable comments of teachers ingratiating themselves to their sponsors. Observations of high levels of achievement, with students explaining the processes they employed to solve problems posed to them, were consistent across private entries in diaries, letters to families and friends never intended for publication, grudging observations in southern papers otherwise hostile to black education, and letters sent by observers to the aid organizations and the Freedmen's Bureau.[29]

Black students learned well despite an enormous gap between the curriculum of their schools and their life experiences. Their own culture was rooted in agrarian rhythms, oral traditions with many African survivals, an ethic of communal self-help, and an expressive religion; the white culture surrounding them was, for most of them, rural, aristocratic or lower class, and traditional. The curriculum they faced employed language, imagery, settings, and ideals that were northern, industrializing, middle class, and Victorian. That curriculum's ideological bias was Whig and Puritan; its literary canon was northern and European; its language was formal, academic, and almost always neutral in affect. In both its written form and its presentation in most classrooms, the curriculum flattened expressiveness by parsing and categorizing language, depoliticized history by silencing most of history's narratives, and sucked the life out of geography through a fetish for memorizing place-names and locations. Despite such a vast chasm, the freed people mastered their lessons.[30]

MEANWHILE, THE PEDAGOGY PRACTICED IN THE FIRST GENERATION OF southern black schools was just as distant culturally from the lives of southern African Americans as was the curriculum. Many of the teachers in the early black schools followed the traditional pedagogy of individual and small-group recitation that was still practiced by midcentury in schools throughout the South and in northern rural schools. Others employed the more modern pedagogies then emerging in northern urban schools. Though distinct from one another in important ways, rooted in contrasting social relationships, both pedagogies were hierarchical, unidirectional, competitive, rationalized, and individualistic. Both tended to privilege passive memorization over active participation, individual achievement over group acquisition, character over intellect.[31] Such pedagogies stood in sharp contrast to a culture that valued mutuality, community, and active engagement.

And yet black students just out of slavery learned with astonishing speed. Black illiteracy dropped dramatically, and would continue to drop throughout the century. Black students continued to fill every classroom that opened. At a point in history when African Americans were as distant from the curriculum of the school as they would ever be, they nonetheless mastered the curriculum. These black learners did not need a culturally appropriate curriculum; they only needed an opportunity.

The demand that black students receive a curriculum that was carefully tailored to their limited cultural experiences was not unknown at the time. Yet even as late as the end of Reconstruction, those calling for such a curriculum—men such as Samuel Chapman Armstrong, Giles B. Cooke, and an emerging cadre of southern white educators who intended to use education to bind southern blacks to the soil—were out of step with most of their contemporaries in the black schools. Those other teachers, including some southern white teachers such as those in Petersburg whose students shone in examinations in languages and arithmetic, assumed that the education that was good for white children was the education that was mandatory for black children. It would not be long before the educational opportunities in Petersburg and throughout the South would be scaled back, however, not out of any failure on the part of ambitious black learners but because of a new generation of educators, northern and southern, who designed a schooling for blacks that would be appropriate for the destiny the nation had determined was appropriate for the race. Those later educators learned from Armstrong, studiously ignoring the manifest lessons available from other teachers.[32]

In the meantime, an implicit curriculum was being enacted, even in classrooms whose teachers may not have been particularly committed to their black charges. The very fact that the teachers expected their black students to master the same curriculum as white students, using exactly the same curricular material, and the students' unmistakable success in mastering that curriculum, taught powerful lessons to the freed people about their teachers' expectations and their own capabilities. They were lessons that would not have been taught as effectively had the teachers insisted upon the presumably more culturally appropriate texts of the *Freedmen's Library* or had they, like Armstrong, restricted the curriculum

To Know All about Our School

to fit presumed racial limitations. The manifest results of the schools contradicted all who argued for a special curriculum. Whether intentionally or unintentionally, the majority of the teachers demonstrated black intellectual equality, and did so under trying conditions. The nation paid no heed to the demonstration, but the freed people no doubt gained confidence and pride from it.

HOW DID THE TEACHERS TEACH IN ORDER TO ACHIEVE THAT LEVEL OF black learning? What was the pedagogy practiced in the early black schools? What are we to make of Wyatt-Brown's claim that the northern, urban pedagogy that the teachers brought into southern, rural schools imposed a symbolic system that created crippling instructional and linguistic distances between the learners' lives and the school? Is it true that, "in fact, the entire discipline of arithmetic, written or mental, was fairly consistently avoided," along with geography, while teachers played to such presumed racial strengths as imitation and memorization?[33]

It is easy to dispense with Wyatt-Brown's charge about the neglect of arithmetic and geography. It is an odd claim, supported by an appeal to three reports from 1863, 1864, and 1866; it is overwhelmed by hundreds of teachers' and superintendents' reports that provide rich descriptions of black students solving arithmetic problems and frequent remarks by teachers that the subject was the favorite among the students. The evidence of their study of, and achievement in, geography, may be the more surprising, given that most of the students had probably never traveled more than ten or twenty miles from their homes. At one point Wyatt-Brown cites John W. Alvord to sustain his claim that the freed people's teachers avoided teaching arithmetic, yet Alvord's twice-yearly reports on the schools prove the opposite. Those reports indicate that for most of the bureau's five years, in fact, more black students were studying arithmetic than any other advanced study, and geography was the third-most-common subject studied. Indeed, of all students at all levels, only those at the most elementary level, those just starting to "spell and read easy lessons," were more numerous than those studying arithmetic, in 1868 and later.[34] The claim that African American students were culturally (or racially) incapable of mastering arithmetic is unsustainable.

The remark about the problem of an urban pedagogy for rural students, however, opens the way to a more complex analysis than Wyatt-Brown intended, but one that may deepen our understanding of the pedagogy and its appropriateness to a newly emancipated people. However, it must first

To Know All about Our School

be recalled that most of the teachers in the first generation of southern black schools were neither northern nor urban, and the pedagogy they imported into the schools had not a trace of either influence. Southern white teachers and southern black teachers, along with not a few northern white and black teachers, had only attended schools that practiced what, for the purposes of this investigation, can only reasonably be considered rural or traditional pedagogy. Making up the rest of the teachers, a distinct minority, were urban northern blacks, many of whom had attended a normal school and some of whom had attended college or an academy or had other contact with a modernizing pedagogy. Further, many, but not all, of the northern white teachers, like their black counterparts, had attended normal school, college, or an academy. What the freed people's schools had, then, were a majority of teachers practicing a traditional pedagogy, and a minority practicing an urban and, it might be fair to say, a modernizing, pedagogy. While those with experience in modernizing schools were certainly a minority, many of them were among the teachers who taught the longest. There were, then, two different and occasionally overlapping pedagogies at work in the schools, not the single urban teaching that Wyatt-Brown claims. Nonetheless, he was on to something of which he was not even aware.

In the North, there were, by midcentury or earlier, two distinct pedagogies, rural or traditional and urban or modern.[35] Traditional and modern modes of teaching differed most clearly in two ways, both of which had an impact on the early black schools, and both of which must be understood if we are to test Wyatt-Brown's critique of urban pedagogy as inappropriate for the freed people. The first difference is that the two depended upon contrasting social and technical relationships within the classroom; the second difference is that while traditional schooling was strictly local and unsystematized, modern pedagogy was deeply implicated in organizing and elaborating educational systems.[36]

First, the change in the social relations between students and teacher between the two pedagogies was dramatic. Traditional education was primarily a face-to-face, one-on-one encounter between parent and child, master and apprentice, teacher and student. In its institutional form, traditional pedagogy was characterized by social relations that relied chiefly on force or the threat of force to achieve two ends simultaneously, classroom order and individual motivation. Schoolmasters wielded the rod against the student who was reciting as well as against other students who, in their boredom, found outlets for their youthful vitality. Modernizers, in contrast,

To Know All about Our School

experimented with many alternatives to classroom violence to humanize the social relations of the classroom. By the 1860s, the modern teacher had, to a large degree, abandoned the traditional reliance on corporal punishment. In its place the teacher was expected to govern through force of personality. Teachers were to maintain order by cultivating an emotional, maternal relationship with learners and to motivate through the child's natural curiosity, a love of learning, and, when necessary, the offer of prizes or, negatively, a withdrawal of acceptance or privileges.[37]

Some teachers in the freedmen's schools deployed those modern proclivities in their classroom discipline practices. At the outset of their four decades of work on the Sea Islands of South Carolina, Ellen Murray and Laura Towne "agreed that no corporal punishment should ever be used," even though they suspected that "to institute moral government among children used to no persuasion but that of the lash, was no easy task."[38] "In the discipline of our schools we do not resort to corporal punishment," a Massachusetts teacher wrote in 1867. "I have myself for many years been greatly opposed to it." She found that "the *threat* of expulsion always proved sufficiently potent to insure good conduct."[39] Another teacher remarked that the freedmen themselves expected the teachers to punish their children by whipping them, but she resisted: "Parents who come into my school often say, 'I can't see how you does get along so straight without whipping.' I tell them it is much easier to govern by love than by fear of the rod. I think the race have had whipping enough for the present and all coming generations, and nothing would induce me to use the *rod*; neither do I believe it necessary."[40] Sarah Williams found that "When the scholars transgress they tell us to whip them, but they are so used to that, that we find other things are often a greater punishment." She confessed, "If I had to use [the whip] I know I would cry as much as the scholars."[41]

The teachers' modern practices were reinforced by the policies of some of the organizations that supported them. The most influential and longest lived of the secular aid societies, the New England Freedmen's Aid Society, told its teachers bluntly that "corporal punishment is strongly objected to, and its use is regarded as evidence of incompetency in the teacher."[42] In a letter to one of its normal schools in Virginia, the society's Teachers Committee succinctly summarized its sense of the link between appropriate modes of discipline and the ideal forms of student motivation and simultaneously summarized the emerging modern notion of appropriate social relations in the classroom. It maintained that corporal punishment lowers the standard of any school; prevents the true relation between pupils & teachers, and that a resort to it argues against the possession of a natural power & ability to govern on the part of a teacher, & therefore indicates that such teacher lacks one of the essential qualifications.

A Normal School, which is to teach true methods & inspire the pupils with the right animus as prospective teachers[,] ought not to resort to any course which brings in an appeal to the lower motives. It should inspire the pupils with the desire to do right & to study for study's sake, by making the lessons attractive, & should inculcate by the daily example of its teachers the necessity of great patience, in explaining difficulties, while demanding thoroughness in all things.[43]

In place of physical force, modern, urban teachers substituted their own force of character, moral suasion, appeals to conscience, and the students' emotional attachments to the teacher. As an observer described a school on St. Helena Island, such schools were "governed on the principle of winning rather than whipping"; and two of the major aid societies affirmed that "the regular attendance and discipline common in Northern schools," though not to be automatically expected of a people "just emerging into the blessings of self-control," could still "be attained without any severity of treatment, but by the persuasions which flow from the teacher's own character and example."[44] Sela G. Wright was certain that teachers could dispense with the rod: "A strong attachment to the teachers is soon manifested by the children and their parents," he reported. "This fact, with proper instruction, in nearly every instance, secures prompt obedience."[45] The principal of a school in Washington, D.C., explained, "Corporeal punishment is not resorted to: we have endeavored to rule by reason and persuasion rather than by force."[46] Charles P. Day reported that after two students got into a fight in school, he "told them that they had done a very wicked thing, had disgraced themselves and the whole school, that I would give them one day to think of it in [sic], and then they might write down whatever they had to say in relation to the matter, and I would read it to the school. They did so."[47]

This shift from force to conscience relied on instilling a sense of personal guilt. "We do not talk much to the children about penalties and punishments, but much about right and wrong, about what we wish and expect from them," Juliet B. Smith wrote from Fernandina, Florida, "about the effects which will come from well-doing, and we refer to suspension always as the worst thing evil-doing can bring down upon them. I believe suspension is the best discipline."[48] Not infrequently, such efforts were inextricably intertwined with religious appeals. In 1862, Martha Schofield, who would go on to work with the freed people for nearly half a century, confided in her diary that she had spent two hours after school "pleading and coaxing the good that I knew *must* be in the heart of one of my most wayward pupils. I conquered at last, though I had to punish him, but my talk brought the repentant tears, and I do sincerely hope, he may be strengthened to do better."[49] William H. Kennedy detained misbehaving students after class: "I keep them and pray with them, and give them the teachings of the Savior, and such treatment has a more lasting effect, I find, than whipping."[50]

Not every disciplinary encounter by teachers bent on moral suasion ended in a lecture, of course. Frances J. Munger, teaching in Greensboro, North Carolina, related the following instance in 1866:

> I saw a boy pass a paper across the aisle, which is a forbidden thing, as it invariably leads to visiting. When he saw that I was looking at him, he naturally stopped; I called him to me and asked him why he stopped? he said because I looked at him and he knew that I would speak to him. Then, said I, you would do a thing if you thought I was not looking, that you would not do if you thought I was? "Yes'm." I must confess that he took away my text for a lecture; and as he is one of the good boys of the school, after a *very* few remarks, I discreetly returned to my geography class.[51]

The abandonment of force and violence in modernizing classrooms extended beyond the prevention of disorder. Modern educators also sought to build social relations in classrooms that would enhance motivation and achievement. Mortimer A. Warren, a Yale graduate who worked for a decade in southern black schools, gave voice to the emerging vision of the modern schoolhouse when, in 1869, he wrote, "I love promptness in a school; but I want it born of hunger for knowledge and ambition to get higher, and not a military precision forced by fear. Our school has not the showy appearance of some, yet the enthusiasm and progress of our pupils compensate for the lack of that drilled exactness which would be so beautiful were it not so costly. I name my plan of government the democratic. This plan of government yields the happiest results."[52] The "secret" of Abby Simmon's decade of success teaching the freed children of Norfolk and Washington, D.C., was "that she so secures the interest and affections of her pupils that they much prefer being in the schoolroom to any other place."[53]

Enthusiasm and affection have their limits as a means to gain motivation, however. Modern teachers had other strategies to fall back upon. Drawing on the labor incentive systems emerging under industrial capitalism, they established competitive reward systems in schools. Joseph Lancaster's monitorial schools had relied almost exclusively on carefully articulated status hierarchies through which students passed on the basis of competitively determined merit. Subsequent modernizing pedagogies in the United States after the 1820s rejected the more mechanistic aspects of monitorial schools, along with Lancaster's privileging of more advanced students as instructors, but they retained and elaborated upon the monitorial schools' promotion rituals and their reliance upon competition, emulation, and rewards to achieve compliance and motivation.[54]

The freed people's teachers employed a variety of positive sanctions as a counterpart of their rejection of force and other negative sanctions. To improve punctuality, for instance, Elizabeth Pennock, a thirty-year-old teacher from Philadelphia, found that giving picture cards to those children who arrived at school on time improved the punctuality of all. Well ahead of the behaviorists, she found that once "the better habit" was established, "the picture-card encouragement is no longer necessary."[55] Laura M. Towne found that the freed people were so eager to learn that she needed only to resort "to a potent factor—emulation."[56]

Ranking and promotion rituals in the form of student grades had not yet been fully codified in northern urban schools by the 1860s.[57] Thus the freedmen's teachers who developed forms of student grades to stimulate competition and to thereby improve discipline and motivation were in the vanguard of the modernizing impulse. S. A. Finney reported "happy results" from her assignment of numeric grades "for lessons, attendance and deportment. My pupils have a perfect dread of getting a low number, and by this method, they are encouraged to *proceed*." She assigned a ten as the highest score, indicating excellence; a five indicated "indifferent"; a zero was "a failure." The effectiveness of her program lay in part in the public approbation or humiliation that accompanied it; she read the students' grades to the class weekly, "& when a five or an *aught*, is read out, the tears flow from the eyes of the child to whom it belongs." It would be difficult to find a more succinct summary of the emerging social relations of the classroom and their roots in forms of hierarchical affectional relations than Finney's description of her philosophy: "My first object with my scholars is to gain their confidence & good will, & when their good will *is* obtained, & they feel assured that although their teacher is their superior in intelligence, she is good & kind & condesending—they are prepared, for the leading sentiments in morality, that all superiority, or true greatness in man, depends upon his goodness, & in this sentiment I lay the foundation of my government, & by it, excite the children to govern themselves."[58]

Emma V. Brown, a free black woman from Georgetown, D.C., had taught in Myrtilla Miner's school for free African American girls before the Civil War, attended Oberlin College briefly, and continued teaching in Georgetown and elsewhere for many years after the Civil War. She found that teaching the children of ex-slaves was quite different from her experiences with the children of free blacks. With the former, she finally resorted to a form of grading, marking the students "for lessons and for conduct, also for punctuality and regularity." Students who were "quiet, earnest and truthful" wore badges in school indicating they had achieved the "rank of 'Truth and Honor.'" The system "has done more toward securing quiet, good lessons and promptness than anything I have ever before tried in school," she wrote in 1866.[59]

At the same time that urban pedagogy reconstructed social relationships in classrooms, it also transformed technical relationships, the relations between human subjects and such technical factors as time, technologies, and objects. When industrial processes began to dictate meticulous obedience to the clock, for example, the clock began to dictate many aspects of classroom practices, altering teachers' and students' relations to the curriculum, to the school, and to one another. From the Lancastrian schools onward, popular education in the nineteenth century taught precise punctuality as a virtue on a par with honesty and piety. Likewise, new pedagogical techniques, essentially new classroom technologies, revolutionized the technical relations of the classroom.

The insistence on clock discipline in an agrarian society made little sense, yet the freedmen's teachers sought relentlessly to promote punctuality, relying on reward systems and threats of expulsion to secure greater promptness. There was a logic to the clock's new prominence in northern classrooms, linked to the need to discipline an industrializing society to punctual attendance upon the machine. However, the efforts of modernizers to reproduce the virtues of punctuality, or reduce the "evils of tardiness," in a fully agrarian context speak to the degree to which the imposition of the urban school in the rural South was largely unreflective.[60] Yet the freedmen's teachers urged punctuality almost as insistently as they culti-

A second group of students from the Capitol Hill School, Washington, D.C., c. 1868. Courtesy of the Trustees of the Boston Public Library/Rare Books.

vated literacy, even as some of them noted the illogic of expecting punctuality from people who did not even own clocks. Caroline Thomas was among those who could excuse her students "for not being on the spot at just the right time; many of them have not the means within their reach of knowing anything about it." Yet in the same breath, Thomas spoke of using humiliation to gain greater punctuality:

> I have had considerable difficulty to impress upon these children the importance of punctuality, and thought for the first few weeks I never should be able to accomplish it; but by dint of perseverance in encouraging those who came early, and in showing my displeasure to those who came late, the habit of promptness is being gradually established. I will give thee an instance of my manner of treating those who are late. When such scholar makes his appearance inside the door, I instantly stop whatever I may be doing, and say "Children, tell (calling the delin-

To Know All about Our School

quent by name) at what hour school commences"; at this they will *sing* out, "School commences at 8 o'clock in the morning." This seems to mortify them, and *I* think is having a good effect; in some cases it has acted like a charm.[61]

More frequently, teachers sought to encourage punctuality with the same incentive systems they used to motivate learning, as when Arthur Sumner and Louise Kellogg gave small testaments to students who were "neither late nor absent" for an entire term.[62]

It is likely, however, that much of the insistence on punctuality had less to do, ultimately, with socializing students to the clock-driven world of industrial society than with other aspects of the urban school itself, particularly its transformed pedagogical methods and systems. Urban schools rapidly replaced the traditional individual and small-group recitation before a schoolmaster with technologies of whole-group teaching through oral instruction. Those modes of instruction required that all be in attendance from the start of the lessons. When the *National Intelligencer* characterized Julia A. Lord's Washington, D.C., classroom as "under the most complete control. Everything in the school moves like clockwork," it was describing classroom technical relations that worked well only when punctuality prevailed.[63]

An early teacher in Memphis, Tennessee, Lucinda Humphrey, related an incident that illustrates the contrast between the technical relations of traditional schools and those in the modern, urban school. Her students, remembering the classrooms they had observed their master's children attending, did not initially believe that whole-group teaching and oral instruction were appropriate school practices. One of her students, "who had been employed in some way about a school-house, thought it 'mighty diff'rent from the Secesh teachin,' and much to my annoyance, assured the rest that 'dey neber could learn nuffin widout lookin' on no books.'" She was gratified by "their great astonishment" when they turned from oral instruction to their books and realized how much they had learned.[64] South Carolina's virtual defunding of the state's black normal school in 1875 meant that the school had no textbooks whatsoever, yet the principal reported that the school's teaching methods—lectures, classroom discussions, and other alternatives to recitations—substituted well in teaching students "to observe, to investigate, to think." "It is interesting to observe their wonder at our book-less instruction deepen into interest, interest into enthusiasm and enthusiasm into gratitude," he wrote. Other teachers like-

To Know All about Our School

wise reported in detail on their practice of oral instruction to whole classes, a practice virtually unheard of in traditional pedagogy.[65]

Other changes in pedagogy common to urban schools also made their appearance in the freed people's schools. Urban educators claimed, for example, to be more interested in intellectual understanding than in mere memorization, implying that the latter end characterized the common goal of traditional recitation methods. Cynthia C. Ranstead was praised for her work in Farmville, Virginia. "She has evidently advanced far upon the ways of the improved systems of teaching," wrote an observer in 1866, "which makes understanding rather than acquisition the basis of intelligence." A colleague in another room of the same school followed the same "system of teaching as generally practiced in the best schools of New England." Her objective was "to have her pupils acquire the greatest amount of substantial knowledge that the time will enable them to do, and no time is given to learning set phrases and verses and other stuff for exhibition." The same observer's description of Eliza P. Dean's teaching encapsulated the ideal of midcentury modern pedagogy:

> Every thing is done well, strictly and with precision, and in such manner as shows a clear understanding of the subject. Her principle of teaching is to pass nothing until it is fully understood and made familiar, so that it can be used appropriately in all its relations. Nothing is pressed upon the understanding; but, on the contrary, by tact and skill the understanding is induced to grasp for and to seek new thoughts and principles, based upon those already known. She is a very highly educated teacher, skilled in all the theories and principles of mental development, thoroughly practical in all her workings, and probably is not excelled as a teacher or disciplinarian by any one in this country.[66]

Another of the more obvious contrasts in the technical relations of modern, urban schools compared to traditional, rural schools was visual. By the time of the Civil War, northern teachers expected a modern school to be filled with visual teaching aids, "maps, black-boards, charts, and tablets of texts,—those indispensable aids in correct teaching," in the words of Emma Bowman.[67] By 1867, a secondary school for the freedmen of Washington, D.C., boasted "blackboards, outline maps, and a variety of useful charts a fine globe, a large black globe, used in drawing maps with chalk, and for other kindred purposes," along with desks "fashioned after the Boston school furniture."[68] Martha A. Wight, teaching in Beaufort, South Carolina, wrote in 1864 that her "blackboard and globe are invaluable aids, but I much wish that I had an Outline Map of the Hemispheres, and one of the United States."[69] Another teacher asserted that blackboards were "absolutely necessary. If I were called upon to decide between blackboards and books, *i.e.*, arithmetics, I should prefer the boards and teach arithmetic orally."[70]

Modern teaching technologies were seldom available at the outset of the southern work, of course. In the primitive conditions of the freedmen's schools, particularly in the early years when a schoolhouse might consist of a tent, a former slave pen, or a damp church basement, the teachers became inventive in creating substitutes for familiar pedagogical aids. In his first months of teaching, without schoolhouse, textbooks, or chalkboard, William Burgess simply moved from cabin to cabin, taught a lesson to the inhabitants, and wrote "chalk letters on the walls about for them to learn by the next day." Many of his learners followed him all day to be sure they got the lesson.[71] Nancy S. Battey reported, "I am thrown wholly upon my own resources in teaching geography, as the school-room is furnished with neither globe or maps," but she procured a large cannon ball to serve as a globe. It "answers very well," she thought, "and, perhaps, gives them as accurate an idea of the shape of the earth as the most finished globe."[72]

Central to industrialization, and thus not surprisingly central to modernizing, urban education, were processes of routinizing, systematizing, and bureaucratizing. While northern school bureaucracies did not gain the level of power or standardization of nineteenth-century European ministries of education, the classifying, supervising, centralizing, and organizing germ infected northern educators. Education's twentieth-century "cult of efficiency" had its roots in the material forces and industrial discourses of the first industrial revolution eight decades earlier. Educators deployed both the language and the mechanics of efficiency as they labored to render teaching and learning more tractable, effective, and efficient. They reconstituted the modes of authority over schools and teachers, displacing traditional, informal community supervision with more systematic surveillance by principals and superintendents. They built data-gathering agencies that, while initially vested with little formal power, realized informal opportunities to shape practices and possibilities by the sorts of information requested on the forms they would increasingly impose on teachers.[73]

Simultaneously, teachers appropriated the same efficiency discourse to reconstitute classrooms and reinvent themselves. Modernizing teachers preferred systematically "graded" classrooms that housed students who were working at the same academic level, and communities pointed with pride to their "graded" schools. Simultaneously, educators created more systematic pedagogies, devised more elaborate school curricula, and constructed schools and a curriculum to educate teachers. Within the early logic of efficiency and routinization, the material and ideological ground was cleared for perhaps the most remarkable aspect of the modern, urban school, the emergence of a predominantly female teaching force.[74]

The freed people's educators most affected by modernization imported those routinizing and systematizing practices into the South. Before the Civil War ended, the nascent southern schools had principals and superintendents who monitored classroom practices and teacher behavior, not infrequently colliding with teachers on matters of policy and personality. For example, as early as April 1862, Solomon Peck had been appointed superintendent of the freedmen's school in Beaufort, South Carolina, overseeing the work of five teachers. Early superintendents such as William F. Mitchell in Tennessee and William F. Allen in South Carolina and Alabama spent more time organizing schools for their aid societies than in supervising teachers. Yardley Warner, little celebrated though perhaps the most remarkable of the superintendents, coordinated, examined, and raised funds for many years for a network of Quaker schools scattered across the upper South. The American Missionary Association was particularly hierarchical, employing several men at relatively high salaries each year to supervise its teachers in larger towns and cities, and turning to women as principals, at much lower salaries, later in the 1860s. Likewise, all of the larger organizations required monthly teachers' reports that they used to cajole contributors and promote freedmen's education, much as early northern educational bureaucracies used school reports to promote the expansion of tax-supported common schools.[75]

Graded schools sprouted across the South, housing sophisticated pedagogy and modern curricular innovations. Virtually as a matter of course, if a freedmen's school had more than one teacher, one was appointed principal. Hundreds of teachers, male and female, had the opportunity to serve as principal if they remained in the South for more than two or three years. In the earliest years, when schools of two or three hundred students met in churches or other large halls without partitions, the principal's job might consist primarily of keeping order amid the confusion of four or five teachers working with different groups. As soon as buildings could be procured that conformed to modern notions of a schoolhouse, however, with separate classrooms for each teacher and his or her class, the principal took on roles more familiar to northern schools, usually consisting of teaching the most advanced class while providing a modicum of supervision and assistance for the teachers under his or her care.[76]

Urban schools organized children with as much zeal as they organized teachers. Where traditional teachers taught students at all levels of proficiency, working with each child individually or teaching small groups of children at similar levels, urban schools were "classified"; that is, the students were divided into classes according to their proficiency in literacy and numeracy skills. No sooner had the freedmen's teachers found buildings for schools than they set about the task of classifying or grading their schools. For instance, by 1864 at Port Royal, South Carolina, the schools of the National Freedmen's Relief Association had been divided into a high school, two levels of intermediate schools, and a primary school. The high school—not yet a secondary school, but the most advanced school—had over fifty students, while the two intermediate schools shared 160 students, and the primary school enrolled 232. Shortly after opening a school in Little Rock, Arkansas, a Quaker teacher reported, "we have adopted a graded system."[77] A year before the war ended, Portsmouth, Virginia, had "been laid out into districts, and, as far as possible, the schools have been *graded*." The superintendent, an educator from Boston, explained, "This gives great advantage to the teachers and scholars. It is so much easier to teach where there is uniformity and order, than where the school is heterogeneous or mixed up."[78] The American Missionary Association even went so far as to enforce its own compulsory attendance rule at Fortress Monroe, Virginia, creating a private force of truant officers from among the older students.[79]

With the advent of the Freedmen's Bureau in 1865, the effort to routinize and organize southern black education accelerated. The bureau was housed in the War Department and headed by a career army officer. Its educational work was more highly organized and more hierarchical than any state educational system of its day. Assistant superintendents and sub-assistant superintendents in each state in the former Confederate states reported to the general superintendent in Washington, who reported in turn to the bureau commissioner. Within months of assuming office, John Alvord, general superintendent of freedmen's schools for the bureau, had created and distributed detailed reporting forms for all teachers from which he distilled ten semiannual reports between 1866 and 1870, without doubt the most complete source of data on educational matters in the Deep South in the nineteenth century. Alvord sought information not simply on the numbers of teachers, schools, and students, but also the number of

Sunday Schools, enrollment in various subject areas, the efforts of teachers to promote temperance, the condition and ownership of schoolhouses, the disposition of white citizens to the educational work, and a multitude of other issues.[80]

In the North, modern schools promoted a modern, elaborate, systematic pedagogy efficiently applied to a broad curriculum. Teachers became self-conscious and deliberate about their pedagogy. Likewise, the freed people's teachers spoke frequently of their teaching methods and the subjects they taught, describing a modern sensibility to teaching and learning. Charles Stearns, for example, explained how his classroom practices, involving the entire class, not individuals, were intended to maximize student attention and understanding:

> Understanding the importance of fixing their attention upon the lessons, we adopted the plan of having them repeat in concert, passages from the Scriptures, usually from the Psalms, and then questioning them as to what they had repeated, and explaining its meaning. Another oral exercise was, for a class to read in the Bible, and then require the remainder of the school to tell what the class had read, thus securing their attention during the reading. We always required each class, at the close of their lessons, to tell in their own language what they had been reading about, so as to fasten in their memories the information given in the books.[81]

Stearns's emphasis on understanding rather than rote memorization was a cornerstone of the new urban pedagogy. It was a mode of teaching that, when practiced best, continuously asked students to explain their reasoning. In teaching her students division of compound numbers, Cordelia N. Buchanan required them not only to derive correct answers but to "explain all the principles and examples accurately" and could report that "in the latter study they delight to excel."[82] The principal of the freedmen's normal school in Baltimore, Henry T. Hartwell, taught for understanding, and taught his future teachers to do the same. "I find it very difficult for most scholars who can perform an example readily upon the slate to give the reasons for their work," he wrote in 1866. "To remedy this defect, we spend much time on Mental Arith. and in explaining examples. Our object is to understand the reason for every step we take." His description of teaching geography illustrates the flexibility of this pedagogy when working with students whose experience might otherwise limit their grasp of the subject. His approach to teaching began with the learner, moving her

To Know All about Our School

from the familiar to the unfamiliar: "Geography commences with a description of the school room, direction of objects, their distance from each other, &c. This is extended to the town in which we are teaching, together with its history, resources, and peculiarities, &c. From the town to the counties, then the state as a whole. For this purpose our room is furnished with a Map of Md. By the aid of text books or the Outline Map of U.S. we are now ready to take up the adjoining state."[83]

Urban pedagogy's concern with more effective teaching extended naturally to reading, the first skill most students must master. Hartwell and others spoke of the "improved" reading methods they used with their students, and one teacher, John C. Zachos, wrote a reading textbook for adult learners based on his work with the freed people at Port Royal, South Carolina.[84] Henry Fish described in detail his method of teaching reading, claiming that, in contrast to traditional methods, "we apply every element learned immediately to its legitimate and ultimate use, the representation of *words* and vocalize their combination in the words." The result, he was certain, was a gain in efficiency, for much time was lost under traditional methods; further, traditional methods caused students to lose "immensely in interest—enthusiasm—by not having mental activity with the exercise of reading; for the more faculties you can awaken in an exercise, the more intense the interest in it."[85]

A particularly rich description of a black school in Washington, D.C., illustrates the apparently successful work of Phebe T. Chamberlain to integrate many aspects of the curriculum into a simple reading lesson while simultaneously keeping her students engaged and thinking. The anonymous observer noted that the lesson was based on a reading lesson from a typical school reader, yet Chamberlain used the passage to test her students' grasp of geography, physiology, science, grammar, definitions, spelling, and history. As the children read, the teacher interrupted, never lecturing, only questioning:

> One passage ran thus: Though you had the manners of a Chesterfield and lacked truth, etc. "Stop there," said Miss Chamberlain, and applying to a little urchin, not surely over nine years, she asked, "Who was Chesterfield?" The reply came on the instant, "An English nobleman, famed for his courteous manners, so that to call one a Chesterfield implies that he is a well-bred gentleman." "When did he live? Where is England? London? Succession since Queen Anne? In whose reign was American independence achieved?"

To Know All about Our School

"Next read. Stop, Lawrence, parse the sentence you have just read, the punctuation of the paragraph, with the rules that govern it?"

"There, Julia, you said Cuba, go and point out Cuba on the map, and tell its chief productions? How and when were the West Indies named? Where did Columbus land, and where was he born? And now that you are at the map, remain there, and point out every place mentioned, while I hear the class." I watched the child and pointer, which, by the way, was at least two-thirds larger than the child, with critical interest, and the dear little creature never once failed with river, city, lake or continent. And thus it went on. "You say *air*, Washington, tell me what air is compose of? With what organ do you breathe? What is the function of the heart? the liver? What is steam? The uses of steam?"[86]

The impulse to routinize and systematize included efforts to assure that all teachers learned and practiced the new pedagogy. As a result, from the 1840s onward in the North, teacher education began to flourish, the earliest teachers' associations emerged, and professional teaching journals appeared. As urban pedagogy extended into the freed people's schools, at least one aid society sent professional journals to its teachers to keep them apprised of current thinking in pedagogy, and teachers and supervisors created teachers' institutes and associations in southern cities to share their skills.[87]

More important, the urge to systematize and routinize education in the rural South included the systematic preparation of the next generation of teachers. Carefully organized teacher education, in special normal schools and normal classes within regular schools, emerged only a quarter-century before the American Civil War. The idea of formal teacher education took root quickly in the modernizing Northeast, spread west, then, under the influence of the freedmen's educators, emerged as unproblematically in the South as had any other feature of urban education. Thus, as early as 1864, the New England Freedmen's Aid Commission had established a normal school in Norfolk, Virginia, Laura Towne had begun systematic teacher education in St. Helena, South Carolina, and the Pennsylvania Freedmen's Relief Association had purchased land in Washington, D.C., for a normal school. Other aid groups quickly followed suit. The National Freedmen's Relief Association announced in 1865 that it intended to turn one of its schools into "a school of some higher grade where the most advanced pupils could be fitted for teachers." The Presbyterians organized a normal school in Baltimore in 1866, and by 1867 the American Mission-

Anna Gardner's school in Charlottesville, Virginia, c. 1868. Note the age range of
the students. The four older students in the upper left, holding what appear to be
diplomas, were her "normal class" who had completed their teacher training with her.
They include Isabella Gibbons, second from the left, and Robert B. Scott and Paul
Lewis, probably the two directly to the right of Gibbons. Gibbons, Scott, and Lewis
went directly from their training under Gardner to long teaching careers.
Courtesy of the Trustees of the Boston Public Library/Rare Books.

ary Association reported seven schools that supported normal classes, along
with four schools under construction that would be either normal schools
or collegiate institutions with normal courses.[88] In other words, four years
after the first schools for freed slaves opened behind Union lines, and two
years after Lincoln released the Emancipation Proclamation, the freedmen's educators had begun establishing centers for the professional education of black teachers for southern black schools. By 1870, nearly ninety
normal schools and normal classes were in operation, scattered from Virginia to Mississippi.[89]

One purpose for systematizing and routinizing the freed people's schools
was to carry the northern system of common schools into the South as part
of the process of reconstruction. The educators' language occasionally betrayed a regional chauvinism, but it also revealed the modernizer's faith in

To Know All about Our School

the efficacy of systems, processes, and routines. They were certain that if modern educational systems were put in place, the South was no more likely to reject them than an industry would neglect an advanced technology. The South needed "a wise and thorough system of public schools," leaders of the Friends Freedmen's Association wrote, "a system of efficient and well conducted schools, ready to be transferred to them as soon as they are prepared to receive them." Their argument, echoed by other aid societies, was steeped in the discourse of system and efficiency: the schools required "thoroughly competent teachers, equipped with all the modern improvements of substantial value in the art of imparting knowledge"; "to organise a system of schools" meant "to collect teachers, books, buildings and other material, and put them into efficient working order"; southern communities would realize "great savings" when they were able to bring the proffered system under their own "management."[90]

IN A REMARKABLY SHORT TIME, PARTICULARLY GIVEN THE CONTEXT OF WAR, dislocation, economic chaos, and sectional and racial hostility, a few thousand teachers established thousands of schools for former slaves in the heart of the old slave kingdom. In the first decade of their work, they extended basic literacy to scores of thousands of freed people, more substantial education to tens of thousands more, and the beginnings of higher education to a few thousand. Yet in their organization, structures, and practices, those schools were creatures of an industrializing, bureaucratizing, urbanizing society riven with the tensions of immigration, modernization, and proletarianization. The South was, and would stubbornly remain for decades, thoroughly traditional and rural. A mechanical view of modernization theory might expect that the transplant would wither in the hostile environment of the South; a naive social meliorist view of institutional efficacy—not unlike the hopes of some of the freedmen's educators—would predict that the transplant would act on the environment, benevolently nurturing the South into grateful surrender to industrial capitalism.

Neither happened, of course. Although education for African Americans in the South suffered from decades of opposition, state neglect, and discrimination, the race's remarkable commitment to formal education kept its schools alive. At the same time, poor white southerners retained their traditional indifference toward formal schooling for decades, despite facilities and opportunities that eventually outstripped those available to poor blacks. Southern social relations did not destroy the idea of mass universal schooling, but neither did the presence of a modern system of schools, established primarily by and for the freed people, move the South effectively toward modernization.

Did the modern, urban form and content of freedmen's education matter, then? It appears that it did. It mattered little how well the modern school fit the exact relations of a premodern South. In its pace, intent, breadth, and potential for human capital formation or for democratic aspirations, the modern school was functionally irrelevant and ideologically foreign to the dominant tendencies in southern society. Dialectically, however, it mattered a good deal that a few thousand teachers carried that particular structure into the rural South at that historic moment.

First, it mattered because the social relations of the modern classroom disrupted the patriarchal relations of the planter regime. Those classroom relations did not, and could not, end nor even significantly alter the stark hierarchical and violent social and political regime under which the freed people toiled. But experiencing classroom relationships based on relative mutuality, affection, enthusiasm, and respect, within which learners were cajoled and enticed rather than threatened when natural curiosity flagged, validated former slaves' hopes for genuine freedom from oppression. Classrooms with modern social relations provided daily object lessons in the possibility of decency and justice.[91] It is little wonder that the freed people filled classrooms to overflowing as soon as teachers could be found.

Similarly, the new technical relations of the modern school may be found to have mattered as well. While the northern school's clock fetish did not translate well to a society still governed by agricultural rhythms, the school's preference for technologies of whole-group teaching appears to have resonated with the communal ethic and group solidarity of the black South, while its inclusion of other educational technologies in the form of blackboards, globes, charts, and other visual learning aids moved formal education away from its tradition of near total reliance on books. Such technologies doubtlessly rendered classrooms more accessible, particularly for a people systematically excluded from the prerequisite cultural capital of books.

Second, it mattered how quickly and how fully the routinizing and systematizing forces within modern education were able to fasten public schooling itself onto the apparatus of the South's postwar and post-Reconstruction states. Within five years of the end of the war, every southern state had written strong educational provisions into its constitution, and some Reconstruction governments had created departments of education patterned

To Know All about Our School

after northern or western models. Redeemer governments slashed state budgets, cut deeply into school support, and dismantled the educational bureaucracy, yet none could undo the democratic vision of education as a public good and a responsibility of the public. Constitutional provisions and state agencies, even those hostile to black education, provided the black community with a mechanism through which to keep alive the ideal of free education for all of its children and to achieve the goal of mass universal education.[92]

It mattered a good deal, too, that the modern school taught a much broader curriculum than traditional schools, leavened with a more flexible and efficient pedagogy directed toward understanding. This broader curriculum essentially moved studies into primary school that had once been the province of those with access to a secondary or higher education. African Americans who had been attending school for no more than a few months were receiving lessons in history, geography, and rudimentary science. In the hands of an astute teacher, that broader curriculum inevitably extended the freedmen's political education; in the grasp of astute learners, such a curriculum opened intellectual doors even under less capable teachers. The curriculum of the modern school held more potential than the curriculum of traditional schools to introduce the freed people to a broader world.

Finally, the modern, urban school in the South mattered, for the modern school's passion for system brought with it teacher training. And it may be that nothing was more important to the history of African American education in the South than the systematic education of southern black teachers in exactly the social and technical relations, the pedagogies, the systems and routines, and the best aspirations of the modern school.

Those who condemned the curriculum of the first generation of southern black schools on the grounds that it was irrelevant to the lives of the freed people denied the imperative in a democracy that all learners have access to the same knowledge, the same skills, the same social capital. Knowing how to write well, grasping the structure of languages, understanding spatial relationships and the peculiarities of geography, deepens political understanding. Learning to think clearly will not make one more subservient, and hence may be opposed by those who desire a more pliant populace, but it is vital to democratic life. Similarly, those who condemned the pedagogy practiced by a minority of the teachers because it was inappropriate to the lives, the culture, and the future of an agrarian, rural people underestimated, misperceived, and denigrated the abilities of the freed people. At its heart, the freed people's emancipation project aimed to appropriate the social and cultural capital of the dominant class. An education that employed a curriculum appropriate to rural life, through a pedagogy tamped down to racist presumptions about the abilities of the freed people, would have denied them access to exactly the knowledge, the codes of power, and the habits of mind that stood, and still stand, at the center of the social and cultural capital the freed people sought and deserved.

Chapter Six

Race, Reconstruction, and Redemption

The Fate of Emancipation and Education, 1861–1876

Fear has driven off some of our teachers.

H. C. Vogell, 1870

Education is a reality with the freedmen *now*, a fixed fact. We have
no quaint or rapturous expressions of thanksgiving or wonder to narrate,
as when schools were first opened, and we introduced books with their
mysteries. Schools are a system; we have classes like those in
other regulated institutions.

Cordelia Jennings Attwell, 1870

They bitterly shut the door of their new schoolhouse and turn away
to their toil, feeling that they have not only been bereaved but wronged.

Ralza M. Manly, 1870

From slavery through Reconstruction and into Redemption, African
Americans fought tenaciously for literacy. Enslaved blacks risked
fearsome punishment to read and write;[1] at the dawn of freedom,
the black quest for schooled knowledge flowered brilliantly. Even before
formal emancipation, and at an accelerated pace thereafter, the freed people built schools, recruited teachers from among the literate in their own
communities, welcomed anyone else willing to teach them, and filled the
schools to overflowing. Black school attendance surged; secondary and
higher institutions for the freed people multiplied. In many southern
states in the late 1860s, newly minted state departments of education, the
fruits of southern interracial politics, geared up to assure free schooling to
all southern children, black and white.[2]

Yet that promising dawn did not usher in a bright new day of educational, social, and political possibilities. Threatening clouds formed early, auguring a storm of reaction, retrenchment, and repression. Within three to four years after their ambitious beginnings, state education bureaucracies were reduced to skeletal structures on eroded foundations. Schools closed; school years were halved; teachers went unpaid. The number of southern white teachers in the black schools rose, though the number of black teachers rose faster, but the growth in teachers for black schools remained woefully behind demand. Only the most fearless of the northern white teachers had the courage and commitment to weather the storm. Systematic educational discrimination sprouted in the storm's eerie aftermath.

Historians have described the process of constructing unequal southern education as almost exclusively legislative and political, what Henry Allen Bullock described as "the chain of legal containment." As part of the white South's effort to restore home rule, Democratic hegemony, and white supremacy during Reconstruction, Redeemers promised black voters that public education would not be abolished under their rule. Once in power, they honored the letter of their promise, retaining state-funded education, though they dismantled the educational bureaucracies created under Republican governments and slashed state school budgets. Still, in the early years of Democratic rule, the funding cuts were relatively equal across white and black schools. Only after the disfranchisement campaigns of the 1880s and 1890s, and after the New South men began to replace the older Bourbon Democrats, did legislatures across the South begin to devise means to assure the greater prosperity of white schools at the expense of black schools.[3]

The assault on educational opportunity did not begin with late nineteenth-century legislative actions, however, nor even with the political chicanery of the 1870s that resulted in the retrenchment of the school bureaucracies that had worked to extend the reach of public education in the middle years of Reconstruction. It began earlier, at the moment of emancipation. It was not only, nor even primarily, an attack on educational opportunity. It was, rather, an assault on a dream, the dream of black independence and freedom through education, the dream of the fullest emancipation through literacy and knowledge. The assault began as soon as the freed people began to act on the dream. White terrorism, systematic, organized, and relentless, targeted the dream with deadly accuracy. The South lost the battles of the Civil War, surrendering its armies and losing slavery and the goal of Confederate independence, but there was no peace treaty after Appomattox, no armistice, and there was no peace. Over the

Race, Reconstruction, and Redemption

subsequent decade the South fought a new war on new terrain with new strategies, holding fast to its most fundamental institution. The South won that war, the war to retain white supremacy.[4]

Crushing the most liberatory aspects of black education was crucial in the South's ultimate victory. Unbridled white resistance, violence, and terror, dating from the beginning of the education of the freed people, took an incalculable psychological and physical toll on the southern black community and its few white supporters and set the stage for a white supremacist reshaping of black education. By the end of the nineteenth century a triumphalist white supremacy reunited the North and South, or, in Edward J. Blum's more provocative rendering, reforged the white republic. Thereafter, northern and southern white elites would begin to work together to reshape black education to better serve their ends.[5]

Many writers have noted some aspects of Reconstruction-era southern white resistance to black education. Few get the dates right; most blame teachers and learners for southern white resistance; and none appreciate the full fury, force, and effect of the resistance. Henry Lee Swint, for example, wrote in 1941 that southerners did not oppose freedmen's education itself, that there was no significant resistance to the black schools prior to the presidential campaign of 1868, and that the teachers brought violence on themselves through their abolitionist-inspired teaching in the black classrooms. Had northern teachers not usurped the field of black education, Edgar Knight added, southerners would gladly have taken up the work themselves and saved southern race relations.[6]

Writing more than three decades later and taking an otherwise revisionist stance, William Preston Vaughn embraced elements of Swint's Dunningite view. The northern teachers' disregard for the "feelings of southern whites" provoked the ire of southerners, Vaughn wrote. He concurred in the opinion that the teachers brought opposition on themselves, implying thereby that conditions for black education would have been better without the northern white teachers. Black teachers, on the other hand, did not face much opposition, according to Vaughn. As with other writers, the probability that southern white attacks on black schools and teachers had a profound impact on the black community seems never to have occurred to Vaughn.[7]

Bertram Wyatt-Brown took a similarly negative stance toward the schools and their teachers, regarding the northern teacher as the central problem, though, as noted earlier, for him the problem was that the teachers' pedagogy and curriculum was so vastly inappropriate to the learners as

Race, Reconstruction, and Redemption

to doom the project from the beginning. Whether or how southern teachers might have improved the process was of little interest to him.[8] Other recent historians have been more sympathetic to the teachers, and a few have found their presumed abolitionism a point of honor rather than censure. Though they have noted the opposition faced by the teachers, they have made little of it beyond observing the toll it took on some of the teachers.[9]

Swint, Vaughn, and Wyatt-Brown got it wrong. Southern white resistance to black education was, first and foremost, opposition to black independence and intellectual striving, no matter who imparted the habits of mind that nurtured such independence and intellect; southern white teachers suffered precisely the same sorts of opposition and violence that northern white teachers faced; black teachers suffered the same level of violent resistance as white teachers.

Further, southern opposition did not begin in the late 1860s as a result of conflict over presidential politics, as Swint and others argued. It began virtually from the outset of freedmen's education, increasing in virulence throughout the Civil War and Reconstruction. By the mid-1860s, it amounted to open terrorism aimed at destroying the black dream of intellectual emancipation through education. The terrorism was directed at both the black franchise and black education, for on one level the black vote and black education merged. Each was an affront to white supremacy and racial paternalism. Together, the franchise and education bespoke black autonomy, agency, and determination; education free of paternalism was essential to a free ballot, and, as it turned out, a free ballot was essential to free and equal education.

The unrelenting terrorism targeted teachers, schoolhouses, and students during and after the Civil War, when blacks acted most forcefully on the dream of black literacy and freedom. The terrorism doubtless reinforced the black community's folk knowledge that white rage against black freedom knew no moral bounds, that open resistance to white power courted deadly force, and that any educational movement intent on emancipating black minds would reawaken the beast of white terrorism. Over the next century that folk knowledge was reinforced by the social relations of sharecropping, by disfranchisement, by poverty, by lynchings, and by the daily indignities of segregation. It was further ramified by aspects of the largely unexplored dark side of post-*Brown* desegregation—the summary firing of tens of thousands of black educators in the 1970s, forms of desegregation that fell with greatest force on black students, the closing of black schools with the consequent loss of school traditions, trophies, mascots, and support systems, and other aspects of desegregation.[10]

THERE ARE MANY PROBLEMS WITH THE TRADITIONAL INTERPRETATION OF southern white resistance to the freed people's schools. Take first the claim that southern resistance was aimed at northern teachers, not at black education. The claim founders on the fact that more than one-half of the teachers in the first generation of southern black schools were native white southerners, including hundreds of former Confederate soldiers. Yet southern teachers faced the same opprobrium and anger as did their northern counterparts. For example, Alfred W. Morris, a white resident of Nixonton, North Carolina, taught the freed people of his community in early 1866 but closed his school after only six weeks, "apprehensive for his safety" because of the "threatening state of public feeling" regarding his work.[11] Mary Bowers established a black school near Chapel Hill, North Carolina, in 1866, occasionally assisted by her husband. Both were lifelong residents of the area, yet their neighbors were outraged that they would attempt to teach the area's former slaves. Bowers wrote that "*no* one seems even to be willing that they should be taught at all," and added, "My neighbors went so far as to say that my Husband and myself ought to be drummed out of the country for teaching the colored people." Two weeks later she observed that she was "teaching night and day though much against the wishes of the white people, they are *very bitter* against me for teaching the colored people."[12]

Silas Outlaw, an elderly native of Alabama, reported in the late 1860s that his neighbors were "trying to run me off" and threatening his life for teaching the freed people.[13] Texan Thomas Collins noted that his neighbors were "down on me with a double vengeance" for teaching the freed people, while the Ku Klux Klan broke up the Clarksville, Texas, school established in 1867 by Charles Goldberg, "an old resident of this county," forcing Goldberg to flee to Arkansas for safety.[14] Another white Texas teacher, an impoverished widowed mother of seven children, Mary F. Orndorf, was driven out of Polk County in 1868 "for teaching a colored school," only to face similar hostility in Huntsville, Texas. Like other southern white teachers, she was not opposed because of any Yankee proclivities; as one writer observed, "Only hunger compels her to teach."[15] Whites in Maxey's, Georgia, threatened to burn down P. H. Gillen's school and to murder him.[16] When the military organized schools in occupied New Orleans during the war, it hired 130 native white teachers to teach in

Race, Reconstruction, and Redemption

the city's black schools. Military officers reported, however, that in spite of their nativity, the teachers had to "bear the jeers and contempt of friends and kindred," and described numerous instances of abuse and attacks on schools and teachers.[17] Few southern whites could have taken positions in black schools without being "conscious of the social sacrifice" they made.[18] None appear to have taught out of any commitment to prewar abolitionist beliefs.

Southern hostility toward native whites teaching in black schools was sufficiently virulent that some southern teachers were punished by being denied the opportunity of subsequent employment in white schools. Ellen M. Buggy, for example, taught in the New Orleans' Colored School No. 2 in 1864, then taught in a white school for two years. When a Democratic school board took over, she was fired. As she explained, despite her southern roots, "I was known as a Yankee, because I had been in the black school, and they thought I was not fit to teach white school."[19] Likewise, Catherine Brim, a white teacher in Dawson, Georgia, noted that "before I took the colored school I was doing well in teaching but it has injured my capacity in taking other schools, and standing in the esteem of the community."[20] Buggy, Brim, and others were victims of a general sense among many southerners that teaching in black schools was degrading—"if you teach niggers, you are no better than a nigger yourself," according to some. Others considered teaching the freed people as treason, fearing the possibility that educating the freed people could lead to social equality.[21]

Status in the community did not mitigate the opposition to southern whites teaching the freed people. Dr. William Hale opened a school in Tennessee to all children regardless of color, though very few white children chose to attend. Yet despite his status as a physician and his willingness to teach all children, he "met with very great opposition."[22] Georgia A. Grimes, the widow of a wealthy physician and Confederate soldier, remarked that "being teacher of a colored school has, as it were, isolated me from the rest of the world. I have communication with but few beyond the limits of my own domicile."[23] Even one's status as a veteran of the Lost Cause did not ease the opposition of southern whites to teaching in the black schools. Robert P. Lindsey, Confederate veteran and son of a Georgia slaveholder, turned to teaching in a black school after the war. When asked about the public sentiment toward schools such as his, he responded, "They are generally treated with contempt."[24] James W. Reese, later to gain a Confederate pension as a Georgia veteran, taught for at least three years after the war in his native Morgan County. In 1869, he wrote to the

Freedmen's Bureau that his neighbors were strongly "against my teaching Freedmen." He added, "I am thinking that they will try and interfere with my school again this next week, and if they do I ask your protection."[25] An aide-de-camp to General Robert E. Lee who established a black school in Petersburg, Giles B. Cooke, paid a heavy social price for his work, despite his conservative intentions.[26]

The issue was not the nativity of the teachers, then. Southern teachers, just like northern teachers, faced opprobrium, social isolation, and occasional violence. Nor was the problem that the teachers were white. Black teachers, whether from the North or the South, faced as much opposition, and occasionally more deadly violence, than did white teachers. Peter Hamilton opened a school in Bonham, Texas, right after the Civil War ended. As soon as Union troops were withdrawn, local whites struck. "Hamilton was driven off, his life threatened, and the school broken up." The former Confederate guardhouse Hamilton used as his schoolhouse was torn down to drive home the point that black schooling was intolerable. Hamilton appears never to have attempted teaching again.[27] In William A. Jones's first two years as a teacher in Mississippi he was shot at several times and wounded once. From his first days until he returned to his home in Elmira, New York, for his father's funeral, he "was persecuted in every shape imaginable. My tormentors even persecuted me up to the moment that I got on the cars" for the trip home. Despite that experience, he taught for at least four more years, but chose to work in Georgia and Texas rather than return to Aberdeen.[28] Solomon Derry faced down Alabama Klansmen who had ordered him to close his school or die. Richard Burke, minister and teacher in Sumter County, Alabama, and Benjamin F. Randolph, Oberlin College graduate, teacher, and state senator in South Carolina, did not fare as well—they were murdered by whites for their educational work. George Ormond and Edwin Belcher in Georgia and George T. Cook in Mississippi were all threatened with violence for teaching the freed people.[29]

The Deep South was not the only place where black teachers faced potentially deadly force from southern whites intent on ending their work. In Maryland, a terrorist "fired with deadly intent" at John Wesley Cromwell, grazing him, and mobs attacked Martha L. Hoy and Mary E. Perry in separate incidents in 1865.[30] When Klansmen confronted Edward Bowman in North Carolina, he escaped a beating, or worse, by leaping out of a window. In Townsville, North Carolina, Klansmen pasted a placard on Samuel Cross's door with the outline of a coffin and spade along with a

Race, Reconstruction, and Redemption

warning to leave.[31] The Tennessee Klan broke up Samuel Lowrey's school in Rutherford County, forcing him to leave the county, while in Franklin County in 1869, opponents of black education burned down the school eight days after the freedmen had built it and threatened its teacher, former slave William Smith.[32] Elsewhere in Tennessee, two Fisk University students established a school at Dresden in the spring of 1869. On 2 September 1869, they were awakened at gunpoint, roped together at the neck, and "dragged more than a mile into the woods," where twelve men took turns beating them "with whips and heavy rods." They were then ordered "to run and as they fled they were followed by a volley of bullets."[33] A white female teacher in Maryland gave a clear answer to claims that black teachers were treated better by southern whites than white teachers. She reported that opponents of her work told her, "If they had sent a black teacher here we would have burnt the old shell, (church), teacher and scholars together before this time." She was convinced that "but one obstacle stood in the way" of violence against her: "the subject in hand was a white woman."[34]

Earlier historians pivoted much of their defense of southern opposition to black schools on the claim that northern teachers were abolitionists and engaged in abolitionist teaching in their classrooms, assuming that the teachers were imparting ideas of equality through their teaching and curriculum. None of those writers ever demonstrated the teachers' abolitionist heritage; the fact that they would teach a reviled race was proof enough of their apostasy. Yet the teaching by southern whites was unlikely to have been prompted by abolitionism. Further, as argued earlier, while a very few of the northern white teachers can be shown to have been abolitionists before the war, most betrayed no abolitionist leanings. The northern teachers were, at best, generically antislavery. More saliently, in their actions in the classrooms and in their daily lives in the South, many northern whites were more likely to have reinforced ideas of inequality than of equality.[35] Only among black teachers and a handful of white teachers might a curriculum of equality have dominated.

Southern resistance to black education, then, had little to do with a widespread abolitionism among the teachers. It arose, rather, from the fundamental effrontery of black education itself. It did not take an abolitionist in the classroom to teach the freed people to expect equality and freedom—the freed people did not need to be taught that expectation by anyone.

Race, Reconstruction, and Redemption

The white South was not monolithic, of course. There were many who were simply indifferent to the black schools. For instance, James P. Butler, a Union veteran who taught for one year in Huntsville, Texas, before becoming a Freedmen's Bureau agent in the city, observed that "the public seems to have no objections to the organization of Schools," but added that white Texans "will furnish no assistance for that purpose, and they are averse to having any Southern person teach them, using such expressions as, 'It is beneath the dignity of a Southern lady or gentleman to teach "niggers." ' "[36] At the other end of the former Confederacy, Thomas Jackson reported "indifference or hostility to educating freedmen with few exceptions" among whites in Virginia.[37] There were also some southern whites who supported black education to one degree or another. In 1867, whites in Sherman, Texas, raised $150 to assist in building a local black school, while the largest landholder in Liberty, Texas, donated a tract of land for a black school. Three years later, citizens in McKinney, Tennessee, assisted the freed people to rebuild a school burned down by opponents of black education.[38] A native white teacher in Macon County, Alabama, thought that public opinion regarding her school by 1870 was "about equally divided" for and against, though that same year another native white teacher with five years' experience in a black school in Coosa County, Alabama, described her neighbors as "very indignant" about her work.[39]

The thousands of southern white teachers who taught the freed people were themselves testimony to some level of support for black literacy, though, as we have seen, many made it clear that they taught black students out of economic desperation, not out of any commitment to intellectual emancipation.[40] Further, it became clear to some of the educators that southern support for black education could also be a means to keep out good teachers and blunt the emancipatory force of education. James Fitz Allen Sisson reported that, in much of rural Georgia, "colored and white teachers are employed that cannot read, and spell correctly, and know nothing beside. The whites are constantly urging the Freed people to employ teachers of the classes mentioned: first, to keep out others, from the North, East, & West, and: second: because they do not wish them to learn beyond just enough to make them contented; but, without much real benefit. They first urge them not to have schools."[41] Yet even though some southern whites supported black education, few were willing to speak up forcefully in its defense, itself a sign of the intensity of resistance among the majority of southern whites.

THE RESISTANCE TO BLACK EDUCATION TOOK MANY FORMS. FOR MOST teachers, resistance and opposition was manifested in daily indignities and petty annoyances. Social ostracism was pervasive, with teachers frequently reporting that local whites refused to recognize their presence or treated them rudely. Insults were common, ranging from simple name calling to spreading malicious rumors of white teachers bearing mulatto babies.[42] Mary Osborne explained that in her first months as the freedmen's teacher in Church Creek, Maryland, she was "the subject of quite as much attention on the street as was agreeable. Men bandied rude, insulting jests, at my expense, and coupled my name with curses, while ladies stood in their doors, or at their gates, and stared me full in the face with curled lips till I had passed them; and even from the children I heard, 'Who cares for her, she's nothing but a d—d nigger teacher.' "[43] Three teachers in Charleston, South Carolina, had begun attending an Episcopal church but, after only two weeks, "they were informed that their presence was not agreeable to the congregation, and therefore the vestry had concluded to withdraw their seats, and request them to worship God in some other temple."[44]

More troubling to the teachers, whether northern or southern, black or white, was intimidation and harassment. "Threats of 'burning of school houses,' 'tarring & feathering' &c are not uncommon, while petty insults and indignities are freely and boldly offered," William L. Coan reported from Lexington, Virginia, in late 1865. "The presence of 'military' *alone* makes it *safe* or *possible* to prosecute our work."[45] Elliot Whipple learned that those who opposed his work intended to poison him, engage him in a quarrel, or in some other way to "drive me off or get me into a scrape to compel me to leave."[46] A Freedmen's Bureau officer described white teacher Jennie Mead's treatment in Hickman, Tennessee: "Her life has been threatened again and again; she has been grievously insulted upon the streets; one of her pupils has been murdered, and the parents of her pupils menaced until the attendance has been diminished to nearly one-half the original number."[47] White college men were at the forefront of some attacks on black schools and their teachers. In 1865, University of North Carolina students attacked freed people who were meeting to discuss black schools in Chapel Hill; University of Virginia students routinely stoned and disrupted a large freedmen's school in Charlottesville; and teachers in Jackson, Mississippi, were "whooped and yelled at on the street by college boys."[48]

White opponents of black education realized, however, that threats and ostracism were of limited effectiveness. A more direct way to limit black

Race, Reconstruction, and Redemption

Mary S. Osborne, twenty-six years old when she began teaching in Church Creek, Maryland, in 1865, taught in the South for four years. Her description of her first year of work, serialized in a Methodist weekly, *Zion's Herald*, provides more insight into her unpleasant encounter with southern poor white culture and into the southern response to northern teachers than glimpses into her work with the freed people. Courtesy of the Trustees of the Boston Public Library/Rare Books.

education was for a community to simply refuse to board the teachers, to deny access to the buildings needed for classrooms, or to decline to sell land or buildings for the use of black students. George F. Bowles informed the Tennessee bureau superintendent that the white families in Fayetteville would not board any white person teaching colored schools, while Warren and Julia Norton boarded with a black family in Bryan, Texas, after they were put out of two consecutive boardinghouses "because we were engaged teaching Freedmen."[49] Jennie Howard notified the Freedmen's Bureau superintendent of education for Virginia, "The family with whom we board are continually harassed, have been warned to 'rid themselves of us as soon as possible.' "[50] Even before Maria C. Hopson arrived in Talladega, Alabama, in 1866, the citizens had agreed among themselves that they would not board her; once she had managed to establish herself despite their efforts, Talladegans made such serious threats against her and the house she lived in that the local Freedmen's Bureau agent felt she would not be safe if Union troops were withdrawn. Mahala Close was forced to leave Brandon, Mississippi, after only three months of teaching when the white citizens refused to board her or to allow blacks to do so. White employers told black sharecroppers in one village in North Carolina that if they boarded the teacher, they would be thrown off their land.[51]

The whites of Jackson, Mississippi, were "bitterly opposed" to a group of Quaker teachers who attempted to open a school there in 1865. "Nothing would induce them to give a room which would be used for the Freedmen in any way," so three teachers taught more than 130 students in the sanctuary of the black church.[52] Although a native of Americus, Georgia, Esther A. Christian could not persuade her fellow citizens to rent space for a school nor to sell schoolbooks to her students, and a bureau agent in Virginia reported that in his vicinity it was "impossible to hire for school purposes, and parties even refuse to sell land if schools or churches for freedpeople are to be erected thereon."[53] A black teacher in North Carolina reported that the few whites who were initially willing to rent or sell buildings or land for a black school were pressured by others to back out of the deals he thought he had secured. The last one to let him down was, he concluded, "like the rest, Faint Hearted," and the majority of the whites "are so much *opposed* to Colard Mens Education that they will do all in thiar power to pull it down." After several months of frustration, he finally closed his school.[54] Elizabeth Granger, for many years thereafter the principal of a black school in Paris, Texas, reported in 1869 that white carpenters refused to build a schoolhouse for the freed people; she intended to do the work herself.[55]

Even when the freed people were able to gain access to a building for school purposes, local whites often found the means to take it away. For instance, Daniel F. Noonan, who described himself as "by birth and principles a white man," was teaching in his own rented room in Atlanta, even though the military authorities had given orders that a church building, owned by a white congregation but used by a black congregation, should be used during the week for school purposes. "As soon as the Trustees became aware of the purpose of occupying the Church for school the[y] took the key from the Sexton and stubbornly refused to deliver it up," Noonan wrote, "claiming that the negroes never paid a cent for the church and therefore only used it on sufrage."[56] Whites in Columbiana, Tennessee, seized the black school founded by Elizabeth Thompson and turned it into a school for white children only.[57]

Harassment and obstruction were just the velvet glove over the iron fist of southern resistance, however. Burning down black schools or the black churches that housed the schools was an effective and terrifying means of disrupting the learning process. Hundreds of black schoolhouses were put to the torch in the 1860s and 1870s; in 1865 and 1866, a dozen schools were burned down in Maryland, and nearly forty were reduced to ashes in mid-1869 in Tennessee. Caroline Croome had only been teaching in New Berne for a few weeks in 1864 when her school burned down. In May 1865, rioters in Memphis particularly targeted black schools, destroying twelve, along with four black churches. The Second Baptist Church in Richmond, Virginia, home to a large black school, was burned down in 1866. The school at Dawson, Georgia, was set afire in 1869. Incendiarism against the black school in Stevenson, Alabama, prompted one of the aid societies to build its Huntsville school of brick. Even well after southern states had taken over education and most northern teachers had left, incendiarism remained a potent means for southern whites to vent their wrath at black education. In 1871, for instance, white Texans burned schools in Chappel Hill and Freestone County, and whites in Alabama attempted to set fire to Talladega College's central building; in 1872, Virginians burned down the black school in Centerville.[58]

Schools taught by black teachers may have been at greater risk for incendiarism than those taught by white teachers. In Clinton, Tennessee, Sally Daffin's school, described by an observer as "one of the best buildings, and one of the best schools, taught by one of the best teachers, in this part of the State," was torched in March 1869.[59] Maggie L. Porter, born enslaved, lost her school in Lebanon, Tennessee, to fire several months after Daffin's. John Wesley Cromwell's school in Maryland was torched in 1866, and in the same year southerners attempted to burn down Edmonia Highgate's school in New Orleans. A school in North Carolina taught by a black teacher, William Smith, burned down in 1869, only eight days after he opened it; he and the freed people rebuilt it in four days. Daniel McGee, probably also a former slave, saw his Troup County, Georgia, school destroyed by fire in 1868. Robert H. McCord, a black teacher in Alabama, James Davis, a black teacher in Tennessee, and Louanna Higgleston, a black teacher in Texas, all lost their schools to incendiaries in that same year.[60] In 1870, arsonists destroyed the school taught by Talladega College student Irving Jenkins; by the end of the year, after reports of more burnings, a Talladega teacher remarked that whites had destroyed "the last *good* schoolhouse they had in the county."[61]

Terrorism through fire was often effective in ending educational efforts and driving away teachers. Arson in Fayetteville, Tennessee, in 1866 caused the local white teacher to give up the cause, and no new school was attempted, while George Childs and his wife left Edgefield, Tennessee, after their school was burned down in the same year. A. G. Perryman, a white man, fled his school in Georgia after it was burned down in 1867 and the white citizens threatened to hang him for teaching. Jordan K. Parker, a black native of Roxboro, North Carolina, quit teaching in 1869 after his school was burned down one year after he opened it.[62] After the Klan destroyed Morris Maier's school in Kaufman, Texas, in 1868, he left the state, and the local bureau agent concluded that "it would be an impossibility to reorganize the school in that town."[63]

Burning down schoolhouses was symbolically potent, striking at the central physical manifestations of black intellectual aspirations, schoolhouses and schoolbooks. Arson had the potential not only to curtail educational work but also to stoke primal fears. Arsonists struck at night when teachers and buildings were most defenseless, using a weapon—the spectacle of flaming buildings—certain to evoke terror and suggesting, sometimes explicitly, that teachers faced the same fate as their schoolhouses if they continued with their work. When the school taught by Robert W. Stokes, a black teacher in Missouri, was burned to the ground, for instance, he was informed that he would be "*treated* in the *same way*" as his schoolhouse if he remained in the state.[64] Further, many of the targets of arson were schools built and paid for by the freed people themselves. Incendiary terrorism against education thereby became economic terrorism as well, depriving the black communities of places of learning (and, frequently, places of worship) and divesting them of scarce communal capital.[65]

Other forms of intimidation were aimed at teachers' living quarters, often, as with arson, at night. The enemies of black education fired shots through open doorways, threw stones at walls and windows, shouted insults and obscenities from the darkness, set fires, invaded households, and in other ways disrupted teachers' lives outside of school. Jennie Starkey withstood intimidation in Humbolt, Tennessee, for most of three years, but finally left after enduring a nighttime raid during which her house was assaulted "with Bricks & other missiles, breaking the windows & greatly endangering the lives of the helpless inmates," as an observer reported.[66] Black students were also terrorized in a bid to discourage their attendance at the black schools. The adult students attending Edmonia Highgate's night school in late 1866 were shot at, though she reported that none had yet been killed, while earlier that year, whites attacked black students in Maryland and vandalized their school. In 1867, the children in

Milliken, Texas, faced such threats that their parents feared sending them to school; in 1868 in Louisiana, the threats were so great that sixteen parishes reported no black schools.[67] In Newton County, Georgia, in 1869, whites with drawn pistols stoned children going to and from school. While the children were in school, they and their teacher were "so loudly, and grossly insulted that children wept, and some, have, through fear, resulting therefrom, remained from school."[68]

White terrorism toward black education did not stop with the symbolic violence of burning down schools or intimidating students and teachers. Teachers were the direct victims of escalating physical violence throughout Reconstruction. Thomas B. Barton built two schoolhouses near Long Creek, North Carolina, and taught in both of them. On 19 December 1866, armed white men took him from his bed, carried him a few miles into the woods, and threatened to kill him, saying, "you damn nigger teacher, we have got you now and will blow your damned Yankees brains out." Rather than killing him, they satisfied themselves by beating him with tree limbs, intending, as they told him, to "mark me so I would not be known." He subsequently armed himself and continued teaching into the spring of 1867, intending to leave in April, having received "nothing for my trouble except the satisfaction that I have done some good among the poor colored people."[69] In August 1869, Edwin Barnetson awoke in the middle of the night surrounded by thirty to forty masked men who demanded that he leave his school in Purdy, Tennessee, within five days. He wrote to a bureau official asking for protection. He was advised to "stick it out," but, with no promise of protection, he chose instead to return to his Angelica, New York, home.[70] In 1867, rioters in Millican, Texas, targeted the teachers, Mr. and Mrs. J. W. Henley, forcing Mr. Henley "to leave to save his life. The school is now closed."[71] Whites drove Union veteran Franklin Shelden out of his school in Columbia, Texas, in 1866. Others assaulted Isaac M. Newton for his teaching in Somerville, Tennessee, in 1868. B. C. Hammond and his wife were physically accosted and forced from their school in 1869. George Holmes, teaching in Hinds County, Mississippi, from 1872, was driven violently from the county in 1875 because he taught in a black school.[72]

Northern teachers received their share of physical violence, but southern teachers, white and black, were also targets. Rebels broke up two different schools that Margaret S. Clark, a white southerner, established in North Carolina in 1868. Dinwiddie County, Virginia, native Leonard A. Birchett taught a black school near his home for two years, but opponents forced him to give it up and flee to Norfolk at the end of 1869; he was

Race, Reconstruction, and Redemption

allowed to return to teach in a white school the next year. William L. Linsey, a native white teacher, was driven from his school in Franklin County, North Carolina, in 1868 "at the hands of White men for teaching colored school."[73] In 1869, an assailant attempted to kill the teacher in Kaufman, Texas; the teacher subsequently fled the state. Also in 1869, terrorists in Gonzalez, Texas, pistol whipped a Moravian teacher in front of his night class, dragged him to a river, and threatened to drown him unless he promised to discontinue his school; he was found the next day and helped onto a stage to escape. In 1870, John J. Strong reported from Talladega College that "two of our teachers have been Kukluxed & others have been threatened so things look rather scary."[74]

Black educator Daniel Broomfield had to flee his school in Warrenton, Georgia, in 1866 in a hail of gunfire; it was 1868 before he ventured to teach again. Black Civil War veteran William H. H. Butler carried a gun constantly while teaching in Kentucky as protection against a promised attack. Black teacher James M. Windgow remained in his school in Richmond, Texas, only two months in 1869, "for times is to unquiet here for me and my life is threatened." He reported being shot at and having brickbats thrown at him.[75] Black teacher and Maryland native William H. Foster left Ferry Neck, where he was "very much liked" by the freed people, after receiving a letter warning him to leave within ten days and hearing that local whites intended to kill him.[76] Lewis A. Fuller, a black Union veteran teaching near Baton Rouge from 1868, fled Louisiana in 1876 after White Leaguers threatened him and hanged several of his neighbors.[77] By 1868, the Freedmen's Bureau officer in Anderson County, Texas, reported that the county had "no schools because the Rebel whites have broken them all up. The freedpeople would give their all to have good schools."[78] Two young black teachers in Alabama, Dallas McClellan and Irving Jenkins, were driven from their schools in 1870. Klansmen forced Jenkins from his schoolroom; he escaped his captors, though they wounded him as he fled. Also in 1870, a Freedmen's Bureau officer in rural Louisiana helped an unidentified elderly black man establish a school in Bossier Parish. Whites objected to the school, flogged the teacher and threatened his life, destroyed the schoolbooks, and burned the schoolhouse. The official sent another teacher to Keachie, DeSoto Parish. Local whites dragged the teacher from his house and warned him to leave in five minutes or be lynched. He went to a second assignment where he "met worse treatment." Whites there burned his saddle, hid his horse, "and were preparing to hang him when a colored man took him out by a secret way and guided him round to where his horse was secreted. He mounted the animal bareback and rode for life."[79]

Charles St. Clair, probably a Union veteran, established an academy for the freed people in Louisiana right after the war; whites assassinated him for his work in 1866 or 1867. In 1868, the teacher in Rock Dam, Texas, possibly William H. Adams, was murdered, as was Franklin Sinclair in Louisiana. Richard Burke established a black school in Sumter County, Alabama, in 1865; the Klan murdered him in 1870. James G. Patterson, a black teacher from Yazoo County, Mississippi, who became a state law-maker, was assassinated in 1875. William and Alzina Haffa, whites from Philadelphia, migrated to Mississippi in 1870 as farmers but were impor-tuned by the local freed people to open schools for them. They taught in two schools near Auburn despite opposition from their white neighbors. Their house was raided in the middle of the night in 1875 by a group of between fifty and seventy-five men who shot and fatally wounded Wil-liam; they also killed a black father and son on an adjoining farm. The assassins refused to allow Alzina to get a physician and kept watch in the house until William died several hours later. They then demanded that Alzina bury him immediately without a coffin and leave the state.[80]

One historian has claimed that women teachers were spared actual physical violence, "perhaps the result of a remnant of chivalry, but more likely because threats alone often sufficed to drive them away."[81] While fewer women than men appear to have suffered direct violence, chivalry did not extend as far as that claim suggests. Three different women teach-ers, Mary E. Perry, Julia F. P. Dickson, and Martha L. Hoy, all northern black women, were assaulted in Maryland in 1865 and 1866. Edmonia G. Highgate, also a northern black teacher, was shot at in her classroom on two different occasions in 1866. Likewise in 1866, an assailant attempted to assassinate Eunice Congdon, a white teacher, in Danville, Virginia. Sarah Dickey, founder of the black women's school Mount Hermon, in Missis-sippi, was shot at in her home in the early 1870s.[82] While threats were often, though not always, effective in driving women teachers away, vio-lence apparently was not as effective: all of those women continued teach-ing after their violent experiences, Hoy, Highgate, Dickson, and Dickey for many more years.[83]

Both the supporters and opponents of black education knew that the presence or absence of Union troops in the South was crucial in determin-ing the level of violence against the schools and teachers, and violence against the freed people in general. Yet throughout Reconstruction, troop levels were constantly drawn down, leaving increasing areas of the South unprotected. A continual theme in letters from Texas in the 1860s, for example, was the near impossibility of establishing schools without the presence of the military to protect the teachers and the freed people, particularly in smaller settlements. The bureau agent from DeWitt County, Texas, reported that there were no schools in Clinton and Yorktown, though each could attract sixty or more students. However, "it would be almost impossible to carry on a school in either of these places without the presence of the Troops, for, if the school, once started, was not broken up by a shower of bullets from the Pistols of a crowd of Drunken Ruffians, it would be unreasonable to expect Teachers to remain where they would be hourly and daily grossly insulted without any means of redress."[84] After describing C. E. Coleman's school in Richmond, Texas, Samuel C. Sloan, the bureau agent and Union army captain, wrote, "I do not think that he, or any other Teacher of Freedmen, could remain here one day without the presense of Union Soldiers." Any teacher attempting to organize a school "would find the presence of the military—I fear—absolutely necessary to protect him from insolence and abuse."[85] Michael O'Regan, who had been a candidate for the state's constitutional convention, felt so intimidated by his fellow white Texans for his educational activities that, when Washington withdrew the few troops remaining in Goliad, Texas, he wrote, "The Soldiers received orders to leave this evening, and, as I dare not remain, I leave with them." He moved to Houston, where he continued teaching under the protection of the military.[86] Joseph Welch, the bureau superintendent for Texas, reported at the end of 1868 that many of the black schools had been discontinued "in consequence of terrorism exercised by disorderly parties, whom it was impracticable to punish."[87]

THE BLOODY RACE RIOTS IN MEMPHIS IN 1865 AND NEW ORLEANS IN 1866 demonstrated the efficacy of terror. Rioters in Memphis burned down a dozen black schools, four black churches, and over ninety black homes, and murdered one teacher. In the days after the riots, other teachers were threatened with death if they did not leave the city. The terrorist intimidation was effective: of the more than forty teachers who taught in black schools in Memphis in 1864–65, only thirteen, or one-third, returned the following year, five of whom were local black teachers. The total teaching force in Memphis in the year following the riots fell to fewer than thirty. Meanwhile, because the New Orleans riot occurred in the summer when most schools were not in session, teachers and schools were less frequently

Race, Reconstruction, and Redemption

the target of terror. The number of teachers in black schools in New Orleans in the year following the riot was actually slightly higher than before the riots (eighty-eight in 1865–66, ninety-three in 1866–67). However, in the latter year, only thirty-two of the teachers, about one-third, were repeaters, and nearly half of those, fifteen in total, were local black teachers. Put another way, four-fifths of the white teachers in each city failed to return in the year following the riots, a higher rate of "drop-outs" from one year to the next than found in other southern cities in the 1860s.[88]

There can be no doubt that the threats and the actual violence and murder that increasingly surrounded the schools and teachers had an impact. We can never know how many teachers left the South or abandoned black education to take up safer work in the South because of terrorism, but the discouragement and fear is clear in many of their letters. T. G. Steward—black Civil War veteran, teacher, AME church leader, chaplain to black troops in the West for many years, and Wilberforce University professor[89]—provides a poignant example. He wrote from Marion, Alabama, in 1871, detailing the growing force of terrorist organizations. Teachers and other activists had been "advertized as subjects of assassination," he wrote, and those still remaining in Marion were "of the opinion that nothing can be gained by our being murdered by these devils. We are not particularly anxious to gain a reputation in that manner. Did we not know that hundreds of good men have been brutally murdered in Alabama in the last three years because they chose to disregard the warnings that were timely, we should be disposed to think that what we *now* see & hear is only a little chivalric blustering." He concluded, "I cannot bear to think of quitting the field and giving up this work that promises so well, but there seems to be no other way left."[90]

The impact on the black community must have been even greater than the impact on teachers. The freed people had given a far greater proportion of their meager funds and labor than either the government or the most generous northern aid groups to obtain land for schools, to buy lumber, and to build schoolhouses. They had sacrificed their and their children's earning potential to attend school. Yet before Reconstruction had run half its course, the Freedmen's Bureau had ceased its operations, northern aid societies had retrenched or withdrawn entirely, and most of the northern white teachers had quit teaching in the black schools. Southern state school systems, initiated auspiciously by Republican governments in some southern states by the late 1860s, were cut back severely as Democratic governments regained power, too often through violence and fraud. Well before the bureau closed its offices, before northern aid had dried up, before southern political processes gutted state systems, systematic violence, arson, and terror had begun to take its toll. A supporter of the black schools in Delaware visited the makeshift school used by the students in Slaughter Neck after their school was destroyed in 1868. "I shall not soon forget the air of sadness resting on the countenances of the older scholars," he wrote, "and I could readily believe the blackened ruins opposite were throwing their shadow over their hearts."[91]

The freed people understood the link between political efficacy and literacy, and even as early as 1870 they knew that they had been betrayed. Ralza M. Manly, Virginia superintendent of education, who would spend many years working in black education, heard as much from the freed people. "They feel and say," he wrote, "that the Government, having given them freedom and franchise, should not leave them in ignorance." As much as they could do, and did do, for themselves, they understood deeply that authentic access to formal education for all of the community required more than they could do alone. As Manly noted, they were "ready to help support schools with all they have or can get, except what is necessary to provide the coarsest food and scantiest clothing, but without teachers or friends to advise, the State doing nothing, and Government, which they thought they could trust to the end, 'gone back on them,' " access would be severely limited. Less than a decade after emancipation, the freed people "bitterly shut the door of their new schoolhouse and turn away to their toil, feeling that they have not only been bereaved but wronged."[92] The dream that an end to slavery would allow African Americans free access to the power of literacy was met not with access and reason but with betrayal, butchery, fire, and force.

A cartoon by Thomas Nast from October 1874 illustrated the relationship between black schooling and Reconstruction-era violence. In the central device, a poor black couple kneels in grief over a dead black child. Before them is a fallen spelling book. Behind them to one side are the smoldering ruins of a schoolhouse, while on the other side is the silhouette of a lynched black man. Above them are a skull and crossbones and the legend, "Worse than slavery." Flanking the device on either side are two armed figures shaking hands above the skull, one a robed Klansman, the other a White Leaguer. Above these figures, in a sunburst, is an American eagle with the words "The Union as it Was. This is a White Man's Government." In that single image, Nast captured the link between the educa-

tional future of African Americans and the violent reassertion of white supremacy.[93]

Historians have studied terrorist violence during Reconstruction almost exclusively in the context of the black franchise. The white South was intent on controlling the black vote and resorted to terror to gain that end. Only later, after the death of Reconstruction, would the South simply disenfranchise black voters. Yet, as Thomas Nast understood, education was also deeply implicated in the terrorist response. Ultimately, education and the franchise cannot be disentangled, for effective use of the franchise was linked to literacy and, for many in the nineteenth century, the point of literacy was the intelligent use of the franchise.

The turn to terror to check black educational aspirations had deep roots in the South's history. In the antebellum years, the white South had elaborated a rigid, hierarchical system of social distinctions extending from wealthy elites, through middling and poor whites, to free blacks and slaves at the bottom. Integral to that social system was a culture that, rejecting Enlightenment rationalism, placed a premium on honor and the defense of honor. The southern culture of honor demanded a response, often violent, to any perceived insult or challenge to personal or collective honor, including any challenge to the social order.[94] Emancipation, black freedom, black education, and the black franchise all constituted direct challenges to the natural social order; worse, they all insulted southern whiteness.

Southern myth justified slavery on the grounds that a divine plan had given the superior race the task of rescuing blacks from African barbarism and savagery so that, through a painfully slow and always tenuous process of tutelage, the black savage might become docile, industrious, and orderly. The civilizing process was uncertain, however, and constant vigilance was necessary to guard against a relapse into savagery. The ideal black slave in such a system, then, was tractable, loyal, affectionate, subservient, industrious, and happy in servitude. Any evidence of independent thought or action, of discontent or surliness, of disloyalty or resistance—any evidence of the feared and hated "uppity nigger"—was evidence of the ever-potent reversion to type, the reemergence of savagery. No savage act by whites to control black savagery was impermissible, and no one dared suggest that what constituted black savagery would, in a white skin, represent nobility and civilization.[95]

If slavery existed to civilize Africans, paternalism emerged as the means to assure that the civilizing process had a moral foundation. Paternalism prescribed mutual obligations between social superiors and inferiors. Slave masters, paternalism insisted, provided protection, direction, and sustenance to slaves who were racially incapable of independent, moral action. Slaves, in turn, owed their masters gratitude, labor, and loyalty. Paternalism pervaded the entire social order; the upper classes expected deference from lower white classes; poor whites gained status in the bargain, for they were far above free and enslaved blacks. Social discipline routinely included violent assaults by superiors on inferiors and duels between wronged equals; racial discipline relied on violence by slave masters on the enslaved and the threat of violence by slave patrols when slaves ventured away from the plantation. At the heart of white violence against black education during Reconstruction, then, was a culture rooted in paternalistic hierarchy and accustomed to collective social and racial control and to violence to assure conformity and punish challenges to the social order.[96]

The determination of African Americans to gain literacy posed a frontal challenge to virtually every aspect of southern honor, and most especially paternalism and racial control. Black literacy, and particularly the rapidly mounting evidence in the 1860s that mastery of literacy was not limited to a handful of more advanced members of the race, gnawed at the roots of the easy belief in insuperable racial differences and the divinely ordained necessity of white paternalistic control. Burgeoning literacy in the freed people's schools provided unavoidable evidence of the inadmissible possibility of black intellectual capacity and of the unimaginable potential that blacks could not merely survive, but could even thrive, without white oversight. The schools and their teachers threatened an entire worldview. Southern whites were daily witnesses to black learners entering schools and black classrooms to recite lessons. They responded to that affront to their beliefs and dignity by pelting schoolhouses with stones and attacking them with fire. They ostracized and threatened teachers to avenge the insult of former slaves achieving what the southern mind believed unachievable. They angrily confronted southern white teachers who collaborated in the apostasy of black schooling.

Decisions to gain an education, to build schoolhouses, to recruit teachers, to spread literacy in their community, bespoke a level of black autonomy and independence that flew in the face of cherished racial beliefs and provoked white rage. The freed people's education project gave the lie to claims that African Americans needed paternal care because they were incapable of independent thought and action in their own best interest. Their spontaneous determination to grasp educational opportunities was assertive and independent. Yet within the perverse logic of southern honor and paternalism, black schooling was not indicative of black agency and intelligence but was a sign of black insolence and ingratitude. At the moment of freedom, the freed people did not remain docile and loyal. Instead, they appropriated the schoolhouse, a central symbol of white privilege.[97] Given white certainty that blacks were incapable of independent action and aspirations, southerners could only attribute the freed people's education project to the meddling of foolish, even dangerous, northern whites. By the same token, in the South's eyes, whites who worked with and for the freed people could only be engaged in such racial heresy for their own personal gain.

Southern myth insisted that only the elite deserved or could benefit from formal education. It was the precondition of governing inferior classes and races. It was a symbol of refinement, leisure, and culture that, by its nature, could not possibly be extended to the masses, much less to the black masses. Black education was an absurdity. For poor whites, who had long accepted their inferior educational place, the notion of African Americans striving for schooling threatened the foundations of their status,

lowly as it was.[98] Thus for many southerners, black aspirations for schooling challenged the hierarchy that defined their world and insulted both
elite status and white status.

Black independence, then, and most especially educated independent
black thought and action, contradicted fond white dreams of a docile,
dependent race. The freed people's entire education project was independent of southern white control. To a people wedded to paternalism and
control, such a project was unthinkable, intolerable, an insult to white
honor. As a result, from throughout the South came reports that southern
sentiment toward the schools was "hostile, ugly, and malicious," "indignant," and "very bitter indeed."[99] Such a project had to be countered,
violently if necessary.

The threats to paternalistic care posed by the growing hundreds of black
schools and thousands of teachers serving black learners reveal the deeper
impulses of southern race relations and expose the malignant side of paternalism. Independent thought and action, the ability to question, to seek
one's own truths, to act on one's own initiative, opened the possibility of
questioning all aspects of social relationships. Independent learning carried the possibility of reaching conclusions heretical to the established and
sanctified southern racial order. The criticality that is always potential
within literacy included the potential to supersede dependence. The reassertion of racial control and paternalism, stripped of its pretensions of
affectionate care and benevolence, was essential to white supremacy.

Literate African Americans undermined a belief in racial inferiority
that was essential to the psychic health of postbellum whites. Worse, black
education and literacy signaled an erosion of racial control. If educated,
blacks would better understand their world and could act more intel-
ligently to shape that world outside the control of whites. That was clearly
the message that a group of terrorists conveyed to Thomas Barton, a northern white teacher in New Hanover County, North Carolina, in January
1867 when they abducted and beat him. "The niggers were bad enough
before you came," they told the teacher, "but since you have been teaching
them, they know too much and are a damn sight worse."[100]

The claim by southern white men that, as a result of schooling, the freed
people "know too much," betrays the sources and intentions of white violence toward black education. Knowledge might, indeed, be power, or lead
to power. The mind of the white South could not imagine power that was
not power over others. Hence, independent access to knowledge had to be
crushed and the remnants of black schooling had to be redirected into safe

Race, Reconstruction, and Redemption

channels. In the black-and-white intellectual universe that southerners had created, whites either had total power and control over their inferiors, or they were powerless and controlled by their inferiors. From such a worldview sprang the bizarre justification that William Haffa's assassins gave his wife for their crime: teachers such as the Haffas "could not rule over them and do as they please with them."[101] From that worldview came the continual battle cry of the last years of Reconstruction that the white South would not tolerate "Negro rule." From that worldview arose an entire historical interpretation of Reconstruction that saw the South as prostrated by scalawags, carpetbaggers, and blacks and that sanctified violence and fraud as "redemption."

The causes of white violence during Reconstruction, then, had their roots deep in a culture that had been nurtured to defend racial slavery and class inequality. Southerners were engaged in a deadly war of attrition against independent black education. Their victory in that war was not total, but their terrorism took an enormous toll. Throughout Reconstruction, hundreds of teachers abandoned their schools out of fear for their lives. An untold number, probably adding up to scores, were killed outright. Others were worn down by the isolation and insecurity of the work and turned away from the freed people. Many of the school buildings that terrorists burned down were rebuilt immediately by courageous black communities and their teachers, but many other schools died in the cooling embers. We can never know the number of potential students who never enrolled because employers threatened to throw families off the land if they did, or who began their studies but withdrew in the face of those sorts of threatened, and occasionally practiced, acts of economic terrorism.

As Reconstruction sputtered to its ignominious end, with nothing reconstructed but with white supremacy redoubled, the dream that education would be a part of the emancipation project, that knowledge might provide a path to autonomy and equality, that an entire people could understand and act upon their world through reason and literacy, was bloodied and bruised. A people's collective struggle for education met the savage rage and fury of overwhelming white power. In the decades to follow, while enduring sharecropping, lynching, Jim Crow social relations, and migrations, southern African Americans would continue to sacrifice greatly for their children's education. They would sustain a vital network of black colleges and universities, law schools and medical colleges. But while a tiny minority gained advanced education, the majority of America's black children absorbed, again and again, the implacable lesson that

Race, Reconstruction, and Redemption

the codes of power were for others and that the surest means to survival lay in the culture and codes of the black community. They were at risk in schools that whites created and controlled; they were safe in the world their fathers and mothers created and controlled.

In the long view of history, the South lost the war to create a new nation, and its gamble cost it one of its most revered institutions, racial slavery. But before the United States had reached its centennial anniversary, the South had won the war to salvage slavery's legacy, white supremacy. Its subsequent enforced construction of generations of at-risk black children, perpetually ill-served in inferior schools, provided victorious and triumphalist whites, northern and southern, with evidence for their self-fulfilling assertions of racial supremacy. The white South's victory in the uncivil war for white supremacy established the terrain for the subsequent battles over the shape and content of black education. That terrain would greatly favor the power of wealthy whites to bend black education to their ends. The freed people's emancipation project was irrelevant to, even subversive of, those ends. The children and grandchildren of the freed people did not abandon that project but, on the terrain of the choosing of the powerful, their efforts were continually blunted and deflected. Laura Towne's prediction that "this race is going to rise" remained the dream, but education as the means to achieve that goal proved, in the final analysis, inadequate in the face of white oppression.

Appendix A

Teachers in the Freed People's Schools,
1861–1876

The Freedmen's Teacher Project is attempting to identify by name every teacher who worked in a school for the freed people between 1861 and 1876. Individuals are included in the database if they taught for at least one month and provided that they are identified by name, the year they taught, and at least the state in which they taught. Beyond that minimum information, the project also collects prosopographical data on race, gender, birth year, all locations and years taught, sponsoring organizations (if any), home, marital status (and changes in marital status), parents' occupation, teachers' occupation before and after teaching in the South, educational attainments, schools attended (academy or normal school and above), evidence of antebellum abolitionism, military experience, religious affiliation, and other data, along with more traditional archival information. The project is ongoing, so quantitative data reported in this volume is subject to revision.

There are rich historical sources from the 1860s, including lists of teachers, where they taught, and, frequently, their homes, published at least annually by most of the major northern freedmen's aid and missionary societies, and the manuscript records of the Bureau of Refugees, Freedmen, and Abandoned Lands, including lists of teachers, letters from and about teachers, and the thousands of monthly reports of the teachers. Those resources identify the majority of the teachers in that decade. Other resources flesh out the teachers from that period. For the 1870s, however, the resources are not as complete. The Freedmen's Bureau closed, for all intents and purposes, in 1870 (very few records were kept in its last two years, 1870–72); the larger secular freedmen's aid societies collapsed; smaller missionary societies retrenched or withdrew; and the remaining northern aid groups reduced their work. Southern states picked up much of the educational work, but most kept poor records or the records have not survived. Incomplete records through which individual teachers can be identified are extant for only five southern states, for two to three years each, and those cover only the years prior to the resumption of Democratic rule. As a result, the project has rich and probably quite complete records for the teachers in the first decade of the southern work, but much less complete records for the second half of Reconstruction. Thus it is likely that the project documents the work of the northern teachers very well, but that it undercounts the southern teachers, black and white, particularly after 1870.

To partially compensate for that undercount, the project has made rough estimates of the number of black and southern white teachers in the freed people's schools. For the methods employed in making those estimates, see Appendix B.

After the teachers were initially identified, the project systematically sought further information on them through a variety of sources. Those include the decennial censuses (1850 to, in some cases, 1920), the records of the Freedmen's Savings and Trust Company (which also provided initial identification of a few score of the teachers), Confederate and Union Civil War military records, military pension records, the records of the Southern Claims Commission, city directories, college and university alumni catalogues and archives, the archives of the aid societies, the archives of southern black colleges and universities, and autobiographies and biographies, among many other sources.

Full data is known for only a minority of the teachers. Those with common names can seldom be located in sources beyond those that initially identified them. Gender cannot be ascertained for some of those identified only by initials rather than full surnames. Misspelling of names in various sources compounds the problem of extending data on individuals. Nonetheless, by a constant process of crosschecking names and other information, mining primary and secondary sources, and linking data, the project continues to locate and eliminate duplicate records and to improve its findings.

The data reported in the tables below is subject to revision as work continues on the Freedmen's Teacher Project. However, given the current size of the database, future work is not likely to substantially change the overall conclusions, particularly regarding northern teachers.

TABLE 1-A. **Gender and Race of All Teachers**
(Total Teachers Currently Identified, 1861–1876: 11,672)

Gender	n	% of Gender Known	% of Total
Male	5,344	47.4	45.8
Female	5,934	52.6	50.8
Unknown	394		3.4
Race	n	% of Race Known	% of Total
Black	4,140	46.8	35.5
White	4,702	53.2	40.3
Unknown	2,829		24.2
Native American	1		

Appendix A

TABLE 2-A. Northern Teachers by Race and Gender 181

Race/Gender	n	% of Race Known	% of Total Northern Teachers
Northern black female	364	9.2	7.0
Northern black male	365	9.3	7.0
Northern black, gender unknown	4	0.1	0.1
Total northern black teachers	733	18.6	14.1
Northern white female	2,115	53.7	40.7
Northern white male	1,047	26.6	20.2
Northern white, gender unknown	41	1.0	0.8
Total northern white teachers	3,203	81.4	61.7
Total northern teachers, race known	3,936		
Northern female, race unknown	904		17.4
Northern male, race unknown	310		6.0
Northern, race and gender unknown	41		0.8
Total northern teachers, race unknown	1,255		24.2
Total identified northern teachers	5,191		

Note: White immigrants who had been in the country before the war began are counted in the region in which they were living by 1861; subsequent immigrants, some of whom immigrated specifically to teach in the southern black schools (n = 63) are counted as northern teachers.

Appendix A

TABLE 3-A. **Southern Teachers by Race and Gender**

Race/Gender	n	% of Race Known	% of Total Southern Teachers
Southern black female	1,251	24.8	19.0
Southern black male	2,081	41.2	31.7
Southern black, gender unknown	75	1.5	1.1
Total southern black teachers	3,408	67.6	51.9
Southern white female	674	13.3	10.2
Southern white male	926	18.3	14.1
Southern white, gender unknown	39	0.8	0.6
Total southern white teachers	1,639	32.4	24.9
Total southern teachers, race known	5,047		
Southern female, race unknown	647		9.8
Southern male, race unknown	659		10.0
Southern, race and gender unknown	229		3.4
Total southern teachers, race unknown	1,535		23.2
Total identified southern teachers	6,582		

TABLE 4-A. **Teachers of Foreign Birth by Race and Gender**

Race/Gender	n	% of Race Known	% of Total Foreign-born
Black female	9	7.0	6.7
Black male	29	22.5	21.6
Total black teachers	38	29.5	28.3
White female	24	18.6	17.9
White male	57	44.2	42.5
Total white teachers	81	62.8	60.4
Total foreign-born teachers, race known	129		
Race unknown, female	4		3.0
Race unknown, male	1		0.7
Total race unknown	5		3.7
Total foreign-born teachers	134		

Note: These teachers are also included in tables 1-A, 2-A, and 3-A.

Appendix A

Teachers	Years
Northern blacks	3.62
Females	3.59
Males	3.66
Southern blacks	2.75
Females	2.83
Males	2.70
Northern whites	2.42
Females	2.61
Males	2.17
Southern whites	1.57
Females	1.66
Males	1.50

TABLE 6-A. **Mean and Median Age at Commencement of Teaching in Freedmen's Schools**

Region/Race/Gender	Mean Age	Median Age
Southern black teachers	26.2	23
Males	27.2	24
Females	23.9	21
Northern black teachers	26.1	24
Males	28.1	25
Females	24.0	22
Southern white teachers	35.2	33
Males	38.1	35
Females	30.0	28
Northern white teachers	30.4	28
Males	33.7	31
Females	28.8	27

Appendix A

Appendix B

Estimating the Number of Black and Southern White Teachers, 1869–1876

As noted above, a significant number of southern whites taught in the southern black schools, roughly half as many as northern whites. A relatively small number of southern white teachers agreed to teach for, or were hired by, a northern aid agency. Significantly more were assisted by or agreed to report to the Freedmen's Bureau. It is clear from state archival records, however, that far more southern white teachers were in the freed people's schools by 1870 than can be positively identified by name. There were likewise far more black teachers in those schools than have been identified to date. To attempt to establish with some level of certainty the proportional participation of northern and southern white teachers and African American teachers in the first generation of southern black education, the Freedmen's Teacher Project used the existing data from South Carolina, supplemented with that from Alabama, to estimate the number of black and southern white teachers from 1870 onward. As noted above, given the nature of the sources available to the project, with nearly complete coverage of the teachers supported by the aid agencies from their beginning to their demise or to the end of Reconstruction, it is likely that the northern white teachers are largely accounted for in the database.

Various sorts of state records that identify individual teachers have survived in only five southern states: Texas, Louisiana, North Carolina, Alabama, and South Carolina. Most date from 1870 to about 1872. The Texas records are particularly voluminous. Unfortunately, they do not indicate the teachers' race nor whether they taught in black or white schools; those who can be identified as black from other sources have been added to the database, but there is no way to determine whether the others taught in black schools. The Louisiana records are incomplete and only extend for two years. In North Carolina, county-level education records extend from 1869 to the late 1870s but cover fewer than one-quarter of the counties. None of those states' records, then, provide sufficiently robust records upon which to base larger estimates.

Records have survived in Alabama that detail every teacher and the race of the school within which they taught, covering most but not all counties, extending from 1870 to 1872, though they are more complete in 1870–71 than subsequently. They are sufficiently robust to provide a provisional baseline for an estimate of the number of black and white teachers in 1870. In South Carolina, the quarterly reports of teachers, with an indication of the race of the school, have survived for 1869–1871, though they are incomplete. Of far greater value, however, are the annual reports of the South Carolina superintendent of education. Throughout the 1870s, those reports provided tabular records of the number of northern white teachers, northern black teachers, southern white teachers, and southern black teachers (except in 1876 and 1878). They also reported the number of black and white students in the state schools.

The South Carolina data merely identifies the total number of teachers; it does not indicate how many taught in white versus black schools. Throughout the decade of the 1870s, however, black students outnumbered white students. By 1875, for example, black students outnumbered white students 63,000 to 47,000. It is likely, however, given the growing discrimination against black schools by the end of Reconstruction, that there were more black students per teacher as compared to white students per teacher. Thus, despite the greater number of black students, the project assumed that about half of the total South Carolina teaching force was working in black schools.

To estimate the number of South Carolina's white teachers in black schools, then, the project assumed that most northern white teachers and all black teachers were teaching in black schools. It subtracted that number of teachers from the half who were in black schools, leaving an estimate of the number of southern white teachers in the black schools.

Establishing the number of black teachers was more straightforward. Archival sources for 1869–70 and the above-referenced state superintendent's annual reports provide solid evidence of the total number of black teachers in South Carolina's schools from 1870 to 1879. Incomplete archival sources in Alabama identify teachers in that state's black schools in 1870–71, many of whose race has been ascertained through the census and other sources; there were at least 214 black teachers in the Alabama freed people's schools.

To arrive at the estimates of southern white and black teachers in the freed people's schools throughout the South, the project took the total number of teachers of both races identified in the Alabama records (1870–71, 590 white teachers, 214 black teachers) and in the published South Carolina records (1870–77, see table 1-A), then divided the white and black 1870 population statistics for each of those states by the number of teachers to arrive at the proportion of each population per teacher. In 1870–71, the results indicate that in Alabama, one of every 884 white citizens was teaching in a black school, and one of every 2,222 black citizens was teaching. In South Carolina, 1 of every 669 white citizens was teaching in a black school, while one of every 1,068 black citizens was teaching. Among white teachers, the difference in proportions between the states differed by about one-quarter; among blacks the proportions differed by a bit more than one-half.

Appendix B

TABLE 1-B. **Teachers in South Carolina Schools, 1870–1879, and Estimated Number in South Carolina Black Schools**

Teachers	1870–71	1871–72	1872–73	1873–74	1874–75	1876–77	1878–79
Northern whites	61	53	62	67	55	42	18
Southern whites	1,390	1,634	1,561	1,655	1,821	1,683	2,072
Northern blacks	23	22	26	36	42	16	12
Southern blacks	424	476	661	778	937	933	1,064
Total	1,898	2,185	2,310	2,536	2,855	2,674	3,166
Half	949	1,092	1,155	1,268	1,427	1,337	1,583
Probable number of southern white teachers in black schools (half total teachers minus northern white and all black teachers)	433	541	406	387	393	346	489

Sources: *Annual Reports of the State Superintendent of Education of the State of South Carolina.* In *Reports and Resolutions of the General Assembly of the State of South Carolina.* Columbia, S.C., 1871–1879; South Carolina Superintendent of Education, "Teacher Reports Submitted by County Commissioners for School Years 1869–70," South Carolina State Archives.

Note: Further, incomplete South Carolina archival records indicate that at least 389 black teachers were teaching in the state in 1869–70.

The Alabama data serves as a check on the South Carolina data; as noted, the Alabama data included most but not all counties, and thus undercounts the total number of white teachers in black schools. Race is uncertain for about one-third of the Alabama teachers; when race has not been established, the teachers are assumed to have been white (which inflates the likely number of actual white teachers and depresses the likely number of black teachers). Still, the numbers for 1871 in Alabama and South Carolina suggest that the proportions in South Carolina may have been higher than the proportions elsewhere. Further, the proportion of whites to blacks in Alabama was near parity (whites outnumbered blacks by less than 5 percent), while the same proportion in South Carolina was 2:3. Throughout the South, however, whites outnumbered blacks 2:1. Thus, the likelihood of whites teaching in black schools was higher in Alabama than in the South as a whole, and highest in South Carolina, where blacks outnumbered whites by a greater proportion than in any other state. In other words, it is reasonable to assume that the higher the proportion of blacks to whites, the more likely a white teacher would find employment in a black school, all other factors being equal; throughout the South, the ratio of white teachers to the white population should be much lower than in South Carolina and Alabama.

To arrive at a conservative estimate of the likely number of white teachers in black schools during Reconstruction, therefore, the project adjusted the South Carolina proportions for white teachers by a factor of three and the South Carolina proportions for black teachers by half. It then divided the adjusted proportions for

Appendix B

TABLE 2-B. **Proportions of Teachers of Each Race to Total Population of Race in South Carolina, Adjusted Proportions, and Resulting Estimate of Total Southern Teaching Force in Southern Black Schools, 1870–1876**

	1869–70	1870–71	1871–72	1872–73	1873–74	1874–75	1875–76
White teachers in black schools as proportion of white population[a]	1:669	1:535	1:713	1:748	1:737	1:837	
Adjusted proportion	1:2,007	1:1,605	1:2,139	1:2,244	1:2,211	1:2,511	
Black teachers as proportion of black population[b]	1:1,068	1:960	1:874	1:629	1:534	1:444	1:446
Adjusted proportion	1:1,602	1:1,440	1:1,311	1:944	1:801	1:666	1:669

Estimated number of African American and southern white teachers in southern black schools, 1869–1876

	Estimated Total Black Teachers	Estimated Total White Teachers
1865–66	700	400
1866–67	1,000	550
1867–68	1,200	600
1868–69	2,000	1,300
1869–70	2,800	3,300
1870–71	3,100	4,600
1871–72	3,400	5,800
1872–73	4,700	4,300
1873–74	5,600	4,100
1874–75	6,700	4,200
1875–76	6,700	3,700

[a]In 1870, the census reported 289,667 white inhabitants in South Carolina; 521,384 in Alabama; and 9,378,068 in the former slaveholding southern states.

[b]In 1870, the census reported 415,814 black inhabitants in South Carolina; 475,510 in Alabama; and 4,495,478 in the former slaveholding southern states.

each year into the total black and white population in the southern states in 1870. The results were then rounded down, again in the interest of producing more conservative and defensible estimates. The results are reported in table 2-B.

Finally, the project worked backward from 1871 (or 1870, in the case of black teachers) to estimate the number of each group from 1865. In the case of southern white teachers, the estimates are based on the assumption that white participation in black education accelerated rapidly after the southern states began supporting

Appendix B

black schools, in 1869 and 1870 in most cases. Many black teachers, as noted in the text, initiated schools without assistance from the bureau or other agencies and thus may not be accounted for among those who have been identified to date; others may have begun their teaching career after the commencement of public support and have not been identified because of poor or missing state-level records.

Notes

All note references to the decennial censuses refer to the manuscript U.S. federal census returns, available on microfilm and online, except where the reference is specifically to the published census compendia.

Abbreviations

AAS	American Antiquarian Society, Worcester, Mass.
ABHMS	American Baptist Home Mission Society
ACWS	American Civil War Soldiers, online database, <www.ancestry.com>
AF	*American Freedman*
AFUC	American Freedmen's Union Commission
AM	*American Missionary*
AMA	American Missionary Association
AMAA	American Missionary Association Archives, Amistad Research Center, Tulane University, New Orleans, La.
ASA	Alabama State Archives, Montgomery, Ala.
BRFAL	Bureau of Refugees, Freedmen, and Abandoned Lands. BRFAL following a state refers to the records of the bureau superintendent of education for that state; BRFAL following Ed. Div. refers to records of the Education Division, i.e., the headquarters of the division within the bureau; BRFAL following other designations refers to other offices within the bureau. BRFAL records were consulted on microfilm; each reference is followed by the National Archives microfilm collection number and the roll number within the collection, e.g., M803:7.
CR	*Christian Recorder*
CSR	Compiled Service Records, manuscripts, National Archives, Washington, D.C.
CU	Cornell University, Olin Library, Special Collections, Ithaca, N.Y.
CWPR	Civil War Pension Records, manuscripts, National Archives, Washington, D.C.
DU	Duke University, Perkins Library, Durham, N.C.
FA	*Freedmen's Advocate*

FF		*Freedmen's Friend*
FFA		Friends Freedmen's Association, the name given to the Friends' Association of Philadelphia and Its Vicinity for the Relief of Colored Freedmen
FJ		*Freedmen's Journal*
FR		*Freedmen's Record*
FSTC		Freedmen's Savings and Trust Co., CD database
GPO		Government Printing Office
HBS		Harvard Business School, Baker Library, Cambridge, Mass.
HC		Haverford College, Magill Library, Philadelphia, Pa.
LASA		Louisiana State Archives, Baton Rouge
LC		Library of Congress, Washington, D.C.
LR		Letters Received
LS		Letters Sent
MdHS		Maryland Historical Society, Baltimore
MHC		Mount Holyoke College, Archives and Special Collections, South Hadley, Mass.
MHS		Massachusetts Historical Society, Boston
NA		National Archives, Washington, D.C.
NCSA		North Carolina State Archives, Raleigh
NEFAS		New England Freedmen's Aid Society
NEYM		Society of Friends, New England Yearly Meeting
NF		*National Freedman*
NFRA		National Freedmen's Relief Association
NOU		New Orleans University, New Orleans, La.
NWFAC		Northwestern Freedmen's Aid Commission
NYYM		Society of Friends, New York Yearly Meeting
OC		Oberlin College, College Archives, Oberlin, Ohio
PFB		*Pennsylvania Freedmen's Bulletin*
PFRA		Pennsylvania Freedmen's Relief Association
RIHS		Rhode Island Historical Society, Providence
SC		Swarthmore College, Philadelphia, Pa.
SCC		Records of the Southern Claims Commission, microfilm and manuscript, National Archives, Washington, D.C.
SCSA		South Carolina State Archives, Columbia
SL		Radcliff Institute, Schlesinger Library, Harvard University, Cambridge, Mass.
SoM		*Spirit of Missions*
SR		School Reports
TMSR		Teachers' Monthly School Reports
TSLA		Texas State Library and Archives, Austin
UNC		University of North Carolina, Wilson Library, Chapel Hill
UP		University of Pennsylvania, Special Collections, Philadelphia
UR		University of Rochester, Department of Rare Books and Special Collections, Rochester, N.Y.

Notes

USC	University of South Carolina, South Caroliniana Library, Columbia
USCWS	U.S. Civil War Soldiers, online database, <www.ancestry.com>
UVA	University of Virginia, Alderman Library, Special Collections, Charlottesville
VHS	Virginia Historical Society, Richmond
WSHS	Wisconsin State Historical Society, Madison
YU	Yale University, New Haven, Conn.

Preface

1. Du Bois, *Souls of Black Folk*, 64, 65.

2. Knight, " 'Messianic' Invasion of the South," 645, 649.

3. Swint, *Northern Teacher in the South*.

4. Ibid., 82–84; Cash, *Mind of the South*, 140.

5. Cash, *Mind of the South*, 141.

6. Hoffert, "Yankee Schoolmarms," 188–201.

7. Jacqueline Jones, *Soldiers of Light and Love*; Selleck, *Gentle Invaders*; Butchart, " 'Army of Civilization,' " 76–87.

8. Horst, *Education for Manhood*; Morris, *Reading, 'Riting, and Reconstruction*; Butchart, *Northern Schools*; Joe M. Richardson, *Christian Reconstruction*; Butchart, "Mission Matters," 1–17; along with sources cited in note 7.

9. McPherson, "The New Puritanism," 611–42, quotation from 619.

10. Jones, *Soldiers of Light and Love*, 30–31; Perkins, "The Black Female American Missionary," 123–24. In fairness, Jones makes her generalizations only for the teachers in Georgia, though it is too easy to read them as more broadly generalizable, as Perkins does. Jones's sample is skewed toward American Missionary Association teachers, a bias she does not recognize, but one that damages conclusions drawn from the sample. Among others who echo this portrayal, see Brady, "Trials and Tribulations," 5–20; Maxine D. Jones, " 'They Are My People,' " 78–89; Small, "Yankee Schoolmarm in Freedmen's Schools," 381–402; Heather Andrea Williams, " 'Clothing Themselves in Intelligence,' " 372–89.

11. An important exception is Morris, *Reading, 'Riting, and Reconstruction*, 85–130. Perkins, "The Black Female American Missionary," and Maxine D. Jones, " 'They Are My People,' " deal with the black teachers among the freed people, but are unaware of the extent of black participation; DeBoer, *His Truth Is Marching On*, deals only with the black teachers employed by the AMA, and does not account for all of them.

12. Jacqueline Jones asserts, for example, that American Missionary Association teachers "were evangelical abolitionists," though she never attempts to demonstrate that: Jones, *Soldiers of Light and Love*, 20.

13. Dykstra, *Bright Radical Star*; Butchart and Rolleri, "Iowa Teachers," 1–29.

14. Jacqueline Jones reports a similar average age for her small sample of teachers yet continues to characterize the teachers as young: Jones, *Soldiers of Light and Love*, 211.

15. Ibid., 31; McPherson, "The New Puritanism," 619.

16. Morris, *Reading, 'Riting, and Reconstruction*, 236–40; Butchart, *Northern Schools*, 130–68.

Chapter 1

1. Du Bois, *Black Reconstruction in America*, 638.

2. The literature on the southern literacy laws is well summarized in Andrea Heather Williams, *Self-Taught*, 7–29; on the general issue of black literacy under slavery, see especially Cornelius, *When I Can Read*; estimates of southern black literacy among slaves and free blacks vary between 5 and 10 percent: see for example Webber, *Deep Like the Rivers*, 131; Du Bois, *Black Reconstruction in America*, 638.

3. Du Bois, *Black Reconstruction in America*, 638.

4. Alvord, *First Semi-Annual Report* (January 1866), 10.

5. Harriet M. Buss to her parents, 22 June 1863, Harriet M. Buss Letters, UP.

6. Report of James Peet, *FA* 1 (May 1864): 17. Likewise, in Richmond, Virginia, in 1865, James Rhodes found one school with 500 students being taught by four teachers, and another with 300 students under the tutelage of another four teachers; altogether 1,500 black students were studying in five schools: James E. Rhoads to Margaret E. Rhoads, 16 May 1865, James E. Rhoads Papers, HC. In Yorktown, Virginia, Eunice Congdon usually shared her 200 students with an assistant but occasionally had to teach the entire class alone; after teaching that large class during the day, she had a night class of 190 adults: Eunice Congdon to Sarah Cope, 9 July 1864, FFA, Women's Aid Committee, LR, Friends Freedmen's Association Papers, SC.

7. Etta Payne, in [Mount Holyoke Female Seminary], *The Second Letter of the Class of '63. October, 1866* (Northampton, Mass.: Metcalf, 1866), 16–17, in Mount Holyoke College Archives, South Hadley, Mass. Likewise, Philena Carkin and Anna Gardner taught more than 200 students in Charlottesville, Virginia: Philena Carkin, "Reminiscences of My Life," UVA.

8. *Loyal Georgian* 1 (27 January 1866): n.p. In the same year, Thomas C. Haines reported over one hundred students in his school in St. Joseph, Missouri: [Friends'] *Freedmen's Record* 1 (March 1866): 10; in Farmville, Virginia, three teachers worked with over 250 students: *PFB* (July 1866): 1–2; even as late as 1868, schools in New Orleans were thronged beyond capacity—many schools had over one hundred students, while citywide the average was eighty-five per teacher: E. S. Stoddard to Frank R. Chase, "Report of Examination and Inspection of the Public Colored Schools of the City of New Orleans, La.," 5 May 1868, Ed. Div. BRFAL, M803:12.

9. Hettie E. Sabattie to J. Murray Hoag, 10 January 1869, Georgia BRFAL, M799:9.

10. Sarah Williams to "Aunt Hettie and the rest," 20 January 1872 (quotation); Williams to same, 30 March 1872, Correspondence of Edward Williams, in Stratton (Maule) Papers, SC.

11. See for example Rice, "Yankee Teacher in the South," 152; *AM* 8 (December 1864): 293; E. Cordelia Hydorn, "The Freedmen's Mission," *Sabbath Recorder* 22 (11

12. E. H. Botume to Ednah Dow Cheney, 3 February 1874, LR, NEFAS Records, MHS.

13. Caroline Alfred to Ednah Dow Cheney, 5 December 1875, LR, NEFAS Records, MHS.

14. Holland, *Diary of Laura M. Towne*, 281.

15. U.S. Office of Education, *Report of the Commissioner of Education for the Year 1880*, lxii; Bond, *Education of the Negro*, vii.

16. Butchart and Rolleri, "Secondary Education and Emancipation: Secondary Schools for Freed Slaves in the American South, 1862–1875," 157–81.

17. All information here is drawn from the Freedmen's Teacher Project.

18. Black literacy in the South in 1860 was 10 percent at best; black literacy in the North was roughly 75 percent. Given the black population at the time, that would mean there were about 456,000 literate African Americans nationwide, or about 1.7 percent of the nation's population, a bit less than one-fiftieth.

19. By the spring of 1865, 1,860 teachers had been engaged in the freed people's schools for at least one term. Over 22 percent of the teachers whose race has been established were black. Of the teachers who had taught by that date, black teachers would go on to average over four years of teaching, while those known to have been white averaged three years. Data drawn from the Freedmen's Teacher Project.

20. *Friends' Intelligencer* 19 (5 April 1862): 57; Du Bois, *Black Reconstruction in America*, 459; Messner, *Freedmen*, 391; Alvord, *Second Semi-Annual Report* (July 1866), 10–11.

21. *FA* 1 (November 1864): 40.

22. [Mary S. Osbourne], "Among the Freedmen in Maryland. No. 3," *Zion's Herald*, 17 January 1865, 2.

23. Georgia Educational Association, "A New Plan for Educating the Freedmen of the South," circular, n.p., (1867), Ed. Div. BRFAL, M803:12; on the association, see also Alvord, *First Semi-Annual Report* (January 1866), 2. Because of black poverty and the opportunism of whites, the association was relatively short-lived: Jacqueline Jones, *Soldiers of Light and Love*, 54.

24. E. Rucker to G. L. Eberhart, 28 November 1865, Register of LR, p. 33, Georgia BRFAL, M799:8.

25. Alvord, *Second Semi-Annual Report* (July 1866), 18.

26. "Report of Freedmen's Schools in North Carolina, For the month ending August 31, 1865," State Superintendents' Monthly SR, Ed. Div., BRFAL, M803:13, emphasis in original.

27. Joel Grant to L. Thomas, 28 February 1866, in Berlin, Reidy, and Rowland, *The Black Military Experience*, 632.

28. Arnold T. Needham to W. W. Patton, 8 March 1864, Needham Correspondence, Chicago Historical Society, Chicago, Ill.

29. Shaffer, *After the Glory*, 17. On the role of the Union army in contributing to black literacy, see also Alvord, *First Semi-Annual Report* (January 1866), 11; Cornish, "Union Army as a School," 368–82; Blassingame, "Union Army as an Education

194 Institution," 152–59; Warren B. Armstrong, "Union Chaplains," 104–15; Bahney, "Generals and Negroes." As Heather Williams has argued, this literature underestimates the role of African American soldiers in expanding and accelerating the army's educational work and overstates the willingness of the army to respond: Heather Andrea Williams, " 'Commenced to Think Like a Man,' " 196–219.

30. Georgia Educational Association, "A New Plan for Educating the Freedmen of the South," circular, n.p., (1867), Ed. Div. BRFAL, M803:12.

31. For the bureau expenditures, see Peirce, *The Freedmen's Bureau*, 82. The estimate of $8 million raised by the aid societies, 1861 to 1870, is mine, based on reported receipts of all the aid societies for whom consistent data could be collected; it excludes the societies' estimates of the value of used goods. The estimate of $2 million expended by the freed people is based on fragmentary and inconsistent data provided in Alvord's semiannual reports. He provided no data on black expenditures in his first two reports; thereafter, he reported the tuition paid by the freed people and indicated the number of schools owned outright the freed people and the number supplied by the bureau (which appears to have included the buildings built or repaired by the freed people to which the bureau contributed, as well as those paid for fully by the bureau), but did not indicate the value of the land that the schools occupied. In his last four reports, 1869 and 1870, Alvord estimated a total of $750,000 expended by the freed people. Extrapolating over the life of the bureau suggests the figure of about $2 million from the freed people. That does not account for the first four years of black educational effort prior to the bureau and, from what can be determined from the reports, excludes the cost of the school grounds, labor, donated material, and the hundreds of schools that did not report to the bureau. For Alvord's data that yields the overall estimate of the freed people's investment, see Alvord, *Seventh Semi-Annual Report* (January 1869), 9; *Eighth Semi-Annual Report* (July 1869), 10; *Ninth Semi-Annual Report* (January 1870), 9; and *Tenth Semi-Annual Report* (July 1870), 5.

32. *FA* 1 (May 1864): 17 (quotation); *FA* 1 (April 1864): 13; [Forten], "Life on the Sea Islands," May 1864; ibid., June 1864; Sallie Daffin, in *CR* 4 (17 September 1864): 149; Mrs. John L. Denman, "Report for September 1867," SR, Georgia BRFAL, M799:21; Robert Harris to H. C. Vogell, 7 June 1869, LR, North Carolina BRFAL, M844:9; J. W. Grady to F. A. Fiske, 11 May 1868, LR, North Carolina BRFAL, M844:7. The education of adult freedmen is explored more fully in Butchart, "Schooling for a Freed People."

33. William R. Hooper, "Shall He be Educated? A Reply to 'The Freedman and His Future,' " *Lippincott's Magazine* 4 (December 1869): 671.

34. L. D. Barrow, in *FA* 1 (February 1864): 5.

35. Fleming, *Civil War and Reconstruction in Alabama*, 458; Bentley, *History of the Freedmen's Bureau*, 170 (quotation).

36. Wesley, "Forty Acres and a Mule," 119.

37. Jonathan W. Harrison, teaching in Cedar Grove, S.C., in *FA* 1 (March 1864): 9.

38. Western Yearly Meeting, Society of Friends, *Minutes of the Western Yearly Meeting of Friends* (n.p., 1867), 31.

39. Eunice Congdon to Sarah Cope, 9 July 1864, LR, FFA, Women's Aid Committee, HC.

40. *AM* 7 (May 1863): 115–16.

41. Martha Johnson to her sisters, 11 April 1863, Johnson Family Papers, Vermont Historical Society, Barre, Vt.; Mary F. Root, writing from Beaufort, S.C., 1 February 1863, in *AM* 7 (April 1863): 90–91.

42. Clarence E. Walker, *Rock in a Weary Land*, esp. 46–81; John L. Bell, "Presbyterian Church and the Negro," 15–36; Ogle, "Brother Against Brother," 137–54; Harry V. Richardson, *Dark Salvation*; H. Sheldon Smith, *In His Image But*, 209–13; W. Harrison Daniel, "Virginia Baptists and the Negro," 340–63; Gravely, "Social, Political and Religious Significance," 3–25.

43. Letter dated 20 November 1865, transcribed p. 24, Anna H. Kidder Collection, SL.

44. Jenkins, *Seizing the New Day*, 78.

45. Richard Sloan to E. M. Wheelock, 4 May 1866, Unregistered LR, Texas BRFAL, M822:10, misspelling *sic*.

46. Robert G. Fitzgerald to F. A. Fiske, 20 February 1868, LR, North Carolina BRFAL, M844:7; Alvord, *Fourth Semi-Annual Report* (July 1867), 50, 74.

47. In Sarah Cadbury, "Letters from Slabtown Virginia 3rd mo. 22nd to 5th mo. 11th 1866 to her family in Germantown Philadelphia," p. 109, Sarah Cadbury Correspondence, HC.

48. In 1865, Congress created the Bureau of Refugees, Freedmen, and Abandoned Lands, popularly known as the Freedmen's Bureau. From the beginning, the bureau was forced to renege on the legislation's promise of forty acres and a mule for all loyal southerners and the freedmen. Perpetually underfunded and often staffed with military and former military officers with little sympathy for the freed people, its authorization expired in 1870. In its brief career, it was moderately successful in providing emergency relief for white refugees and the freed people, in regularizing labor contracts in the aftermath of the collapse of chattel slavery, and in providing some coordination and aid to southern black schools. Cimbala, *Under the Guardianship*; Cimbala and Miller, *Freedmen's Bureau and Reconstruction*; Crouch, *Freedmen's Bureau and Black Texans*; Finley, *From Slavery to Uncertain Freedom*; Bentley, *History of the Freedmen's Bureau*.

49. Quoted in Alvord, *Tenth Semi-Annual Report* (July 1870), 13.

50. L. C. Lockwood, *Independent*, 5 February 1863, 1.

51. Quoted in *AF* 2 (February 1868): 364, spelling *sic*.

52. Quoted in C. R. Bent to [George W. Giles], undated, in Unregistered LR, Ed. Div., BRFAL, M803:13.

53. Philip S. Foner, "Address of Frederick Douglass," 177.

54. John Sweeney to Clinton Fisk, 8 October 1865, in Berlin, Reidy, and Rowland, *The Black Military Experience*, 615. The freedmen's quest for manhood loomed very large in the decisions of thousands of black men to join the Union forces during the Civil War, and often carried explicitly gendered meanings for them: see Shaffer, *After the Glory*, 3–17.

55. My notion of black literacy as part of the freed people's emancipation project draws from an extensive recent historical literature that understands African American emancipation as a process, not merely an event, though to date that literature has done little with literacy and education as a part of the process. See Ransom and Sutch, *One Kind of Freedom*; Litwack, *Been in the Storm So Long*; Eric Foner, *Nothing but Freedom*; Foner, *Forever Free*; Magdol, *A Right to the Land*; Mohr, *On the Threshold of Freedom*; Cohen, *At Freedom's Edge*; and the volumes in the *Documentary History of Emancipation* series, edited by Ira Berlin and others.

56. Butchart, "Remapping Racial Boundaries," 61–78; Butchart, " 'We Best Can Instruct,' " 27–49.

57. The number of freedmen's teachers who can be shown to have held clear abolitionist views before the war was remarkably small. Most of the northern teachers who spoke about their purposes for teaching said nothing about the needs of the freed people; their motivations were primarily self-referential. See Butchart, *Northern Schools*, 115–34; Butchart, "Perspectives on Gender," 15–32; and particularly Butchart, "Mission Matters," 1–17.

58. Mary Bowers to F. A. Fiske, 11 April 1866, Unregistered LR, North Carolina BRFAL, M844:10.

59. This argument is developed below, Chapter 3.

60. Swint, *Northern Teacher in the South*, 72. See also Knight, *Influence of Reconstruction on Education*; Knight, " 'Messianic' Invasion of the South," 645–51; Noble, *Forty Years*; de Roulhac, "Freedmen's Bureau in North Carolina," 53–67, 154–63; Bentley, *History of the Freedmen's Bureau*. Cf. Du Bois, "Reconstruction and Its Benefits," 781–99; and Du Bois, *Black Reconstruction in America*, 637–69.

61. Jenkins, *Seizing the New Day*, 71.

62. McPherson, "Some Thoughts on the Civil War," 17, n. 28. McPherson estimates a 400 percent increase in literacy, beginning from a supposition of 10 percent literacy in 1865. If the literacy rate was lower, as some scholars argue, the increase would, of course, be higher.

63. This and the following four paragraphs first appeared in Butchart, "Remapping Racial Boundaries," 61–64. Reproduced here by the generous permission of Stichting Paedagogica Historica.

64. Genovese, *Roll, Jordan, Roll*, 561–63: Cornelius, *When I Can Read*, 18, 32–33; Woodson, *The Education of the Negro*; Heather Andrea Williams, *Self-Taught*, 7–21, 203–13.

65. Genovese, *Roll, Jordan, Roll*, 135, 617–19; Cornelius, *When I Can Read*, 65–67; Philip S. Foner and Josephine F. Pacheco, *Three Who Dared*, esp. 57–95. Cornelius makes the important observation that antiliteracy laws were seldom enforced, yet "slaves recognized their symbolic power" (64). So, one might add, did most southern whites.

66. Butchart, *Northern Schools*, 169–80; Heather Andrea Williams, *Self-Taught*, 30–173.

67. Among many sources, see for example Lemann, *Redemption*; Perman, *Reunion without Compromise*; Eric Foner, *Reconstruction*, 77–123, 176–215, 412–59;

Chapter 2

1. Richard Wells, Application #75, 14 February 1867, Tallahassee Branch, Register of Signatures of Depositors in Freedmen's Savings and Trust Company; 1870 census, Fla., Leon Co., Southern portion, 34/33, p. 637; 1880 census, Fla., Leon Co., Precinct 13, 108/109, p. 351C; Canter Brown Jr., *Florida's Black Public Officials*, 137. On Kirksey and his son, Lafayette, and their holdings, see 1860 census, Fla., Leon Co., Tallahassee, 205/205, p. 23; and 1860 census, Slave Schedules, Fla., Leon Co., pp. 247, 251, 279, 292–93.

2. Samuel H. Smothers: 1860 census, Ind., Wayne Co., New Garden, 563/574, p. 801; Co. C, 45 USCT, CSR; 1880 census, Tex., Dallas Co., Dist. 59, 112/121, p. 134D; 1900 census, Tex., Brazoria Co., Justice Precinct 7, 527/527, p. 150A; on his education, see <http://www.indianahistory.org/library/manuscripts/collection$weguid es/African-American$wemss.html>, accessed 29 March 2008.

3. Harris family: 1850 census, Mich., Monroe Co., Monroe 1 Ward, 139/142, pp. 355–56; 1860 census, Ohio, Lorain Co., Oberlin, 375/371, p. 209; AMA, *Eighteenth Annual Report* (1864), 25; AMA, *Twentieth Annual Report* (1866), 3; *AM* 11 (April 1867): 77; *FF* 1 (December 1868): 3; *FF* 1 (April 1871):4; *CR* 13 March 1869, 34; *FF* 1 (January 1874): 6; Oberlin College, *Seventy-Fifth Anniversary General Catalogue*, 423–24; O'Hara, Mrs. James E. [Lizzie Harris] File, Graduates and Former Students, OC; Wassom, Mrs. George T. [Frankie Emma Harris] File, Graduates and Former Students, OC; Majors, *Noted Negro Women*, 30–32, 71–74.

4. Small, "Yankee Schoolmarm in Freedmen's Schools," 381–402; Wolfe, "Women Who Dared"; Hoffert, "Yankee Schoolmarms," 188–201; Horst, *Education for Manhood*; Jacqueline Jones, *Soldiers of Light and Love*; Butchart, *Northern Schools*; Engs, *Educating the Disfranchised and Disinherited*; Swint, *Northern Teacher in the South*.

5. There are scattered studies that take seriously the central role of African Americans, some quite good. In general, however, those studies have not yet modified the dominant thrust of the literature. See for example James D. Anderson, "Ex-Slaves"; Heather Andrea Williams, *Self-Taught*; Butchart, "Edmonia G. and Caroline V. Highgate"; Butchart, " 'We Best Can Instruct' "; Maxine D. Jones, " 'They Are My People' "; Morris, *Reading, 'Riting, and Reconstruction*, 85–130; Perkins, "The Black Female American Missionary Association"; DeBoer, *His Truth Is Marching On*.

6. Small, "Yankee Schoolmarm in Freedmen's Schools," 381–402; Hoffert, "Yankee Schoolmarms," 188–201; Jacqueline Jones, *Soldiers of Light and Love*; Selleck, *Gentle Invaders*.

7. Northern, southern, and foreign-born black teachers together numbered 4,140; northern white teachers numbered 3,203. White teachers outnumber black teachers only when southern whites are included. See Appendix A. As argued in this

study, southern white teachers must be considered separately from northern white teachers since they had distinctly different objectives and agendas. These numbers are subject to revision as the Freedmen's Teacher Project continues to generate data.

8. Of the 8,842 teachers whose race is known, 4,140, or 46.8 percent, were black. If the 2,790 teachers whose race remains unknown were all white (unlikely), those 4,140 black teachers were 35.5 percent of the teachers. Data drawn from the Freedmen's Teacher Project.

9. Of the 4,140 black teachers, 733 were from northern states. In 1870, there were 339,628 African Americans living in all northern states. Thus, one out of every 463 northern blacks taught. Northern whites accounted for no more than 4,296 of the teachers (and probably fewer, since race is not yet known for all northern teachers). In 1870, there were 23,825,051 whites in the North. Thus, one out of every 5,546 northern whites spent any time in the southern black schools (5,546/463 = 11.98). Population data calculated from U.S. Bureau of the Census, *Ninth Census*, 1:xvii.

10. Across northern states, white illiteracy for those twenty-one years of age and older was 4 to 6 percent, with Ohio having about the lowest rate at 4.2 percent. Black illiteracy for the same group ranged from 14 percent to 26 percent; the highest black illiteracy was in the Midwest, where access to free education for African Americans was particularly constrained. Black illiteracy in Ohio was 24.7 percent; Indiana had a black illiteracy rate of 25.9 percent. Connecticut and Massachusetts, with the most liberal access to education for blacks, had black illiteracy rates of 13.8 percent. With an average of 20 percent black illiteracy versus 5 percent white illiteracy, northern blacks were fifteen to eighteen times more likely to have taught in the South than were northern whites. Calculations derived from data in U.S. Bureau of the Census, *Ninth Census*, 1:xvii, 396. On black access to education in the North, see for example McCaul, *The Black Struggle*; Arnie Cooper, "A Stony Road"; Mabee, *Black Education in New York State*; Ballard, *The Education of Black Folk*; McGinnis, *The Education of Negroes in Ohio*; Savage, "Early Negro Education"; Marion M. Wright, *Education of Negroes in New Jersey*; Carroll, "The Beginnings of Public Education."

11. Northern black men taught an average of 3.66 years, while northern black women taught an average of 3.59 years; southern black men averaged 2.7 years, and southern black women averaged 2.8 years. See Appendix A, table 5-A, for comparable figures for northern and southern white teachers. Compiled from the Freedmen's Teacher Project.

12. The five black teachers were Sarah A. Gray (1861 to the 1890s), Eliza Ann Cook and George F. T. Cook (1861 to at least the 1880s), Emma V. Brown and Sarah Daffin (1862 to the 1880s). The five white teachers with uninterrupted careers in the southern black schools beginning in 1862 were Martha Clary Hale, Laura Towne, Ellen Murray, Elizabeth Hunn, and Elizabeth Hyde Botume.

13. U.S. Office of Education, *Special Report*, 200, 216–17, 239, 257, 272–74; Lillian G. Dabney, *The History of Schools*, 58–61, table III; U.S. Office of Education, *Report of the Commissioner of Education* (1871), 398–99; ibid., (1874), 475; *FA* 1 (September 1864): 32; "George F. T. Cook," *Crisis* 5 (January 1913): 11. Among the

other early teachers in Washington was Maria W. Stewart, the noted black abolitionist speaker and writer. She was sixty years old when she began teaching in 1863;
she remained in the classroom for seven years. Flexnor, "Maria W. Stewart," 377–
78; Marilyn Richardson, *Maria W. Stewart*, 96, 103–4.

14. U.S. Office of Education, *Special Report*, 285, 288, 311; Mansfield, "That
Fateful Class," 64–66, 258; "Monthly Report of Sub-Assistant Commissioner (or
Agent), 5th and 6th Ed'l Sub-Dists, State of Virginia, February 1869," Monthly
Statistical School Reports, Virginia BRFAL, M1053:12; Robinson, TMSR, Novem-
ber 1869, Virginia BRFAL, M1053:17; C. Robinson to Samuel Austin, 6 October
1866, and "A Brief Sketch of the 'Beulah' School," both in Records of the Rhode
Island Association for Freedmen, RIHS. Robinson returned to Pennsylvania to
continue his education at Lincoln University in 1867.

15. Berry: 1860 census, Md., Baltimore 12 Ward, 1361/1592, p. 913; Fleetwood:
1860 census, Md., Baltimore Co., Baltimore 19 Ward, 486/583, p. 74; *Baltimore City
Directory* (1863–64), 455–56; (1865–66), 480–81; (1867–68), 567, 583; (1868–
69), 620–21; (1870), 700; (1871), 694–95; Fortie: 1870 Federal Census, Maryland,
Baltimore Co., Baltimore 5 Ward, —/—, p. 158.

16. Joseph C. Corbin, later the Arkansas Superintendent of Education and founder and principal of Branch Normal College in Pine Bluff, Arkansas, also taught
with Adams and Gibson in the late 1840s and early 1850s. Gibson left the school
from 1862 to 1866 due to wartime conditions in Louisville but continued teaching
during those four years. *CR* 5 (3 June 1865): 86; Simmons, *Men of Mark*, 545–48,
798–800, 829–33; Richings, *An Album of Negro Educators*; Kimball, "Freedom's
Harvest," 283; Kimball, "Education for Negroes in Kentucky," 61; Application
#6627, 21 August 1873, Louisville Branch, Register of Signatures, FSTC.

17. On Davis, see AMA, *Sixteenth Annual Report* (1862), 42; *FJ* 1 (September
1865): 34; Mansfield, "That Fateful Class," 25; Horst, *Education for Manhood*, 28.
On Spivery, see *AM* 12 (April 1868): 73; *AM* 13 (May 1869): 99; *AM* 14 (June 1870):
122; DeBoer, *His Truth Is Marching On*, 256. On Williams, see A. S. Flagg, "Report
of Schools for Freedmen in 1st District, State of Virginia, during the month of
February 1866," Monthly Statistical School Reports, Virginia BRFAL, M1053:12;
"Assistant Sub-Assistant Commissioner's (or Agent's) Monthly Report on Education
of Freedmen and Refugees in 1st Div., 1st Sub-District, State of Virginia . . ., January
1868," Monthly School Reports of Assistant Subassistant Commissioners and
Agents, Virginia BRFAL, M1053:13. The most celebrated of the early teachers,
Mary Peake, illustrates a persistent problem with the current scholarship. Peake
appears to have instructed small groups of students in the 1850s and was persuaded
by an agent of the American Missionary Association to reengage in teaching after
September 1861. She died several months later of consumption. She began her work
later than Davis, Spivery, and Williams, none of whom appear to have had any
encouragement from the AMA or any other white organization, she taught fewer
students, and she taught only briefly. Her greater fame resulted from a biographical
sketch published by the AMA as a means to raise funds and increase interest in the
association's work. The sketch caught the fancy of many readers because it emphasized Peake's near-white complexion and physiognomy (stressed both in the text

200

and in an etching purported to be her likeness) and because it played on the early Victorian trope of the noble, dying heroine. See Lockwood, *Mary S. Peake.*

18. *CR* 6 (10 February 1866): 22; "Assistant Sub-Assistant Commissioner's (or Agent's) Monthly Report on Education of Freedmen and Refugees in 1st Div., 3rd Sub-District, State of Virginia . . ., January 1868," Monthly School Reports of Assistant Subassistant Commissioners and Agents, Records of Supt. of Ed., Virginia, BRFAL, M1053:13.

19. Weston: AMA, *Nineteenth Annual Report* (1865), 24; AMA, *Twentieth Annual Report* (1866), 26; Thomas Holt, *Black over White,* 70; Beard: Pegues, *Our Baptist Ministers and Schools,* 145; Stromer: Powers, "Black Charleston," 257. Beaird: E. R. Carter, *Biographical Sketches of Our Pulpit,* 147–48; Trowbridge, *The South,* 490–91.

20. "School Report of Lucinda Jackson," 1 January 1866, and "School Report of Miss Jane Deveaux," 1 January 1866, both in SR, Georgia BRFAL, M799:20 (in response to the report form's question, "How long has your School been organized?" Deveaux responded, "30 years"); *CR* 5 (15 April 1865): 58; James Porter, "Report of Oglethorpe School," 30 June 1866, SR, Georgia BRFAL, M799:20; Albert Otto, "Two Centuries of Educational History in Chatham County" (typescript, n.d., unpaginated; "Minutes of the Board of Education, Savannah," vol. 2, (ms., in Chatham County Public Schools, Board of Education Office), pp. 72–3, 10 March 1873; Drago, *Black Politicians and Reconstruction,* 27, 98; Du Bois, *Black Reconstruction in America,* 507; Foner, *Freedom's Lawmakers,* 173.

21. Personal correspondence, Barbara Sellers Darden, 24 November 1999; Marrs, *Life and History*; *FA* 1 (November 1864): 40; Henry D. Smith, Application #264, 27 April 1872, Natchez Branch; and Application #693, 14 April 1874, Natchez Branch, Register of Signators, FSTC; C. L. Tambling to E. M. Gregory, 31 October 1865, and L. A. Wheelock, "Report of Schools for Freedmen," October 1866, both in SR, Texas BRFAL, M822:11; Sarah Wren, 1870 census, Tex., Brazos Co., Bryan, 54/36, p. 21.

22. In addition to the northern and southern black teachers, a small handful, thirty-eight teachers, were foreign-born. Four were more or less directly from Africa, a dozen were from the Caribbean Islands, but most were from Canada. Virtually all of the latter had roots in the American South. Data drawn from the Freedmen's Teacher Project.

23. FFA, *Annual Report* (1865), 26; NYYM, *Third Report* (1864), 3–5; *FR* 1 (December 1865): 203; NYYM, *Fifth Report* (1866), 4–5; Sterling, *We Are Your Sisters,* 74; Yellin, "Written by Herself," 486.

24. Walter spent four years in the civil service, 1886–1890; Moses taught to at least 1880. 1880 census, La., Lafayette Parish, Vermillionville, 48/48, p. 434C; 1900 census, La., Lafayette Parish, Lafayette, 191/202, p. 9B; Beverly Babin Woods, "Walter H. Williams, Sr."

25. AMA, *Nineteenth Annual Report* (1865), 25; ibid. (1866), 29; *AM* 11 (April 1867): 75; *AM* 14 (June 1870): 126; *AM* 15 (May 1871): 99; *AM* 16 (May 1872): 99; *AM* 17 (September 1873): 200; *AM* 19 (February 1875): 34; 1880 census, La., Iberia Parish, New Iberia, 408/421 and 422, p. 441B; 1900 census, La., Iberia Parish, New Iberia, Dist. 34, 84/89, p. 4B; Joe M. Richardson, " 'Labor is Rest to Me,' " 5–20.

26. Hood, *One Hundred Years,* 202; *AM* 11 (April 1867): 74; *AM* 12 (April 1868):

74; *AM* 13 (May 1869): 100; *AM* 14 (June 1870): 122; Maxine D. Jones, " 'They Are My People,' " 80–81; Huddle, "To Educate a Race," 135–60; West, "The Harris Brothers," 126–38; Joe M. Richardson, *Christian Reconstruction*, 195.

27. 1870 census, Ky., Nelson Co., Bloomfield, 6/56, p. 102; Charles W. Keyes to J. W. Alvord, 5 February 1870, Ed. Div., BRFAL, M803:11; C. W. Harris, 5 August 1871, Letter H88, p. 143, Register of LR, Vol. 1., Supt. of Public Instruction, State of Texas, Ms. 2-7/760; Register of Teachers' Certificates, 1871–1873, Supt. of Public Instruction, State of Texas, Ms. 2-7/646, pp. 286–87, TSLA; 1880 census, Tex., Liberty Co., 54/54, p. 231B; personal correspondence, Mark A. Furnish, 6 June 2007.

28. It is often not possible to establish the slave or free status of African Americans. If they appear in the decennial census, they were most likely free. However, many free blacks avoided census takers, and census takers may have not bothered to enumerate free blacks. See Adele Logan Alexander's remarkable study of free blacks in Georgia, *Ambiguous Lives: Free Women of Color in Rural Georgia, 1789–1879*.

29. For examples of those writing in a practiced hand, see for example Josephine Tipton, raised in Augusta, Georgia, but teaching in Dallas County, Ala., in 1869: Tipton, TMSR, April 1869, SR, Alabama BRFAL, M810:7; Solomon Derry, definitely a former slave who taught for many years and wrote in a particularly clear, firm hand: Solomon Derry to R. D. Harper, 20 April 1868, LR, Alabama BRFAL, 810:2; or Thomas J. White, a native Tennessean who began teaching in Columbia, Tenn., in 1864: Thomas J. White to D. Burt, 30 October 1866, LR, Tennessee BRFAL, M1000:3.

30. About 37 percent of the southern black teachers were women. In the fifteen years covered by this study, southern black male teachers taught for an average of 2.7 years, while southern black women taught for more than 2.8 years. Note, however, that the gender disparity may be in part an artifact of the sources used to identify the teachers. Particularly after the collapse of the Freedmen's Bureau and of many of the northern aid societies, the census is one of the more-important sources for identifying teachers and their total years served. However, southern census takers commonly failed to indicate women's occupations, or simply noted them as "keeping house" or "at home." Many women teachers, black and white, may have continued teaching beyond the end of the bureau records, but their careers are now lost to historians.

31. The mean age of the black teachers in their first year of teaching was 26.1, while for white teachers the mean was 31.9 years. Black men were significantly older than black women when they began teaching. See Appendix A, table 6-A. Data drawn from the Freedmen's Teacher Project.

32. The percentage of married women was slightly higher for southern black teachers (32 percent) than for northern black teachers (28 percent); about one in ten is known to have been a widow (33 of 372 were referred to as Mrs.). The marital status of about one-fifth of the black women teachers is not yet known. Because men's marital status is not indicated in the common honorifics (Mrs. and Miss in contrast to Mr. or Rev.), men's marital status is less often known for men in the Freedmen's Teacher Project.

33. The social class of northern white teachers is explored in Chapter 4. In 1850, 1860, and 1870, the decennial federal census asked individuals about their financial worth. In 1850, the question asked for an estimate of total wealth; in the following two censuses, the question asked for an estimate of two forms of wealth, real estate and personal estate (the latter included most forms of wealth other than land, including the value of slaves). The data must be used cautiously, of course, since it was self-reported; respondents may have intentionally inflated or deflated their estimates for any of a number of reasons. Further, if the wealth holder was not at home when the census taker arrived, others estimated the wealth, probably inaccurately. Still, with caveats, historians have found the data to have some value. Among many others, see Soltow, "Economic Inequality," 822–39; Steckel, "Poverty and Prosperity," 275–85; Winkle, "U.S. Census as a Source," 565–77; and Soltow, *Men and Wealth.*

34. The median wealth for the black teachers was $500 in 1860; by 1870, with many southern black teachers included in the data, the median wealth was $0. Because of a few very wealthy teachers or families of teachers, the mean wealth for the black teachers in 1860 ($n = 99$) was $2,708; in 1870 ($n = 535$) the mean was $896. On national wealth estimates, see Soltow, "Economic Inequality"; Kearl and Pope, "Wealth Mobility: The Missing Element," 461–88.

35. 1860 census, Penn., Philadelphia 3 Ward, 1026/1242, p. 381; 1870 census, Penn., Philadelphia 3 Ward, 1077/1293, p. 549; *AF* 3 (April 1869): 15; Mary E. Cornish to W. L. Vanderlip, 4 October 1870, LR, Ed. Div., BRFAL, M803:10.

36. 1860 census, N.Y., Chemung Co., Elmira, 1197/1160, p. 536; J. M. Langston to O. O. Howard, 25 July 1867, LR, Ed. Div., BRFAL, M803:7; William A. Jones to George W. Whipple, 14 October 1868, AMAA; *AM* 13 (May 1869): 101; *AM* 14 (June 1870): 128; *AM* 15 (May 1871): 100; *AM* 16 (May 1872): 100; 1880 census, N.Y., Chemung Co., Elmira, Dist. 70, 193/270, p. 283A. The Jones family cannot be found in the 1870 census; the 1880 census did not record family wealth.

37. 1870 census, Ala., Mobile Co., Mobile, 1002/1189, p. 203; 1900 census, Ala., Mobile Co., Mobile Dist 94, 38/39, p. 2B; Horton and Horton, *In Memory of You,* 38.

38. Francis P. Johnson, TMSR, October 1867, SR, Georgia BRFAL, M799:21; Frank Johnson, 1870 census, Ga., Richmond Co., Augusta, 422/501, p. 173; Francis P. Johnson, Application #4935, 2 September 1872, Augusta Branch, Register of Signators, FSTC; 1880 census, Ga., Richmond Co., Augusta, 176/180, p. 374A. On the Freedmen's Savings and Trust Company, see Osthaus, *Freedmen, Philanthropy, and Fraud.*

39. 1850 census, N.C., Warren Co., Warren Twp., 779/779, p. 56; 1860 census, N.C., Warren Co., Warrenton, 96/96, p. 244; 1870 census, N.C., Warren Co., Twp. 19, Littleton PO, 148/148, p. 510.

40. Mosko Barte [*sic*], 1870 census, Md., Baltimore Co., Baltimore 19 Ward, 1139/1413, p. 329. Most of his wealth, $20,000, was in real estate.

41. Martha attended Oberlin Academy from 1860 to 1866, Mary from 1863 to 1870: Oberlin College, *Seventy-fifth Anniversary General Catalogue,* 514; AMA, *Twentieth Annual Report* (1866), 34; *AM* 11 (April 1867): 77; *AM* 12 (April 1868): 78; *AM* 13 (May 1869): 105; *AM* 16 (May 1872): 99; *AM* 17 (September 1873): 197;

AMA, *28th Annual Report* (1874), 39: *AM* 19 (February 1875): 32; Thomas Jarvis, 203 1860 census, Ohio, Lorain Co., Russia Twp., Oberlin, 231/232, p. 199; 1870 census, Ohio, Lorain Co., Oberlin, 261/258, p. 627.

42. Alfred Jones, 1860 census, D.C., Washington 1 Ward, 1469/1465, p. 410; 1870 census, D.C., Washington 1 Ward, 667/870, p. 184; 1880 census, D.C., Washington, 249/347, p. 266D. One of his daughters, Matilda, attended Oberlin College for two years and had been a student of Myrtilla Miner prior to that; the other two sisters who taught probably also attended the Miner School: Oberlin College, *Seventy-fifth Anniversary General Catalogue*, 532; ABHMS, *Baptist Home Missions*, 563; U.S. Office of Education, *Special Report*, 263; Washington, D.C. Superintendent of Colored Schools of Washington and Georgetown, *Annual Report* (1871–72), 48; ibid. (1872–73), 54; ibid. (1873–74), 48.

43. Northern black teachers attended at least eighteen different northern colleges and universities. Four of the black teachers had attended institutions outside the country: King's Institute and University of Toronto (Ontario, Canada); Codrington College (British West Indies); and the University of Glasgow (Scotland). Four of the northern colleges were self-consciously interracial: Eleutherian, Iberia, New York Central, and Oberlin.

44. All of these numbers are conservative. They constitute all the teachers in the Freedmen's Teacher Project who have been positively identified as having attended those schools.

45. William F. Allen Diary, 30 November 1864 and 23 December 1864, typescript, 68, 80–81 (quotation 81), WSHS, all spelling *sic*.

46. [Edward L. Pierce], "The Freedmen at Port Royal," *Atlantic Monthly* 12 (September 1863): 307.

47. Ruth A. Grimes to E. A. Ware, 29 February 1868, LR, Georgia BRFAL, M799:10.

48. Felix Smith, TMSR, December 1869, January and March 1870, SR, Virginia BRFAL, M1053:18; C. S. Schaeffer to R. M. Manly, 7 February 1870, LR, Virginia BRFAL, M1053:5.

49. Robinson's school was first described in NYYM, *Report of a Committee*, 8; Robinson provided a synopsis of the school's history in C. Robinson to John H. Cook, 6 June 1870, LR, Ed. Div., BRFAL, M803:10; C. Robinson to John H. Cook, 2 December 1870, LR, Ed. Div., BRFAL, 803:11; see also "A Brief Sketch of the 'Beulah' School" (flyer, undated but after June 1866), in Records of the Rhode Island Association of Freedmen, 1864–1867, RIHS; on the next six institutions for teacher education, see Sarah E. Chase to Fred W. G. May, 18 November 1864, Chase Family Papers, AAS; *NF* 1 (July 1865): 203; *FR* 1 (March 1865): 42; *FR* 1 (July 1865): 110; *FR* 1 (August 1865): 129; *FR* 1 (September 1865): 139; *FF* 1 (December 1867): 117; United Presbyterian Church of North America, *Minutes of the Seventh General Assembly*, vol. 2, no. 2, p. 187; Presbyterian Church USA, *First Annual Report* (1866), 17–19; *AM* 11 (January 1867): 11–12; on subsequent development of teacher education for southern African Americans, see Butchart and Rolleri, "Secondary Education and Emancipation," 157–81.

50. In addition to Beulah Normal, these include a high school in Tarboro, N.C.,

established by James H. M. Jackson; the J. P. Butler Institute in Jamesville, N.C.; the Sumner School (later Howard School) in Fayetteville, N.C.; Payne College, Newberry, S.C.; and Caine Institute in Charleston, S.C. Compiled from "List of High or Normal Schools, Colleges and Universities in the State of North Carolina," in H. C. Vogell to John W. Alvord, 6 June 1870, LR, North Carolina BRFAL, M844:11; Manning and Booker, *Martin County History*, 1:119; Foner, *Freedom's Lawmakers*, 34; Huddle, "To Educate a Race," 135–60; Benjamin W. Arnett, comp. and ed., *The Budget; Containing the Annual Reports*, 19–21; Alvord, *Tenth Semi-Annual Report* (July 1870), 52; and Klein, *Survey of Negro Colleges*, 471–72.

51. Lincoln Institute, *Lincoln Institute*; Henry Sullivan Williams, "Development of the Negro Public School System," 152–53.

52. Georgia Educational Association, "A New Plan for Educating the Freedmen of the South," circular, n.p. (1867), Ed. Div. BRFAL, M803:12.

53. Butchart and Rolleri, "Secondary Education and Emancipation," 157–70.

54. "Department of the South. The Educational Progress," *FA* 1 (March 1864): 10. On normal classes, see also Alvord, *Sixth Semi-Annual Report* (July 1868), 67.

55. *PFB* (April 1866): 5–6; William F. Mitchell to James Miller McKim, 6 December 1867, AFUC Papers, CU (emphasis in original).

56. *PFB* (April 1866): 5–6; *FF* 1 (March 1868): [2]; AMA, *Twenty-first Annual Report* (1867), 16–17; history and organization of Friends' Freedman Association, in M. E. Sherman to J. W. Alvord, 27 November 1867, LR, Ed. Div., BRFAL, M803:6 (quotation).

57. *AM* 11 (January 1867): 11–12.

58. *CR*, 18 July 1868: 66. Waring had studied at Oberlin Academy and for two years at Oberlin College before starting his career in Florence. He taught among the freed slaves for the Freedmen's Bureau in Florence from 1867 to 1869, and for the Presbyterian Committee on Missions to the Freedmen in Winchester, Va., from 1869 to 1872. He subsequently earned a law degree and may have practiced law briefly but returned to education, teaching mathematics at Alcorn College, serving as principal of a high school in Louisville, then becoming the first black principal at Charles Sumner High School in St. Louis, serving there from 1879 until his retirement in 1908. St. Louis named an elementary school in his honor, the Oscar M. Waring Elementary School, in 1940. C. W. Buckley to J. W. Alvord, 14 February 1867, LR, Ed. Div., BRFAL, M803:6; *CR*, 18 July 1868: 66; Oscar M. Waring, Grads & Formers File, Alumni Records, OC.

59. Jane B. Smith to Friend Fuller Fiske, 12 January 1868, Jane Briggs Smith Fiske Papers, AAS.

60. Adam H. Erwin to F. A. Fiske, 14 January 1868, and Erwin to Fiske, 18 February 1868, LR, North Carolina BRFAL, M844:7.

61. Monroe Fullenwider, 1870 census, N.C., Lincoln Co., Ironton Twp., Lincolnton PO, 31/39, p. 165.

62. J. L. Evans, Register of LR, North Carolina BRFAL, M844:6; Thomas H. Hay to F. A. Fiske, 22 June 1868, LR, ibid., M844:8; William P. Hays to F. A. Fiske, 6 May 1868, ibid., M844:7.

63. Laura Holt to J. R. Lewis, 19 August 1869, LR, Georgia BRFAL, M799:13;

William A Clark to J. R. Lewis, 31 July 1869, ibid.; Annie V. Bond to D. Burt, 26 June 1867, LR, Tennessee BRFAL, M1000:3; Bond to James Thompson, 14 November 1868, ibid., M1000:4.

64. C. C. Singleton to J. R. Lewis, 27 July 1869, LR, Georgia BRFAL, M799:13.

65. Laura Holt to J. R. Lewis, 19 August 1869, LR, Georgia BRFAL, M799:13.

66. Deveaux was well educated, judging from his letters to the bureau, was from Savannah, and was no doubt related to Jane Deveaux, the long-time Savannah black educator, though no firm evidence has yet been located to confirm that.

67. William P. Lloyd to W. P. Carlin, 18 November 1868, LR, Tennessee BRFAL, M1000:4.

68. See for example Jacob D. Enos to J. R. Lewis, 15 September 1869, LR, Georgia BRFAL, M799:13; Hermann Bokum to D. Burt, 2 March 1867, LR, Tennessee BRFAL, M1000:3; John Durdin to G. L. Eberhart, 19 November 1866, LR, Georgia BRFAL, M799:8; J. L. McDowell to Theodore S. Palmer, 14 March 1869, LR, Tennessee BRFAL, M1000:4; Reuben P. Clark to E. D. Compton, 7 June 1869, ibid. On the bureau's education work, see Cimbala, "Making Good Yankees," 5–18; Kenneth B. White, "The Alabama Freedmen's Bureau"; Hornsby, "The Freedmen's Bureau Schools," 397–417; Joe M. Richardson, "The Freedmen's Bureau," 460–67; Abbott, "The Freedmen's Bureau," 65–81; Lowe, "The Freedmen's Bureau and Education," 29–39; Alderson, "The Freedmen's Bureau," 64–90; Luther P. Jackson, "The Educational Efforts," 1–40.

69. Butchart, *Northern Schools*, 97–114.

70. Lucy Brown to F. A. Fiske, 21 March 1868, LR, North Carolina BRFAL, M844:7; Fiske to Brown, 9 April 1868, LS, ibid., M844:3; Lem K. Harris to H. C. Vogell, 22 October 1868, LR, ibid., M844:8.

71. Allen A. Williams, TMSR for May through December 1866, SR, Alabama BRFAL, M810:6; W. H. H. Peck to C. D. Kinsman, 26 April 1866, Register of LR, ibid., M810:3 (emphasis in original); Charles C. Arms to C. W. Buckley, 25 February 1867, ibid.; Arms to Buckley, 4 March 1867, ibid.; Allen Williams, 1870 census, Ala., Montgomery Co., Twp. 14, Range 20, 1014/1014, p. 163.

72. Solomon Derry to R. D. Harper, 20 April 1868, LR, Alabama BRFAL, M810:2; Derry to Harper, 27 April 1868, LR, ibid.

73. R. D. Harper to Solomon Derry, 23 April 1868, Letterbook, Vol. 2, LS, Alabama BRFAL, M810:1.

74. Derry to Harper, 27 April 1868, LR, Alabama BRFAL, M810:2, grammatical construction *sic*.

75. H. M. Bush to Solomon Derry, 1 May 1868, Letterbook, vol. 2, LS, Alabama BRFAL, 810:1.

76. There were several teachers' reports from Union Springs prior to the spring of 1867, but none thereafter; the school there apparently remained an independent endeavor even after the state began supporting black schools, for neither the school nor Derry appear in the manuscript state school reports in the Alabama state archives. On Derry's career, see Hood, *One Hundred Years*, 370–74; on Atwater, see R. S. Rush to R. D. Harper, 9 April 1868, LR, Alabama BRFAL, M810:2; *FF* 1 (May 1869): 12; *FF* 1 (November 1869): 5.

77. Hermann Bokum to D. Burt, 2 March 1867, LR, Tennessee BRFAL, M1000:3.

78. Data drawn from the Freedmen's Teacher Project.

79. D. Burt to William P. Carlin, 8 May 1867, LS, Letter Press Book, p. 332, Tennessee BRFAL, M1000:1.

80. "Sub-Assistant Commissioner's (or Agent's) Monthly Report on Education of Freedmen and Refugees in 2nd Div., 9th Sub-District, State of Virginia . . ., April 1868," SR, Virginia BRFAL, M1053:13; "Monthly School Report of the 9th Sub-District, District of Virginia, [November 1868]," ibid., M1053:12; TMSR, April 1869, ibid., M1053:15; TMSR, October 1869, ibid., M1053:17; TMSR, December 1869, ibid., M1053:18; *AM* 13 (May 1869): 100; *AM* 14 (June 1870): 122. William had been enslaved in Virginia but freed himself early in the war. He moved to Massachusetts, where he met Sarah and attended school before returning to Virginia. He died in 1873, just after he and Sarah moved to Savannah—he as a minister, she as teacher: *AM* 17 (September 1873): 214.

81. Junius B. Jones, 1860 census, Ohio, Lorain Co., Oberlin, 282/283, p. 202; Junius B. Jones to James Thompson, 8 January 1869, LR, Tennessee BRFAL, M1000:4; *AM* 13 (May 1869): 103; Jones, Grads & Formers File, Alumni Records, OC.

82. Long, *History of the A.M.E. Church*, 188–89. Waterman's sister, G. G. Waterman, began teaching in Lake City in 1875; she established Finley High School in Lake City in 1889: ibid., 189.

83. Frank McKeel: 1870 census, Ala., Randolph Co., Louina Twp., 184/184, p. 583; "Annual Report of T. W. Greer, County Supt. for Chambers County, Ala., for year 1871," in Reports on Conditions of Schools, 1868–1869, [*sic*], Ala. Supt. of Public Instruction, ASA; 1880 census, Ga., Decatur Co., Bainbridge, 68–69, p. 118B; 1900 census, La., Caddo Parish, Shreveport 5 Ward, 403/549, p. 18B; Hicks, *History of Louisiana Negro Baptists*, 198.

84. Bryant: Register of Monthly Rents for School Buildings, p. W, Misc. Records, North Carolina BRFAL, M844:16; *AM* 17 (September 1873): 194; Wake County, N.C., County Board of Education, Minutes, 1872–1885, p. 26, NCSA; 1880 census, N.C., Wake Co., South East Raleigh, 615/691, p. 274B. Moore: AMA, *Twentieth Annual Report* (1864), 24; *AM* 13 (May 1869): 100; Application #3426, 7 March 1873, New Bern Branch, Register of Signatures, FSTC; Hood, *One Hundred Years*, 285–87. Swanson: TMSR, September 1868, SR, Georgia BRFAL, M799:22; TMSR, April 1869, ibid., M799:23; TMSR, June 1869, ibid., M799:24; 1880 census, Ga., Fulton, Atlanta, 127/210, p. 221C.

85. Bomar: Inez Moore Parker, *The Rise and Decline*, 187–88. Chresfield: Presbyterian Church USA, *First Annual Report* (1866), 12; ibid., *Second Annual Report* (1867), 27; ibid., *Third Annual Report* (1868), 32; ibid., *Fourth Annual Report* (1869), 55; ibid., *Fifth Annual Report* (1870), 25; Presbyterian Church USA, *Report of the Presbyterian Committee of Missions for Freedmen* (1870), 5; ibid. (1874), n.p. Mary Chresfield died after five years of teaching, but James was supported by the Presbyterian Church into the late 1870s or beyond; he remarried in 1873, and his new wife also taught with him. Billings: *FR* 2 (March 1866): 59; *FR* 2 (November 1866): 203; *FR* 3 (November 1867): 176; *FR* 4 (May 1868): 84; *FR* 4 (November

1868): 180; *FR* 5 (January 1871): 103; "Schools & Teachers, NEFAS," p. 78, and
"Schools & Teachers, NEFAS," p. 84, NEFAS Records, MHS. Miller: *AM* 13 (May
1869): 100; *AM* 14 (June 1870): 122; *AM* 15 (May 1871): 98; *AM* 16 (May 1872): 98;
AM 17 (September 1873): 194; AMA, *Twenty-eighth Annual Report* (1874), 42; *AM*
19 (February 1875): 31. Mallory: *AM* 11 (April 1867): 76; *AM* 12 (April 1868): 76;
AM 13 (May 1869): 103; *AM* 15 (May 1871): 99; *AM* 16 (May 1872): 99; *AM* 17
(September 1873): 197; *AM* 19 (February 1875): 33; Congregational Church, *Con-
gregational Yearbook* (1893), 31.

86. Daffin: AMA, *Eighteenth Annual Report* (1864), 25; AMA, *Nineteenth Annual Report* (1865), 19; AMA, *Twentieth Annual Report* (1866), 17; *AM* 11 (April
1867): 73; Robert R. Corson to Sarah L. Daffin, 13 October 1867, FFA, Letterbook of
the Instruction Committee, vol. 2, Department of Records, Philadelphia Society of
Friends, Philadelphia, Pa.; D. Burt to Sallie L. Daffin, 25 March 1868, LS, Letterbook, p. 723, LS, Tennessee BRFAL, M1000:1; James Thompson to John W. Alvord,
11 January 1869, LR, Ed. Div., BRFAL, M803:12. Thompson: U.S. Office of Education, *Special Report*, 290; *AF* 3 (April 1869): 11; *FR* 5 (January 1871): 102; NEFAS,
"Daily Journal, 1871–1873," pp. 33, 40, NEFAS Papers, MHS. Alexander: *AM* 11
(April 1867): 75; AMA, *American Missionary Association*, 6; *FF* 1 (April 1872): 1;
Louisa L. Alexander, Graduates and Formers Files, College Archives, OC; Oberlin
College, *Seventy-fifth Anniversary General Catalogue*, 12. Miles: Mary E. Miles "To
the Ladies of the Woman Aid Association," 1 June 1866, LR, FFA, Women's Aid
Committee, HC; *SoM* 31 (December 1867): 820; *SoM* 33 (April 1868): 326; *FF* 1
(November 1869): 2; *FF* 1 (December 1870): 2; *FF* 1 (December 1871): 6; *FF* 1
(December 1872): 6; *FF* 1 (January 1874): 4; *FF* 1 (November 1874): 2; *FF* 1 (January
1875): 1.

87. Patterns of aid society hiring deduced from data in the Freedmen's Teacher
Project.

88. *AM* 10 (November 1866): 242.

89. Alvord, *Seventh Semi-Annual Report* (January 1869), 24.

90. Sara G. Stanley to George Whipple, 6 October 1864, AMAA; Sears, *Camp
Nelson, Kentucky*, lvi–lvii, lxxvii, n. 210.

91. Joe M. Richardson, *Christian Reconstruction*, 190–91; McPherson, "White
Liberals and Black Power," 1357–86.

92. *FA* 1 (Sept 1864): 29; *Charleston Courier*, 28 June 1867, 1; "Bi-Monthly Report
of Schools in 1st Sub-Dist BRF and A Lands District of Virginia in accordance with
Cir. No. 17. . . . For the two (2) Months Ending on the 30th Day of April 1868," SR,
Virginia BRFAL, M1053:14; Fannie B. Waring, TMSR, April 1869, SR, Virginia
BRFAL, M1053:15; "A Brief Sketch of the 'Beulah' School" (flyer, undated, probably
1866), in "Records of the Rhode Island Association of Freedmen, 1864–1867,"
RIHS; Robert Harris, "Superintendent's Monthly Report of Schools," February
1867, AMAA; Louis B. Toomer, "Report of Oglethorpe School," 30 June 1866, SR,
Georgia BRFAL, M799:20; FFA, "Statistics of Schools, 1866–1868," FFA Papers, SC.

93. American Baptist Free Mission Society, *Twenty-first Annual Report* (1864),
11; *FA* 1 (January 1864): 3; *FA* 1 (June 1864): 21; *FA* 1 (November 1864): 40; *NF* 1
(February 1865): 38; *NF* 2 (June 1866): 181; *NF* 2 (September 1866): 232; *AF* 2 (July

1867): 255; *AF* 2 (October 1867): 301; *AF* 3 (October 1868): 11; *AF* 3 (April 1869): 11; American Freedmen's Union Commission, "Commission Book," n.p., in AFUC Papers, CU; Application #272, 14 December 1867, Richmond Branch, Register of Signatures, FSTC; Application #3839, 5 April 1870, Beaufort Branch, Register of Signatures, FSTC; Application #8390, 4 December 1873, Vicksburg Branch, Register of Signatures, FSTC; Harry V. Richardson, *Dark Salvation*, 192–93; Clarence E. Walker, *A Rock in a Weary Land*, 66.

94. Dyson, *Howard University*, 242, 383–84; Logan, *Howard University*, 51; ABHMS, *Baptist Home Missions*, 583; *AM* 16 (May 1872): 100; *AM* 17 (September 1873): 200; AMA, *Twenty-eighth Annual Report* (1874), 40; Foner, *Freedom's Lawmakers*, 180–81, 211–12. Other information compiled from Freedmen's Teacher Project.

95. The Freedmen's Teacher Project has, to date, positively identified 242 black Union veterans who taught in the freed people's schools, using Compiled Service Records, the Civil War Pension Records, ACWS, and USCWS. It is likely that upwards of double that number actually served in the Union forces. However, because of the number of black soldiers with names similar to the names of known teachers, positive identification is often impossible.

96. Swails: Co. F, 54 Mass. Inf., CSR; Pension Cert. No. 357160, CWPR. Clark: Pension Cert. No. 930554, CWPR. Nocho: Beatrice Suggs Banner, "Jacob Robert Nocho," typescript, undated, in Nocho Park File, Vertical File, Museum Archives, Greensboro Historical Museum.

97. NEFAS, "Daily Record. Freedmen's Aid Society. [7 January 1865 to 11 September 1866]," p. 136; *FR* 1 (July 1865): 119; and *FR* 2 (April 1867): 205; ABHMS, *Baptist Home Missions*, 611; Mary J. R. Richards to G. L. Eberhardt, 22 February 1867, LR, Georgia BRFAL, M799:8; Mary J. R. Richards, TMSR, April 1867, SR, ibid., M799:20. Richards first told her story of working for the Union secret service in *AF* 2 (April 1867): 205; the story is verified and amplified in Varon, *Southern Lady, Yankee Spy*, 28–30, 165–68.

98. Foner, *Freedom's Lawmakers*, 180–81; Marszalek, *Black Congressman*; *FA* 1 (January 1864): 3; *NF* 1 (February 1865): 38; Powers, *Black Charlestonians*, 150; William C. Harris, "James Lynch," 40–61; Rothrock, "Joseph Carter Corbin," 277–314; Joe M. Richardson, "Jonathan C. Gibbs," 363–68.

99. Based on data from Freedmen's Teacher Project and analyses of the city directories for the District of Columbia, Baltimore, Petersburg, and Charleston, 1865–1880.

100. Quoted in Joe M. Richardson, *Christian Reconstruction*, 192. Booth went on to teach in Missouri and Texas for several years.

101. G. W. Bryant to Samuel Shellabarger, February 1867, LR, Ed. Div., BRFAL, M803:8.

102. Robert Harris to H. C. Vogell, 12 November 1868, Unregistered LR, North Carolina BRFAL, M844:10.

103. C. C. McKinney to "Gentlemen of the American Missionary Association," 11 December 1865, AMAA.

104. Quoted in Mansfield, "That Fateful Class," 189, emphasis in original.

105. Mary A. Best to W. W. Holden, 2 February 1869, Unregistered LR, North Carolina BRFAL, M844:11. Holden forwarded Best's letter to the Freedmen's Bureau; neither the state nor the bureau appears to have assisted her.

106. Robert P. Martin to F. A. Fiske, 30 September 1867, LR, North Carolina BRFAL, M844:7.

107. Robert Harris to H. C. Vogell, 7 June 1869, LR, North Carolina BRFAL, M844:9.

108. Edmonia G. Highgate to S. S. Jocelyn, 30 January 1864, AMAA; *CR* 6 (7 July 1866): 105. Leon Litwack has argued that among black teachers, as among white teachers in the freedmen's schools, moral concerns overwhelmed political concerns in education. There is little in the black teachers' expression of their motivations or in their teaching practices that sustains the claim, particularly in contrast to white teachers. Litwack, *Been in the Storm So Long*, 455–62. On the issue of racial uplift as it played itself out in the twentieth century, see Gaines, *Uplifting the Race*; on the discourse of black manhood in the postbellum black community, see Shaffer, *After the Glory*, esp. Chapter 1.

109. On the evolution of racial uplift ideology, the heir to the language of elevation, see Gaines, *Uplifting the Race*.

110. Charles Highgate, 1860 census, N.Y., Onondaga Co., Syracuse 7 Ward, 430/552, p. 68; *New York Weekly Anglo-African*, 28 December 1861; *Binghamton Standard*, 31 December 1862; Edmonia G. Highgate to M. E. Strieby, 17 December 1866, AMAA; D. H. Cruttenden "To the Friends of Education," 26 January 1864, AMAA. The date of Charles Highgate's death is approximate; he is listed in the 1860 census, but Hannah Francis Highgate is listed as widow of Charles in the 1862 Syracuse *City Directory*. For a more-complete biography of two of the sisters, from which portions of the following sketch is drawn, see Butchart, "Edmonia G. and Caroline V. Highgate," 1–13.

111. Edmonia G. Highgate to S. S. Jocelyn, 30 January 1864, AMAA.

112. Highgate to S. S. Jocelyn, 17 February 1864; Highgate to M. E. Strieby, telegram, 6 March 1865; Highgate to George Whipple, 13 April 1864; Highgate, "Monthly Report of Darlington School for the Month of March, 1865"; H. F. Highgate to N. Noyes, 5 July 1865, all in AMAA.

113. *CR* 6 (17 March 1866): 41; *CR* 6 (7 July 1866): 105.

114. *CR* 6 (7 July 1866): 105.

115. U.S. Congress, House Reports, "New Orleans Riots"; Rable, *But There Was No Peace*, 43–58.

116. *CR* 6 (18 August 1866): 129; Highgate to M. E. Strieby, 17 December 1866, AMAA (quotation); *CR* 6 (3 November 1866): 173, *CR* 7 (6 July 1867): 1.

117. "Report of Committee on Colored Schools," 16 September 1867, in Orleans Parish School Board, Minutes, August 29, 1865–June 2, 1869 (no. 7, pp. 209–10), Orleans Parish School Board Meetings and Related Committees, NOU. Louisiana was the only southern state to attempt to sustain racially integrated schools during Reconstruction. The interviews with the black teachers were apparently related to efforts to add a segregation clause to the state constitution. See Harlan, "Desegregation in New Orleans Public Schools," 663–75; Vaughn, *Schools for All*, 78–102.

118. Frank R. Chase to J. W. Alvord, 2 March 1867, LR, Ed. Div., BRFAL, M803:6; *CR* 7 (16 November 1867): 183; *AF* (April 1869): 15.

119. *AF* 3 (October 1868): 9; *CR* 9 (16 January 1869): 2; Charles Highgate, Co. B, 185th N.Y. Inf., CSR.

120. Quoted in Sterling, *We Are Your Sisters*, 301.

121. Current, *Those Terrible Carpetbaggers*, 179–80; A. T. Morgan, *Yazoo*, 345–46.

122. E. G. Highgate to E. P. Smith, 23 June 1870, AMAA.

123. Sterling, *We Are Your Sisters*, 301–4.

124. [Lincoln University] *Alumni Magazine* 1 (February 1885): 36; Lincoln University, *Statistical Catalogue*, 19; Talbert, *Sons of Allen*, 74–75. It is not yet clear how long Hannah Francis, James, or Willella taught, though some evidence suggests they were still teaching in Mississippi to at least mid-decade.

125. H. F. Highgate to George Whipple, 23 April 1864, AMAA.

126. Edmonia G. Highgate, "Monthly Report of Darlington School for the Month of March, 1865," AMAA.

127. James D. Anderson, *Education of Blacks in the South*, 4–32; Butchart and Rolleri, "Secondary Education and Emancipation," 157–81.

128. Ida S. Marshall to O. O. Howard, 7 March 1867, LR, Ed. Div., BRFAL, M803:7.

Chapter 3

1. Stell had migrated to Texas from Florida with her family before 1860; while in Florida, the family had owned eight slaves: 1850 census, Slave Schedule, Fla., Jacksonville, Div. 4, p. 371; 1850 census, Fla., Jacksonville, Div. 4, 305/314, p. 305 (identified as Mary J. Stell); 1860 census, Tex., DeWitt Co., 96/96, p. 462 (identified as Josephine Stell); Josie Stell to Joseph Welch, 7 March 1868, LR, Texas BRFAL, M822:8; Stell to Gov. Pease, 9 June 1868, ibid.; A. K. Foster to Joseph Welch, 8 October 1868, LR, Texas BRFAL, M822:5; Stell to Welch, 8 Sept 1869, ibid.

2. John Caldwell: 1860 census, Ga., Coweta Co., Newnan, 166/154, p. 694; 1860 census, Slave Schedule, Ga., Coweta Co., Newnan, p. 159; Assistant Commissioner's Monthly Report . . . for the District in Charge of Major John S. [illegible], February 1868, SR, Georgia BRFAL, M799:17; John Caldwell to O. O. Howard, 10 October 1868, LR, Ed. Div., BRFAL, M803:6; John H. Caldwell, *Reminiscences of the Reconstruction*; Lawrence, *Methodist Preachers in Georgia*, 27; Daniel W. Stowell, "We Have Sinned," 1–38.

3. Groner: 1860 census, N.C., Gaston Co., Dallas, 1365/1253, p. 90; R. G. Dun Collection, North Carolina, vol. 11, Gaston Co., p. 474a, HBS; 1870 census, N.C., Lincoln Co., Ironton, Lincolnton PO, 122/133, p. 171; William Birnie to H. C. Vogell, 30 November 1868, Unregistered LR, North Carolina BRFAL, M844:10 (quotation); "Sub-Assistant Commissioner's (or Agent's) Monthly Report on Education of Freedmen and Refugees in Sub-District, State of North Carolina, in charge of William Birnie for the month of August 1868 . . .," SR, North Carolina BRFAL, M844:15; "List of vouchers paid by Chief Disbursing Officer," in George W. Bullock to H. C. Vogell, 26 March 1870, SR, North Carolina BRFAL, M844:16.

4. The only major study of freedmen's education that deals seriously with southern teachers is Morris, *Reading, 'Riting, and Reconstruction*, 131–48. While useful, the chapter includes a number of mistaken identifications of teachers and problematic conclusions.

5. Knight, " 'Messianic' Invasion of the South," 647. See also Knight, *Influence of Reconstruction on Education*; Swint, *Northern Teacher in the South*; and Cash, *Mind of the South*.

6. South Carolina, State Superintendent of Education, *First Annual Report* (1869), 236–37; ibid., *Fourth Annual Report* (1873), 433; *Ninth Annual Report* (1877), 612.

7. In 1864, 130 of 162 teachers in New Orleans were southern whites: U.S. Army, *Report of the Board of Education*, 7–12; other data above compiled from the Freedmen's Teacher Project database. Southern white teachers comprise more than one-eighth of the teachers identified by the project. However, most of the teachers after 1870 are yet to be identified. As the data above indicates, increasing numbers of southern whites began teaching the freed people in the later years of Reconstruction.

8. For a full description of the source of these estimates, see Appendix B.

9. Over 1,600 teachers have been positively identified as southern whites. Race has not yet been determined for another 1,535; half or more were probably white. As noted earlier, the total number of southern white teachers was far higher than that, but most have not been recovered and many probably never can be. Men constituted roughly 58 percent of the southern white teachers. See table 3.

10. The mean age of southern white men in their first year of teaching was 38.1 years (median = 35 years); the mean age of southern white women was 30.0 years (median = 28 years).

11. Of the southern white women whose marital status is known, 238 were married, 63 were widowed, and 261 were single. In contrast to the 10 percent of southern white women who were widows, only 3 percent of northern white women were widows.

12. Faust, *Mothers of Invention*, 81.

13. R. M. Manly to O. O. Howard, 30 June 1869, LR, Virginia BRFAL, M1053:4. Prewar occupations have been determined for 455 of the 926 southern white male teachers whose race is certain. Data drawn from the Freedmen's Teacher Project.

14. Southern white women taught for an average of 1.66 years, while southern white men taught 1.5 years; the average across genders was 1.57 years. Data compiled from the Freedmen's Teacher Project.

15. *FR 2* (June 1866): 124; *FR 2* (November 1866): 204; Julia A. Wilson, 6 October 1868, TMSR, September 1868, SR, Georgia BRFAL, M799:22 (quotation, all spelling *sic*); Willson [*sic*], 1860 census, Ga., Talbot Co., Talbotton Twp., 426/426, p. 613; 1870 census, Ga., Talbot Co., Flinthill Dist, 1643/1639, p. 62.

16. *AF 1* (March 1867): 180; U.S. Army, *Report of the Board of Education*, 7–12; A. Toomer Porter, *Led On!* 223–24; *Petersburg (Va.) Daily Index*, 3 September 1868, 3; Freedmen's Teacher Project database.

17. Jacob Reed Ballard, TMSR, January 1870, and E. S. Thorpe, TMSR, October 1869, both in SR, Alabama BRFAL, M810:7; W. L. Coan to R. M. Manly, undated,

marked "Dec 1865" by recipient, Monthly Statistical School Reports, Virginia BRFAL, M1053:12. The Freedmen's Bureau standard monthly report form asked for teachers' perceptions of local sentiment toward education, black and white, along with extensive data on enrollment, attendance, and curriculum. As a result, literally thousands of comments on the teachers' sense of southern white attitudes toward black schools, and education for the poor in general, have survived, extending from 1866 to 1870. A majority report negative attitudes, usually toward the education of both blacks and poor whites, though more-favorable reports are not uncommon. There appears to be no clear tendency across time toward either more-favorable or less-favorable sentiments.

18. For the purposes of the Freedmen's Teacher Project, any teacher known to have lived in the South less than five years before the Civil War was identified in the database as a northerner. Those living longer in the South, and particularly those having married a southerner, are presumed to have imbibed enough southern culture to generally identify with southern values and southern racial attitudes (though, of course, the North and South were not far apart on issues of race, whatever their stances on slavery). Length of time in the South has been estimated from census notations of the ages and birthplaces of children when more-direct evidence is missing.

19. Mary A. Neely, TMSR, March 1867, May 1870, SR, Alabama BRFAL, M810:6 and 7; Annual Report of H. M. Coffey, County Supt. for Lowndes Co., Ala., for year 1871, in Reports on Conditions of Schools, 1868–1869 [sic], ASA; 1870 census, Ala., Lowndes Co., Lowndesboro, 262/283, p. 255. Grover: Harriet R. Burke to C. W. Buckley, 14 August 1867, Register of LR, Alabama BRFAL, M810:3; A. Taylor to H. M. Bush, 25 February 1868, Register of LR, Alabama BRFAL, M810:2; Edmund Grover, TMSR, October 1867 through April 1869, SR, Alabama BRFAL, M810:6 and 7; 1860 census, Ala., Macon Co., So. Div., 110/120, p. 713; 1870 census, Ala., Lowndes Co., Calhoun, 2/2, p. 422.

20. George Mutch, 1860 census, Ga., Richmond Co., Augusta 2 Ward, 516/508, p. 767; 1870 census, Ala., Lee Co., Opelika, 22/22, p. 230; George Mutch, TMSR, June 1866, LR, Alabama BRFAL, M810:6; C. W. Buckley to J. W. Alvord, 14 February 1867, LR, Ed. Div., BRFAL, M803:6.

21. Thomas Hart to Charles Haughn, 28 April 1869, LR, Texas BRFAL, M822:6; Thomas Hart, "Report of School for Freedmen," June 1870, SR, Texas BRFAL, M822:16; F. Meir to E. C. Bartholomew, 7 October 1869, LR, Texas BRFAL, M822:6; "Treasurer's Office. Payments to School Teachers, 1871–1872," 71, and "Register of Teacher Certificates 1871–1873," 282–83, Texas State Department of Public Instruction Collection, TSLA.

22. Presbyterian Church USA, Second Annual Report of the General Assembly's Committee, 26; ibid., Third Annual Report (1868), 31; ibid., Fourth Annual Report (1869), 55; Nevins, Encyclopedia of the Presbyterian Church, 1189.

23. S. C. Armstrong, "Normal-School Work Among the Freedmen," 176.

24. Morris, Reading, 'Riting, and Reconstruction, 135. There are a number of problems with his thesis, not least of which is his tendency to conflate postwar

Republican party affiliation with wartime loyalty. Genuine Unionists could be, and often were, as opposed to African American rights as were staunch secessionists. But the largest problem is the empirical claim that Unionists accounted for "a major portion" of the southern teaching cadre. The research into southern white teachers, male and female, does not sustain the claim.

25. Testimony of N. Maria Taylor, U.S. Congress, House Reports, "New Orleans Riots," 239, 392. Of eighteen teachers dismissed for their Unionist sentiments, only Mary Ann Armstrong and L. M. Richardson sought to continue teaching in African American schools. A third dismissed teacher, Clara McBride, was a northerner who had only been in New Orleans since 1860; she taught for two years in the freed people's schools: "New Orleans Riots," 398–400, 427–30; Frank R. Chase to J. W. Alvord, 2 March 1867, LR, Ed. Div., BRFAL, M803:6; Report of Committee on Colored Schools, 16 September 1867, 6 November 1867, in Orleans Parish School Board, Minutes, August 29, 1865–June 2, 1869, NOU.

26. After an exhaustive search of the Southern Claims Commission records, matching claimants against the names in the Freedmen's Teacher Project, only eighteen teachers (or parents or spouses of teachers) could be found among those who sought compensation on the grounds of loyalty to the Union—and four of those were African Americans. On the total number of claimants, see Mills, *Southern Loyalists in the Civil War*, x.

27. To date, 308 of the teachers have been positively identified as Confederate veterans; it is likely that three to six times that many of the southern white teachers in the freed people's schools had fought for the Confederacy, however. Two major problems attend the process of identifying Confederate soldiers who taught in southern black schools. First, southern military records often identify soldiers only by first initial and last name. As a result, it is virtually impossible to determine, for instance, whether one of the seven men who served from Alabama identified as either J. Stuart or James Stuart is the James H. Stuart who taught in Montgomery, Alabama, in 1871–72. The more common the last name, the more difficult it is to make positive identifications. Second, the identification of teachers in black schools is more problematic in the later years of Reconstruction than earlier. There were hundreds, if not thousands, of teachers whose names can probably never be recovered because of the paucity of school records after the early 1870s; many of those teachers doubtless were Confederate veterans.

28. "Register of Students' Names—Wofford College—Aug. 1854–Oct. 1 1880," handwritten ms., Wofford College Archives, Spartanburg, S.C.; Harris: 1860 census, S.C., Abbeville Co., 1700/1663, p. 114; 1860 census, Slave Schedule, S.C., Abbeville Co., p. 120; Alonzo Harris, Co. G, 1 S.C. Inf., ACWRD; Lawrence, *Methodist Preachers in Georgia*, 232; Harris, TMSR, SR, Georgia BRFAL, M799:21; Harris, 1870 census, Ga., Oglethorpe Co., Maxey's, 525/524, p. 225.

29. William McKell, Co. C, 14 Miss. Inf., ACWRD: "Roster of Teachers of Freedmen's Schools in the State of Mississippi," in H. R. Pease to O. O. Howard, 31 January 1870, Ed. Div., BRFAL, M803:11; McKell, 1870 census, Miss., Okibbeha Co., Police Beat 5, 494/494, p. 436.

30. Bell, *11th Virginia Infantry*, 83; *AF* 2 (July 1867): 255; *AF* 2 (October 1867): 301; *AF* 2 (January 1868): 347; *AF* 3 (October 1868): 11; *FR* 5 (April 70): 86; Lazenby: 1870 census, Va., Bedford Co., Staunton Twp., 64/62, p. 340.

31. Edwin Miller to J. T. Kirkman, 31 July 1867, LR, Texas BRFAL, M822:4 (quotation); see also, for example, R. M. Manly to H. T. Owen, 5 March 1866, LS, Virginia BRFAL, M1053:1.

32. E. T. Lamberton to H. C. Vogell, 31 August 1868, LR, North Carolina BRFAL, M844:8.

33. F. W. Boyd: 1860 census, Miss., Adams Co., Natchez PO, 890/890, p. 123; 1860 census, Slave Schedule, Miss., Adams Co., p. 40; *SoM* 33 (August 1868): 660–61.

34. The lone exception, at this point in the research, was John Thomas Clark, an Episcopal minister in Virginia who held 108 slaves in 1860. Nearly two-thirds of his $208,000 in total wealth in 1860 was human property; a decade later he was worth $27,000, still a wealthy man in 1870 Virginia. He taught the freed people for three years, 1865–68. His wife, Mary A. Clark, assisted him for two years, his son, William A. Clark, for one year. 1860 census, Va., Halifax Co., Roanoke, 862/838, p. 717; 1860 census, Slave Schedule, Va., Halifax Co., Northern Dist., pp. 332–33; 1870 census, Va., Halifax Co., Roanoke, 13/13, p. 621; J. R. Stone, "Supplement to School Report for December 1866 for 2nd Dist." Monthly Statistical School Reports; Stone, "Supplement to School Report for June 1867," Monthly Statistical School Reports; "District Superintendent's Monthly School Report on Education of Freedmen and Refugees . . ., November 1867, 11th Sub-District . . .," Monthly Statistical School Reports; "District Superintendent's Monthly School Report on Education of Freedmen and Refugees . . ., February 1868, 11th Sub-District . . .," Monthly Statistical School Reports, Virginia BRFAL, M1053:12; *SoM* 31 (December 1866): 728; *SoM* 31 (December 1867): 820; *SoM* 33 (April 1868): 326.

35. Goodman: 1860 census, Va., Louisa Co., Northern Dist., 407/407, p. 819; 1860 census, Slave Schedule, Va., Louisa Co., Northern Division, p. 277; George A. Goodman, Co. C, 13 Va. Inf., ACWRD; 1870 census, Va., Louisa Co., Northern District, 1613/1542, p. 365; Virginia Superintendent of Public Instruction, *Virginia School Report* (1871), 88; ibid. (1878), 99. Goodman continued to teach after 1878, but whether in black or white schools is not known: 1880 census, Va., Louisa Co., 243/265, p. 193.

36. Flake: 1860 census, N.C., Anson Co., Lanesboro, 442/402, p. 247; 1860 census, Slave Schedule, N.C., Anson Co., Lanesboro, p. 41; Francis Flake, Co. K, 43 N.C. Inf., ACWRD; William McFarland, "Sub-Assistant Commissioner's (or Agent's) Monthly Report . . . For the Month of July 1868," North Carolina BRFAL, M844:15; ibid., August 1868; ibid., September 1868; McFarland to H. C. Vogell, 26 October 1868, Unregistered LR, North Carolina BRFAL, M844:10; 1870 census, N.C., Anson Co., Lanesboro, 33/31, p. 351. Of Flake's four slaves, two were small children and a third was ten years of age; the adult, presumably the mother of the children, was his only adult slave.

37. Rain: 1860 census, Ala., Washington Co., City of St. Stephens, 25/25 and 26/26, p. 964; 1860 census, Slave Schedule, Ala., Washington Co., p. 440; Benton Rain, Co. H, Murphy's Batt. Ala. Cav., and Co. K, 15 Ala. Cav., ACWRD; 1870 census,

1872, 311; ibid., 1873, 297; ibid., 1874, 295; ibid., 1876, 302; Rain Family File, Local
History and Genealogy Library, Mobile Public Library.

38. Hixon: 1860 census, Ala., Butler Co., Precinct 11, 1661/1661, p. 202; Ezra
Hixon, Co. D, 59 Ala. Inf., USCWS; "Consolidated Monthly Report of Wm. Seawell,
Supt. of Ed. for Butler Co, 31 July 1870," Butler Co., Ala. Dept. of Ed. Papers, ASA;
"Annual Report of J. M. Thigpen, County Supt. for Butler County, Ala, for the Year
1871," in "Annual Report on the Condition of Education in Each County," Ala. Dept.
of Ed., ASA; "Consolidated Monthly Report of Wm. Seawell, Supt of Education for
Butler Co, Jan, Feb, and March, 1874," Butler Co., Ala. Dept. of Ed., ASA; "Quarterly
Report of J. M. S. Thigpen, County Supt. of Education for Butler Co, Ala, January,
February, March, April, May, and June, 1877, Colored Schools," Butler Co., Ala.
Dept. of Ed., ASA; Hixon, 1880 census, Ala., Butler Co., 416/435, p. 381B.

39. McCondichie: 1860 census, Ala., Wilcox Co., Eastern Div., 299/333, p. 1058;
1860 census, Slave Schedule, Ala., Wilcox Co., Eastern Div., p. 48; Jay McCondichie,
Co. C, 44 Ala. Inf., USCWS; 1870 census, Ala., Wilcox Co., Snow Hill, 538/539, p.
469; George Shockley to C. W. Buckley, 16 December 1867, LR, Alabama BRFAL,
M810:2; McCondichie, TMSR, October 1867, SR, Alabama BRFAL, M810:6; "Quarterly
Report of E. D. Morrill, County Supt. for Wilcox County, Ala, for the Year 1871
& 2," and "Annual Report of E. D. Morrill, County Supt for Wilcox Co. Ala, for the
year 1874," both in Ala. Dept. of Ed., Annual Financial Statements, Wilcox Co.,
ASA; "Annual Report of E. D. Morrill Supt. For Wilcox County, Ala, for year 1871,"
in Reports on Conditions of Schools, 1868–1869 [*sic*], Ala. Dept. of Ed., ASA.

40. The Protestant Episcopal Freedmen's Commission was created in 1865.
Within three years, it was sustaining sixty-six teachers, but its revenues dropped
dramatically thereafter, a source of constant complaint by the commission. In
1868–69, it was supporting only seven teachers. It remained at that low level of
operation for a few more years and disappeared from the church's missionary
publication, *Spirit of Missions*, after 1876.

41. Methodist Episcopal Church, South, *Minutes of the South Carolina Conference
of the Methodist Episcopal Church, South, for 1864, 1865, and 1866* (Charleston,
S.C.: Methodist Episcopal Church, South, 1867), 14 (quotation); W. Harrison
Daniel, "Virginia Baptists and the Negro," 361. See also Alvord, *Second Semi-Annual*
Report (July 1866), 1; Daniel W. Stowell, " 'The Negroes Cannot Navigate Alone,' "
65–90; George Braxton Taylor, *Virginia Baptist Ministers*, 348–55; Corey, *History
of the Richmond Theological Seminary*, 55–57; Robert Ryland, 1860 census, Slave
Schedule, Va., Henrico Co., Western Subdiv., pp. 90, 98.

42. The role of the Baltimore Yearly Meeting of Friends in extending black
education in North Carolina, along with assisting the North Carolina Quakers in
rebuilding their own devastated system of schools, is traced briefly in Hickey,
"Pioneers of the New South," 3–7. Quakers had 1.6 percent of all North Carolina
church "sittings" (a rough measure of church size) in 1870: U.S. Bureau of the
Census, *Ninth Census*, 1:506, 512.

43. Alfred H. Jones to H. C. Vogell, 5 December 1868, Unregistered LR, North
Carolina BRFAL, M844:10 (quotation); *FF* 1 (April 1866): 105; *FF* 1 (December

1867): [116]; *FF* 1 (March 1868): [3]; *FF* 1 (November 1869): 2; *FF* 1 (April 1871): 2; *FF* 1 (April 1872): 2; *FF* 1 (January 1874): 6; *FF* 1 (March 1874): 6; *FF* 1 (January 1876): 4; *FF* 1 (January 1877): 1; H. C. Vogell to W. C. Welborn, 24 November 1868, LS, North Carolina BRFAL, M844:4; George Dixon to F. A. Fiske, 18 April 1867, Unregistered LR, North Carolina BRFAL, M844:10.

44. Edward Payson Hall to F. A. Fiske, 7 August 1867, LR, North Carolina BRFAL, M844:7 (quotation, emphasis in original); note appended to E. P. Hall, "The Sacrifice," dated 8 November 1865, Delphinia E. Mendenhall Papers, Friends Historical Collection, Hege Library, Guilford College, Greensboro, N.C.; *FF* 1 (April 1866): 100; *FF* 1 (December 1867): [116]; *FF* 1 (December 1868): 2; *FF* 1 (November 1869): 2; *FF* 1 (June 1871): 4; on his work with black teachers, see his report in *FF* 1 (December 1868): 2; Anscombe, "The Contribution of the Quakers," 274.

45. Mary Bowers to F. A. Fiske, 11 April 1866, Unregistered LR, North Carolina BRFAL, M844:10, emphasis in original; Mrs. J. F. Durbin to "the Provost Marshall of Amite City," 17 September 1865, LR, Louisiana BRFAL, M1026:8.

46. Genovese, *Roll, Jordan, Roll*, 183–93; Oakes, *The Ruling Race*, 105–22; Tise, *Proslavery*; Boles, *Masters and Slaves*.

47. Sarah J. Percival, from a note on the back of her TMSR, January 1868, SR, Virginia BRFAL, M1053:15.

48. "Report of [Esther] Christian School," 30 September 1866, SR, Georgia BRFAL, M799:20.

49. James E. Rhodes to Margaret E. Rhodes, 16 May 1865, James Rhodes Collection, HC; Mary Bowers to F. A. Fiske, 20 September 1866, Unregistered LR, North Carolina BRFAL, M844:10.

50. Thompson, TMSR, October 1867, SR, Alabama BRFAL, M810:6; Carswell, TMSR, September 1868; SR, Georgia BRFAL, M799:26; Lawley, TMSR, February 1869; Westmoreland, TMSR, June 1867; S. S. Dupress, TMSR, May 1868, all in SR, Alabama BRFAL, M810:6.

51. J. M. Jennings, TMSR, SR, Alabama BRFAL, M810:6. Jennings served as a captain in Co. F, 3 Ala. Inf.: USCWS.

52. Isaiah Bodenhamer to F. A. Fiske, 24 March 1868, LR, North Carolina BRFAL, M844:7.

53. Louis N. Poole, TMSR, November 1867, SR, Georgia BRFAL, M799:21, spelling *sic*. Poole went on to teach in white schools, along with his wife, in Spartanburg, S.C.: Poole, 1870 census, S.C., Spartanburg Co., Spartanburg CH, 115/115, p. 17.

54. John Silsby to M. E. Strickley, 22 October 1866, LS, Alabama BRFAL, M810:1.

55. Blum, *Reforging the White Republic*, 13, 30, 88, 91–92.

56. J. C. Currin to Miss Hubbard [*sic*: Hubard], 6 February 1869; Currin to Miss Hubard, 12 April 1869; Edward P. Smith to S. W. Hubard, 26 April 1869, and letters to and from Sue W. Hubard, 1868 and 1869, in Hubard Family Papers, UNC.

57. Correspondence Received Relating to Employment (Applications), 1864, Louisiana BRFAL, M1026:7–8.

58. Cornelia Hancock to Mother, fragment, 19 February 1866, Cornelia Hancock Papers, SC.

59. R. M. Manly to O. O. Howard, 30 June 1869, LR, Virginia BRFAL, M1053:4.

60. J. McMahon to Joseph Welch, 5 May 1869, LR, Texas BRFAL, M822:6; Charles Haughn to [Welch], 24 March 1869, ibid.

61. Stacy Mayfield to Joseph Welch, 13 August 1869, LR, Texas BRFAL, M822:6; on her ownership of slaves, see Haughn to [Welch], 24 March 1869, ibid.

62. Data on southern white women based on 1870 census data on 136 women located to date. About one-sixth (515) of southern white teachers of both genders have been found in the 1870 census. In 1870, half reported real estate and personal estates combined of $400 or less; 215 reported no wealth at all. Proportions are likely to change somewhat as the project continues, but, given this sample size, they are not likely to change dramatically. Data drawn from the Freedmen's Teacher Project.

63. M. Cochrane to "Gentlemen," 30 March 1864, Correspondence Received Relating to Employment, Louisiana BRFAL, M1026:7; see also M. T. Cochrane to "Gentlemen," 14 September 1864, ibid.; Maria Cochrane, "Semi-Monthly Report of Louisiana Schools," Assumption Parish, 30 November 1865, ibid., M1026:4; "Semi-Monthly Report . . .," Assumption Parish, 15 January 1866, ibid., M1026:5; "Semi-Monthly Report . . .," Assumption Parish, May 1868, ibid., M1026:6.

64. C. C. Arms to C. W. Buckley, 6 February 1867, Register of LR, Alabama BRFAL, M810:3.

65. William H. Henderson and others "To the Board of Education," 16 April 1864, Correspondence Received Relating to Employment, Louisiana BRFAL, M1026:7, emphasis in original, misspelling *sic*.

66. Harriet A. Hart to Edward Smith, 23 February 1872, AMAA. Setzer: Morris, *Reading, 'Riting, and Reconstruction*, 147; Bowman: C. S. Drake to C. W. Buckley, 2 March 1867, Register of LR, Alabama BRFAL, M810:3A; Bennett to Mr. Bush, 27 February 1868, LR, Alabama BRFAL, M810:2; Sarah Bowman: 1870 census, Ala., Sumter County, Livingston, 118/107, p. 223. Bullock: "Annual Report of Thomas J. Emmons, County Superintendent of Education for Monroe Co, Ala., for the Scholastic Year ending Sept 30, 1873," Alabama Dept. of Ed. Annual Financial Statements, Monroe Co., ASA; Sarah Bullock: 1870 census, Ala., Monroe Co., Dennards Bluff, 1039/1039, p. 469. Elam: Petersburg (Va.) *Daily Index*, 3 October 1868, 3; *Daily Index*, 8 July 1871, 3; *Daily Index*, 31 January 1872, 3; *Daily Index*, 18 July 1872, 3; Petersburg (Va.) *Index and Appeal*, 17 September 1874, 3; *Index and Appeal*, 27 August 1875, 31; *Index and Appeal*, 10 January 1876, 3; Elizabeth Elam: 1870 census, Va., Dinwiddie Co., Petersburg 5 Ward, 1/1; 1880 census, Va., Dinwiddie Co., Petersburg, 4 Ward, 132/159, p. 400.

67. Report of Esther Christian, 27 October 1865, SR, Georgia BRFAL, M799:20.

68. Georgia A. Grimes to "Superintendent of F. A. Society of M. E. Church," 13 May 1870, LR, Tennessee BRFAL, M1000:5.

69. Savilla Edge: 1870 census, Ala., Randolph Co., Wedowee, 862/862, p. 561; Kenneth B. White, "The Alabama Freedmen's Bureau and Black Education: The Myth of Opportunity," 121.

70. Four hundred seventy-four of the southern white teachers had the title of Mrs., 508 were designated Miss; the marital status of the remaining southern white women has not yet been established. Of the 177 married women who have been

located in the census, seventy-seven were widows, 105 were married. Of the married and widowed women, half reported total family wealth of $250 or less; thirty-one reported no wealth at all.

71. Davis: 1870 census, Ala., Calhoun Co., Cross Plains, 130/130, 659; Welch: 1870 census, S.C., Charleston Co., St. Stephens, 156/151, p. 473; Winn: 1870 census, Ala., Jackson Co., Kirbys Mill, 51/51, p. 223.

72. 1870 census, S.C., Newberry Co., Newberry Twp., 58/58, p. 640; 1870 census, S.C., Newberry Co., Newberry Twp., 244/244, p. 650; 1870 census, S.C., Georgetown Co., Santee Twp., 1335/1384, p. 373; 1870 census, Ala., Talladega Co., Twp. 22, 26/26, p. 658.

73. Wigg: 1870 census, S.C., Richland Co., Columbia 2 Ward, 213/265, p. 118; Faggard: "Annual Report of M. H. Serby, County Supt. for Hale County, Ala, for year 1871," in Reports on Conditions of Schools, 1868–1869 [sic], Ala. Dept. of Ed., ASA; also as Thaggard in State of Alabama, Dept. of Public Instruction, *Report of Joseph H. Speed, Superintendent of Public Instruction of the State of Alabama, for the Scholastic Year Ending October 1st, 1873* (Montgomery, Ala., 1873), 53; Faggard: 1870 census, Ala., Hale Co., Greensboro, 471/502, p. 63.

74. Adams: 1860 census, La., Orleans Co., New Orleans Ward 11, 2688/2949, p. 0; Henderson, 1870 census, S.C., Union Co., Unionville, Fishdam Twp., 135/154, p. 399; Freeman: 1870 census, Ala., Sumter Co., Earbee, 327/327, p. 167. For examples of single southern white teachers' wealth, see Sarah Smith, 1870 census, Ga., Newton Co., Covington Twp., 566/11, p. 56; Mary A. Brinkman, 1870 census, Ala., Elmore Co., Wetumpka, 1295/1319, p. 50; Sarah A. Smallwood, 1880 census, S.C., Charleston Co., Charleston, 744/563, p. 42B; M. W. Gilbert, 1870 census, Ala., Mobile Co., Mobile, 48/54, p. 220.

75. McCurry, *Masters of Small Worlds*; Lockley, "Spheres of Influence: Working White and Black Women in Antebellum Savannah," 102–20; Whites, *Civil War as a Crisis in Gender*, 41–63; Censer, *Reconstruction of White Southern Womanhood*; Faust, *Mothers of Invention*, 80–113. Faust concludes that southern white women's "new sense of self" that moved them toward work such as teaching "was based not in the experience of success but in desperation, in the fundamental need simply to survive" (243). In *Women's Work? American Schoolteachers, 1650–1920*, Perlmann and Margo attempt to argue that the feminization of teaching occurred more slowly than has long been held, and was particularly retarded in the South, even after the Civil War. Their study relies almost exclusively on sampling the federal censuses, however, a source that is demonstrably inaccurate regarding women's work, particularly in the South; the process of feminization moved much faster in the South than they claim.

76. Credit report, S. M. Adams, R. G. Dun Collection, Alabama, vol. 21, Pike Co., p. 156, HBS; Adams: 1860 census, Ala., Pike Co., Troy PO, 230/233, p. 211; Sam Adams, Co. G, 9 Ala. Inf., USCWS; "Annual Report of W. C. Menefee, County Supt. for Pike County, Ala, for year 1871," in "Reports on Conditions of Schools, 1868–1869" [sic], Ala. Dept. of Ed., ASA.

77. Credit report, R. A. Burnett, R. G. Dun Collection, Alabama, vol. 7, Choctaw Co., p. 111, HBS; R. A. Burnett: 1860 census, Ala., Choctaw Co., Northern Div.,

113/116, p. 484; 1860 census, Slave Schedules, Ala., Choctaw Co., Northern Div., p. 408; Robert Burnett, Co. C, 38 Ala. Inf., ACWRD; 1870 census, Ala., Butler Co., Greenville, illeg/260, p. 421; "Annual Report of V. R. Williams, County Supt. for Choctaw County, Ala, for year 1871," in Reports on Conditions of Schools, 1868–1869 [*sic*], ASA.

78. William McKeown: 1860 census, S.C., Chester Co., Chester, 555/515, p. 34; William McKeown, Co. C, 17 S.C. Inf., USCWS; "Teacher Reports Submitted by York County Commissioners for School Year 1869–1870," S.C. Supt. of Ed. Papers, SCSA; 1870 census, S.C., Chester Co., Blackstock Twp., 115/122, p. 195.

79. Carstarphen: 1860 census, Mo., Ralls Co., Spencer Twp., 259/255, p. 38; 1860 census, Slave Schedule, Mo., Ralls Co., Spencer, p. ?; 1870 census, Tenn., Davidson Co., Nashville 3 Ward, 10/11, p. 213; J. G. Carstarphen to C. E. Compton, 24 May 1870, LR, Tennessee BRFAL, M1000:5.

80. Billingsley: 1860 census, Tex., Travis Co., Precinct 5, 350/350, p. 262; 1870 census, Tex., Travis County, Austin, 533/578, p. 241; James Oakes to J. P. Richardson, 31 December 1867, TX, roll 7 (quotation); "School Records" (22) p. 127, "Record of Schools" (23), p. 80, and "List of Houses Rented and Teachers Employed," p. 24, all in Misc Records, Texas BRFAL, M822:18.

81. Bush: 1860 census, S.C., Richland District, Gadsden PO, 158/161, p. 93; 1870 census, S.C., Richland Co., Twp. 4, 2267/2573, p. 291; South Carolina, Supt. of Ed., Teacher Reports Submitted by County Commissioners for School Years 1868–1869, 1869–1870: Richland County, 1869–70, in S.C. Supt. of Ed. Papers, SCSA.

82. Louiza and Lockey Simmons, TMSR, September 1869, North Carolina BRFAL, M844:15.

83. M. A. Chambers to E. C. [*sic*: H. C.] Vogell, 27 August 1869; see also Chambers to Vogell, 26 July 1869, both in Unregistered LR, North Carolina BRFAL, M844:11.

84. *PFB* (February 1868), 12.

85. C. D. Elliot: 1850 census, Tenn., Davidson Co., Nashville, 777/879, p. 143; 1860 census, Tenn., Davidson, Dist. 13, Nashville PO, 863/843; 1870 census, Tenn., Davidson Co., Nashville 5 Ward, 259/319, p. 316.

86. Carswell: 1870 census, Ga., Wilkinson Co., Irwinton, 166/181, p. 390. Steer: *Friends' Intelligencer* 23 (23 June 1866), 251; "Schedule of Schools under the Friends Association for the Aid and Elevation of the Freedmen," 30 June 1869, Ed. Div., BRFAL, M803:11; Steer, 1870 census, Va., Northern Div., Loudon Co., Waterford, 2/2, p. 35. Webster: 1860 census, Ala., Perry Co., Woodville, 581/581, p. 586; 1870 census, Ala., Perry Co., Marion, 56/56, p. 180; Alabama Dept. of Public Instruction, *Report of Joseph H. Speed*, 78; Webster appears not to have held slaves immediately before the war.

87. H. A. Hart to J. W. Alvord, 29 January 1868, LR, Ed. Div., BRFAL, M803:7; 1860 census, Ga., Liberty Co., Dist. 15, 63/51, p. 738; 1860 census, Slave Schedule, Ga., Liberty Co., Dist. 15, p. 60.

88. Harriet A. Hart to J. W. Alvord, 29 January 1868, LR, Ed. Div., BRFAL, M803:7 (first and second quotations); Hart to Mr. Edward Smith, 23 February 1872, AMAA (third and fourth quotations).

89. Denied Claim #4299, Harriet Atwood Hart, McIntosh, Georgia, Records of

the Southern Claims Commission, National Archives, microfilm; Harriet Atwood Newell Hart to "The Honorable Claim Commissioners," 12 March 1878, in ibid. (quotation). Hart's reference to starting her school in 1869, repeated in another extant letter, is contradicted by her first report of her school from January 1868, which clearly indicates that she started the school earlier than the date of the report; see Hart to Alvord, 29 January 1868, LR, Ed. Div., BRFAL, M803:7.

90. Stewart: 1850 census, Ga., Troup Co., LaGrange, 27/29, p. 114; Witham: 1850 census, Ga., Meriwether Co., Div. 59, 509/509, p. 342; 1860 census, Ga., Troup Co., LaGrange, 929/856, p. 310; 1860 census, Slave Schedule, Ga., Troup Co., LaGrange, p. 184; John D. Witham, Co. C, 14 Battalion Ga. Light Artillery, USCWS; other information and all quotations from R. G. Dun Collection, vol. 34, Georgia, Troup Co., p. 21, HBS; "Assistant Commissioner's Monthly Report" for LaGrange, Ga., February 1868, Georgia BRFAL, M799:17; 1870 census, Ga., Troup Co., LaGrange, 47/47, p. 224.

91. Cooke: 1850 census, Va., Norfolk Co., Portsmouth, 893/971, p. 181; 1850 census, Slave Schedule, Va., Norfolk Co., Portsmouth, p. 329; 1860 census, Va., Prince George, City Point, 363/363, p. 376; Anonymous, "Giles B. Cooke," 2–4.

92. On paternalism during slavery, see Oakes, *Ruling Race*; Genovese, *Roll, Jordan, Roll*; Genovese, *World the Slaveholders Made*; on the continuing hold of paternalism after emancipation, see especially Williamson, *Rage for Order*, 10–14.

93. *Petersburg (Va.) Daily Index*, 3 October 1868, 3; ibid., 6 July 1871, 3; ibid., 11 July 1872, 3; *Petersburg (Va.) Daily Progress*, 27 July 1871, 3; *Petersburg (Va.) Daily Index*, 28 July 1871, 3; ibid., 14 September 1872, 3.

94. *SoM* 37 (April 1872): 248 (quotation); "Giles B. Cooke," 5.

95. *SoM* 37 (April 1872): 248; *Baltimore Sun*, 12 May 1935, clipping in Giles Buckner Cooke Papers, VHS (second and third quotations); "Giles Buckner Cooke," 5 (fourth quotation); A. Toomer Porter, *Led On!* 199 (last quotation).

96. From manuscript biography of Giles B. Cooke, handwritten notes to Chapter 7, page 3, Giles Buckner Cooke Papers, VHS.

97. R. M. Manly to O. O. Howard, 30 June 1869, LR, Virginia BRFAL, M1026:4.

Chapter 4

1. Mary Mead: 1850 census, Mich., Hillsdale Co., Hillsdale, 177/180, p. 511; 1860 census, Mich., Hillsdale Co., Hillsdale, 319/315, p. 661; NWFAC, *Second Annual Report* (1865), 15; NYYM, *Fifth Report* (1866), 9; *Freed-Man* (May 1866): 247; *AM* 12 (April 1868): 74; *AM* 13 (May 1869): 103; *AM* 14 (June 1870): 124; *AM* 15 (May 1871): 98; *AM* 16 (May 1872): 98. In 1860, Mead's wealth was estimated at $4,500, not quite double the median wealth nationally; by 1870, while teaching in Selma, she was worth an estimated $6,000. She returned to Hillsdale after teaching the freed people: 1870 census, Ala., Dallas Co., Selma, 22/30, p. 68; 1880 census, Mich., Hillsdale Co., Hillsdale, 51/54, p. 115A.

2. Walter McDonald, Co. G, 7 N.H. Vols., CSR; Walter McDonald, TMSR, December 1868, Georgia BRFAL, M799:22; *AM* 13 (May 1869): 101; George W. Farnham to J. W. Alvord, 3 February 1870, LR, Ed. Div., BRFAL, M803:10.

3. *NF* 2 (June 1866): 181; *AM* 11 (April 1867): 74; Martin, *"Dear Sister,"* esp. xxiii (quotation); *AM* 15 (May 1871): 99; Benedict: 1870 census, Tenn., Davidson Co., Nashville 10 Ward, 84/103.

4. Forty percent of northern white teachers whose homes are certain came from the six states that make up New England. Of 3,202 northern white teachers identified to date, 2,115 were women; gender is not known for 41. See Appendix A, table 2-A. Data drawn from the Freedmen's Teacher Project.

5. 1850 census, Conn., Litchfield Co., Woodbury, 208/208, p. 366; 1860 census, Conn., Fairfield Co., Huntington, 1158/1219, p. 559.

6. Northern white women averaged over two and one-half years each; northern white men averaged less than two and one-quarter years. See Appendix A, table 5-A, for comparative figures for other groups. Compiled from the Freedmen's Teacher Project database.

7. Morris, *Reading, 'Riting, and Reconstruction*, "The Army of Civilization," title to Chapter 1; Jacqueline Jones, *Soldiers of Light and Love*; Knight, " 'Messianic' Invasion of the South," 645–51; Selleck, *Gentle Invaders*. The Freedmen's Teacher Project has, to date, positively identified 4,458 teachers as northerners, but only 3,203 as white. Some of those whose race has not been established may have been black. It is probably safe to conclude that at least 4,200 were white.

8. The comparisons above speak only to the teachers who have been positively identified in the Freedmen's Teacher Project. As noted in Chapter 3 and explained in Appendix B, when estimates of teachers not yet identified are added, the work of northern white teachers pales even further. If conservative estimates are included, northern white teachers were eclipsed by 1865–66, were one-quarter of all teachers by the following year, and a tiny fraction by 1870. See table 3.

9. Stoutenburg: 1865 N.Y. State census, Dutchess Co., Poughkeepsie Twp., 2nd Election Dist., 11/12; Julia A. Wilbur to J. Miller McKim, 10 Jan 1866; M. H. Stoutenburg to Crammond Kennedy, 21 August 1867; Charles A. Dixon and others to Mrs. Stoutenburg, 31 July 1867, all in AFUC Papers, CU; "Assistant Sub-Assistant Commissioner's (or Agent's) Monthly Report on Education of Freedmen and Refugees in 1st Div., 6th Sub-District, State of Virginia . . .," January 1868," SR, Virginia BRFAL, M1053:13; ABHMS, *Baptist Home Missions*, 610.

10. Five hundred and nineteen teachers were married, both spouses teaching; 122 individuals were in larger family groups headed by a mother and father; 66 were in mother-child groups, most often mother-daughter, while 55 were in father-child groups; independent of other family members, 323 sisters taught together, and another 100 were in sister-brother groups. Only 31 brothers taught together without a parent or sister with them. Data drawn from the Freedmen's Teacher Project.

11. In the antebellum era, there was a greater range of higher education institutions available to students than subsequently. They ranged from colleges through academies, female seminaries, and normal schools. Many academies and female seminaries were as rigorous as the colleges of their day. Men attended at higher rates than women, though the first women's colleges, the earliest coeducational colleges, and academically oriented female seminaries had been established by the 1830s and expanded throughout the rest of the antebellum era. See among others

Nash, *Women's Education in the United States*; Kelley, *Learning to Stand and Speak*; Ogren, *American State Normal School*; Geiger, *American College in the Nineteenth Century*; Solomon, *In the Company of Educated Women*; Thelin, *History of American Higher Education*; Shmurak and Handler, " 'Castle of Science,' " 315–42; Sweet, "The Female Seminary Movement," 41–55.

12. Compiled from the Freedmen's Teacher Project database. On Oberlin and Mount Holyoke, see also Butchart, "Mission Matters," 1–17.

13. The mean age for northern white male teachers when they began their teaching was 30.4 years; the mean age for northern white female teachers was 28.8. See Appendix A, table 6-A.

14. There are serious impediments to accurately gauging women's work, however. Those whose occupations were identified through letters were likely to highlight their work as teachers, to the neglect of other occupations, since they were applying for teaching positions. For this study, most occupations were identified through the census. The census is, however, a source with its own biases. Many of the women teachers are noted in the census as "keeping house" or "at home" even in years when they were teaching. The problem is much greater for women in the South. There was probably much higher female workforce participation—and more women teachers—than the census reveals, and the female teachers studied here probably held a greater range of occupations than the data available can indicate.

15. L. Tandy to Samuel Hunt, 3 October 1865, AMAA; Beal: 1855 New York State census, Allegany Co., Angelica Twp., 39/42; 1860 census, Allegany Co., Angelica Twp., 520/27, p. 352; H. S. Beals to S. Jocelyn, 19 February 1862, AMAA; all other information here compiled from Freedmen's Teacher Project.

16. Woodbury: 1860 census, Kalamazoo Co., Village of Kalamazoo, 400/397, p. 461; Curtis: 1860 census, Conn., Litchfield Co., Woodbury, 403/414, p. 46; *NF* 1 (October 1865): 311; *NF* 2 (June 1866): 181; Ireson sisters: 1850 census, Mass., Essex Co., Lynn, 505/688, p. 255; 1860 census, Mass., Essex Co., Lynn 6 Ward, 2676/3717, p. 884; 1870 census, Mass., Essex Co. Lynn 6 Ward, 414/563, p. 672; *FR* 1 (April 1865): 65; *FR* 1 (July 65): 118; *FF* 1 (December 1864): 21; *FF* 1 (August 1865): 69; *AM* 9 (October 1865): 220.

17. Fenner: 1860 census, R.I., Providence Co., Providence 5 Ward, 998/1442, p. 154; 1870 census, R.I., Providence Co., Providence 8 Ward, 524/880, p. 322; *AM* 17 (September 1873): 193; AMA, *Twenty-eighth Annual Report* (1874): 32; *AM* 19 (February 1875): 30. Whitehouse: 1860 census, Me., Kennebec Co., Pittston, 304/302, p. 219; 1870 census, Me., Kennebec Co., Pittston, 420/431, p. 433 (for her family); 1870 census, Va., Henrico Co., Richmond, Jefferson Ward, 1440/1650, p. 512 (for Melissa); 1870 Richmond *City Directory*, p. 207; "Names of Persons to Whom Certificates of Qualifications as Teachers have been Given from Oct. 1st to December 31st 187," New Hanover County School Records, 1856–1884, NCSA; Hanover County School Records, County Examiners Letterbook 1869–1874, p. 42, NCSA.

18. Wealth data was compiled from all teachers identified to date in the 1850, 1860, and 1870 censuses. For 1860, when median wealth nationally was $2,500, the mode for the northern white freed people's teachers (*n* = 672) was $2,500, but the

median was double that at $5,906. For the 1870 sample ($n = 503$), the mode is much lower at $1,300, while the median is moderately lower at $5,810. The sharp difference between mean and mode indicates the skewed nature of the data, with a few very wealthy individuals at the top end offsetting the larger number at the bottom end with no wealth.

Historians and economists working with census wealth data note that average wealth varied greatly depending on the region of the country being considered. Western and southern states had lower average wealth than eastern states. The range provided above is from Ohio, probably a rough measure of northern wealth averages. See Klingaman and Vedder, *Essays in Nineteenth-Century Economic History*, 177–90; Kearl, Pope, and Wimmer, "Household Wealth in a Settlement Economy," 471–96; Soltow, "Economic Inequality in the United States," 822–39; Blackburn and Ricards, "Unequal Opportunity on a Mining Frontier," 19–38.

19. This estimate is based on the assumption that the Freedmen's Teacher Project has been able to identify about one-half of all veterans who taught the freed people. To date, the project has positively identified nearly 300 of the teachers as white Union veterans. Many can never be positively identified because of the large number of men with the same names.

20. Higginson: NEFAS, *Second Annual Report* (1864), 24; Samuel S. Higginson, Co. S, 9 USCI, CSR; Higginson, Cert. No. 982227, CWPR; Carruthers: AMA, *Seventeenth Annual Report* (1863), 32; AMA, *Eighteenth Annual Report* (1864), 27; George N. Carruthers, Co. F, 51 USCI, CSR: Carruthers, Cert. No. 388263, CWPR; Olds: AMA, *Seventeenth Annual Report* (1863), 32; AMA, *Eighteenth Annual Report* (1864), 27; Abner D. Olds, Co. F, 59 USCI, CSR; Doolittle: *FA* 1 (May 1864): 17; Oscar E. Doolittle, Co. E, 5 USCI, CSR; Doolittle, Cert. No. 111195, CWPR; Calahan: McGranahan, *Historical Sketch*, 17; *FA* 1 (January 1864): 2; Thomas Callahan, [*sic*], Co. F, 48 USCI, CSR; Calahan, Cert. No. 739601, CWPR.

21. Butler, *Awash in a Sea of Faith*, esp. 225–88.

22. Butchart, *Northern Schools*, 3–12, 33–52; Joe M. Richardson, *Christian Reconstruction*, 145–59; Morris, *Reading, 'Riting, and Reconstruction*, 3.

23. Hamm, *Quakers in America*; Barbour and Frost, *The Quakers*; Selleck, *Gentle Invaders*.

24. Butchart, *Northern Schools*, 77–95.

25. Jane Briggs Smith to Friend Fuller Fiske, 18 January 1867; see also Smith to Fiske, 25 June 1865. Jane Briggs Smith Fiske Papers, AAS.

26. McPherson, "The New Puritanism," 611–42, quotation from 619.

27. The decennial censuses obtained four sorts of information on denominations: the number of church buildings, the number of "accommodations" (in 1860) or "sittings" (in 1870), the value of the property owned by the denominations or individual churches within a denomination, and, in 1870, the number of "organizations," which allowed the census to include churches that did not meet in a church edifice. No data was collected regarding membership. To estimate relative sizes of the denominations, then, a rough estimate can be made by the number of parishioners who could be accommodated, assuming that excess capacity would be roughly equal across denominations. The data on the number of edifices, number of

224 church organizations, and value of property provides a second level of rough comparison. Using those measures, in 1860, the Friends, or Quakers, constituted 1.4 percent of all accommodations, 1.4 percent of all church buildings, and 1.3 percent of value of church property; by 1870, the sect had declined to 1.0 percent of sittings, 0.9 percent of church organizations and church edifices, and 1.7 percent of value of church property. The Unitarian church was about one-third smaller, with 0.7 percent of total church sittings in 1870. Together, Quakers and Unitarians amounted to 1.75 percent of all church sittings in 1870. U.S. Bureau of the Census, *Eighth Census*, 2:497–501; U.S. Bureau of the Census, *Ninth Census*, 1:506–23.

28. While the Freedmen's Teacher Project includes religious affiliation as one of its variables, the religious data is incomplete. Although most of the missionary societies indicated a preference for hiring only members of their own denomination, there were enough exceptions that no automatic assumptions could be made that a teacher working for the Baptists, for example, was, ipso facto, a Baptist. Religious affiliation, then, has been coded into the database only when there is clear evidence —letters from teachers or others, biographical or autobiographical identification, and other relatively unequivocal sources. Additionally, Quaker teachers can often be identified in letters and diaries by their use of the familiar second person pronoun and avoiding the pagan names of months. As a result of those problems, no attempt has been made in this study to compare other denominations with one another, and estimates of the numbers of Quaker teachers are probably conservative.

29. Dyson, *Howard University*, 241, 246, 413, 453, 468, 475, 477, 485; Inez Moore Parker, *The Rise and Decline*, 112–15; Wilmoth A. Carter, *Shaw's Universe*, 3–26; Jay S. Stowell, *Methodist Adventures in Negro Education*, 169; Summerville, *Educating Black Doctors*, 6–7. The other long-serving presidents of black institutions of higher education include Samuel Chapman Armstrong at Hampton Institute, Daniel Phillips at what became Roger Williams College, Edund Asa Ware at Atlanta University, Charles J. Corey at Richmond Theological Seminary, Nathan A. Brackett at Storer College, John G. Fee at Berea College, Luke P. Dorland at Scotia Seminary, and George M. P. King at Wayland Seminary. Tupper, Braden, Corey, Brackett, Ware, Phillips, and Armstrong all remained in office to their deaths.

30. Ninety-eight northern white men have been positively identified as having taught in black higher education before 1876; another twenty-one men also taught in higher schools, but racial identification has not yet been established.

31. Seventy-five have been positively identified as white; another fifteen women also taught in higher education institutions, and most are probably white, but racial identification has not yet been established for them.

32. Dyson, *Howard University*, 165, 241, 413, 452–53, 457, 459, 474, 478; Bumstead, "Mrs. Lucy E. Case," 24–41; Booker, *And There Was Light!* 3–13; Plotner information from alumni files, Ohio Wesleyan University Historical Collection, Delaware, Ohio.

33. *FF* 1 (April 1865): 44; Anscombe, "The Contribution of the Quakers," 176, 183–89; Kennedy, "Southland College," 207–38; McPherson, *Abolitionist Legacy*, 156, 171; Selleck, *Gentle Invaders*, 12–13, 194–95, 199.

34. Herbig, "Friends for Freedom"; Butchart, "Caroline F. Putnam," 389–96.

35. Robbins, "Laura Towne," 40–54; Wolf, "Laura M. Towne," 375–405; see also Butchart, "Laura Towne and Ellen Murray."

36. Schofield School, *Fourteenth Annual Report* (1882); Smedley, "Martha Schofield and the Rights of Women," 195–210; Smedley, *Martha Schofield*.

37. Ednah D. Cheney to Miss Lowell, 17 February 1872, Jeanette Bailey Cheek Collection, SL; Knoxville, Tenn., Public Schools, *Commencement Annual, 1881–1903*, 3–4; Beck Cultural Exchange Center, *History of Blacks in Knoxville*, 23.

38. Correspondence File, Dickey, Sarah A., Class of 1869, Alumnae File, MHC; Wilkins, "Education for Freedom"; Griffith, *Dauntless in Mississippi*.

39. Reynolds, *Baptist Missionary Pioneers Among Negroes*, 58; Joe M. Richardson, *Christian Reconstruction*, 178.

40. Cornelia Hancock Papers, SC; Jaquette, *South after Gettysburg*.

41. Butchart, "Lucelia E. Williams," 486.

42. *FR* 1 (April 1865): 65; *FR* 1 (December 1865): 203; *FR* 2 (December 1866): 218; *FR* 3 (November 1867): 176; *FR* 4 (November 1868): 180; *FR* 5 (November 1869): 54; *FR* 5 (January 1871): 103; Botume, *First Days amongst the Contrabands*; Botume to Booker T. Washington, 1 January 1902, in *Booker T. Washington Papers*, ed. Harlan, Smock, and Kraft, 6:368–69.

43. Beadie, "Emma Willard's Idea," 543–62; Scott, "The Ever Widening Circle," 3–20; Woody, *History of Women's Education*; Sklar, *Catharine Beecher*; Vinovskis and Bernard, "Beyond Catharine Beecher," 856–69; Burstyn, "Catharine Beecher," 386–403; Melder, "Ipswich Female Seminary," 223–40; Porterfield, *Mary Lyon*.

44. Mandle, "Re-Establishment of the Plantation Economy," 68–88; Mandle, *The Roots of Black Poverty*; Williamson, *Crucible of Race*; Foner, *Nothing but Freedom*; Ransom and Sutch, *One Kind of Freedom*; Davis, *Good and Faithful Labor*.

45. On the curriculum in these schools, see my sketches of four of them: Butchart, "Laura Towne and Ellen Murray"; Butchart, "Caroline F. Putnam," 389–96; Butchart, "Lucelia E. Williams," 518–19; and Butchart, "Martha Schofield," 416–18.

46. Holland, *Letters and Diary of Laura M. Towne*, 247, 248, 249, 259, 276, 300; Ellen Murray, eulogy for Towne, in Penn School, *Report of the Penn Normal, Industrial and Agricultural School*, 18; Herbig, "Friends for Freedom," 272–76; Smedley, *Martha Schofield*, 238, 255.

47. Philena Carkin, "Reminiscences of my Life," 1:39–44, UVA; Smallwood, *Time of Hope*, 89; Sarah A. Dickey to "My Dear Classmates," 4 March 1872, in Correspondence File, Dickey, Sarah A., Class of 1869, Alumnae File, MHC, spelling and punctuation *sic*.

48. Clark, Gardner, Hancock, Munro, and Schofield had all been raised in Quaker homes; Holley, Botume, and Towne were Unitarian. Putnam embraced Unitarianism as an adult.

49. William L. Webb, Co. F., 13 Conn. Vols., Pension Cert. No. 349355, CWPR; he initially joined Co. H, 2 Conn. Inf.: CSR; Teacher Reports Submitted by County Commissioners for School Years 1868–1869, 1869–1870, in S.C. Supt. of Ed. Records, SCSA; 1870 census, S.C., Georgetown Co., Waccamaw Twp., 1107/1221, p. 412; 1880 census, S.C., Georgetown Co., Santee Twp., Dist 154, 860/860, p. 415C.

50. Porter: Eliza C. Porter, "Report of School for Freedmen," April 1870, SR, Texas BRFAL, M822:16; *AM* 14 (June 1870): 128; Mary H. Porter, *Eliza Chappell Porter*, 170–78. Neil: Presbyterian Church USA, *First Annual Report* (1866), 11; ibid., *Second Annual Report* (1867), 25; ibid., *Third Annual Report* (1868), 30; ibid., *Fourth Annual Report* (1869), 59; ibid., *Fifth Annual Report* (1870), 29; ibid., *Annual Report of the Presbyterian Committee of Missions* (1871), 14; ibid. (1872), 20; ibid. (1873), n.p.; ibid. (1874), n.p.; ibid., (1875), n.p.; Barber, *A History of the Work*, 30; Inez Moore Parker, *The Rise and Decline*, 14, 59–60; Swann, *Bread Upon the Waters*, 21–23.

51. Campbell: AMA, *Nineteenth Annual Report* (1865), 31; Fannie Campbell, TMSR, SR, Texas BRFAL, M822:11; Fannie Campbell to E. M. Wheelock, 11 February 1867, LR, ibid., M822:3; Clarence Mauck to Charles A. Vernon, 31 May 1868, LR, ibid., M822:7; E. Gay to Charles A. Vernon, 30 June 1868, LR, ibid., M822:7. Loomis: *NF* 1 (October 1865): 311; *NF* 2 (June 1866): 181; *AF* 2 (July 1867): 255; *AF* 2 (October 1867): 301; *AF* 2 (January 1868): 347; *Fifth Annual Report of the State Superintendent of Education of the State of South Carolina, 1873*, in *Reports and Resolutions of the General Assembly of the State of South Carolina* (1874), 397; *Sixth Annual Report, 1874*, in ibid. (1875), 399; Thomason, *Foundations of the Public Schools*, 211. Loomis apparently stayed in South Carolina as a teacher; by 1884, she was on the faculty of Charleston's Avery Institute: Avery Normal Institute, *Catalogue of Avery Normal Institute*, 3. Branch: Pension Certificate #417977, CWPR; ABHMS, *Baptist Missions*, 608; NWFAC, *Second Annual Report* (1865), 15; *AM* 11 (April 1867): 77; Colby to George W. Bulloch, 2 November 1869, LS, Arkansas BRFAL, M980:1.

52. FFA, *Fourth Annual Report* (1867), 20; Mary E. F. Smith to John E. Bryant, 11 November 1866, John Bryant Papers, DU; *FA* 1 (October 1864): 34; NEYM, *Report to the Committee in Charge of Friends' Mission*, 2.

53. In 1867, NEFAS paid Bessie Canedy $700 per year as principal, the same amount it paid to Arthur Sumner for the same job: "Records of the Teachers Committee," February 1866–September 1870, entry for 28 August [1867] (for Canedy), and ibid., entry for 8 January 1868 (for Sumner), NEFAS Records, MHS; in its last year of operation, the AFUC paid its principals $500 regardless of gender: Daniel G. Fort to Michael E. Strieby, 2 August 1869, AMAA. The AMA, by contrast, appears to have always discriminated in its pay for teachers and principals depending on gender and appointed few women to leadership positions.

54. Holland, *Letters and Diary of Laura M. Towne*, 147; Robbins, "Laura Towne," 48, 51; Wolf, "Laura M. Towne," 395, 396; George W. Farnham to J. W. Alvord, 3 February 1870, LR, Ed. Div., BRFAL, M803:7; NEYM, "Minutes," various dates, RIHS; Ada W. Smith to Isabella James, fragment [1867], Isabella Batchelder James Correspondence, SL.

55. Jacqueline Jones, "Women Who Were More Than Men," 47–59.

56. Mary [E. Clark] to G. D. Pike, 18 October 1868, AMAA, spelling *sic*.

57. FFA, "Minutes of the Instruction Committee," 20 June 1864, HC; *Freedmen's Reporter* 1 (October 1867): 87; *FR* 3 (May 1867): 85.

58. [S. S. Jocelyn?] to George Whipple, 17 July 1867, AMAA.

27 August 1868, AMAA.

60. Compiled from the Freedmen's Teacher Project. The choice of examining those teaching for seven or more years was arbitrary, constituting those who taught for not quite half the period covered by this study.

61. AMA, *Eighteenth Annual Report* (1864), 25; AMA, *Nineteenth Annual Report* (1865), 21; AMA, *Twentieth Annual Report* (1866), 24, 29; *AM* 11 (April 1867): 74–75; *AM* 12 (April 1868): 74–75; *AM* 13 (May 1869): 100–101; *AM* 14 (June 1870): 123; *AM* 15 (May 1871): 99; Sarah E. Cargill, Application #6872, 18 March 1871, Charleston, S.C. Branch, Register of Signatures, FSTC; *AM* 15 (May 1871): 98; *AM* 16 (May 1872): 98; *FF* 1 (April 1871): 1, 2; *FF* 1 (December 1871): 7; *FF* 1 (December 1872): 2; *FF* 1 (January 1874): 5; *FF* 1 (November 1874): 2; *FF* 1 (January 1876): 4; *FF* 1 (January 1877): 1; *FF* 1 (November 1878): 1.

62. Presbyterian Church USA, *Fourth Annual Report* (1869), 55; ibid., *Fifth Annual Report* (1870), 25; ibid., *First Annual Report of the Presbyterian Committee of Missions for Freedmen* (1871), 11; ibid., *Second Annual Report* (1872), 17; ibid., *Third Annual Report* (1873), n.p.; ibid., *Fourth Annual Report* (1874), n.p.; ibid., *Fifth Annual Report* (1875), n.p.; FFA, "Minutes of the Instruction Committee, 1868–1875," entry for 23 August 1870, HC; *FF* 1 (December 1868): 2–4; *FF* 1 (November 1869): 1; *FF* 1 (November 1870): 1–2, 4; *FF* 1 (June 1871): 2; *FF* 1 (December 1871): 5; *FF* 1 (December 1872): 1; *FF* 1 (January 1874): 2; *FF* 1 (November 1874): 2; *FF* 1 (June 1880): 1; *Daily Danville (Va.) News*, 20 November 1877; *FR* 4 (November 1868): 180; *FR* 5 (November 1869): 54; *FR* 5 (January 1871): 103; NEFAS, "Records of the Teachers Committee, Sept 1870–Nov 1876," entry for 14 February 1876, and letters from Alfred to Ednah Dow Cheney, NEFAS Papers, MHS.

63. H. J. T. Hudson to Caroline Alfred, 3 August 1875, NEFAS Papers, MHS.

64. Christine Jacobson Carter, *Southern Single Blessedness*; Delfino and Gillespie, *Neither Lady Nor Slave*; Ginzberg, *Women and the Work of Benevolence*; Kerber, "Separate Spheres, Female Worlds," 9–39; Chambers-Schiller, *Liberty a Better Husband*; Matthews, *The Rise of Public Woman*; Cogan, *All-American Girl*; Jo Anne Preston, "Domestic Ideology" 531–51.

65. Welter, "The Cult of True Womanhood," 422–61; Mary P. Ryan, *Cradle of the Middle Class*; Rotundo, *American Manhood*; Boylan, "Evangelical Womanhood," 62–80; Mary P. Ryan, "A Women's Awakening," 602–23; Jean E. Friedman, *Enclosed Garden*; Censer, *Reconstruction of White Southern Womanhood*; Burton, "Effects of the Civil War," 205–24; Friend and Glover, *Southern Manhood*.

66. Chambers-Schiller, *Liberty a Better Husband*, 205; Christine Jacobson Carter, *Southern Single Blessedness*. On the growth in women's education in the nineteenth century, see Nash, *Women's Education in the United States*; Kelley, *Learning to Stand and Speak*; on women's education in the North, see Burstyn, "Catharine Beecher," 386–403; Nancy Green, "Female Education and School Competition," 129–42; Bunkle, "Sentimental Womanhood and Domestic Education," 13–30; Shmurak and Handler, " 'Castle of Science,' " 315–42; on women's education in the South, see Farnham, *Education of the Southern Belle*; Trey Berry, "History of Women's Higher Education," 303–19.

67. Round: Widow's Pension cert. no. 345486, CWPR; *FA* 1 (April 1864): 15. Hyslop: L. H. Hyslop to Whipple, 5 July 1864, AMAA; AMA, *Nineteenth Annual Report* (1865), 19. Fullenwider: S. Fullenwider to George Whipple, 13 October 1864, AMAA; AMA, *Eighteenth Annual Report* (1864), 27; *FA* 1 (May 1864): 17.

68. John Conant, Pension Cert. No. 833603, CWPR; AMA, *Seventeenth Annual Report* (1863), 32; AMA, *Eighteenth Annual Report*, 26; W. E. Wording to O. O. Howard, 22 February 1869, LR, Ed. Div., BRFAL, M803:8; Conant: 1870 census, S.C., Beaufort Co., Beaufort, 169/230, p. 15; 1880 census, S.C., Beaufort Co., Dist. 41, 411/535, p. 23A.

69. *FF* 1 (December 1868): 7; "Assistant Sub-Assistant Commissioner's (or Agent's) Monthly Report on Education of Freedmen and Refugees in, 8th Sub-District, State of Virginia . . ., January 1868," and similar report, October 1868, SR, Virginia BRFAL, M1053:13; 1870 census, Va., Lunenburg Co., Lewiston Twp., 58/57, p. 525.

70. F. H. Bartlett to "Prof. McNair," 13 December 1864, Orleans Parish file, State Board of Education Records, LASA.

71. Carrie Baker to Board of Education, 22 January [1864], LR, Louisiana BRFAL, M1026:7.

72. William C. Gannett to Kate Tilden, 11 December 1864, William Channing Gannett Papers, UR; Cornelia A. Drake to George Whipple, 5 July 1864, AMAA; Lucy M. Doolittle and Olive M. Whitney to Whipple, 17 November 1865, AMAA; see also Emily Knapp to Samuel Hunt, 1 September 1866, AMAA; Eliza H. Twitchell to Samuel Hunt, 27 August 1866, AMAA; Emeline N. Stanton to E. M. Cravath, 2 February 1874, AMAA. Doolittle, Knapp, and Stanton taught for one year each; Whitney was either not offered a position or did not accept; Twitchell, who did mention the freed people in passing, remained in the work for nine years.

73. Of the 1,283 northern white teachers in southern black schools in 1865–66, 815 (63.5 percent) were teaching for the first time; 373 (45.8 percent) of those teachers did not return the following year.

74. Olive J. Emerson Morrow to Miss Edwards, 8 December 1903, Olive J. Emerson Alumnae File, Class of 1865, College Archives, MHC.

75. M. A. Babcock to S. S. Jocelyn, 11 November 1863, AMAA; see also, for example, Amelia J. Twitchell to ME Strieby, 30 July 1864, AMAA.

76. Melvina A. Babcock to S. S. Jocelyn, 19 March 1864, AMAA.

77. E. P. Bond to J. J. Woolsey, 23 Aug 1866, AFUC Papers, CU; Henry H. Griffin to George Whipple, 27 February 1864, AMAA.

78. Amelia J. Twitchell to M. E. Strieby, 30 July 1864, AMAA.

79. Emily Knapp to Samuel Hunt, 1 September 1866, AMAA; Eunice Knapp to Samuel Hunt, 1 September 1866, AMAA, spelling *sic*, emphasis in original.

80. Caroline H. Merrick to Lydia Shattuck, 25 October 1862, Letters of Lydia Shattuck, Alumnae File, MHC.

81. John C. Tucker to S. S. Jocelyn, 28 January 1864, AMAA; Eliza H. Twichell to Samuel Hunt, 9 August 1866, AMAA; Twitchell to Hunt, 27 August 1866, AMAA; George C. Carpenter to Whipple, 20 August 1866, AMAA; Mary J. Kimball to Ellen Collins, 12 September 1866, AFUC Papers, CU.

82. M. Jerusha Rice to "Kind Sir," 4 November 1864, AMAA.

83. Matilda M. Atkinson to Corresponding Secretary of the American Miss. Ass., 8 February 1864, AMAA.

84. S. S. Smith to "the Christian Missionary Assocn.," 16 February 1864, AMAA.

85. Harriet Hoffman to Corresponding Secretary, 19 March 1864, AMAA.

86. S. S. Smith to "the Christian Missionary Assocn.," 16 February 1864, AMAA.

87. Maggie Webster to Samuel Hunt, 6 November 1866, AMAA.

88. On women's role in domestic and foreign missions in the antebellum years and the language of mission, see Robert, *American Women in Mission*; Porterfield, *Mary Lyon*; Porterfield, "A Sister to Oneida," 1–13; Welter, "She Hath Done What She Could," 624–38; Welter, "The Feminization of American Religion," 137–57; Devens, " 'If We Get the Girls,' " 219–38; Crumpler, "The Role of Women," 25–33; Banker, " 'They Made Haste Slowly,' " 123–32; Yohn, *A Contest of Faiths*; Yohn, "The Validity of Pluralism," 343–64; Coleman, "Not Race, but Grace," 41–60; Vickers, "Models of Womanhood," 41–53; Andrew, "Educating the Heathen," 331–42; Brumberg, *Mission for Life*.

89. Jessie L. Paterson to Samuel Hunt, 10 September 1866, AMAA.

90. L. H. Hyslop to Whipple, 16 June 1864, AMAA; see also C. L. Lloyd to E. P. Smith, 18 September 1869, AMAA; C. L. Tambling to S. S. Jocelyn, 21 January 1864, AMAA; Eunice Knapp to Samuel Hunt, 30 August 1866, AMAA.

91. McKivigan, *The War Against Proslavery Religion*, 3–20, quotation 19; see also Hardman, *Charles Grandison Finney, 1792–1875*; Asa, "Theology and Methodology of Charles G. Finney"; Moorhead, "Social Reform," 416–30.

92. R. S. Walk to George Whipple, 20 April 1864, AMAA; Charles Strong to S. S. Joceylin [*sic*], 26 October 1863, AMAA, spelling *sic*.

93. Without, as yet, making a concerted effort to explore the issue, the Freedmen's Teacher Project has identified, to date, sixty teachers who moved from the freed people's schools to foreign missions, missions to the Native Americans, and other mission fields. Most worked among the freed people for one or two years, though a few taught in the South for up to seven years.

94. Strong: 1875 New York State census, Cattaraugus Co., Town of Randolph Twp., 242/257; *Gazetteer and Business Directory of Cattaraugus County*, 272; *Historical Gazetteer and Biographical Memorial of Cattaraugus County*, 1033–34; Walk: 1870 census, Pa., Philadelphia 15 Ward, 628/732, p. 156; 1870 census, Pa., Philadelphia 15 Ward, 540/641, p. 144.

95. W. L. Clift to Samuel Hunt, 26 September 1866, AMAA; Louise Small to Cyril Pearl, 13 February 1865, AMAA.

96. W. Treadwell to Samuel Hunt, 21 December 1865, AMAA.

97. Mary H. Seymour to S. S. Jocelyn, 26 May 1863, AMAA.

98. Swint, *Northern Teacher in the South*; Jacqueline Jones, *Soldiers of Light and Love*, 18–23.

99. Eunice Browne to Samuel Hunt, 18 November 1865, AMAA; Walter L. Clift to Samuel Hunt, 29 October 1866, AMAA.

100. George F. Mosher to Strieby, 9 February 1865, AMAA (Mosher was not commissioned, however, as noted below).

101. George Grinell to "Dear Sir," 6 January 1863, AMAA, spelling *sic*; Alma Baker to S. S. Jocelyn, 1 October 1863, AMAA.

102. Josephine F. Smith to J. Miller McKim, 8 August 1866, AFUC Papers, CU.

103. John Dodd to Jocelyn, 24 August 1863, AMAA, describing Harriet Arnold.

104. Julia M. Marshall to George Whipple, 5 August 1864, AMAA.

105. John C. Tucker to S. S. Jocelyn, 28 January 1864, AMAA.

106. Sorin, *Abolitionism*, 86–87, 130–45; Dillon, *Slavery Attacked*; Huston, "Experiential Basis," 609–40; McKivigan, *The War Against Proslavery Religion*; Sernett, *Abolition's Axe*; David Brion Davis, "Reflections on Abolitionism," 797–812; Dykstra, *Bright Radical Star*; Magdol, *Antislavery Rank and File*.

107. Holland, *Letters and Diary of Laura M. Towne*, p. 8, 17 April 1862.

108. M. O. Quaiffe to T. W. Conway, 21 September 1865, LR, Louisiana BRFAL, M1026:8 (quotation); George W. Honey to Strieby, 17 September 1866, AMAA.

109. The Freedmen's Teacher Project attempted to identify as many of the teachers as abolitionists as possible. The project looked for any who clearly self-identified as abolitionists in letters, diaries, or other written material, any whose biographies and autobiographies identified them as abolitionists, other direct evidence, such as membership in an antislavery society, signing antislavery petitions, or corresponding with the editors of antislavery papers, and secondary source identifications, such as the list of abolitionists in McPherson, *Abolitionist Legacy* and similar sources. To date, 220 of the nearly 4,300 northern white teachers have been documented as abolitionists, or as having evidence that suggests the likelihood of abolitionism. Those with the clearest evidence of abolitionism averaged 4.9 years in the southern black schools before 1876; those for whom there is presumptive evidence of abolitionism averaged 4.5 years. The mean number of years for those without evidence of abolitionism falls to 2.4 years.

110. The policy of the American Baptist Free Mission Society was "to entrust the management of funds and labors to the colored people themselves, and thus work through them rather than *for* them." Nathan Brown to J. W. Alvord, 14 September 1869, LR, Ed. Div., BRFAL, M803:8. On the ABFMS, see McKivigan, "American Baptist Free Mission Society," 340–55; McKivigan, *The War against Proslavery Religion*; Marshall, "Eleutherian College," 201–2 [Eleutherian College was founded by ABHMS as an interracial abolitionist college]; on the AMA, see Joe M. Richardson, *Christian Reconstruction*. Sehat, "Civilizing Mission of Booker T. Washington," 328–37, 352–53, provides a particularly compelling critique of the AMA.

111. Elvira Leland to S. S. Jocelyn, 16 November 1863, AMAA.

112. Rhodelle Miller to S. S. Jocelyn, 25 December 1863, AMAA, capitalization *sic*; Mrs. J. Pennell Stephens to George Whipple, 26 February 1864, AMAA.

113. Mary J. Lane to Cyril Pearl, 1 February 1865, AMAA; George F. Mosher to Michael E. Strieby, 9 February 1865, AMAA.

114. *AM* 10 (July 1866): 152. The AMA did, in 1867, "renew" its principal that no one who harbored racial prejudice "ought to be appointed or sustained," though the number of embarrassing incidents of teacher racism indicates how difficult it was to follow the principle; see AMA, *Twenty-first Annual Report* (1867): 4.

115. Mary S. Williams to E. P. Smith, 20 July 1868, AMAA.

116. Katherine A. Dunning to George Whipple, 1 September 1865, AMAA; Dunning to M. E. Strieby, 6 October 1865, AMAA; Dunning to Samuel Hunt, 27 March 1866, AMAA.

117. John Lowrey to S. S. Jocelyn, 27 January 1863, AMAA.

118. Maria Benson to S. S. Jocelyn, 2 March 1864, AMAA.

119. May Merry to D. E. Emerson, 15 August 1877, AMA, emphasis added.

120. On women's war work, see especially Jane E. Schultz, *Women at the Front*; Silber, *Daughters of the Union*; Attie, *Patriotic Toll*; Oates, *Woman of Valor*; Brumgardt, *Civil War Nurse*.

121. Terry: 1860 census, Mass., Worcester Co., Sutton, 1245/1762, p. 899; Esther Asenath Terry to "My Dear Brother" [William Terry], 3 June 1864; Terry to William Terry, 7 July 1864 (quotation), Terry-Slocum Papers, YU.

122. Terry to William Terry, 26 September 1864; Terry to "My Dear Annie," 26 March 1866 (quotation), Terry-Slocum Papers, YU.

123. AMA, *Twentieth Annual Report* (1866), 19; *AM* 11 (April 1867): 75; Terry to [William Terry], 5 December 1866; Terry to "My Dear Brother & Sister," 7 November 1867 (quotation), Terry-Slocum Papers, YU.

124. Terry to William Terry, 8 June 1870 (first quotation); Terry to "My Dear Brother & Sister," 3 August 1870 (second quotation), Terry-Slocum Papers, YU.

125. Buss: 1860 census, Mass., Worcester Co., Sterling, 2529/2520, p. 1033; Harriet Buss to "Dear Parents," 12 March 1850, emphasis in original (first quotation), Harriet M. Buss Papers, UP.

126. Buss to parents, 7 March 1860, Buss Papers, UP.

127. Buss to "Dear Parents," 27 January 1860, ibid.

128. Buss to parents, 7 March 1860, ibid.

129. Buss to "Dear Parents," 27 June 1859, writing from Freedom, Pa. (quotation); Buss to her parents, 14 September 1861, in ibid.

130. NFRA, *Monthly Paper*, May 1863: 2; Harriet Buss to her parents, 31 March 1863 (quotation), Buss Papers, UP.

131. *FA* 1 (January 1864): 3; *FA* 1 (June 1864): 21; Buss to parents, 14 June 1866 (quotation), Buss Papers, UP.

132. Buss to parents, 15 January 1868, Buss Papers, UP.

133. Buss to parents, 26 November 1868, ibid.; Buss to C. L. Woodworth, 1 May 1868, AMAA; *AM* 13 (May 1869): 99; ABHMS, *Baptist Missions*, 602.

134. Harriet Buss to her parents, 26 November 1868; Buss to parents, 19 December 1868 (quotation), Buss Papers, UP.

135. Smith: 1850 census, Mass., Plymouth Co., Hanson, 25/32, p. 121; 1870 census, Mass., Plymouth Co., Hanson, 194/216, p. 286; *FR* 1 (July 1865): 118; *FR* 1 (December 1865): 203; *FR* 2 (November 1866): 203; *FR* 3 (November 1867): 176; *FR* 4 (November 1868): 180; *FR* 5 (November 1869): 54; *FR* 5 (February 1870): 70; Jane Briggs Smith Diary, entry for 4 April 1871, Jane Briggs Smith Fiske Papers, AAS.

136. Jane Briggs Smith to Friend Fuller Fiske, 25 June 1865, Smith Fiske Papers, AAS.

137. Smith to Fiske, 20 August 1865, ibid., emphasis in original.

138. Smith to Fiske, 31 July 1866, ibid.

139. George W. Williams to J. C. Churchill, 2 September 1868, in Churchill to O. O. Howard, 8 September 1868, LR Ed. Div., BRFAL, M803:6; Matilda M. Atkinson to Corresponding Secretary of the American Miss. Ass., 8 February 1864, AMAA.

140. Luthera [?] Hill to S. S. Jocelyn, 22 February 1864, AMAA.

141. The phrase is from Kent, *Converting Women*, 4 and passim; see also Stephanie Wright, "Education and the Changing Social Identities."

Chapter 5

1. Teachers, locations, and years drawn from the Freedmen's Teacher Project.

2. Blum, *Reforging the White Republic*, esp. 51–86.

3. In an otherwise remarkably perceptive study, Edward J. Blum engages in an uncritical celebration of the freemen's aid movement. His take on the movement is contradicted by virtually all the scholarship of the last four decades. He makes no effort to refute that scholarship, but rather simply ignores its findings while citing much of the scholarship. As a result, he is blind to the ways much of the movement contributed directly to the return to racial solidarity that stands at the center of his argument. See ibid., 51–86.

4. Botume, *First Days Amongst the Contrabands*, 19.

5. Rose, *Rehearsal for Reconstruction*; McPherson, *Struggle for Equality*, esp. 401–5; Browning, " 'Bringing Light to our Land,' " 1–17; Butchart, *Northern Schools*.

6. See especially McPherson, *Abolitionist Legacy*; see also Inez Moore Parker, *The Rise and Decline*; James P. Brawley, *Two Centuries of Methodist Concern*.

7. Fleming, *Civil War and Reconstruction in Alabama*, 518.

8. S. C. Armstrong, "Normal-School Work among the Freedmen," 175, 179.

9. Ibid., 176.

10. Wyatt-Brown, "Black Schooling during Reconstruction," 154–55, 157.

11. Horst, *Education for Manhood*, 195; American Tract Society, *Fortieth Annual Report*, 65; AMA, *Twentieth Annual Report*, 15, 18.

12. For a full description and analysis of the American Tract Society texts, see Butchart, *Northern Schools*, 136–51. Cf. Heather Andrea Williams, *Self-Taught*, 126–37; Blum, *Reforging the White Republic*, 56–59.

13. Child, *Freedmen's Book*, iii. Child intended to donate any profits from the book to freedmen's education: Lydia Maria Child to Samuel May, 11 January 1866, AFUC Papers, CU.

14. *Freedmen's Torchlight* 1 (December 1866): 1–4.

15. *NF* 2 (April 1866): 119; R. M. Manly to William C. Child, 25 June 1866, LS, Virginia BRFAL, M1053:1; Orville T Andrews to D. Burt, 27 December 1866, LR, Tennessee BRFAL, M1000:3; Reuben P. Clark to D. Burt, 29 January 1867, LR, Tennessee BRFAL, M1000:3. James M. McPherson claims that Child's book "was used as a primer and textbook in freedmen's schools," and Robert C. Morris asserts that her book "is representative of teaching materials used throughout the Reconstruction era." Neither claim is accompanied by evidence of actual classroom use of

the material: McPherson, *Struggle for Equality*, 388; Morris, *Reading, 'Riting, and Reconstruction*, 182.

16. J. A. Lane, "Minutes of Meeting of 9–10 June 1865," AMAA.

17. Philena Carkin, "Reminiscences of My Life," UVA; for examples of the textbooks used, see *AF* 1 (January 1867): 154; *NF* 1 (August 1865): 214–15; Delaware Association for the Moral Improvement and Education of the Colored People, "Minutes," 12 October 1867, Historical Society of Delaware; New England Educational Commission, *First Annual Report*, 33–34; "The Freedmen at Port Royal," *Atlantic Monthly* 12 (September 1963): 303.

18. Arthur Sumner to Ednah Dow Cheney, 6 November 1873, NEFAS Collection, MHS.

19. Holland, *Letters and Diary of Laura M. Towne*, entry for 13 June 1865, pp. 163–64, confusion of predicate for subject *sic*.

20. *AF* 2 (April 1868): 398. Among other schools reporting the study of history, composition, and physiology, see *FF* 1 (May 1869): 6; *FF* 1 (May 1865): 55; *FA* 1 (September 1864): 29; Cornelia Hancock to Sarah [Hancock?], 11 March 1866, Cornelia Hancock Manuscripts, SC; Holland, *Letters and Diary of Laura M. Towne*, 163–64, letter written 13 June 1865; H. T. Hartwell to Mr. Graham, 24 July 1866, AMAA; *AF* 2 (April 1868): 39.

21. *AF* 1 (March 1867): 186; *FF* 1 (February 1873): 4.

22. Jane B. Smith to Friend Fiske, 12 January 1868, Jane Briggs Smith Fiske Papers, AAS.

23. Manuscript copies of the Teachers' Monthly School Reports have been preserved in the records of the bureau's state superintendents. They were consolidated twice yearly and reported in Alvord, *Semi-Annual Reports on Schools for Freedmen* (Washington, D.C.: GPO, 1866–1870).

24. *Petersburg (Va.) Daily Appeal*, 12 July 1873, 3.

25. Mortimer A. Warren, "The State Normal School, South Carolina," ms. First Annual Report of the South Carolina State Normal School, 1875, USC.

26. S. C. Armstrong, "Normal-School Work among the Freedmen," 175.

27. See, among many other examples, Holland, *Letters and Diary of Laura M. Towne*, 163–64; Reilly, *Sarah Jane Foster*, 76, 128–29; Jane Briggs Smith Fiske Collection, AAS; Lydia Atkinson, "Diary of Lydia Atkinson," SC; Cornelia Hancock Manuscripts, SC; letters of Josephine Elizabeth Strong in Strong Family Papers, YU; *Petersburg (Va.) Daily Courier*, 7 July 1871, 3.

28. *PFB* 1 (December 1865): 65.

29. See, for example, William F. Allen Diary, 19 June 1864, William F. Allen Collection, Wisconsin Historical Society; *Petersburg (Va.) Daily Index*, 7 July 1871, 3; George McK. Mitchell to G. L. Eberhart, 31 October 1866, LR, Georgia BRFAL, M799:8; C. R. Bent to ?, undated, in George W. Gile to John W. Alvord, 13 July 1869, LR, Ed. Div., BRFAL, M802:12; *FA* 1 (May 1864): 17; *Fourth Annual Report of the Barnard Freedmen's Aid Society of Dorchester*, 4; Mary F. Wells to E. P. Smith, 18 February 1867, LR, Alabama BRFAL, M810:1; Park Brewster to [James Thompson], 5 September 1868, LR, Tennessee BRFAL, M1000:4.

30. The best study of nineteenth-century textbooks remains Elson, *Guardians of Tradition*; on the curriculum in northern schools, see Cremin, *American Education*, though Cremin would not agree with my characterization of the curriculum.

31. See Katz, *Irony of Early School Reform*; William R. Johnson, " 'Chanting Choristers' "; Nash, " 'Cultivating the Powers of *Human Beings*' "; Hogan, "Market Revolution and Disciplinary Power"; Hogan, "The Organization of Schooling"; Robarts, "Quest for a Science of Education"; Finkelstein, "Pedagogy as Intrusion," though none of those sources would agree fully with this particular characterization.

32. Watkins, *White Architects of Black Education*; James D. Anderson, *Education of Blacks in the South*; James D. Anderson, "Historical Development of Black Vocational Education," 180–222; Bond, *Negro Education in Alabama*; Sherer, *Subordination or Liberation*; Spivey, *Schooling for the New Slavery*.

33. Wyatt-Brown, "Black Schooling during Reconstruction," 152–57, quotation 155; his remark about the equal neglect of geography is in note 30.

34. Arithmetic was reported as having the highest enrollment of all subjects in three reports (Alvord, *Third Semi-Annual Report* [January 1867], 4; Alvord, *Fifth Semi-Annual Report* [January 1868], 12–14; and Alvord, *Sixth Semi-Annual Report* [July 1868], 6–7), but was more often reported as having the second- or third-highest enrollment (Alvord, *Fourth Semi-Annual Report* [July 1867], 5; Alvord, *Seventh Semi-Annual Report* [January 1869], 6–8; etc.).

35. The language of rural and urban pedagogies employed here should not be read too literally. Some rural teachers adopted modern, or "urban," modes of teaching, while many urban teachers continued to follow very traditional modes of teaching. However, the northern urban areas tended to see more pedagogical innovation in the first half of the nineteenth century, from the work of Joseph Lancaster onward, than did rural schools. The movement from one form of pedagogy to the other was part of what has been called modernization, and I occasionally refer to urban or modern pedagogy as "modernizing." I do not mean the term normatively, however. Modernization has not assured unproblematic progress. See, for example, Lasch, *The True and Only Heaven*.

36. The history of actual classroom practices in the nineteenth century has been neglected, though the prescriptive literature has been covered well. My argument here is drawn in part from the following: Robarts, "Quest for a Science of Education"; David Hamilton, "Adam Smith"; Hogan, "Modes of Discipline"; Hogan, "Market Revolution and Disciplinary Power"; William R. Johnson, " 'Chanting Choristers' "; Katz, "The Emergence of Bureaucracy"; Katz, *Irony of Early School Reform*, 132–38; and Katz, "The 'New Departure' in Quincy."

37. Hogan, "Examinations, Merit, and Morals," 31–78; Hogan, "Market Revolution and Disciplinary Power"; Butchart, "Punishments, Penalties, Prizes, and Procedures"; Glenn, "School Discipline and Punishment."

38. Towne, "Pioneer Work," 7.

39. *FR* 3 (January 1867): 7. See also, for example, Kilham, "Sketches in Color," 35–36.

40. *FR* 2 (December 1866): 212; see also *AM* 13 (March 1869): 55.

41. Sarah Williams to "Aunt Annie," 14 March 1869, Correspondence of Edward Williams, in Stratton (Maule) Papers, SC.

42. NEFAS, "Letter of Instruction to Teachers," printed circular letter, undated, c. 1866, in William Channing Gannett Collection, UR. PFRA's "Instructions to Teachers" were clearly based on NEFAS's rules, adapting this particular rule to provide a bit more leeway for teachers: "Corporal punishment should be very rarely resorted to, and its frequent use is regarded as an evidence of incompetency in the teacher." *PFB* (October 1866): 1. Many teachers who opposed corporal punishment were quick to add that they would not entirely abandon it; it had its place for extreme cases. For example, William G. Tackaberry, reporting on his observations in South Carolina and Florida in the spring of 1864, wrote, "A mild and gentle discipline answers every purpose in the schools, except in a few cases, where it is necessary to resort to the rod, or expulsion from school, to remedy abuses." *FA* 1 (June 1864): 23.

43. "To the Teachers of the Normal School, Elizabeth City [Virginia]," 22 February 1871, copied in NEFAS, "Daily Journal [1869–1871]," 339, NEFAS Papers, MHS. The Baltimore Normal School, sustained by the AFUC and the Baltimore Association for the Moral and Educational Improvement of the Colored People, also explicitly prohibited corporal punishment: Baltimore Normal School, "Rules and Regulations adopted by the Normal School Committee for the Government of the Normal & Model Schools," undated, pp. 3–4, enclosed in Baltimore Normal School "Minute Book," vol. 1, MdHS.

44. *PFB* 2 (July 1866): 3; "Instructions for Teachers," *PFB* 2 (October 1866): 1. Identical language appears in New England Freedmen's Aid Society, "Letter of Instruction to Teachers," printed circular letter, undated, c. 1866, William Channing Gannett Collection, UR.

45. *AM* 8 (August 1864): 192.

46. *PFB* 1 (August 1865): 49, spelling *sic*.

47. *AM* 9 (March 1865): 49.

48. *AF* 2 (January 1868): 350–51.

49. Martha Schofield, Diary, 15 January 1862, p. 115, handwritten ms., Martha Schofield Papers, SC.

50. *AM* 8 (July 1864): 178.

51. *FF* 1 (April 1866): 102.

52. Quoted in AMA, *Twenty-third Annual Report* (1869), 27.

53. *AF* 2 (January 1868): 348.

54. Hamilton, "Adam Smith," 281–98; Hogan, "Examinations, Merit, and Morals," 31–78; Hogan, "From Contest Mobility to Stratified Credentialing," 21–42; Hogan, "Modes of Discipline," 1–56.

55. *FF* 1 (May 1869): 9; two teachers handled a school of over 120 students with reported ease, their "judicious system of rewards and punishment disposing of most cases" of insubordination: *FA* 1 (May 1864): 18.

56. Towne, "Pioneer Work," 7; see also her letter of 11 December 1864, reprinted in *PFB* 1 (February 1865): 6, where she describes emulation in action: "Position in

class is the object of the liveliest ambition. They study hard to attain the head, and feel keenly the pleasure of getting there, or the mortification of losing rank."

57. Little has been written on the origins of grading or ranking systems in the nineteenth century, though teachers were clearly beginning to experiment with such systems by the 1860s. See Hogan, "From Contest Mobility to Stratified Credentialing," 21–42; and Labaree, *Making of an American High School*, 17, 27, 52–60.

58. S. A. Finney to E. L. Deane, 28 February 1870, Unregistered LR, Ed. Div., BRFAL, M810:12, spelling *sic*. A similar system of grades, with opportunities for what modern students would recognize as "extra credit," is described in *PFB* 1 (June 1867): 5.

59. *PFB* 2 (December 1866): 11.

60. Quotation from A. E. Newton, in *AF* 2 (January 1868): 348.

61. Caroline Thomas to Friends' Association for the Aid and Elevation of the Freedmen, 26 August 1866, *Friends' Intelligencer* 23 (29 September 1866): 475.

62. *FA* 1 (May 1864): 18; see also Stearns, *Black Man of the South*, 65.

63. Quoted in *AF* 1 (March 1867): 186.

64. *AM* 7 (May 1863): 115–16.

65. Mortimer A. Warren, Report of the State Normal School, Columbia, South Carolina, 30 June 1876, ms., South Carolina Normal School, USC. Warren had reported in his 1874–75 report, that "in spite" of the lack of texts, "we have prospered. . . . I think our pupils have become more independent than if they had books." Warren, 28 June 1875, ibid. Others reporting whole-class teaching include Jane M. Slocum's description of her oral instruction for the entire class: "It consists of chart instruction, object teaching, mental arithmetic, numeration, and whatever else I chance to think of." *FF* 1 (March 1865): 36. Henry Fish provided a remarkably thorough description of his mode of teaching reading and writing, which depended primarily on oral, group instruction in contrast to the "irksome method" of "solitary study" common to traditional schooling: *FA* 1 (July–August 1864): n.p. See also *FF* 1 (May 1869): 9; Stearns, *Black Man of the South*, 64–66; New England Educational Commission, *First Annual Report*, 35–36; Kilham, "Sketches in Color," 36–37; among many others.

66. *PFB* 1 (July 1866): 1–2.

67. *FF* 1 (February 1870): [2].

68. *AF* 1 (March 1867): 186, quoting the *National Intelligencer*.

69. *FA* 1 (July/August 1864): 25.

70. *PFB* (December 1866): 11; see also *FF* 1 (April 1866): 102.

71. [Friends Freedmen's Association] "Circular Letter," 24 December 1863, HC.

72. *FF* 1 (March 1865): 36–37. By 1867, the Friends' Freedmens Association was routinely supplying its teachers with maps, globes, dictionaries, and thermometers: FFA, Minutes of Instruction Committee, 19 March 1867, 26 March 1867, Friends Freedmen's Association Papers, SC.

73. Callahan, *Education and the Cult of Efficiency*; Katz, "The Emergence of Bureaucracy," 155–88, 318–47; Katz, Doucet, and Stern, *Social Organization of Early Industrial Capitalism*; Stanley K. Schultz, *Culture Factory*, 103–53; Tyack, *The One Best System*, 28–77.

74. Kaestle, *Pillars of the Republic*, 69–70, 132–34; Stanley K. Schultz, *Culture Factory*, 107–9, 125–31; Herbst, "Teacher Preparation," 213–56; Fitts, "Una and the Lion," 140–57; Strober and Lanford, "Feminization of Public School Teaching," 212–35.

75. NEFAS, *First Annual Report* (1863), 26–27. Mitchell's work is documented in AFUC, "Minutebook," AFUC Papers, CU; Allen's work is documented in the William F. Allen Papers, WSHS; on Warner, see Warner, *Yardley Warner*; and *FF* 1 (May 1869): 6. Regarding the AMA's supervision, see AMA, *Annual Reports*, 1863–1875; J. A. Nichols to Samuel Hunt, 16 December 1865, AMAA; G. D. Pike to E. P. Smith, 25 July 1868, AMAA; and [Laura J. Noble] to E. P. Smith, 25 July 1868, AMAA; on monthly teachers' reports, see for example C. C. Leigh to Esther H. Hawks, 2 March 1863, J. M. Hawks and Esther Hawks Papers, LC; and examples of reports in AMAA or AFUC Papers, CU. Data from the reports were systematically compiled and used in the aid society publications and in John W. Alvord's *Semi-Annual Reports*.

76. *AM* 8 (September 1864): 214–15; NEFAS, "Letter of Instruction to Teachers," c. 1866; PFRA, "Instructions for Teachers," in *PFB* 1 (October 1866): 1.

77. *FA* 1 (July–August 1864): n.p.; quotation from [Friends'] *FR* 1 (April 1866): 7. See also, among others: *FF* 1 (February 1866): 96; *FF* 1 (May 1869): 9; *AF* 2 (January 1868): 350–55; *AM* 9 (April 1865): 76; *AM* 9 (July 1865): 159.

78. W. S. Bell, 31 October 1864, in *AM* 8 (December 1864): 293, emphasis in original.

79. George Whipple to O. O. Howard, 16 May 1865, LR, Office of the Commissioner, BRFAL, M752:3.

80. See Alvord, *Semi-Annual Reports* (1866–70). Thousands of the bureau's Teachers' Monthly School Reports have survived, scattered through various divisions of the Freedmen's Bureau Papers; a few also have found their way into the archives of the individual aid societies and the early papers of state superintendents of education in some of the southern states. The bureau's report form was relatively complex, leading one assistant to complain that if it were any more difficult, "one fourth of the teachers will not properly fill it."

81. Stearns, *Black Man of the South*, 64–65.

82. *AF* 2 (April 1868): 398.

83. H. T. Hartwell to Mr. Graham, 24 July 1866, AMAA.

84. John C. Zachos, *The Phonic Primer and Reader*, 1864. Zachos was among the first teachers sent to Port Royal to teach the former slaves on the Sea Islands: see Butchart, "John C. Zachos," 209–10.

85. Henry Fish in *FA* 1 (September 1864): 29, emphasis in original.

86. *PFB* (March 1867): 1–4.

87. FFA, Minutes of Instruction Committee, vol. 1, 20 March 1866; 3 April 1866; 19 March 1867; 26 March 1867, Friends Freedmen's Association Papers, SC; Alvord, *Fourth Semi-Annual Report* (July 1867), 77–78; Alvord, *Fifth Semi-Annual Report* (January 1868), 25; *NF* 1 (15 December 1865): 363–64; [A. E. Newton], *First Annual Report*, 38–39; James D. Arnold to John Ogden, 11 October 1865, AMAA; Swint, "Reports from Educational Agents," 65–71. On early professionalization of

teaching in the North, see for example Ogren, *American State Normal School*; Mattingly, *Classless Profession*; Mattingly, "Educational Revivals," 39–71; Mac-Mullen, *In the Cause of True Education*; and Herbst, "Teacher Preparation in the Nineteenth Century," 213–36.

88. Sarah E. Chase to Fred W. G. May, 18 November 1864, Chase Family Papers, AAS; *PFB* 1 (February 1865): 6; *FR* 1 (March 1865): 42; *FR* 1 (July 1865): 110; *FR* 1 (August 1865): 129; *FR* 1 (September 1865): 139; *NF* 1 (July 1865): 203 (quotation); Presbyterian Church USA, *First Annual Report* (1866), 17–19; AMA, *Twenty-first Annual Report* (1867), 16–17.

89. See Chapter 2.

90. *FF* 1 (December 1867): [117]; see also NFRA, *Fifth Annual Report* (1867), 26; *Report of the West-Roxbury Branch*, 5; *AF*, Extra, 1 (November 1867): 4; Mortimer Warren, "Scheme of Study for Free Common Schools," Appendix B, in *Reports and Resolutions of the General Assembly of the State of South Carolina* (1875), 415–48.

91. I should hasten to add that I do not mean by the above description that I hold any romantic view of nineteenth-century classrooms as implicitly liberating or ideologically unproblematic. Freedom from physical force came often at the cost of psychological manipulation; classroom reward systems grew directly out of analogous oppressive wage systems; the gentler social relations of the classroom had their roots in the social relations of industrial capitalism. Yet, in the setting of the postwar South, those classrooms symbolized a disruption of hegemony and were, dialectically, progressive.

92. James D. Anderson, *Education of Blacks in the South*, 9–18.

Chapter 6

1. Genovese, *Roll, Jordan, Roll*, 135, 561–63, 617–19; Cornelius, *When I Can Read*, 18, 32–33, 65–67; Woodson, *Education of the Negro*; Heather Andrea Williams, *Self-Taught*, 7–21, 203–13.

2. Eric Foner, *Reconstruction*, 365–68.

3. Bullock, *A History of Negro Education*, 66 (quotation), 89–93; Harlan, *Separate and Unequal*, 3–44; Charles William Dabney, *Universal Education in the South*, 1:vii–ix; Bond, *Education of the Negro*, 76–78; James D. Anderson, *Education of Blacks in the South*, 20–23.

4. Historians increasingly understand Reconstruction as a battle for white supremacy in which terrorism was a central tool. See, for example, Lemann, *Redemption*; Rable, *But There Was No Peace*; Gillette, *Retreat from Reconstruction*; Perman, *The Road to Redemption*; DeBlack, *With Fire and Sword*, esp. 174–233; and Shaffer, *After the Glory*, 23–43. Most historians focus primarily on white terrorism as a means to curb black voting, to the exclusion of the southern attack on education.

5. Watkins, *White Architects of Black Education*; James D. Anderson, *Black Education in the South*, 79–109; Blum, *Reforging the White Republic*.

6. Swint, *Northern Teacher in the South*, 94–142. Other writers who took a similarly negative view of the teachers and blame the teachers for their dangerous

meddling include Knight, " 'Messianic' Invasion of the South," 645, 649; and Cash, *Mind of the South*, 140.

7. Vaughn, *Schools for All*, 25–38, quotation 25.

8. Wyatt-Brown, "Black Schooling during Reconstruction," 146–65.

9. Jacqueline Jones, *Soldiers of Light and Love*; Morris, *Reading, 'Riting, and Reconstruction*; Horst, *Education for Manhood*; Selleck, *Gentle Invaders*; Butchart, *Northern Schools*; Butchart, "Recruits to the 'Army of Civilization,' " 76–87.

10. Irons, *Jim Crow's Children*; Cecelski, *Along Freedom Road*; Patterson, *Brown v. Board of Education*.

11. "Report of Freedmen's Schools in North Carolina, For the month ending Feb. 28, 1866," State Superintendent's Monthly School Reports, North Carolina BRFAL, M844:13.

12. Mary Bowers to F. A. Fiske, 20 September 1866, and Bowers to Fisk, 10 October 1866, emphases in original; punctuation *sic*. Unregistered LR, North Carolina BRFAL, M844:10; see also testimony of William G. Bowers, Orange City, N.C., particularly response to question 19, Report #7, Office #507, Denied Claim, SCC.

13. Silas Outlaw, TMSR, October 1869 and January 1870, SR, Alabama BRFAL, M810:7; see similarly H. H. Mitchell, letter of 10 May 1867, in Register of LR, vol. 1, p. 84, Tennessee BRFAL, M1000:2.

14. Thomas Collins, manuscript school report, 16 January 1867, LR, Texas BRFAL, M822:3; C. S. Roberts to J. T. Kirkman, 23 August 1867, ibid., M822:4; Charles Goldberg to Roberts, 30 May 1868, ibid., M822:9; Charles F. Rand to Joseph Welch, 30 June 1868, LR, Texas BRFAL, M822:13; Roberts to Kirkman, 23 August 1867, ibid., M822:4 (quotation).

15. W. H. Howard to Joseph Welch, 26 August 1868, LR, Texas BRFAL, M822:6; Haughn to "My dear Sir" [probably Joseph Welch], 24 March 1869, ibid., M822:6; Orndorf to C. S. Roberts, 22 March 1869, and Orndorf to H. L. Dicks, 23 May 1869, ibid., M822:7.

16. P. H. Gillen to J. R. Lewis, 30 August 1869, LR, Georgia BRFAL, M799:13.

17. [U.S. Army], *Report of the Board of Education*, 7–12.

18. James E. Rhoads to Margaret E. Rhoads, 16 May 1865, Rhoads Collection, HC.

19. *FA* 1 (January 1864): 3; Journal of Accounts of the Board of Education, April 1864 to June 1865, pp. 1, 15, Louisiana BRFAL, M1026:10; U.S. Congress, House Reports, "New Orleans Riots," 430–31, quotation 431. Buggy subsequently taught in another black school for one more year in Carroll Parish: District Superintendent's Monthly School Reports for October 1868, December 1868, and February 1869, Carroll Parish, SR, Louisiana BRFAL, M1026:4.

20. C. F. Brim to "Free School Agent," LR, Georgia BRFAL, M799:13.

21. W. Harrison Daniel, "Virginia Baptists and the Negro," 361.

22. L. F. Drake to C. E. Compton, 4 August 1869, LR, Tennessee BRFAL, M1000:5; similarly, Dr. W. W. Lewis, a native white physician teaching in Brunswick Co., Virginia, described public sentiment toward his school with one word: "Unfriendly." W. W. Lewis, TMSR, January 1869, SR, Virginia BRFAL, M1053:15.

23. Georgia A. Grimes to Superintendent of F. A. Society of M. E. Church, 13 May

1870, LR, Tennessee BRFAL, M1000:5; Grimes: 1860 census, Ga., Heard Co., Franklin PO, 809/794, p. 781; 1870 census, Tenn., Wilson Co., Dist. 5, Lebanon PO, 160/160, p. 412.

24. Robert P. Lindsey, TMSR, June 1869, SR, Georgia BRFAL, M799:24. Lindsey's father had been a small planter, holding ten enslaved African Americans in 1850, and twelve by 1860; by 1870, the family had lost over 90 percent of its prewar wealth; see Lindsey: 1850 census, Slave Schedule, Ga., Butts Co., Dist. 8, p. 780; 1860 census, Slave Schedule, Ga., Butts Co., Dublin District, p. 250; 1860 census, Ga., Butts Co., Dublin Dist., Indian Springs, 111/113, p. 117; 1870 census, Ga., Butts Co., Subdivision 13, Indian Springs, 829/841, p. 528. Lindsey had served in the 35th Georgia Infantry: ACWRD.

25. James W. Reese, TMSR, April 1869, SR, Georgia BRFAL, M799:23; James W. Reese, Pension application filed in Morgan County, Georgia, 6 February 1902, Pension Applications and Supporting Documents, Pension Office, Record Group 58, Georgia Confederate Pensions and Records Department, Georgia State Archives.

26. Unpublished manuscript biography of Giles B. Cooke, handwritten notes to Chapter 7, page 3, Giles Buckner Cooke Papers, VHS.

27. F. Tolman to "Sir," 31 March 1867, LR, Texas BRFAL, M822:4.

28. William A. Jones to George W. Whipple, 14 October 1868, AMAA; *AM* 13 (May 1869): 101; *AM* 14 (June 1870): 128; *AM* 15 (May 1871): 100; *AM* 16 (May 1872): 100. Joe M. Richardson, *Christian Reconstruction*, 192, 196, misidentifies Jones as the William A. Jones who attended Oberlin College, graduating in 1857. Both were black, but the latter was a dentist by 1864 and made his fortune in British Columbia. The William A. Jones who taught in southern schools was from Elmira, N.Y., where he had grown up; he did not attend college. In 1867 he went to Mississippi to teach, without a sponsoring agency; the following year he went to Darien, Georgia, under AMA, then to Brazoria, Texas, where he remained until at least 1872, when he was still listed on AMA's rolls, though his school was receiving state support; it is highly likely that he continued to teach in Texas.

29. Hood, *One Hundred Years*, 370–74; *Harper's Weekly*, 21 November 1868, 740; Eric Foner, *Freedom's Lawmakers*, 15–16, 32, 165; Lemann, *Redemption*, 151. Derry, Ormond, and Cook all continued teaching after their encounters with the Klan and other opponents of their work.

30. D. W. Culp, *Twentieth Century Negro Literature*; Gregory, "Education of Blacks in Maryland," 154.

31. Hampton Normal and Agricultural Institute, *Twenty-Two Years' Work*, 24; letter of S. G. Cross, *AF* 2 (June 1868): 427.

32. Simmons, *Men of Mark*, 145; Scruggs, *Women of Distinction*, 359; Vaughn, *Schools for All*, 71–72; William Smith to "Sir," 22 November 1869, LR, Tennessee BRFAL, M1000:5.

33. H. S. Bennett to Michael E. Strieby, 13 September 1869, LR, Tennessee BRFAL, M1000:5.

34. [Mary S. Osborne], "Among the Freedmen in Maryland. No. 4," *Zion's Herald*, 7 February 1865, 24.

35. Small, "Yankee Schoolmarm in Freedmen's Schools," 381–402; Maxine D. Jones, "The American Missionary Association," 103–11; Butchart, "Mission Matters," 1–17; Butchart, "Perspectives on Gender," 15–32.

36. James P. Butler, "Sub-Assistant Commissioner's (or Agent's) Monthly Report on Education of Freedmen and Refugees in Sub-District, State of Texas, in charge of James P. Butler, for the Month of February, 1868 . . .," SR, Texas BRFAL, M822:12; see also for example "Sub-Assistant Commissioner's (or Agent's) Monthly Report on Education of Freedmen and Refugees in Sub-District, State of North Carolina, in charge of C. W. Dodge for the month of March 1868 . . .," SR, North Carolina BRFAL, M844:15.

37. Thomas Jackson, "Sub-Assistant Commissioner's (or Agent's) Monthly Report on Education of Freedmen and Refugees in 11th Sub-District, State of Virginia . . ., April 1868," SR, Virginia BRFAL, M1053:13.

38. Anthony Bryant to Charles Garretson, 30 September 1867, LR, Texas BRFAL, M822:3; A. H. Mayer to J. T. Kirkman, 10 May 1867, LR, Texas BRFAL, M822:4; *McKinney Messenger* 15 (18 June 1870) and 15 (16 July 1870), <http://www.geocit ies.com/collincotx/mmvol15.html?20055>, retrieved 5 April 2005.

39. Mrs. F. A. M. Shaver, TMSR, January 1870, SR, Alabama BRFAL, M810:7; Elizabeth S. Thompson, TMSR, SR, January 1870, Alabama BRFAL, M810:7.

40. See for example Stacy Mayfield to Joseph Welch, 13 August 1869, LR, Texas BRFAL, M822:6; W. H. Howard to Joseph Welch, 26 August 1868, ibid.; Maria Cochrane to "Gentlemen," 30 March 1864, Correspondence Received Relating to Employment, Louisiana BRFAL, M1026:7.

41. James Fitz Allen Sisson to J. R. Lewis, 2 September 1869, LR, Georgia BRFAL, M799:13, all punctuation *sic*.

42. *Liberator*, 8 April 1864, 57; Smallwood, *Time of Hope*, 80–81; A. L. Snow to C. E. Compton, 7 November 1869, LR, Tennessee BRFAL, M1000:5.

43. [Osborne], "Among the Freedmen in Maryland. No. 5," *Zion's Herald*, 14 March 1866, 44. See similar comments in C. M. Cummings, TMSR, January 1866, SR, Georgia BRFAL, M799:20; Jesse H. Rupert, TMSR, March 1870, SR, Virginia BRFAL, M1053:19.

44. *PFB* (December 1866): 2.

45. W. L. Coan to R. M. Manly, undated, marked "Dec 1865" by recipient, Monthly Statistical School Reports, SR, Virginia BRFAL, M1053:12, emphasis in original; see also Maria C. Hopson to Wager Swayne, 10 March 1866, Register of LR, Alabama BRFAL, M810:3; [Osborne], "Among the Freedmen in Maryland. No. 4," *Zion's Herald*, 7 February 1865, 24.

46. Elliot Whipple to C. W. Buckley, 15 June 1867, LR, Alabama BRFAL, M810:3.

47. Alvord, *Seventh Semi-Annual Report* (January 1869), 44.

48. Rable, *But There Was No Peace*, 29; Philena Carkin, "Reminiscences of my Life," 1:39–44, UVA; Sarah A. Dickey to "My Dear Classmates," 4 March 1872, in Correspondence File, Dickey, Sarah A., Class of 1869, Alumnae File, MHC (quotation).

49. G. Bowles to D. Burt, 22 November 1866, LR, Tennessee BRFAL, M1000:3; Warren Norton to Louis W. Stevenson, 8 March 1870, LR, Texas BRFAL, M822:7.

50. Jennie E. Howard to R. M. Manly, 15 June 1866, Unregistered LR, Virginia

BRFAL, M1053:6; see also for example Edmonia G. Highgate to M. E. Strieby, 17 December 1866, AMAA.

51. Thomas Taylor to C. W. Buckley, 28 March 1866, Register of LR, Alabama BRFAL, M810:3; Hopson to Wager Swayne, 10 March 1866, ibid.; Maria C. Hopson to Buckley, 22 April 1866, ibid. Despite the difficulties of her first year in Talladega, Hopson continued to teach there from 1866 to 1869; J. M. Langston to O. O. Howard, 10 July 1867, LR, Ed. Div., BRFAL, M803:7. A Lynchburg, Virginia, native claimed that her family was the only family in the city who would have anything to do with the teachers there; see *PFB* (February 1868): 12; Margaret S. Clark to F. A. Fiske, 30 May 1868, LR, North Carolina BRFAL, M844:7.

52. [Friends'] *FR* 1 (December 1865): 9.

53. Esther A. Christian, TMSR, 27 October 1865, SR, Georgia BRFAL, M799:20; John A. McDonnell, "Sub-Assistant Commissioner's (or Agent's) Monthly Report . . . 1st Div., 9th Sub-District, State of Virginia . . ., January 1868," SR, Virginia BRFAL, M1053:13.

54. William Elliott to F. A. Fiske, 14 April 1866, Unregistered LR, North Carolina BRFAL, M844:10, spelling and emphasis *sic*; William Elliott to F. A. Fiske, 16 May 1866, ibid. Elliott was more successful elsewhere in the state; he taught for at least four more years.

55. Lizzie Granger to "Dear Sir," 26 July 1869, LR, Texas BRFAL, M822:5.

56. Daniel F. Noonan to "Sir" [G. L. Eberhard], 24 October, 1865, LR, Georgia BRFAL, M799:20, spelling *sic*. Rev. S. S. Murkland, for many years a Presbyterian minister in North Carolina, was locked out of his church when he opened a black school in it; he had to continue the school in his home: Sidney S. Murkland to F. A. Fiske, 31 October 1867, LR, North Carolina BRFAL, M844:7.

57. E. S. Thompson to R. D. Harper, 14 October 1868, Register of LR, Alabama BRFAL, M810:2; see also G. B. Mitchell to J. R. Lewis, 18 March 1869, LR, Georgia BRFAL, M799:12, regarding a similar case in Richmond County, Georgia.

58. Gregory, "Education of Blacks in Maryland," 154; Vaughn, *Schools for All*, 47; Horace James, *Annual Report of the Superintendent of Negro Affairs in North Carolina. 1864. With an Appendix, Containing the History and Management of the Freedmen in this Department up to June 1st, 1865* (Boston: W. F. Brown & Co., [1865]), 20–21; Rable, *But There Was No Peace*, 39; R. M. Manly to William George Hawkins, 4 April 1866, LS, Virginia BRFAL, M1053:1; C. F. Brim to "Free School Agent," 29 June 1869, LR, Georgia BRFAL, M799:13; R. S. Rust in Cincinnati to Rev. R. D. Harper, 20 November 1868, Register of LR, Alabama BRFAL, M810:2; T. McHugh, Letter M160, 19 Sept 1871, p. 252, Register of LR, Vol. 1, Texas Supt of Public Instruction, TSLA; C. H. Prowell, Letter P126, 30 November 1871, p. 309, ibid.; J. J. Strong to E. M. Cravath, 14 August 1871, AMAA; NEFAS, "Daily Journal, 18 May 1871–Sept 1873," p. 111, NEFAS Records, MHS.

59. S. Daffin to J. Thompson, 7 March 1869, LR, Tennessee BRFAL, M1000:4; Samuel Walker to James Thomson, 9 March 1869, ibid. (quotation).

60. G. D. Pike, *The Jubilee Singers and Their Campaign for Twenty Thousand Dollars* (Boston: Lee and Shepard, 1873), 63–67; J. B. T. Marsh, *The Story of the Jubilee Singers, With their Songs*, rev. ed. (Boston: Houghton, Mifflin and Company,

[1880]), 93–95; Culp, *Twentieth Century Negro Literature*, n.p.; *CR* 6 (18 August 1866): 129; Daniel McGee, TMSR, September 1868, SR, Georgia BRFAL, M799:22; H. H. Burt of Eufala to O. L. Sheppard, 9 April 1868, Register of LR, Alabama BRFAL, M810:2; Alvord, *7th Semi-Annual Report* (January 1869), 44; E. Gay to Charles A. Vernon, 30 June 1868, LR, Texas BRFAL, M822:7.

61. H. E. Brown to E. M. Cravath, 19 September 1870, Alabama file, AMA; H. E. Brown to E. M. Cravath, 13 October 1870, Alabama file, AMA (quotation). Among many other black teachers who experienced incendiarism, see for example Alvord, *7th Semi-Annual Report*, pp. 41, 42, 45.

62. G. Bowles to D. Burt, 22 November 1866, LR, Tennessee BRFAL, M1000:3; D. I. Robinson to C. B. Fisk, 26 June 1866, Unregistered LR, Tennessee BRFAL, M1000:5; William Payne, TMSR, November 1867, SR, Georgia BRFAL, M799:21; Jordan K. Parker to Dear Sir [H. C. Vogell], 25 October 1868, LR, North Carolina BRFAL, M844:8; H. C. Vogell to Parker, 24 November 1869, LS, North Carolina BRFAL, M844:5.

63. Thomas C. Griffin to Joseph Welch, 9 September 1868, LR, Texas BRFAL, M822:5; Louis W. Stevenson to C. S. Roberts, 26 April 1869, ibid. (quotation).

64. Quoted in Christensen, "Schools for Blacks: J. Milton Turner in Reconstruction Missouri," 35 (quotation). See also William Smith to "Sir," 22 November 1869, LR, Tennessee BRFAL, M1000:5.

65. The bureau papers are filled with requests by teachers and agents applying for funds to replace schools destroyed by fire and describing the economic loss to the black community. In most cases, the bureau could provide little or no compensation. See for example Alvord, *7th Semi-Annual Report*, p. 12; Samuel Walker to James Thompson, 9 March 1869, LR, Tennessee BRFAL, M1000:4; H. H. Burt to O. L. Sheppard, 9 April 1868, Register of LR, Alabama BRFAL, M810:2.

66. W. H. Stilwell to C. E. Compton, 29 January 1870, LR, Tennessee BRFAL, M1000:5. In Virginia, an arsonist attempted to burn down the house in which teachers were sleeping: see Sarah Cadbury to John W. Cadbury, 6 April 1866, Sarah Cadbury Correspondence, HC. See also, for example, Jessie H. Rupert, TMSR, March 1870, SR, Virginia BRFAL, M1053:19; Sarah A. Dickey to "My Dear Classmates," 4 March 1872, in Correspondence File, Dickey, Sarah A., Class of 1869, Alumnae File, MHC; and Alvord, *7th Semi-Annual Report* (January 1869), 46.

67. Edmonia G. Highgate to M. E. Strieby, 17 December 1866, AMAA; Gregory, "Education of Blacks in Maryland," 154; N. H. Randlett to Joseph Welch, 20 August 1867, LR, Texas BRFAL, M822:13; Frank R. Chase to Lucius H. Warren, 19 May 1868, LR, Ed. Div., BRFAL, M803:12.

68. James Fitz Allen Sisson to J. R. Lewis, 2 September 1869, LR, Georgia BRFAL, M799:13.

69. Thomas B. Barton to F. A. Fiske, 24 March 1867, Unregistered LR, North Carolina BRFAL, M844:10.

70. Edwin Barnetson to Fredrick S. Palmer, 11 August 1869, Letters Received, Records of Supt. of Ed., Tennessee, roll 5; Palmer to Barnetson, 13 August 1869, ibid.; R. M. Thompson to Palmer, 28 August 1869, ibid.; Mark Edwards to C. E. Compton, 20 September 1869, ibid.

71. N. H. Randlett to Joseph Welch, 20 August 1867, LR, Texas BRFAL, M822:13.

72. Franklin Shelden to E. M. Gregory, 15 May 1866, Unregistered LR, Texas BRFAL, M822:10; Isaac M. Newton to James Thompson, 1 July 1868, LR, Tennessee BRFAL, M1000:4; Lemann, *Redemption*, 117–18; R. S. Rust to J. W. Alvord, 28 May 1869, LR, Ed. Div., BRFAL, M803:6. See also, among other examples, the cases of Amos Sanders, a Quaker teacher in Macon, Mississippi, who received a death threat because of his work: Lemann, *Redemption*, 154; or Ellen L. Benton, whose life was threatened in Tuscaloosa, Alabama: E. L. Benton to Mr. Bush, 28 March 1868, LR, Alabama BRFAL, M810:2. Benton returned to Alabama the next year, but went to Selma instead of Tuscaloosa, the former being safer; see Benton, TMSR, SR, ibid., M810:7.

73. Margaret S. Clark to F. A. Fiske, 30 May 1868, LR, North Carolina BRFAL, M844:7; L. A. Birchett to J. H. Hawes, 8 February 1870, LR, Virginia BRFAL, M1053:5; regarding Birchett's subsequent work as a teacher, see Birchett: 1870 census, Va., Dinwiddie Co., Dist. 2, 450/450, p. 133. A similar case is documented in Charles F. Rand to Joseph Welch, 30 June 1868, LR, Texas BRFAL, M822:13; William L. Linsey, 9 January 1869, Register of LR, North Carolina BRFAL, M844:6 (quotation); see also Linsey to F. A. Fiske, 20 July 1868, ibid., M844:8.

74. Thomas C. Griffin to Joseph Welch, 9 September 1868, LR, Texas BRFAL, M822:5; James Ramsay to Joseph Welch, 29 September 1869, ibid., M822:7; J. J. Strong to E. M. Cravath, 14 August 1871, AMAA (quotation). The Gonzalez teacher, a Mr. Sanders, appears not to have attempted to teach again. See also, among many other examples, William H. Howard to Charles A. Vernon, 31 July 1868, LR, Texas BRFAL, M822:7.

75. Daniel Broomfield to J. P. Beard, 23 March 1866, John Emory Bryant Papers, DU; information on Broomfield's subsequent career from Freedmen's Teacher Project; Richard R. Wright, *Centennial Encyclopaedia*, 54–55; James M. Windgow to Joseph Welch, 6 August 1869, LR, Texas BRFAL, M822:9 (quotation), grammar and spelling *sic*; see also copy of F. Tolman to "Sir," 31 March 1867, LR, Texas BRFAL, M822:4.

76. Griffin, *Beloved Sisters and Loving Friends*, 245 (quotation); NEFAS, "Daily Journal, 18 May 1971–Sept 1873," p. 5, NEFAS Papers, MHS; Foster: 1870 census, Md., St. Marys Co., Dist. 2, 174/174, p. 521.

77. Lewis A. Fuller, "Claimant's affidavit," 14 December 1897, Pension Cert. No. 508403, CWPR.

78. John H. Morrison to Charles A. Vernon, 30 November 1868, LR, Texas BRFAL, M822:7.

79. H. E. Brown to E. M. Cravath, 19 September 1870, AMAA; James McClurg to John W. Alvord, 25 April 1870, LR, Ed. Div., BRFAL, M803:12.

80. Pegues, *Our Baptist Ministers and Schools*, 260; Lizzie A. Wilson to General Reynolds, 16 November 1868, LR, Texas BRFAL, M822:9; Alvord, *Seventh Semi-Annual Report* (January 1869), 32; "Record of Schools," p. 87, Miscellaneous Records, Texas BRFAL, M822:18; Eric Foner, *Freedom's Lawmakers*, 32, 167; U.S. Congress, Senate Reports, *On Alleged Frauds* 1:483–90.

81. Small, "Yankee Schoolmarm in Freedmen's Schools," 387.

82. Gregory, "Education of Blacks in Maryland," 154; Griffin, *Beloved Sisters*, 168; Edmonia G. Highgate to M. E. Strieby, 17 December 1866, AMAA; *FF* 1 (July 1866): 113–14; Sarah A. Dickey to "My Dear Classmates," 4 March 1872, in Correspondence File, Dickey, Sarah A., Class of 1869, Alumnae File, MHC.

83. Congdon taught for one more year; Perry for two more; Hoy taught for at least ten years in southern schools, perhaps longer; Dickson and Highgate both taught for six years (Highgate was returning for a seventh year, starting a new career as an instructor in a southern black normal school, where it is likely she would have remained much longer had she not died as a result of a botched medical procedure); Dickey taught black students in Mississippi for more than a third of a century until her death in 1904.

84. John Scott to C. C. Morse, 23 February 1866, Unregistered LR, Texas BRFAL, M822:10.

85. Samuel C. Sloan to Chauncy C. Morse, 20 February 1866, Unregistered LR, Texas BRFAL, M822:10, spelling *sic*.

86. M. O'Regan to E. M. Wheelock, 30 September 1866, in monthly "Report of Schools for Freedmen," September 1866, SR, Texas BRFAL, M822:11; "Sub-Assistant Commissioner's (or Agent's) Monthly Report on Education of Freedmen and Refugees in charge of T[?] B. Pease, for the Month of February, 1868," ibid., M822:12; John Scott to C. C. Morse, 23 February 1866, Unregistered LR, ibid., M822:10.

87. Alvord, *Seventh Semi-Annual Report*, 36.

88. Rable, *But There Was No Peace*, 33–58; longevity data derive from Freedmen's Teacher Project.

89. On Steward, see Albert G. Miller, *Elevating the Race*.

90. T. G. Steward to E. M. Cravath, 5 April 1871, AMAA; see also Caroline Alfred to Mrs. Ednah Dow Cheney, 4 April 1875, NEFAS Papers, MHS.

91. William Aikman, an officer of the Delaware Association for the Moral Improvement and Education of the Colored People, in Alvord, *Seventh Semi-Annual Report*, 12. On education in Reconstruction and Redemption, see, among others, Perman, *The Road to Redemption*, 172–210; Eric Foner, *Reconstruction*, esp. 365–68, 422, 424.

92. Manly quoted in Alvord, *Tenth Semi-Annual Report* (July 1870), 13.

93. Thomas Nast cartoon, October 1874, retrieved 9 July 2007 from <http://www.csubak.edu/gsantos/img0053.html>.

94. Wyatt-Brown, *Southern Honor*; Wyatt-Brown, *Honor and Violence*; Wyatt-Brown, *The Shaping of Southern Culture*; Williamson, *A Rage for Order*, 3–43; Rable, *But There Was No Peace*.

95. Friedman, *The White Savage*, esp. 3–76.

96. Williamson, *Rage for Order*, 10–14; Genovese, *Roll, Jordan, Roll*, 110–20, 142–47.

97. Butchart, "Remapping Racial Boundaries in Reconstruction," 621–78.

98. When asked about public sentiment regarding schools for poor whites and the freed people, one observer wrote, "the property owners and intelligent whites are as a general thing opposed to educating either class," an observation echoed by

others. They also noted the lack of educational aspirations among poor whites. Jonathan W. Jordan, "Sub-Assistant Commissioner's (or Agent's) Monthly Report . . . 4th Div., 9th Sub-District, State of Virginia . . ., April 1868," Virginia BRFAL, M1053:13; see also C. G. McClelland, "Sub-Assistant Commissioner's (or Agent's) Monthly Report . . . 6th Div., 6th Sub-District, State of Virginia . . ., May 1868," ibid.; and Frank R. Chase to Lucius H. Warren, 19 May 1968, LR, Ed. Div., BRFAL, M803:12. Chase wrote that the bureau agents in Louisiana "report to me 'Public Sentiment as to the education of the Freedmen and Poor Whites as adverse, against, bitter, very bitter.'"

99. "Sub-Assistant Commissioner's (or Agent's) Monthly Report on Education of Freedmen and Refugees in Rutherford and Cannon Counties Sub-District, State of Tennessee for the Month of April 1868," Special Reports, September 1865–June 1870, Tennessee BRFAL, M1000:6; E. S. Thorpe, TMSR, October 1869, SR, Alabama BRFAL, M810:7; Bryant Edmundson, TMSR, April 1868, ibid., M810:6.

100. Roberta Sue Alexander, *North Carolina Faces the Freedmen*, 154.

101. U.S. Congress, Senate Reports, *On Alleged Frauds*, 488.

Bibliography

Primary Sources

Manuscripts

Atlanta, Ga.
    Atlanta University, Trevor Arnett Library
        Frederick Ayer Papers
        Edmund Asa Ware Papers
    Georgia State Archives
        Georgia Pension Office. Pension Applications and Supporting Documents.
          Georgia Confederate Pensions and Records Department
Austin, Tex.
    Archives and Information Services Division, Texas State Library and Archives
        Commission
    Texas State Department of Public Instruction Collection
Baltimore, Md.
    Maryland Historical Society
        Baltimore Association for the Moral and Educational Improvement of the
          Colored People. Minute Book of the Executive Committee.
        Baltimore Normal School Minute Books, 1867–1908
Barre, Vt.
    Vermont Historical Society
        Johnson Family Papers
Baton Rouge, La.
    Louisiana State Archives
        Louisiana State Superintendent of Education. Department of Education,
          1864–1920. Department of Education Records.
        Payroll of the Public Schools of the City of New Orleans
Boston, Mass.
    Harvard University, Harvard Business School, Baker Library
        R. G. Dun Collection
    Massachusetts Historical Society
        New England Freedmen's Aid Society Records

248   Cambridge, Mass.

Harvard University, Radcliffe Institute, Schlesinger Library

James Chaplin Beecher Papers, 1828–1886

Jeanette Bailey Cheek Collection

Holt-Messer Family Papers

Anna H. Kidder Papers

Selma Wesselhoft Papers

Chapel Hill, N.C.

University of North Carolina, Wilson Library, Special Collections

Thomas D. Howard, Sophia W. Howard, and Sally B. Howard, "Charles Howard Family Domestic History," Elizabeth H. Andrews, ed. Cambridge, Mass., bound typescript, 1956.

Hubard Family Papers

Mears-DeRosset Family Papers

Henry E. Simmons Papers

J. B. Willis Papers, 1874–1877

Charleston, S.C.

College of Charleston, Avery Research Center

Avery Normal Institute Records, 1862–1954

Avery School Memorabilia Collection

Holloway Scrapbook

Charlottesville, Va.

University of Virginia, Alderman Library, Special Collections

Philena Carkin, "Reminiscences of my Life and Work among the Freedmen of Charlottesville, Virginia, From March 1st, 1866 to July 1st, 1875."

Chicago, Ill.

Chicago Historical Society

Needham Correspondence

Columbia, S.C.

South Caroliniana Library, University of South Carolina

Schofield Normal and Industrial School Papers

South Carolina Normal School Records

South Carolina State Archives

South Carolina Superintendent of Education. County School Commissioners' Lists of Teachers' Claims for School Years 1868–69, 1869–70.

Teacher Reports Submitted by County Commissioners for School Years 1868–69, 1869–70

Delaware, Ohio

Ohio Wesleyan University

Ohio Wesleyan University Historical Collection

Durham, N.C.

Duke University, Perkins Library

John Emory Bryant Papers

William Righter Fisher and Mary Wager Fisher Papers

Fleming Family Papers

George Gage Papers

Nathan H. Hill Papers

Kate Nowlin Papers, 1869–1874

William C. Russel Papers

Laura Stebbins Papers

Framingham, Mass.

Framingham State College, College Archives

Framingham Normal School Registration and Graduation Record Book, 1839–1849

Gloucester Point, Va.

Harriot Williams Murray, "Journal of Harriot Williams Murray, 1863–1866." Typescript, edited by Linda Harriot Voorhis Breaks, in possession of Ms. Breaks.

Greensboro, N.C.

Guilford College, Hege Library, Friends Historical Collection

Letter Book of Francis King, 1865–1875. Friends Association to Advise and Assist Friends of Southern States.

Delphinia E. Mendenhall Papers

Isham Cox Papers

Greensboro Historical Museum

Nocho Park, Vertical File, Museum Archives

Hampton, Va.

Hampton University, University Archives

Samuel Chapman Armstrong, General Correspondence

Helen Ludlow Files

Jane Stuart Woolsey Papers

Ithaca, N.Y.

Cornell University, Olin Library, Special Collections, Anti-Slavery Collection

American Freedmen's Union Commission Papers

Madison, Wisc.

Wisconsin Historical Society

William F. Allen Diary

Mobile, Ala.

Mobile Public Library, Local History and Genealogy Library

Family History Files

Montgomery, Ala.

Alabama State Archives

Alabama Department of Education Papers, 1869–1880

New Haven, Conn.

Yale University, Special Collections

Strong Family Collection

Terry-Slocomb Family Papers

New Orleans, La.

Amistad Research Center, Tulane University

American Missionary Association Archives

250   New Orleans University, Special Collections
          Orleans Parish School Board Meetings and Related Committees, Minutes
    Oberlin, Ohio
      Oberlin College, College Archives
        Graduates and Formers Files
    Oskaloosa, Iowa
      Iowa Yearly Meeting of Friends, Records Room
        Iowa Yearly Meeting of Friends, Book of Proceedings, Iowa Yearly Meeting
          Interests of Freedmen
    Philadelphia, Pa.
      Haverford College, Magill Library, Quaker Miscellany
        Sarah Cadbury Correspondence
        Cope-Evans Family Papers
        Friends Freedmen's Association, Women's Aid Committee, 1863–1866
        James E. Rhoads Papers
        Taylor Family Papers
      Swarthmore College, Friends Historical Library
        Lydia Atkinson, Diary
        Friends Freedmen's Association Papers
        Cornelia Hancock Manuscripts
        Emily Howland Papers
        New York Yearly Meeting of Friends. Minutes, New York Yearly Meeting of
          Friends [Hicksite], 1846–1872.
        New York Yearly Meeting of Friends. Minutes, New York Yearly Meeting of
          Friends [Orthodox], 1848–1863.
        New York Yearly Meeting of Friends. Meeting for Suffering Minutes
          [Orthodox], 1849–1870.
        New York Yearly Meeting of Friends. New York Yearly Meeting [Orthodox]
          Women's Minutes, 1853–68.
        Martha Schofield Papers
        Stratton (Maule) Papers
      Philadelphia Society of Friends, Department of Records
        Friends Freedmen's Association. Minutes of the Executive Board. 3 vols.,
          1863–1880.
        Friends Freedmen's Association. Minutes of the Instruction Committee.
          3 vols., 1864–1875.
        Friends Freedmen's Association. Letterbook of the Instruction Committee.
          3 vols., 1866–1868.
      University of Pennsylvania
        Harriet M Buss Letters, 1850–1871
    Providence, R.I.
      Rhode Island Historical Society
        Rhode Island Association for Freedmen Records
    Raleigh, N.C.
      North Carolina State Archives

County Records, North Carolina, 1865–1876

Richmond, Va.
    Library of Virginia
        William Henry Ruffner Papers, 1848–1907
    Virginia Historical Society
        Sarah S. Carter, "Account of a Visit to Richmond and Elsewhere, 3rd Mo.,
            1866," Typescript, 1966
        John Thomas Clark File
        Giles Buckner Cooke Papers
        Sarah A. Payne Papers
Rochester, N.Y.
    University of Rochester, Department of Rare Books and Special Collections
        William Channing Gannett Papers, 1857–1956
St. Augustine, Fla.
    St. Augustine Research Library
        Sarah Ann Mather File
Savannah, Ga.
    Chatham County Public Schools, Board of Education Office
        Albert Otto, "Two Centuries of Educational History in Chatham County."
            Typescript, n.d.
South Hadley, Mass.
    Mount Holyoke College, College Archives
        Alumnae File
Spartanburg, S.C.
    Wofford College, College Archives
        Register of Students' Names—Wofford College—Aug., 1854–Oct. 1 1880
Tallahassee, Fla.
    Florida State Archives
        C. Thurston Chase, Draft, Annual Report of the Florida Superintendent of
            Public Instruction, 1870.
        Department of the South, Census of the District of Florida, 1864.
Washington, D.C.
    Library of Congress, Manuscripts Division
        J. M. Hawks and Esther Hawks Papers
    National Archives
        Bureau of Refugees, Freedmen, and Abandoned Lands. Record Group 105.
        Records of the Assistant Commissioner and Subordinate Field Offices for the
            State of Florida, Bureau of Refugees, Freedmen, and Abandoned Lands,
            1865–1872. Microfilm M1869.
        Records of the Assistant Commissioner for the State of Mississippi, Bureau of
            Refugees, Freedmen, and Abandoned Lands, 1865–1869. Microfilm
            M826.
        Records of the Assistant Commissioner for the State of South Carolina,
            Bureau of Refugees, Freedmen, and Abandoned Lands, 1865–1870.
            Microfilm M869.

Records of the Education Division of the Bureau of Refugees, Freedmen, and Abandoned Lands, 1865–1871. Microfilm M803.

Records of the Field Offices for the State of Georgia, Bureau of Refugees, Freedmen, and Abandoned Lands, 1865–1872. Microfilm M1903.

Records of the Mississippi Freedmen's Department ("Pre-Bureau Records"), Office of the Assistant Commissioner, Bureau of Refugees, Freedmen, and Abandoned Lands, 1863–1865. Microfilm M1914.

Records of the Superintendent of Education for the District of Columbia, Bureau of Refugees, Freedmen, and Abandoned Lands, 1865–1872. Microfilm M1056.

Records of the Superintendent of Education for the State of Alabama, Bureau of Refugees, Freedmen, and Abandoned Lands, 1865–1870. Microfilm M810.

Records of the Superintendent of Education for the State of Arkansas, Bureau of Refugees, Freedmen, and Abandoned Lands, 1865–1872. Microfilm M980.

Records of the Superintendent of Education for the State of Georgia, Bureau of Refugees, Freedmen, and Abandoned Lands, 1865–1870. Microfilm M799.

Records of the Superintendent of Education for the State of Louisiana, Bureau of Refugees, Freedmen, and Abandoned Lands, 1864–1869. Microfilm M1026.

Records of the Superintendent of Education for the State of North Carolina, Bureau of Refugees, Freedmen, and Abandoned Lands, 1865–1870. Microfilm M844.

South Carolina. Assistant Commissioner. Records.

Records of the Superintendent of Education for the State of Tennessee, Bureau of Refugees, Freedmen, and Abandoned Lands, 1865–1870. Microfilm M1000.

Records of the Superintendent of Education for the State of Texas, Bureau of Refugees, Freedmen, and Abandoned Lands, 1865–1870. Microfilm M822.

Records of the Superintendent of Education for the State of Virginia, Bureau of Refugees, Freedmen, and Abandoned Lands, 1865–1870. Microfilm M1053.

Registers and Letters Received by the Commissioner of the Bureau of Refugees, Freedmen, and Abandoned Lands, 1865–1872. Microfilm M752.

Civil War Military Records

Civil War Pension Records

Records of the Fifth Agency, Port Royal Correspondence, 1861–1862, Record Group 366.

Registers of Signatures of Depositors in Branches of the Freedmen's Savings and Trust Company, 1865–1874: Huntsville, Ala. (microfilm); Memphis, Tenn. (microfilm); Nashville, Tenn. (microfilm); nationwide (CD)

Southern Claims Commission Records

Bibliography

Historical Society of Delaware
    Delaware Association for the Moral Improvement and Education of the
        Colored People Minutes
Worcester, Mass.
    American Antiquarian Society
        Chase Family Papers
        Jane Briggs Smith Fiske Papers, 1806–1923

Database Records

Ancestry.com, <http://www.ancestry.com>
    Decennial U.S. censuses, 1850–1920
        Military records
            American Civil War Soldiers (Historical Data Systems, comp.)
            U.S. Civil War Soldiers, 1861–1865 (National Park Service, comp.)

Reports

Alabama Department of Public Instruction. *Report of Joseph H. Speed,*
    Superintendent of Public Instruction of the State of Alabama, for the Scholastic
    Year Ending October 1st, 1873. Montgomery, Ala.: Arthur Bingham, 1873.
Alvord, John W. *Semi-Annual Reports on Schools for Freedmen.* 1st–10th.
    Washington, D.C.: GPO, 1866–1870.
American Baptist Free Mission Society. *Annual Reports of the American Baptist*
    Free Mission Society. New York: American Baptist Free Mission Society, 1846–
    1869.
American Baptist Home Mission Society. *Reports of the American Baptist Home*
    Mission Society. New York: American Baptist Home Mission Society, 1862–
    1876.
American Missionary Association. *Annual Reports of the American Missionary*
    Association and the Proceedings at the Annual Meeting. New York: American
    Missionary Association, 1859–1880.
American Tract Society. *Annual Reports of the American Tract Society.* New York:
    American Tract Society, 1861–1872.
Baltimore Association for the Moral and Educational Improvement of the Colored
    People. *Annual Reports of the Baltimore Association for the Moral and*
    Educational Improvement of the Colored People. Baltimore: for the Association,
    1866–1868.
Barnard Freedmen's Aid Society. *Annual Reports of the Barnard Freedmen's Aid*
    Society of Dorchester. [Boston]: Barnard Freedmen's Aid Society, 1864–1867.

254   Cincinnati Contraband's Relief Commission. *Report by the Committee of the Contrabands' Relief Commission of Cincinnati, Ohio. Proposing a Plan for the Occupation and Government of Vacated Territory in the Seceded States.* Cincinnati, Ohio: Gazette Steam Printing House, 1863.

Friends' Association of Philadelphia for the Aid and Elevation of the Freedmen. *Annual Reports of the Friends' Association of Philadelphia for the Aid and Elevation of the Freedmen.* Philadelphia: Merrihew and Son, 1865–1872.

Indiana Freedmen's Aid Commission. *Report of the Board of Managers of the Indiana Freedmen's Aid Commission, to the First Annual Meeting, Held at Indianapolis, September 7th, 1864.* Indianapolis: Indiana Freedmen's Aid Commission, 1864.

Institute for Colored Youth. *Annual Reports of the Board of Managers of the Institute for Colored Youth* [title varies]. Philadelphia: Institute for Colored Youth, 1859–1875.

Lincoln Freedmen's Aid Society. *Annual Reports of the Lincoln Freedmen's Aid Society, Roxbury [Massachusetts].* Roxbury, Mass.: George H. Monroe, 1864–1867.

Methodist Episcopal Church, South. *Minutes of the South Carolina Conference of the Methodist Episcopal Church, South.* Charleston, S.C.: Methodist Episcopal Church, South, 1861–1875.

Methodist Episcopal Freedmen's Aid Society. *Annual Reports of the Freedmen's Aid Society of the Methodist Episcopal Church.* Cincinnati: Western Methodist Book Concern, 1868–1876.

Michigan Freedmen's Aid Commission. *Annual Report of the Freedmen's Aid Commission of the State of Michigan.* Detroit: Joseph Warren, 1866–1867.

National Freedmen's Relief Association of New York. *Annual Reports of the National Freedmen's Relief Association of New York* [title varies]. New York: NFRA, 1863–1867.

New England Educational Commission. *First Annual Report of the Educational Commission for Freedmen.* Boston: NEFAS, 1863.

New England Freedmen's Aid Society. *Annual Reports of the Executive Committee of the New England Freedmen's Aid Commission* [title varies]. Boston: NEFAS, 1864–1865.

Northwestern Freedmen's Aid Commission. *Annual Reports of the Board of Directors of the Northwestern Freedmen's Aid Commission.* Chicago: James Barnet, 1864–1865.

Penn School. *Report of the Penn Normal, Industrial and Agricultural School, St. Helena Island, South Carolina,* 1901.

Presbyterian Church in the U.S.A. *Annual Reports of the General Assembly's Committee on Freedmen of the Presbyterian Church in the United States of America.* Pittsburg: Presbyterian Church, U.S.A., 1866–1870.

———. *Annual Reports of the Presbyterian Board of Missions for Freedmen, of the Presbyterian Church, in the United States of America.* Pittsburg: Presbyterian Church, U.S.A., 1870–1880.

——. *Minutes of the General Assembly of the Presbyterian Church in the United States of America.* New York: Presbyterian Publication Committee, 1862–1869.

——. *The Report of the Eastern Committee for the Education of the Freedmen, Appointed by the General Assembly of the Presbyterian Church in the United States of America, at Their Meeting in Newark, N.J., 1864. Presented at their Meeting in Pittsburg, Pa., May 1865.* Philadelphia: By the committee, 1865.

Protestant Episcopal Freedmen's Commission. *Freedmen's Commission of the Protestant Episcopal Church. December 1866. Selections.* N.p.: [PEFC], 1866.

Report of the West-Roxbury Branch of the New England Freedmen's Aid Society, 1870. Boston: privately printed, 1870.

Schofield School. *Annual Reports of the Schofield School of Aiken, South Carolina.* Aiken, S.C.: School Job-Press, 1870–1882.

Society of Friends. Associated Yearly Meetings of the West. *Report of a Committee on Freedmen, in Parts of Tennessee and the Mississippi Valley, to Friends Board of Control, Third Month, 1865.* Cincinnati: R. W. Carroll, 1865.

Society of Friends. New England Yearly Meeting. *Reports of the Proceedings of the Executive Committee of New England Yearly Meeting of Friends, in Behalf of the Freed People of Color.* New Bedford, Mass.: E. Anthony & Sons, 1864–1866.

Society of Friends. New England Yearly Meeting. *Report to the Committee in Charge of Friends' Mission in Washington, for the Relief of the Freed People of Color.* New Bedford, Mass.: n.p., 1865.

Society of Friends. New York Yearly Meeting. *Reports of a Committee of the Representatives of the New York Yearly Meeting of Friends upon the Condition and Wants of the Freedmen.* New York: NYYM, 1862–1872.

Society of Friends. Philadelphia [Orthodox] Yearly Meeting. *Annual Reports of the Executive Board of the Friends' Association of Philadelphia and Its Vicinity for the Relief of Colored Freedmen . . .* Philadelphia: Sherman, 1864–1867.

United Presbyterian Church of North America. *Minutes of the General Assembly of the United Presbyterian Church of North America.* N.p., 1862–1875.

U.S. Army. *Report of the Board of Education for Freedmen, Department of the Gulf.* New Orleans, La.: True Delta, 1865.

Western Freedmen's Aid Commission. *The Second Annual Report of the Western Freedmen's Aid Commission, Cincinnati, Ohio.* Cincinnati: Methodist Book Concern, 1865.

Government Reports

[Cardozo, T. W.]. *Annual Report of the [Mississippi] State Superintendent of Public Instruction for the Scholastic Year 1874.* Jackson, Miss.: Pilot Publishing, 1875.

District of Columbia Board of Trustees of Public Schools. *Annual Report of the Public Schools of Washington County, D.C., 1871–72.* N.p., [1872?].

Eaton, John. *Report of the General Superintendent of Freedmen, Department of the Tennessee and State of Arkansas for 1864.* Memphis: Published by permission, 1865.

James, Horace. *Annual Report of the Superintendent of Negro Affairs in North*

Carolina. 1864. With an Appendix, Containing the History and Management of the Freedmen in this Department up to June 1st, 1865. Boston: W. F. Brown, [1865].

Kansas. Superintendent of Public Instruction. *Annual Reports of the Superintendent of Public Instruction of the State of Kansas.* Various places: For the State of Kansas, 1861–1875.

Knoxville, Tennessee, City Schools. *Annual Report of the Knoxville City Schools.* Knoxville, 1874–78.

[Newton, A. E.]. *First Annual Report of the Superintendent of Colored Schools for Washington and Georgetown, D.C., for the Year Ending June 30, 1868.* Washington, D.C.: Judd and Detweiler, 1870.

St. Louis Public Schools. *Thirteenth Annual Report of the Board of Directors of the St. Louis Public Schools, for the Year Ending August 1, 1867.* St. Louis, Mo.: Board of Education, 1867.

South Carolina General Assembly. *Reports and Resolutions of the General Assembly of the State of South Carolina, at the Regular Session, 1873–74 and 1874–75.* Columbia, S.C.: Republican Printing Company, 1874–75.

South Carolina. State Superintendent of Education. *Annual Reports of the State Superintendent of Education of the State of South Carolina.* Columbia: State of South Carolina, 1869–1880.

U.S. Bureau of the Census. *Eighth Census of the United States, 1860.* Vol. 1, *Population.* Washington: GPO, 1864.

——. *Eighth Census of the United States, 1860.* Vol. 2, *Statistics.* Washington: GPO, 1866.

——. *Ninth Census of the United States, 1870.* Vol. 1, *Statistics.* Washington: GPO, 1872.

U.S. Office of Education. *Special Report of the Commissioner of Education on the Condition and Improvement of Public Schools in the District of Columbia.* Washington: GPO, 1871.

——. *Reports of the Commissioner of Education.* Washington: GPO, 1870–1880.

U.S. Congress. House Reports. "New Orleans Riots." *Reports of the Committees of the House of Representatives.* 39th Cong., 2d sess., no. 16, 1867. Washington: GPO, 1867.

U.S. Congress. Senate Reports. *Report of the Joint Select Committee to Inquire into the Condition of Affairs in the Late Insurrectionary States.* 42nd Cong., 2d sess., No. 41, 1872. 13 vols. Washington, D.C.: GPO, 1872.

——. Senate Reports. *On Alleged Frauds in the Recent Election in Mississippi.* 44th Cong., 1st sess., no. 527, 1876. 2 vols. Washington: GPO, 1876.

Virginia. Superintendent of Public Instruction. *Virginia School Report. Annual Report of the Superintendent of Public Instruction.* Richmond, Va.: Superintendent of Public Printing, 1871–1880.

Washington, D.C. Superintendent of Colored Schools of Washington and Georgetown. *Annual Reports of the Superintendent of Colored Schools of Washington and Georgetown.* Washington, D.C., 1871–72 to 1873–74.

American Freedman
American Missionary
Christian Recorder
Crisis
Freedmen's Advocate
Freedmen's Friend
Freedmen's Journal
Freedmen's Record
[Friends'] *Freedmen's Record*
Freedmen's Reporter
Friends' Intelligencer
Friends' Review
Independent
Lippincott's Magazine
Loyal Georgian
Missionary Advocate
Missionary Reporter of the A.M.E. Church
National Freedman
Pennsylvania Freedmen's Bulletin
Sabbath Recorder
Spirit of Missions
Zion's Herald and Wesleyan Journal

Books

American Baptist Home Mission Society. *Baptist Home Missions in North America; Including a Full Report of the Proceedings and Addresses of the Jubilee Meeting, and a Historical Sketch of the American Baptist Home Mission Society, Historical Tables, Etc. 1832–1882.* New York: Baptist Home Mission Rooms, 1883.

American Missionary Association. *American Missionary Association: Its Missionaries, Teachers, and History.* [New York?]: American Missionary Association, 1869.

Ames, Mary. *From a New England Woman's Diary in Dixie in 1865.* Springfield, Mass.: Plimpton Press, 1906.

Archer, H. P. *A Historic Sketch of Public Schools in Charleston, S.C., 1710–1886.* Charleston, S.C.: Walker, Evans & Cogswell, 1887.

Arnett, Benjamin W., comp. and ed. *The Budget; Containing the Annual Reports of the General Officers of the African M.E. Church of the United States . . .* Xenia, Ohio: Torchlight Printing, 1881.

——. *The Budget: Containing Biographical Sketches, Quadrennial and Annual Reports of the General Officers of the African Methodist Episcopal Church.* Dayton, Ohio: Christian Publishing House, 1884.

——. *Proceedings of the Semi-Centenary Celebration of the African Methodist*

258   *Episcopal Church of Cincinnati, Held in Allen Temple . . . 1874 . . .* Cincinnati, Ohio: H. Watkins, 1874.

Billington, Ray Allen, ed. *The Journal of Charlotte Forten: A Free Negro in the Slave Era.* New York: Collier Books, 1953.

Booth, Charles Octavius. *The Cyclopedia of the Colored Baptists of Alabama: Their Leaders and Their Work.* Birmingham: Alabama Publishing Company, 1895.

Botume, Elizabeth Hyde. *First Days among the Contrabands.* 1898. Reprint, New York: Arno, 1968.

Brockett, L. P., and Mary C. Vaughn. *Woman's Work in the Civil War: A Record of Heroism, Patriotism and Patience.* Philadelphia: Zeigler, McCurdy, 1867.

Caldwell, John H. *Reminiscences of the Reconstruction of Church and State in Georgia.* Wilmington, Del.: J. Miller Thomas, 1895.

Carter, E. R. *Biographical Sketches of Our Pulpit.* Atlanta: n.p., 1888.

Child, Lydia Maria. *Freedmen's Book.* 1865. Reprint, New York: Arno, 1968.

Colman, Lucy N. *Reminiscences.* Buffalo, N.Y.: H. L. Green, 1891.

Colyer, Meriwether. *History of Higher Education in South Carolina, with a Sketch of the Free School System.* Bureau of Education, Circular of Information No. 3, 1888. Washington, D.C.: GPO, 1889.

Corey, C. H. *A History of the Richmond Theological Seminary, with Reminiscences of Thirty Years' Work among the Colored People of the South.* Richmond, Va.: J. W. Randolph Company, 1895.

Doherty, Robert R. *Representative Methodists. Biographical Sketches and Portraits of the Members of the Twentieth Delegated General Conference of the Methodist Episcopal Church, Held in the City of New York, May, 1888.* New York: Phillips & Hunt, 1888.

Ferebee, London R. *A Brief History of the Slave Life of Rev. L. R. Ferebee, and the Battles of Life, and Four Years of His Ministerial Life. Written from Memory. To 1882.* Raleigh: Edwards, Broughton, 1882.

Gardner, Anna. *Harvest Gleanings.* New York: Fowler and Wells, 1881.

Gibbs, Jonathan. *Report of the Superintendent of Public Instruction of the State of Florida for the Year Ending September 30, 1873.* Tallahassee, Fla.: Hamilton Jay, 1874.

Glasgow, W. Melancthon. *History of the Reformed Presbyterian Church in America, with Sketches of All Her Ministry, Congregations, Missions, Institutions, Publications, Etc., and Embellished with Over Fifty Portraits and Engravings.* Baltimore: Baltimore, Hill and Harvey, 1888.

Haviland, Laura S. *A Woman's Life Work: Including Thirty Years' Service on the Underground Railroad and in the War.* 5th ed. Grand Rapids, Mich.: S. B. Shaw, 1881.

Heard, William H. *From Slavery to the Bishopric in the A.M.E. Church.* 1924. Reprint, New York: Arno Press, 1969.

Holland, Rupert Sargent, ed. *Letters and Diary of Laura M. Towne, Written from the Sea Islands of South Carolina, 1862–1884.* Cambridge, Mass.: Riverside Press, 1912.

Hubbard, G. W., comp. *A History of the Colored Schools of Nashville, Tennessee.*
Nashville: Wheeler, Marshall & Bruce, 1874.

Jones, Charles Edgeworth. *Education in Georgia.* Bureau of Education, Circular of Information No. 4, 1888. Washington, D.C.: GPO, 1889.

Lincoln Institute. *Centennial Review of the Rise, Progress and Condition of Lincoln Institute, Near Jefferson City, Missouri.* N.p., 1876.

——. *Lincoln Institute. Full History of its Conception, Struggles, and Triumph. The Dedicatory Speech of Colonel David Branson.* [Missouri?]: Lincoln Institute, [1871].

Lockwood, Lewis C. *Mary S. Peake: The Colored Teacher at Fortress Monroe.* Boston: American Tract Society, 1865.

Lynch, James. *A Few Things About the Educational Work Among the Freedmen of South Carolina and Georgia, Also, Addresses Delivered at Augusta and Nashville.* Baltimore: Wm. K. Boyle, 1865.

Marrs, Elijah P. *Life and History of the Rev. Elijah P. Marrs, First Pastor of Beargrass Baptist Church, and Author.* Louisville, Ky.: Bradley & Gilbert, 1885.

McGranahan, Ralph Wilson, ed. *Historical Sketch of the Freedmen's Missions of the United Presbyterian Church, 1862–1904.* [Knoxville, Tenn.]: Knoxville College, 1904.

McKay, C. E. *Stories of Hospital and Camp.* 1876. Reprint, Freeport, N.Y.: Books for Libraries Press, 1971.

Morgan, A. T. *Yazoo; or, on the Picket Line of Freedom in the South. A Personal Narrative.* 1884. Reprint, New York: Russell and Russell, 1968.

Murray, Frances Elizabeth. *Memoir of LeBaron Botsford, M.D.* Saint John, New Brunswick: J. & A. McMillan, 1892.

Nevins, Alfred, ed. *Encyclopedia of the Presbyterian Church in the United States of America, including the Northern and Southern Assemblies.* Philadelphia: Presbyterian Publishing, [1884?].

Pearson, Elizabeth Ware, ed. *Letters from Port Royal, 1862–1868.* Boston: W. B. Clarke, 1906.

Phillips, C. E. *History of the Colored Methodist Episcopal Church in America.* Jackson, Tenn.: Publishing House CME Church, 1898.

Porter, A. Toomer. *History of the Holy Communion Church Institute of Charleston, South Carolina, Founded by Rev. A. Toomer Porter.* New York: D. Appleton, 1875.

——. *Led on! Step by Step. Scenes from Clerical, Military, Educational, and Plantation Life in the South, 1828–1898. An Autobiography.* New York: G. P. Putnam's Sons, 1898.

Porter, Mary H. *Eliza Chappell Porter: A Memoir.* Chicago: For the Oberlin Missionary Home Association, 1892.

Randolph, Paschal Beverly. *P. B. Randolph, His Curious Life, Works, and Career.* Boston: Randolph Publishing House, 1872.

Rankin, Melinda. *Twenty Years Among the Mexicans, a Narrative of Missionary Labor.* Cincinnati: Central Book Concern, 1881.

Stearns, Charles. *The Black Man of the South, and the Rebels; or, the Characteristics of the Former, and the Recent Outrages of the Latter.* 1872. Reprint, New York: Kraus Reprint Co., 1969.

Taylor, Susan King. *Reminiscences of My Life in Camp with the 33d United States Colored Troops, Late 1st S.C. Volunteers.* Boston: By the Author, 1902.

Towne, Laura M. *Letters and Diary of Laura M. Towne, Written from the Sea Islands of South Carolina, 1862–1884.* Edited by Rupert S. Holland. Cambridge, Mass.: Riverside Press, 1912.

Trowbridge, John. *The South: A Tour of Its Battlefields and Ruined Cities.* Hartford, Conn.: L. Stebbins, 1866.

Yearbook of the City of Charleston, 1880. Charleston, S.C.: News and Courier Book Press, 1880.

Articles

Armstrong, S. C. "Lessons from the Hawaiian Islands." *Journal of Christian Philosophy*, January 1884, 200–29.

———. "Normal-School Work among the Freedmen." In National Educational Association, *Addresses and Proceedings of the National Educational Association, 1872.* Washington, D.C.: National Educational Association, 1872. Pp. 174–81.

[Forten, Charlotte]. "Life on the Sea Islands." *Atlantic Monthly* 13 (May 1864): 587–96; (June 1864): 666–76.

Kilham, Elizabeth. "Sketches in Color. Second." *Putnam's Magazine* 5 (January 1870): 31–38.

[Pierce, Edward L.]. "The Freedmen at Port Royal." *Atlantic Monthly* 12 (September 1963): 291–315.

Rice, Elizabeth G. "A Yankee Teacher in the South: An Experience in the Early Days of Reconstruction." *Century Magazine* 62 (1901): 151–54.

Secondary Sources

Catalogues, Indexes, etc.

Adams, William, ed. *Historical Gazetteer and Biographical Memorial of Cattaraugus County.* Syracuse, N.Y.: Lyman, Horton, 1893.

Amherst College. *Amherst College Biographical Record, 1973: Biographical Record of the Graduates and Non-Graduates of the Classes of 1822–1971 Inclusive.* Amherst, Mass.: Trustees of Amherst College, 1973.

———. *General Catalogue of Amherst College, Including the Officers of Government and Instruction, the Alumni, and Honorary Graduates, 1821–1905.* Amherst, Mass.: Amherst College, 1905.

Antioch College. *Register of Alumni and Ex-students. Antioch College, Yellow Springs, Greene County, Ohio.* Antioch College Bulletin, vol. 17, no. 4, February 1922.

Atlanta University. *Catalogue of the Normal and Preparatory Departments of Atlanta University.* Atlanta: Atlanta University, 1870–1880.

Avery Normal Institute. *Catalogue of Avery Normal Institute, 35 Bull Street, Charleston, S.C. 1883–84.* Charleston, S.C.: Avery Normal Institute, 1884.

Bisbee, Marvin Davis. *Dartmouth College Necrology, 1897–98*. Hanover, N.H.:
Dartmouth Press, 1898.

——. *General Catalogue of Dartmouth College and the Associated Schools, 1769–1900,
including a Sketch of the College*. Hanover, N.H.: Dartmouth College, 1900.

Bowdoin College. *General Catalogue of Bowdoin College and the Medical School of
Maine, 1794–1912*. Brunswick, Maine: Bowdoin College, 1912.

Brown University. *The Historical Catalogue of Brown University, 1764–1934*.
Providence, R.I.: Brown University, 1936.

Chapman, George T. *Sketches of the Alumni of Dartmouth College, from the First
Graduation in 1771 to the Present Time, with a Brief History of the Institution*.
Cambridge, Mass.: Riverside Press, 1867.

Columbia University. *Columbia University Alumni Register, 1754–1931*. New York:
Columbia University Press, 1932.

Congregational Church. *Congregational Yearbook*. Annual, 1878–1911. Boston:
Fort Hill Press.

Dartmouth College. *Dartmouth College and Associated Schools General Catalogue,
1769–1940*. Hanover, N.H.: Dartmouth College Publications, 1940.

Framingham Normal School. *Catalogue of Graduates of the State Normal School
at Framingham, Mass. 1839–1889*. Boston: Wright and Potter, 1889.

Gazetteer and Business Directory of Cattaraugus County, N.Y., for 1874–5.
(Syracuse, N.Y.: 1874).

Hampton Normal and Agricultural Institute. *Twenty-Two Years' Work of the
Hampton Normal and Agricultural Institute at Hampton, Virginia: Records of
Negro and Indian Graduates and Ex-Students*. Hampton, Va.: Normal School
Press, 1893.

Harvard University. *Quinquennial Catalogue of the Officers and Graduates 1636–
1930*. Cambridge, Mass.: Harvard University, 1930.

Haverford College. *Biographical Catalog of the Matriculates of Haverford
College . . . Prepared by a Committee of the Alumni Association*. Philadelphia:
Haverford College Alumni Association, 1922.

Hicks, William. *History of Louisiana Negro Baptists from 1804 to 1914*. Nashville:
National Baptist Publishing Board, [1915].

Hillsdale College. *Third Record of the Alumni Association of Hillsdale College*.
Hillsdale, Mich.: Hillsdale Standard, 1908.

Hinshaw, William Wade. *The William Wade Hinshaw Index to Iowa Quaker
Meeting Records*. Orthodox Records, 8 vols. Conservative Records, 3 vols.
Hicksite Records, 1 vol. Iowa Quaker Records, 2nd Series, 3 vols. N.p., n.d.,
typescript.

Knoxville, Tenn., Public Schools. *Commencement Annual, 1881–1903: Austin High
School*. Knoxville, Tenn.: W. B. Scott, Foreman Industrial Messenger, 1903.

Lamb, Daniel Smith. *Howard University Medical Department, Washington, D.C.:
A Historical, Biographical and Statistical Souvenir*. Washington, D.C.: Medical
Faculty of Howard University, 1900.

Lincoln University. *Alumni Directory of Lincoln University*. Lincoln University,
Pa.: Lincoln University, [1946].

262 ——. *Lincoln University College and Theological Seminary Biographical Catalogue, 1918.* Lancaster, Pa.: For the University, 1918.

——. *Statistical Catalogue of the Students of the Collegiate and Theological Departments of Lincoln University, 1912.* N.p., 1912.

Miami University. "Alumni Directory, Miami University, 1826–1873, 1888–1940. Oxford College, 1833–1928." *Miami University Bulletin*, ser. 39, no. 11 (July 1941).

——. *General Catalogue of the Graduates and Students of Miami University, Including Members of the Board of Trustees and Faculty during Its First Century, 1809–1909.* [Oxford, Ohio: Miami University, 1909?].

Millard, Eleanor R., comp. *A General Catalog of Trustees, Officers, Professors, and Students of Union Theological Seminary in Virginia.* Montreat, N.C.: Presbyterian Historical Foundation, 1979.

Mount Holyoke College. *One Hundred Year Biographical Directory, Mount Holyoke College, South Hadley, Massachusetts, 1837–1937.* South Hadley, Mass.: Alumnae Association of Mount Holyoke College, 1937.

Newton Theological Institution. *General Catalogue of the Newton Theological Institution, 1826–1943 . . .* Newton Center, Mass.: Newton Theological Institution, 1943.

New York Central College. *Catalogue of the Officers and Students of New York Central College for the Year 1852–3, McGrawville, N.Y.* Homer, N.Y.: For the College, 1853.

Oberlin College. *Seventy-fifth Anniversary General Catalogue of Oberlin College, 1833–1908, Including an Account of the Principal Events in the History of the College, with Illustrations of the College Buildings.* Oberlin, Ohio: Oberlin College, 1909.

Ohio Wesleyan University. "The Ohio Wesleyan University Alumni Directory, 1846–1927." *Ohio Wesleyan University Bulletin* 27 (June 1928): 9–33.

Princeton University. *Princeton University General Catalogue, 1746–1906.* Princeton, N.J.: By the University, 1908.

Rutgers College. *Catalogue of the Officers and Alumni of Rutgers College in New Brunswick, N.J., 1766 to 1916.* Trenton, N.J.: State Gazette Publishing Co., 1916.

St. Lawrence University. *Saint Lawrence University General Catalogue of the Officers, Graduates, and Non-Graduates, 1856–1925.* Canton, N.Y.: By the University, 1926.

Union Theological Seminary. *General Catalogue of Union Theological Seminary in the City of New York. 1836–1908.* Charles Ripley Gillett, comp. New York: Union Theological Seminary, 1908.

University of Vermont. *General Catalogue of the University of Vermont and State Agricultural College, Burlington, Vermont, 1791–1900.* Burlington, Vt.: Free Press Association, 1901.

Western Theological Seminary. *Bulletin of the Western Theological Seminary and Biographical Catalogue.* Allegheny, Pa.: Trustees of the Western Theological Seminary of the Presbyterian Church in the United States of America, 1909.

Westtown School. *Catalog of Westtown Through the Years: Officers, Students and Others, 1799–1945.* Westtown, Pa.: Westtown Alumni Association, 1945.

Williams College. *General Catalogue of the Officers, Graduates, and Non-Graduates of Williams College, 1930.* Williamstown, Mass.: Williams College, 1930.

———. *The Williams Obituary Record.* Williamstown, Mass.: Society of Alumni, 1860–1925.

Yale College. *Obituary Record of Graduates of Yale College Deceased during the Academical Year . . . Presented at the Annual Meetings of the Alumni . . .* [Title varies]. New Haven: Yale College, 1860–1930.

Yale University. *Catalogue of the Officers and Graduates of Yale University in New Haven, Connecticut, 1701–1895.* New Haven: Tuttle, Morehouse & Taylor Press, 1895.

Books

Adams, Myron W. *A History of Atlanta University.* Atlanta: Atlanta University Press, 1930.

Alexander, Adele Logan. *Ambiguous Lives: Free Women of Color in Rural Georgia, 1789–1879.* Fayetteville: University of Arkansas Press, 1991.

Alexander, Roberta Sue. *North Carolina Faces the Freedmen: Race Relations During Presidential Reconstruction, 1865–67.* Durham, N.C.: Duke University Press, 1985.

Anderson, Eric, and Alfred A. Moss Jr., eds. *The Facts of Reconstruction: Essays in Honor of John Hope Franklin.* Baton Rouge: Louisiana State University Press, 1991.

Anderson, James D. *Education of Blacks in the South, 1860–1935.* Chapel Hill: University of North Carolina Press, 1988.

Anderson, Margo J. *The American Census: A Social History.* New Haven, Conn.: Yale University Press, 1988.

Attie, Jeanie. *Patriotic Toll: Northern Women and the American Civil War.* Ithaca, N.Y.: Cornell University Press, 1998.

Augst, Thomas. *The Clerk's Tale: Young Men and Moral Life in Nineteenth-Century America.* Chicago: University of Chicago Press, 2003.

Ayers, Edward L. *The Promise of the New South: Life after Reconstruction.* New York: Oxford University Press, 1992.

Bacote, Clarence A. *The Story of Atlanta University: A Century of Service, 1865–1965.* Atlanta: Atlanta University, 1969.

Baker, Webster B. *History of Rust College.* Greensboro, N.C.: By the Author, 1924.

Ballard, Allen B. *The Education of Black Folk: The Afro-American Struggle for Knowledge in White America.* New York: Harper and Row, 1973.

Barber, Jesse Belmont. *A History of the Work of the Presbyterian Church among the Negroes in the United States of American.* New York: Board of National Missions of the Presbyterian Church in the U.S.A., 1936.

———. *Climbing Jacob's Ladder: Story of the Work of the Presbyterian Church U.S.A.* New York: Presbyterian Board of National Missions, 1952.

Barbour, Hugh, and William J. Frost. *The Quakers.* New York: Greenwood Press, 2003.

264   Beck Cultural Exchange Center. *The History of Blacks in Knoxville, Tennessee: The First One Hundred Years 1791–1891*. Knoxville, Tenn.: Beck Cultural Exchange Center, 1990.

Bell, Robert T. *11th Virginia Infantry*. Lynchburg, Va.: H. E. Howard, 1985.

Bentley, George R. *A History of the Freedmen's Bureau*. Philadelphia: University of Pennsylvania Press, 1955.

Bercaw, Nancy. *Gendered Freedoms: Race, Rights, and the Politics of Household in the Delta, 1861–1875*. Gainesville: University Press of Florida, 2003.

Berlin, Ira. *Many Thousands Gone: The First Two Centuries of Slavery in North America*. Cambridge, Mass.: Belknap Press of Harvard University Press, 1998.

———. *Slaves Without Masters: The Free Negro in the Antebellum South*. New York: New Press, 1974.

Berlin, Ira, and Leslie S. Rowland, eds. *Families and Freedom: A Documentary History of African American Kinship in the Civil War Era*. New York: New Press, 1997.

Berlin, Ira, Joseph P. Reidy, and Leslie S. Rowland, eds. *Freedom: A Documentary History of Emancipation, 1861–1867, Series II, The Black Military Experience*. New York: Cambridge University Press, 1982.

Bernhard, Virginia, Betty Brandon, Elizabeth Fox-Genovese, Theda Perdue, and Elizabeth H. Turner, eds. *Hidden Histories of Women in the New South*. Columbia: University of Missouri Press.

Berry, L. L. *A Century of Missions of the African Methodist Episcopal Church, 1840–1940*. New York: Gutenberg Printing Co., 1942.

Blassingame, John W. *Black New Orleans, 1860–1880*. Chicago: University of Chicago Press, 1973.

Bleser, Carol, ed. *In Joy and Sorrow: Women, Family, and Marriage in the Victorian South, 1830–1900*. New York: Oxford University Press, 1991.

Blum, Edward J. *Reforging the White Republic: Race, Religion, and American Nationalism, 1865–1898*. Baton Rouge: Louisiana State University, 2005.

Boles, John B., ed. *Masters and Slaves in the House of the Lord: Race and Religion in the American South*. Lexington: University Press of Kentucky, 1988.

Bond, Horace Mann. *Education for Freedom: A History of Lincoln University, Pennsylvania*. Lincoln University, Pa.: Lincoln University, 1976.

———. *The Education of the Negro in the American Social Order*. 1930. Reprint, New York: Octagon Books, 1966.

———. *Negro Education in Alabama: A Study in Cotton and Steel*. 1939. Reprint, New York: Atheneum, 1969.

Booker, Robert J. *And There Was Light! The 120-Year History of Knoxville College, Knoxville, Tennessee, 1875–1995*. [Knoxville, Tenn.?]: Robert J. Booker, 1994.

Braden, Mary E. *John Braden: A Pioneer in Negro Education*. Morristown, Tenn.: By the Author, 1935.

Bragg, George F. *The Colored Harvest in the Old Virginia Diocese*. [Baltimore]: n.p., 1901.

———. *History of the Afro-American Group of the Episcopal Church*. Baltimore: Church Advocate Press, 1922.

Brawley, Benjamin. *History of Morehouse College.* Atlanta: Morehouse College, 1917.　**265**

Brawley, James P. *The Clark College Legacy: An Interpretive History of Relevant
Education, 1869–1975.* Atlanta: Clark College, 1977.

———. *Two Centuries of Methodist Concern: Bondage, Freedom and Education of
Black People.* New York: Vantage Press, 1974.

Brewer, J. Mason. *Negro Legislators of Texas and their Descendants.* Dallas, Tex.:
Mathis Publishing, 1935.

Brown, Canter, Jr. *Florida's Black Public Officials, 1867–1924.* Tuscaloosa:
University of Alabama Press, 1998.

Brown, Canter, Jr., and Larry Eugene Rivers. *For a Great and Grand Purpose: The
Beginnings of the AMEZ Church in Florida, 1864–1905.* Gainesville: University
Press of Florida, 2004.

Brown, Hugh Victor. *A History of the Education of Negroes in North Carolina.*
Raleigh: Irving Swain Press, 1961.

Brown, Thomas J., ed. *Reconstructions: New Perspectives on the Postbellum United
States.* New York: Oxford University Press, 2006.

Brumberg, Joan Jacobs. *Mission for Life: The Judson Family and American
Evangelical Religious Culture.* New York: New York University Press, 1980.

Brumgardt, John R., ed. *Civil War Nurse: The Diary and Letters of Hannah Ropes.*
Knoxville: University of Tennessee Press, 1980.

Bryant, Jonathan M. " 'We Have No Chance of Justice before the Courts': The
Freedmen's Struggle for Power in Greene County, Georgia, 1865–1874." In
*Georgia in Black and White: Explorations in the Race Relations of a Southern
State, 1865–1950,* edited by John C. Inscoe, 13–37. Athens: University of Georgia
Press, 1994.

Bryant, Lawrence C., ed. *Negro Lawmakers in the South Carolina Legislature,
1868–1902.* Orangeburg, S.C.: By the Editor, 1968.

Bullock, Henry Allen. *A History of Negro Education in the South: From 1619 to the
Present.* New York: Praeger Publishers, 1970.

Butchart, Ronald E. *Northern Schools, Southern Blacks, and Reconstruction:
Freedmen's Education, 1862–1875.* Westport, Conn.: Greenwood Press, 1980.

Butler, Jon. *Awash in a Sea of Faith: Christianizing the American People.*
Cambridge, Mass.: Harvard University Press, 1990.

Butt, Israel L. *History of African Methodism in Virginia, or Four Decades in the
Old Dominion.* Hampton, Va.: Hampton Institute Press, 1908.

Caldwell, A. B. *History of the American Negro: Virginia Edition.* Vol. 5. Atlanta:
A. B. Caldwell, 1921.

Callahan, Raymond E. *Education and the Cult of Efficiency.* Chicago: University
of Chicago Press, 1962.

Cansler, Charles W. *Three Generations: The Story of a Colored Family of Eastern
Tennessee.* N.p.: Privately printed, 1939.

Carter, Christine Jacobson. *Southern Single Blessedness: Unmarried Women in the
Urban South, 1800–1865.* Chicago: University of Illinois Press, 2006.

Carter, Wilmoth A. *Shaw's Universe: A Monument to Educational Innovation.*
Raleigh: Shaw University, 1973.

266   Cash, Wilbur J. *The Mind of the South*. New York: Knopf, 1941.

Cecelski, David S. *Along Freedom Road: Hyde County, North Carolina, and the Fate of Black Schools in the South*. Chapel Hill: University of North Carolina Press, 1994.

———. *The Waterman's Song: Slavery and Freedom in Maritime North Carolina*. Chapel Hill: University of North Carolina Press, 2001.

Censer, Jane Turner. *The Reconstruction of White Southern Womanhood, 1865–1895*. Baton Rouge: Louisiana State University Press, 2003.

Chadwick, John White, ed. *A Life for Liberty: Anti-Slavery and Other Letters of Sally Holley*. New York, G. P. Putnam's Sons, 1899.

Chambers-Schiller, Lee Virginia. *Liberty a Better Husband: Single Women in America: The Generations of 1780–1840*. New Haven, Conn.: Yale University Press, 1984.

Cimbala, Paul A. *Under the Guardianship of the Nation: The Freedmen's Bureau and the Reconstruction of Georgia, 1865–1870*. Athens: University of Georgia Press, 1997.

Cimbala, Paul A., and Randall M. Miller, eds. *The Freedmen's Bureau and Reconstruction: Reconsiderations*. New York: Fordham University Press, 1999.

Clark, Kathleen Ann. *Defining Moments: African American Commemoration and Political Culture in the South, 1863–1913*. Chapel Hill: University of North Carolina Press, 2005.

Click, Patricia C. *Time Full of Trial: The Roanoke Island Freedmen's Colony, 1862–1867*. Chapel Hill: University of North Carolina Press, 2001.

Clinton, Catherine, and Nina Silber, eds. *Divided Houses: Gender and the Civil War*. New York: Oxford University Press, 1992.

Cogan, Frances B. *All-American Girl: The Ideal of Real Womanhood in Mid-Nineteenth Century America*. Athens: University of Georgia Press, 1989.

Cohen, William. *At Freedom's Edge: Black Mobility and the Southern White Quest for Racial Control, 1861–1915*. Baton Rouge: Louisiana State University Press, 1991.

Cornelius, Janet Duitsman. *When I Can Read My Title Clear: Literacy, Slavery, and Religion in the Antebellum South*. Columbia: University of South Carolina, 1991.

Cozart, Leland Stanford. *A Venture of Faith: Barber-Scotia College, 1867–1967*. [Concord, N.C.]: Barber-Scotia College, 1976.

Cremin, Lawrence. *American Education: The National Experience, 1783–1876*. New York: Harper and Row, 1980.

Crouch, Barry A. *The Freedmen's Bureau and Black Texans*. Austin: University of Texas Press, 1992.

Crum, Mason. *The Negro in the Methodist Church*. New York: Board of Missions and Church Extension of the Methodist Church, 1951.

Culp, D. W., ed. *Twentieth Century Negro Literature; or A Cyclopedia of Thought on the Vital Topics Relating to the American Negro. By One Hundred of America's Greatest Negroes*. 1902. Reprint, New York: Arno Press, 1969.

Current, Richard Nelson. *Those Terrible Carpetbaggers*. New York: Oxford University Press, 1988.

Curry, Leonard. *The Free Black in Urban America, 1800–1850: The Shadow of the Dream*. Chicago: University of Chicago Press, 1981.

Dabney, Charles William. *Universal Education in the South*. 2 vols. Chapel Hill: University of North Carolina Press, 1936.

Dabney, Lillian G. *The History of Schools for Negroes in the District of Columbia, 1807–1947*. Washington, D.C.: Catholic University of America, 1949.

Daniel, W. A. *The Education of Negro Ministers*. New York: J. & J. Harper Editions, 1969.

Davis, Ronald L. F. *Good and Faithful Labor: From Slavery to Sharecropping in the Natchez District, 1860–1890*. Westport, Conn.: Greenwood Press, 1982.

Davis, William R. *The Development and Present Status of Negro Education in East Texas*. New York: Teachers College, Columbia University, 1934.

DeBlack, Thomas A. *With Fire and Sword: Arkansas, 1861–1874*. Fayetteville: University of Arkansas Press, 2003.

DeBoer, Clara Merritt. *His Truth Is Marching On: African Americans Who Taught the Freedmen for the American Missionary Association, 1861–1877*. New York: Garland Publishing, 1995.

Delfino, Susanna, and Michele Gillespie, eds. *Neither Lady Nor Slave: Working Women of the Old South*. Chapel Hill: University of North Carolina Press, 2002.

DeVore, Donald E., and Joseph Logsdon. *Crescent City Schools: Public Education in New Orleans, 1841–1991*. New Orleans: Orleans Parish School Board, 1991.

Dillon, Merton L. *Slavery Attacked: Southern Slaves and Their Allies, 1619–1865*. Baton Rouge: Louisiana State University Press, 1990.

Drago, Edmund L. *Black Politicians and Reconstruction in Georgia: A Splendid Failure*. Baton Rouge: Louisiana State University Press, 1982.

——. *Initiative, Paternalism, and Race Relations: Charleston's Avery Normal Institute*. Athens: University of Georgia Press, 1990.

Du Bois, W. E. Burghardt. *Black Reconstruction in America: An Essay Toward a History of the Part Which Black Folk Played in the Attempt to Reconstruct Democracy in America, 1860–1880*. 1935. Reprint, Cleveland: World Publishing Company, 1964.

——. *The Souls of Black Folk*. New York: New American Library, 1903.

Duncan, Russell. *Freedom's Shore: Tunis Campbell and the Georgia Freedmen*. Athens: University of Georgia Press, 1986.

Dykstra, Robert R. *Bright Radical Star: Black Freedom and White Supremacy on the Hawkeye Frontier*. Cambridge, Mass.: Harvard University Press, 1993.

Dyson, Walter. *Howard University: The Capstone of Negro Education. A History: 1867–1940*. Washington, D.C.: Howard University, 1941.

Edwards, Laura F. *Gendered Strife & Confusion: The Political Culture of Reconstruction*. Urbana: University of Illinois Press, 1997.

——. *Scarlett Doesn't Live Here Anymore: Southern Women in the Civil War Era*. Urbana: University of Illinois Press, 2000.

268   Elson, Ruth Miller. *Guardians of Tradition: American Schoolbooks of the Nineteenth Century*. Lincoln: University of Nebraska Press, 1964.

Engs, Robert Francis. *Educating the Disfranchised and Disinherited: Samuel Chapman Armstrong and Hampton Institute, 1839–1893*. Knoxville: University of Tennessee Press, 1999.

Epstein, Barbara L. *The Politics of Domesticity: Women, Evangelism, and Temperance in Nineteenth-Century America*. Middletown, Conn.: Wesleyan University Press, 1981.

Evans, Matilda. *Martha Schofield; Pioneer Negro Educator*. Columbia, S.C.: DuPre, 1916.

Farnham, Christie Anne. *The Education of the Southern Belle: Higher Education and Student Socialization in the Antebellum South*. New York: New York University Press, 1994.

Faulkner, Carol. *Women's Radical Reconstruction: The Freedmen's Aid Movement*. Philadelphia: University of Pennsylvania Press, 2004.

Faust, Drew Gilpin. *Mothers of Invention: Women of the Slaveholding South in the American Civil War*. New York: Vintage Books, 1996.

Finley, Randy. *From Slavery to Uncertain Freedom: The Freedmen's Bureau in Arkansas, 1865–1869*. Fayetteville: University of Arkansas Press, 1996.

Fitzgerald, Michael W. *Urban Emancipation: Popular Politics in Reconstruction Mobile, 1860–1890*. Baton Rouge: Louisiana State University Press, 2002.

Fleming, Walter L. *Civil War and Reconstruction in Alabama*. New York: Columbia University Press, 1905.

Foner, Eric. *Forever Free: The Story of Emancipation and Reconstruction*. New York: Alfred A. Knopf, 2005.

———. *Freedom's Lawmakers: A Directory of Black Officeholders During Reconstruction*. Rev. ed. New York: Oxford University Press, 1996.

———. *Nothing but Freedom: Emancipation and Its Legacy*. Baton Rouge: Louisiana State University Press, 1983.

———. *Reconstruction: America's Unfinished Revolution, 1863–1877*. New York: Harper & Row, 1988.

Foner, Philip S., and Josephine F. Pacheco. *Three Who Dared: Prudence Crandall, Margaret Douglass, Myrtilla Miner—Champions of Antebellum Black Education*. Westport, Conn.: Greenwood, 1984.

Franklin, John Hope. *Reconstruction After the Civil War*. 2nd ed. Chicago: University of Chicago Press, 1994.

Friedman, Jean E. *The Enclosed Garden: Women and Community in the Evangelical South, 1830–1900*. Chapel Hill: University of North Carolina Press, 1985.

Friedman, Lawrence J. *The White Savage: Racial Fantasies in the Postbellum South*. Englewood Cliffs, N.J.: Prentice-Hall, 1970.

Friend, Craig Thompson, and Lorri Glover, eds. *Southern Manhood: Perspectives on Masculinity in the Old South*. Athens: University of Georgia Press, 2004.

Fuller, T. O. *History of the Negro Baptists of Tennessee*. Memphis, Tenn.: Roger Williams College, 1936.

Bibliography

Gaines, Kevin K. *Uplifting the Race: Black Leadership, Politics, and Culture in the*
Twentieth Century. Chapel Hill: University of North Carolina Press, 1996.

Geiger, Roger, ed. *The American College in the Nineteenth Century*. Nashville,
Tenn.: Vanderbilt University Press, 2000.

Genovese, Eugene D. *Roll, Jordan, Roll: The World the Slaves Made*. New York:
Vintage Books, 1971.

———. *The Slaveholders' Dilemma: Freedom and Progress in Southern Conservative
Thought, 1820–1860*. Columbia: University of South Carolina Press, 1992.

Gillette, William. *Retreat from Reconstruction, 1869–1879*. Baton Rouge:
Louisiana State University Press, 1979.

Ginzberg, Lori D. *Women and the Work of Benevolence: Morality, Politics, and
Class in the 19th Century United States*. New Haven: Yale University Press,
1990.

Gore, Blinzy L. *On a Hilltop High: The Origins and History of Claflin College to
1984*. Spartanburg, S.C.: Claflin College National Alumni Association, 1994.

Griffin, Farah Jasmine. *Beloved Sisters and Loving Friends: Letters from Rebecca
Primus of Royal Oak, Maryland, and Addie Brown of Hartford, Connecticut,
1854–1868*. New York: Ballentine, 1999.

Griffith, Helen. *Dauntless in Mississippi: The Life of Sarah A. Dickey, 1838–1904*.
South Hadley, Mass.: Dinasaur Press, 1965.

Gutman, Herbert. *The Black Family in Slavery and Freedom, 1750–1925*. New
York: Pantheon, 1976.

Hahn, Stephen. *The Roots of Southern Populism: Yeoman Farmers and the
Transformation of the Georgia Upcountry, 1850–1890*. New York: Oxford
University Press, 1983.

Halliburton, Cecil D. *A History of St. Augustine's College, 1867–1937*. Raleigh: St.
Augustine's College, 1937.

Hamm, Thomas D. *Quakers in America*. New York: Columbia University Press,
2003.

Hardman, Keith J. *Charles Grandison Finney, 1792–1875: Revivalist and Reformer*.
Syracuse, N.Y.: Syracuse University Press, 1987.

Harlan, Louis R. *Separate and Unequal: Public School Campaigns and Racism in the
Southern Seaboard States, 1901–1915*. 1958. Reprint, New York: Atheneum, 1968.

Harlan, Louis R., Raymond W. Smock, and Barbara S. Kraft, eds. *Booker T.
Washington Papers*. 14 vols. Urbana: University of Illinois Press, 1977.

Harvey, Paul. *Freedom's Coming: Religious Culture and the Shaping of the South
from the Civil War Through the Civil Rights Era*. Chapel Hill: University of
North Carolina Press, 2005.

———. *Redeeming the South: Religious Cultures and Racial Identities among
Southern Baptists, 1865–1925*. Chapel Hill: University of North Carolina Press,
1997.

Heintze, Michael R. *Private Black Colleges in Texas, 1865–1954*. College Station:
Texas A&M University Press, 1985.

Henderson, Lillian, ed. *Roster of the Confederate Soldiers of Georgia, 1861–1865*.
Atlanta: Georgia Division, United Daughters of the Confederacy, 1994.

Higginbotham, Evelyn Brooks. *Righteous Discontent: The Women's Movement in the Black Baptist Church, 1880–1920.* Cambridge, Mass.: Harvard University Press, 1993.

Hildebrand, Reginald F. *The Times were Strange and Stirring: Methodist Preachers and the Crisis of Emancipation.* Durham, N.C.: Duke University Press, 1995.

Holmes, Dwight Oliver Wendell. *The Evolution of the Negro College.* 1934. Reprint, New York: AMS Press, 1970.

Holt, Sharon Ann. *Making Freedom Pay: North Carolina's Freedpeople Working for Themselves, 1865–1900.* Athens: University of Georgia Press, 2000.

Holt, Thomas. *Black over White: Negro Political Leadership in South Carolina during Reconstruction.* Urbana: University of Illinois Press, 1977.

Hood, J. W. *One Hundred Years of the African Methodist Episcopal Zion Church; or, the Centennial of African Methodism.* New York: A.M.E. Zion Book Concern, 1895.

Horst, Samuel L. *Education for Manhood: The Education of Blacks in Virginia during the Civil War.* Lanham, Md.: University Press of America, 1987.

Horton, Leonard, and Paulette Horton. *In Memory of You: An Educational Legacy.* Mobile, Ala.: Privately printed, 1996.

Hoskins, Charles Lwanga. *Yet with a Steady Beat: Biographies of Early Black Savannah.* Savannah, Ga.: Charles Lwanga Hoskins, 2001.

Howard, Victor B. *Black Liberation in Kentucky: Emancipation and Freedom, 1862–1884.* Lexington: University Press of Kentucky, 1983.

———. *Religion and the Radical Republican Movement, 1860–1870.* Lexington: University Press of Kentucky, 1990.

Hunter, Tera W. *To 'Joy My Freedom: Southern Black Women's Lives and Labors After the Civil War.* Cambridge, Mass.: Harvard University Press, 1997.

Ingle, Edward. *The Negro in the District of Columbia.* Edited by Herbert B. Adams. Johns Hopkins University Studies in History and Political Science, 11th series, 3–4. Baltimore: Johns Hopkins Press, 1893.

Inscoe, John C., ed. *Georgia in Black and White: Explorations in the Race Relations of a Southern State, 1865–1950.* Athens: University of Georgia Press, 1994.

Inscoe, John C., and Robert C. Kenzer. *Enemies of the Country: New Perspectives on Unionists in the Civil War South.* Athens: University of Georgia Press, 2001.

Irons, Peter. *Jim Crow's Children: The Broken Promise of the Brown Decision.* New York: Viking, 2002.

Jackson, Luther Porter. *Negro Office-Holders in Virginia, 1865–1895.* Norfolk, Va.: Guide Quality Press, 1945.

Jaquette, Henrietta S., ed. *South After Gettysburg: Letters of Cornelia Hancock, 1863–1868.* New York: 1956.

Jaynes, Gerald David. *Branches Without Roots: Genesis of the Black Working Class in the American South, 1862–1882.* New York: Oxford University Press, 1986.

Jeffrey, Julie Roy. *The Great Silent Army of Abolitionism: Ordinary Women in the Anti-Slavery Movement.* Chapel Hill: University of North Carolina Press, 1998.

Jenkins, Wilbert L. *Climbing Up to Glory: A Short History of African Americans*
  during the Civil War and Reconstruction. Wilmington, Del.: SR Books, 2002.
———. *Seizing the New Day: African Americans in Post–Civil War Charleston.*
  Bloomington: Indiana University Press, 1998.
Johnson, Michael P., and James L. Roark. *No Chariot Let Down: Charleston's Free*
  People of Color on the Eve of the Civil War. Chapel Hill: University of North
  Carolina Press, 1984.
Jones, Jacqueline. *Soldiers of Light and Love: Northern Teachers and Georgia*
  Blacks, 1865–1873. Chapel Hill: University of North Carolina Press, 1980.
Jones, Maxine D., and Joe M. Richardson. *Talladega College: The First Century.*
  Tuscaloosa: University of Alabama Press, 1990.
Kaestle, Carl F. *Pillars of the Republic: Common Schools and American Society,*
  1780–1860. New York: Hill and Wang, 1983.
Katz, Michael B. *The Irony of Early School Reform: Educational Innovation in*
  Mid-Nineteenth Century Massachusetts. Boston: Beacon Press, 1968.
Katz, Michael B., Michael J. Doucet, and Mark J. Stern. *The Social Organization of*
  Early Industrial Capitalism. Cambridge, Mass.: Harvard University Press, 1982.
Kaufman, Polly Welts. *Women Teachers on the Frontier.* New Haven, Conn.: Yale
  University Press, 1984.
Kelley, Mary. *Learning to Stand and Speak: Women, Education, and Public Life in*
  America's Republic. Chapel Hill: University of North Carolina Press, 2006.
Kent, Eliza F. *Converting Women: Gender and Protestant Christianity in Colonial*
  South India. New York: Oxford University Press, 2004.
Klein, Arthur J., ed. and comp. *Survey of Negro Colleges and Universities.*
  Department of the Interior, Bureau of Education, Bulletin No. 7. Washington,
  D.C.: GPO, 1929.
Klingaman, David C., and Richard K. Vedder, eds. *Essays in Nineteenth Century*
  Economic History: The Old Northwest. Athens: Ohio University Press, 1975.
Klingman, Peter D. *Josiah Walls: Florida's Black Congressman of Reconstruction.*
  Gainesville: University Presses of Florida, 1976.
Knight, Edgar W. *The Influence of Reconstruction on Education in the South.* New
  York: Teachers College, Columbia University, 1913.
Kremer, Gary R. *James Milton Turner and the Promise of America: The Public*
  Life of a Post–Civil War Black Leader. Columbia: University of Missouri Press,
  1991.
Labaree, David F. *The Making of an American High School: The Credentials*
  Market and the Central High School of Philadelphia, 1838–1939. New Haven,
  Conn.: Yale University Press, 1988.
Langhorne, Orra. *Southern Sketches from Virginia, 1881–1901.* Edited by Charles E.
  Wynes. Charlottesville: University Press of Virginia, 1964.
Lasch, Christopher. *The True and Only Heaven: Progress and Its Critics.* New
  York: W. W. Norton, 1991.
Lawrence, Harold, ed. and comp. *Methodist Preachers in Georgia, 1783–1900.*
  Tignall, Ga.: Privately published, 1984.

——, ed. *Methodist Preachers in Georgia, 1783–1900: A Supplement*. Milledgeville, Ga.: Boyd Publishing, 1995.

Lawson, Ellen NicKenzie, and Marlene D. Merrill, eds. *The Three Sarahs: Documents of Antebellum Black College Women*. New York: Edwin Mellen Press, 1984.

Lebsock, Suzanne. *The Free Women of Petersburg*. New York: W. W. Norton, 1984.

Lemann, Nicholas. *Redemption: The Last Battle of the Civil War*. New York: Farrar, Straus and Giroux, 2006.

Link, William A. *A Hard Country and a Lonely Place: Schooling, Society, and Reform in Rural Virginia, 1870–1920*. Chapel Hill: University of North Carolina Press, 1986.

Litwack, Leon F. *Been in the Storm So Long: The Aftermath of Slavery*. New York: Alfred A. Knopf, 1979.

Litwack, Leon, and August Meier, eds. *Black Leaders of the Nineteenth Century*. Urbana: University of Illinois Press, 1988.

Logan, Rayford W. *Howard University, the First Hundred Years, 1867–1967*. New York: New York University Press, 1969.

Logan, Rayford W., and Michael R. Winston, eds. *Dictionary of American Negro Biography*. New York: W. W. Norton, 1982.

Long, Charles Sumner, comp. *History of the A.M.E. Church in Florida*. Philadelphia: A.M.E. Book Concern, 1939.

Mabee, Carleton. *Black Education in New York State: From Colonial to Modern Time*. Syracuse, N.Y.: Syracuse University Press, 1979.

MacMullen, Edith Nye. *In the Cause of True Education: Henry Barnard and Nineteenth-Century School Reform*. New Haven: Yale University Press, 1991.

Magdol, Edward. *The Antislavery Rank and File: A Social Profile of the Abolitionists' Constituency*. Westport, Conn.: Greenwood Press, 1986.

——. *A Right to the Land: Essays on the Freedmen's Community*. Westport, Conn.: Greenwood Press, 1977.

Majors, Monroe A. *Noted Negro Women: Their Triumphs and Activities*. Chicago: By the author, 1893.

Mandle, Jay R. *The Roots of Black Poverty: The Southern Plantation Economy after the Civil War*. Durham, N.C.: Duke University Press, 1978.

Manning, Francis M., and W. H. Booker. *Martin County History*. Williamston, N.C.: Enterprise Publishing Company, 1977.

Margo, Robert A. *Race and Schooling in the South, 1880–1950: An Economic History*. Chicago: University of Chicago Press, 1990.

Marszalek, John F. *A Black Congressman in the Age of Jim Crow: South Carolina's George Washington Murray*. Gainesville: University Press of Florida, 2006.

Martin, Josephine W., ed. *"Dear Sister": Letters Written on Hilton Head Island, 1867*. Beaufort, S.C.: Beaufort Book Co., 1977.

Matthews, Glenna. *The Rise of Public Woman: Woman's Power and Woman's Place in the United States, 1630–1970*. New York: Oxford University Press, 1992.

Mattingly, Paul H. *The Classless Profession: American Schoolmen of the Nineteenth Century*. New York: New York University Press, 1975.

McAfee, Ward M. *Religion, Race, and Reconstruction: The Public School in the*
    Politics of the 1870s. Albany: State University of New York Press, 1998.

McCaul, Robert L. *The Black Struggle for Public Schooling in Nineteenth-Century*
    Illinois. Carbondale: Southern Illinois University Press, 1987.

McCurry, Stephanie. *Masters of Small Worlds: Yeomen Households, Gender*
    Relations, and the Political Culture of the Antebellum South Carolina Low
    Country. New York: Oxford University Press, 1995.

McGinnis, Frederick A. *The Education of Negroes in Ohio.* Wilberforce, Ohio: By
    the Author, 1962.

———. *A History and Interpretation of Wilberforce University.* Wilberforce, Ohio:
    By the Author, 1941.

McKivigan, John R. *The War against Proslavery Religion: Abolitionism and the*
    Northern Churches, 1830–1865. Ithaca, N.Y.: Cornell University Press, 1984.

McMillan, Lewis K. *Negro Higher Education in the State of South Carolina.* N.p.:
    By the Author, 1952.

McPherson, James M. *The Abolitionist Legacy: From Reconstruction to the*
    NAACP. Princeton, N.J.: Princeton University Press, 1975.

———. *The Struggle for Equality: Abolitionists and the Negro in the Civil War and*
    Reconstruction. Princeton, N.J.: Princeton University Press, 1964.

Megginson, W. J. *African American Life in South Carolina's Upper Piedmont.*
    Columbia: University of South Carolina Press, 2006.

Messner, William F. *Freedmen and the Ideology of Free Labor.* Lafayette, La.:
    Center for Louisiana Studies, 1978.

Miller, Albert G. *Elevating the Race: Theophilus G. Steward, Black Theology, and*
    the Making of an African American Civil Society, 1865–1924. Knoxville:
    University of Tennessee Press, 2003.

Miller, Randall M., Harry S. Stout, and Charles Reagan Wilson, eds. *Religion and*
    the American Civil War. New York: Oxford University Press, 1998.

Mills, Gary B. *Southern Loyalists in the Civil War: A Composite Directory of Case*
    Files Created by the U.S. Commissioner of Claims, 1871–1880, Including Those
    Appealed to the War Claims Committee of the U.S. House of Representatives and
    the U.S. Court of Claims. Baltimore: Genealogical Publishing Co., 1994.

Mitchell, Michele. *Righteous Propagation: African Americans and the Politics of*
    Racial Destiny after Reconstruction. Chapel Hill: University of North Carolina
    Press, 2004.

Mohr, Clarence L. *On the Threshold of Freedom: Masters and Slaves in Civil War*
    Georgia. Athens: University of Georgia Press, 1986.

Mohr, James C., ed. *State Politics during Reconstruction: Radical Republicans in*
    the North. Baltimore: Johns Hopkins University Press, 1976.

Montgomery, David. *Beyond Equality: Labor and the Radical Republicans, 1862–*
    1872. New York: Vintage Books, 1967.

Montgomery, William E. *Under Their Own Vine and Fig Tree: The African-*
    American Church in the South, 1865–1900. Baton Rouge: Louisiana University
    Press, 1993.

Moore, John Jamison. *History of the A.M.E. Zion Church, in America.* York, Pa.:
    Teachers' Journal Office, 1884.

274 Morgan, T. J. *Forty Years' Work for the Negroes by the American Baptist Home Mission Society*. New York: American Baptist Home Mission Society, 1901.

Morris, Robert C. *Reading, 'Riting, and Reconstruction: The Education of Freedmen in the South, 1861–1870*. Chicago: University of Chicago Press, 1981.

Morrow, Diane Batts. *Persons of Color and Religious at the Same Time: The Oblate Sisters of Providence, 1828–1860*. Chapel Hill: University of North Carolina Press, 2002.

Morrow, Ralph E. *Northern Methodism and Reconstruction*. East Lansing: Michigan State University Press, 1956.

Murray, Andrew E. *Presbyterians and the Negro—A History*. Philadelphia: Presbyterian Historical Society, 1966.

Murray, Pauli. *Proud Shoes: The Story of an American Family*. New York: Harper & Row, 1978.

Nash, Margaret A. *Women's Education in the United States, 1780–1840*. New York: Palgrave Macmillan, 2005.

Noble, Stuart Grayson. *Forty Years of the Public Schools in Mississippi, with Special Reference to the Education of the Negro*. New York: Teachers College, Columbia University, 1918.

Norris, James D. *R. G. Dun & Co., 1841–1900: The Development of Credit-Reporting in the Nineteenth Century*. Westport, Conn.: Greenwood Press, 1978.

Oakes, James. *The Ruling Race: A History of American Slaveholders*. New York: Alfred A. Knopf, 1982.

Oates, Stephen B. *A Woman of Valor: Clara Barton and the Civil War*. New York: Free Press, 1994.

Ogren, Christine A. *The American State Normal School: "An Instrument of Great Good."* New York: Palgrave Macmillan, 2005.

Osthaus, Carl R. *Freedmen, Philanthropy, and Fraud: A History of the Freedmen's Savings Bank*. Urbana: University of Illinois Press, 1976.

Oubre, Claude F. *Forty Acres and a Mule: The Freedmen's Bureau and Black Land Ownership*. Baton Rouge: Louisiana State University Press, 1978.

Painter, Jacqueline Burgin. *The Season of Dorland-Bell*. Asheville, N.C.: Biltmore Press, 1987.

Painter, Nell Irvin. *Southern History across the Color Line*. Chapel Hill: University of North Carolina Press, 2002.

Parker, Inez Moore. *The Rise and Decline of the Program of Education for Black Presbyterians of the United Presbyterian Church U.S.A., 1865–1970*. San Antonio, Tex.: Trinity University Press, 1977.

Parrish, C. H. *Golden Jubilee of the General Association of Colored Baptists in Kentucky*. Louisville, Ky.: Mayes Printing Co., 1915.

Patterson, James T. *Brown v. Board of Education: A Civil Rights Milestone and Its Troubled Legacy*. New York: Oxford University Press, 2001.

Peabody, Francis Greenwood. *Education for Life: The Story of Hampton Institute*. Garden City, N.Y.: Doubleday, Page, 1918.

Pegues, A. W. *Our Baptist Ministers and Schools*. Springfield, Mass.: Willey, 1892.

Peirce, Paul Skeels. *The Freedmen's Bureau: A Chapter in the History of Reconstruction*. Iowa City: University of Iowa, 1904.

Perlmann, Joel, and Robert A. Margo. *Women's Work? American Schoolteachers, 1650–1920*. Chicago: University of Chicago Press, 2001.

Perman, Michael. *Reunion without Compromise: The South and Reconstruction, 1865–1868*. Cambridge, U.K.: Cambridge University Press, 1973.

———. *The Road to Redemption: Southern Politics, 1869–1879*. Chapel Hill: University of North Carolina Press, 1984.

Porterfield, Amanda. *Mary Lyon and the Mount Holyoke Missionaries*. New York: Oxford University Press, 1997.

Powell, William S., ed. *Dictionary of North Carolina Biography*. Chapel Hill: University of North Carolina Press, 1979, 1986.

Powers, Bernard E., Jr. *Black Charlestonians: A Social History, 1822–1885*. Fayetteville: University of Arkansas Press, 1994.

Rabinowitz, Howard N., ed. *Southern Black Leaders of the Reconstruction Era*. Urbana: University of Illinois Press, 1982.

Rable, George C. *But There Was No Peace: The Role of Violence in the Politics of Reconstruction*. Athens: University of Georgia Press, 1984.

Rachleff, Peter. *Black Labor in Richmond, 1865–1890*. Urbana: University of Illinois Press, 1989.

Range, Willard. *The Rise and Progress of Negro Colleges in Georgia, 1865–1949*. Athens: University of Georgia Press, 1951.

Ransom, Roger L., and Richard Sutch. *One Kind of Freedom: The Economic Consequences of Emancipation*. Cambridge, U.K.: Cambridge University Press, 1977.

Reilly, Wayne E., ed. *Sarah Jane Foster: Teacher of the Freedmen*. Charlottesville: University Press of Virginia, 1990.

Reynolds, Mary C., and others. *Baptist Missionary Pioneers Among Negroes*. Nashville, Tenn.: Sunday School Publication Board, 1902.

Richardson, Harry V. *Dark Salvation: The Story of Methodism as It Developed Among Blacks in America*. Garden City, N.Y.: Anchor Press/Doubleday, 1976.

Richardson, Heather Cox. *The Death of Reconstruction: Race, Labor, and Politics in the Post–Civil War North, 1865–1901*. Cambridge, Mass.: Harvard University Press, 2001.

———. *West From Appomattox: The Reconstruction of America after the Civil War*. New Haven: Yale University Press, 2007.

Richardson, Joe M. *Christian Reconstruction: The American Missionary Association and Southern Blacks, 1861–1890*. Athens: University of Georgia Press, 1986.

———. *A History of Fisk University, 1865–1946*. University: University of Alabama Press, 1980.

Richardson, Marilyn. *Maria W. Stewart: America's First Black Woman Political Writer*. Bloomington: Indiana University Press, 1987.

Richings, G. F. *An Album of Negro Educators*. [Philadelphia]: n.p., 1900.

Richter, William L. *Overreached on All Sides: The Freedmen's Bureau Administrators in Texas, 1865–1868*. College Station: Texas A&M University Press, 1991.

276   Roark, James L. *Masters Without Slaves: Southern Planters in the Civil War and Reconstruction.* New York: W. W. Norton, 1977.

Robert, Dana L. *American Women in Mission: A Social History of Their Thoughts and Practices.* Charlottesville: University of Virginia Press, 1990.

Robinson, Wilhelmena S. *Historical Negro Biographies.* International Library of Negro Life and History. New York: Association for the Study of Negro Life and History, 1970.

Ronnick, Michele Valerie, ed. *The Autobiography of William Sanders Scarborough: An American Journey from Slavery to Scholarship.* Detroit, Mich.: Wayne State University Press, 2005.

Rose, Willie Lee. *Rehearsal for Reconstruction: The Port Royal Experiment.* New York: Vintage Books, 1964.

Rotundo, E. Anthony. *American Manhood: Transformations in Masculinity from the Revolution to the Modern Era.* New York: Basic Books, 1993.

Rubin, Anne Sarah. *A Shattered Nation: The Rise and Fall of the Confederacy, 1861–1868.* Chapel Hill: University of North Carolina Press, 2005.

Ryan, Mary P. *Cradle of the Middle Class: The Family in Oneida County, New York, 1790–1865.* New York: Cambridge University Press, 1981.

Saville, Julie. *The Work of Reconstruction: From Slave to Wage Laborer in South Carolina, 1860–1870.* New York: Cambridge University Press, 1996.

Schafer, Judith Kelleher. *Becoming Free, Remaining Free: Manumission and Enslavement in New Orleans, 1846–1862.* Baton Rouge: Louisiana State University, 2003.

Schultz, Jane E. *Women at the Front: Hospital Workers in Civil War America.* Chapel Hill: University of North Carolina Press, 2004.

Schultz, Stanley K. *The Culture Factory: Boston Public Schools, 1789–1860.* New York: Oxford University Press, 1973.

Schwalm, Leslie. *A Hard Fight for We: Women's Transition from Slavery to Freedom in South Carolina.* Urbana: University of Illinois Press, 1997.

Schwartz, Gerald, ed. *A Woman Doctor's Civil War: Esther Hill Hawks' Diary.* Columbia: University of South Carolina Press, 1984.

Schwartz, Marie Jenkins. *Born in Bondage: Growing up Enslaved in the Antebellum South.* Cambridge, Mass.: Harvard University Press, 2000.

Scott, Anne Firor. *Making the Invisible Woman Visible.* Urbana: University of Illinois Press, 1984.

———. *Natural Allies: Women's Associations in American History.* Urbana: University of Illinois Press, 1991.

Scruggs, L. A. *Women of Distinction: Remarkable in Works and Invincible in Character.* Raleigh: L. A. Scruggs, 1893.

Sears, Richard D. *Camp Nelson, Kentucky: A Civil War History.* Lexington: University Press of Kentucky, 2002.

Selleck, Linda B. *Gentle Invaders: Quaker Women Educators and Racial Issues During the Civil War and Reconstruction.* Richmond, Ind.: Friends United Press, 1995.

Sernett, Milton C. *Abolition's Axe: Beriah Green, Oneida Institute, and the Black Freedom Struggle.* Syracuse, N.Y.: Syracuse University Press, 1986.

Shaffer, Donald R. *After the Glory: The Struggles of Black Civil War Veterans.* Lawrence: University Press of Kansas, 2004.

Sherer, Robert G. *Subordination or Liberation? The Development and Conflicting Theories of Black Education in Nineteenth Century Alabama.* Tuscaloosa: University of Alabama Press, 1977.

Silber, Nina. *Daughters of the Union: Northern Women Fight the Civil War.* Cambridge, Mass.: Harvard University Press, 2005.

Simmons, William J. *Men of Mark: Eminent, Progressive and Rising.* 1887. Reprint, New York: Arno Press, 1968.

Simpson, Matthew, ed. *Cyclopaedia of Methodism. Embracing Sketches of Its Rise, Progress, and Present Conditions. With Biographical Notices and Numerous Illustrations.* Rev. ed. Philadelphia: Louis H. Everts, 1880.

Sizer, Lyde Cullen. *The Political Work of Northern Women Writers and the Civil War, 1850–1872.* Chapel Hill: University of North Carolina Press, 2000.

Sklar, Kathryn Kish. *Catharine Beecher: A Study in American Domesticity.* New York: W. W. Norton, 1976.

Smallwood, James. *Time of Hope, Time of Despair: Black Texans During Reconstruction.* Port Washington, N.Y.: Kennikat Press, 1981.

Smedley, Katherine. *Martha Schofield and the Re-Education of the South, 1839–1916.* Lewiston, N.Y.: Edwin Mellen Press, 1987.

Smith, Charles Spencer. *A History of the African Methodist Episcopal Church, being a Volume Supplemental to a History of the African Methodist Episcopal Church, by Daniel Alexander Payne, D.D., LL.D., Late One of Its Bishops, Chronicling the Principal Events in the Advance of the African Methodist Episcopal Church from 1856 to 1922.* Philadelphia: Book Concern of the A.M.E. Church, 1922.

Smith, H. Sheldon. *In His Image, But . . . : Racism in Southern Religion, 1780–1910.* Durham, N.C.: Duke University Press, 1972.

Smith-Rosenberg, Carroll. *Disorderly Conduct: Visions of Gender in Victorian America.* New York: Knopf, 1985.

Solomon, Barbara Miller. *In the Company of Educated Women: A History of Women and Higher Education in America.* New Haven: Yale University Press, 1985.

Soltow, Lee. *Men and Wealth in the United States, 1850–1870.* New Haven, Conn.: Yale University Press, 1975.

Sorin, Gerald. *Abolitionism: A New Perspective.* New York: Praeger, 1972.

Spivey, Donald. *Schooling for the New Slavery: Black Industrial Education, 1868–1915.* Westport, Conn.: Greenwood Press, 1978.

Sterling, Dorothy. *We Are Your Sisters: Black Women in the Nineteenth Century.* New York: W. W. Norton, 1984.

Stowell, Jay S. *Methodist Adventures in Negro Education.* New York: Methodist Book Concern, 1922.

Summerville, James. *Educating Black Doctors: A History of Meharry Medical College.* University: University of Alabama Press, 1983.

Swann, Vera P. *Bread Upon the Waters: The Lives of Caroline Coulter and*

Samantha Neil. Cheraw, S.C.: Coulter Memorial Academy National Alumni
         Association, 1901.

Swint, Henry Lee. *The Northern Teacher in the South, 1862–1870*. Nashville,
         Tenn.: Vanderbilt University Press, 1941.

——, ed. *Dear Ones at Home: Letters from Contraband Camps*. Nashville, Tenn.:
         Vanderbilt University Press, 1966.

Talbert, Horace. *The Sons of Allen: Together with a Sketch of the Rise and Progress
         of Wilberforce University, Wilberforce, Ohio*. Xenia, Ohio: Aldine Press, 1906.

Talbot, Edith Armstrong. *Samuel Chapman Armstrong: A Biographical Study*.
         New York: Doubleday, Page, 1904.

Taylor, Alrutheus Ambush. *The Negro in Tennessee, 1865–1880*. Washington, D.C.:
         Associated Publishers, 1941.

Taylor, George Braxton. *Virginia Baptist Ministers*. 4th ser. Lynchburg, Va.: J. P.
         Bell, 1913.

Terry, Adolphine Fletcher. *Charlotte Stephens: Little Rock's First Black Teacher*.
         Little Rock: Academic Press of Arkansas, 1973.

Thelin, John R. *A History of American Higher Education*. Baltimore: Johns
         Hopkins University Press, 2004.

Thomas, I. L., ed. *Methodism and the Negro*. New York: Eaton and Mains, 1910.

Thomason, John Furman. *The Foundations of the Public Schools of South Carolina*.
         Columbia, S.C.: State Company, 1925.

Thompson, Patrick H. *History of Negro Baptists in Mississippi*. Jackson, Miss.:
         R. W. Bailey Printing Co., 1898.

Tise, Larry E. *Proslavery: A History of the Defense of Slavery in America, 1701–
         1840*. Athens: University of Georgia Press, 1987.

Tyack, David B. *The One Best System: A History of American Urban Education*.
         Cambridge, Mass.: Harvard University Press, 1974.

Varon, Elizabeth R. *Southern Lady, Yankee Spy: The True Story of Elizabeth Van
         Lew, a Union Agent in the Heart of the Confederacy*. New York: Oxford
         University Press, 2003.

Vaughn, William Preston. *Schools for All: Blacks and Public Education in the
         South, 1865–1877*. Lexington: University Press of Kentucky, 1974.

Venet, Wendy Hamand. *Neither Ballots Nor Bullets: Women Abolitionists and the
         Civil War*. Charlottesville: University Press of Virginia, 1991.

Vincent, Charles. *Black Legislators in Louisiana During Reconstruction*. Baton
         Rouge: Louisiana State University, 1976.

Vinovskis, Maris A., ed. *Toward a Social History of the American Civil War*.
         Cambridge, U.K.: Cambridge University Press, 1990.

Wagner, Clarence M. *Profiles of Black Georgia Baptists*. Atlanta: Bennett Brothers
         Printing Company, 1980.

Walker, Alice O., comp. *Registers of Signatures of Depositors in the Augusta,
         Georgia, Branch of the Freedmen's Savings and Trust Company*. Vol. 1, *Nov.
         1870–June 1872*. Augusta, Ga.: Augusta-Richmond County Public Library,
         1998.

Walker, Clarence E. *A Rock in a Weary Land: The African Methodist Episcopal*

Church During the Civil War and Reconstruction. Baton Rouge: Louisiana State
University Press, 1982.

Warner, Stafford Allen. *Yardley Warner: The Freedman's Friend. His Life and
Times with His Journal and Letters Reproduced in an Appendix.* Didcot [Great
Britain]: Wessex Press, 1957.

Waterbury, M. *Seven Years among the Freedmen.* Chicago: T. B. Arnold, 1893.

Watkins, William H. *The White Architects of Black Education: Ideology and
Power in America, 1865–1954.* New York: Teachers College Press, 2001.

Wayman, Alexander W. *Cyclopaedia of African Methodism.* Baltimore, Md.:
Methodist Episcopal Book Depository, 1882.

Webber, Thomas L. *Deep Like the Rivers: Education in the Slave Quarter
Community, 1831–1865.* New York: W. W. Norton, 1978.

Westerkamp, Marilyn J. *Women and Religion in Early America, 1600–1850: The
Puritan and Evangelical Traditions.* New York: Routledge, 1999.

White, Charles L. *A Century of Faith.* Philadelphia: American Baptist Home
Mission Society, 1932.

White, Deborah Gray. *Ar'n't I a Woman? Female Slaves in the Plantation South.*
New York: W. W. Norton, 1985.

Whites, Lee Ann. *The Civil War as a Crisis in Gender: Augusta, Georgia, 1860–
1890.* Athens: University of Georgia Press, 1995.

———. *Gender Matters: Civil War, Reconstruction, and the Making of the New
South.* New York: Palgrave Macmillan, 2005.

Williams, Heather Andrea. *Self-Taught: African American Education in Slavery
and Freedom.* Chapel Hill: University of North Carolina Press, 2005.

Williams, M. W., and George W. Watkins. *Who's Who among North Carolina
Negro Baptists.* N.p., 1940.

Williamson, Joel. *After Slavery: The Negro in South Carolina During
Reconstruction, 1861–1877.* Chapel Hill: University of North Carolina Press,
1965.

———. *The Crucible of Race: Black-White Relations in the American South Since
Emancipation.* New York: Oxford University Press, 1984.

———. *A Rage for Order: Black-White Relations in the American South Since
Emancipation.* New York: Oxford University Press, 1986.

Winch, Julie, ed. *The Elite of Our People: Joseph Willson's Sketches of Black
Upper-Class Life in Antebellum Philadelphia.* University Park: Pennsylvania
State University Press, 2000.

Wood, Forrest G. *Black Scare: The Racist Response to Emancipation and
Reconstruction.* Berkeley: University of California Press, 1968.

Woodson, Carter G. *Early Negro Education in West Virginia.* Institute, W.Va.:
West Virginia Collegiate Institute, 1921.

———. *The Education of the Negro Prior to 1861.* Washington, D.C.: Associated
Publishers, 1919.

———. *Mis-Education of the Negro.* Washington, D.C.: Associated Publishers, 1933.

Woody, Thomas. *A History of Women's Education in the United States.* New York:
Science Press, 1929.

280   Work, Monroe N., ed. *Negro Yearbook: An Annual Encyclopedia of the Negro, 1925–26.* Tuskegee, Ala.: Negro Book Publishing Co., 1925.

Wright, Gavin. *Old South, New South: Revolutions in the Southern Economy Since the Civil War.* Baton Rouge: Louisiana State University Press, 1986.

Wright, Marion M. *The Education of Negroes in New Jersey.* New York: Teachers College, Columbia University, 1941.

Wright, Richard R. *The Bishops of the African Methodist Episcopal Church.* Nashville, Tenn.: A.M.E. Sunday School Union, 1963.

——. *A Brief Historical Sketch of Negro Education in Georgia.* Savannah, Ga.: Robinson Printing House, 1894.

——. *Centennial Encyclopaedia of the African Methodist Episcopal Church.* Philadelphia: [Book Concern of the A.M.E. Church], 1916.

Wyatt-Brown, Bertram. *Honor and Violence in the Old South.* New York: Oxford University Press, 1986.

——. *The Shaping of Southern Culture: Honor, Grace, and War, 1760s–1880s.* Chapel Hill: University of North Carolina Press, 2000.

——. *Southern Honor: Ethics and Behavior in the Old South.* New York: Oxford University Press, 1983.

Yee, Shirley J. *Black Women Abolitionists: A Study in Activism, 1828–1860.* Knoxville: University of Tennessee Press, 1992.

Yohn, Susan M. *A Contest of Faiths: Missionary Women and Pluralism in the American Southwest.* Ithaca, N.Y.: Cornell University Press, 1995.

Articles and Essays

Abbott, Martin. "The Freedmen's Bureau and Negro Schooling in South Carolina." *South Carolina Historical Magazine* 57 (April 1956): 65–81.

Alderson, William T., Jr. "The Freedmen's Bureau and Negro Education in Virginia." *North Carolina Historical Review* 29 (1952): 64–90.

Alexander, Roberta Sue. "Hostility and Hope: Black Education in North Carolina During Presidential Reconstruction, 1865–1867." *North Carolina Historical Review* 53 (April 1976): 113–32.

Allmendinger, David F., Jr. "Mount Holyoke Students Encounter the Need for Life Planning, 1837–1850." *History of Education Quarterly* 19 (Spring 1979): 27–46.

Anderson, James D. "Ex-Slaves and the Rise of Universal Education in the New South, 1860–1880." In *Education and the Rise of the New South,* edited by Ronald K. Goodenow and Arthur O. White, 1–25. Boston: G. K. Hall & Co., 1981.

——. "The Historical Development of Black Vocational Education." In *Work, Youth, and Schooling: Historical Perspectives on Vocationalism in America,* edited by Harvey Kantor and David B. Tyack, 180–222. Stanford, Calif.: Stanford University Press, 1982.

Andrew, John. "Educating the Heathen: The Foreign Mission School Controversy and American Ideals." *Journal of American Studies* 12 (1978): 331–42.

Anonymous. "Giles B. Cooke." *Tyler Quarterly Historical and Genealogical Magazine* 19 (July 1937): 2–4.

Armstrong, Warren B. "Union Chaplains and the Education of the Freedmen." *Journal of Negro History* 52 (April 1967): 104–15.

Ash, Stephen V. "Poor Whites in the Occupied South, 1861–1865." *Journal of Southern History* 57 (February 1991): 39–62.

Banker, Mark T. " 'They Made Haste Slowly': Presbyterian Mission Schools and Southwestern Pluralism." *American Presbyterians* 69 (Summer 1991): 123–32.

Banks, Willa Young. "A Contradiction in Antebellum Baltimore: A Competitive School for Girls of 'Color' Within a Slave State." *Maryland Historical Magazine* 99 (Summer 2004): 132–63.

Beadie, Nancy. "Emma Willard's Idea Put to the Test: The Consequences of State Support of Female Education in New York." *History of Education Quarterly* 33, no. 4 (Winter 1993): 543–62.

Beck, Scott A. L. "Freedmen, Friends, Common Schools and Reconstruction." *The Southern Friend: Journal of the North Carolina Friends Historical Society* 17 (Spring 1995): 5–31.

Belding, Robert E. "The Dubuque Female Seminary: Catharine Beecher's Blueprint for Nineteenth Century Women's Education." *Palimpsest* 63 (March/April 1982): 34–38, 40–41.

Bell, John L. "Samuel Stanford Ashley, Carpetbagger and Educator." *North Carolina Historical Review* 72 (October 1995): 456–83.

——. "The Presbyterian Church and the Negro in North Carolina During Reconstruction." *North Carolina Historical Review* 40 (January 1963): 15–36.

Bendroth, Margaret L. "Women and Missions: Conflict and Changing Roles in the Presbyterian Church in the United States of America, 1870–1935." *American Presbyterians* 65 (Spring 1987): 49–59.

Berlin, Ira, Steven F. Miller, and Leslie S. Rowland. "Afro-American Families in the Transition from Slavery to Freedom." *Radical History Review* 42 (Fall 1988): 89–121.

Bernard, Richard M., and Maris A. Vinovskis. "The Female School Teacher in Antebellum Massachusetts." *Journal of Social History* 10 (Spring 1977): 332–45.

Berry, Trey. "A History of Women's Higher Education in Mississippi, 1819–1882." *Journal of Mississippi History* 53 (November 1991): 303–19.

Bethel, Elizabeth. "The Freedmen's Bureau in Alabama." *Journal of Southern History* 14 (February 1948): 49–92.

Bigelow, Martha Mitchell. "Public Opinion and the Passage of the Mississippi Black Codes." *Negro History Bulletin* 33 (January 1970): 11–16.

Biggleston, W. E. "Oberlin College and the Negro Student, 1865–1940." *Journal of Negro History* 56 (July 1971): 198–219.

Birnie, C. W. "Education of the Negro in Charleston, South Carolina, Prior to the Civil War." *Journal of Negro History* 12 (January 1927): 13–21.

Blackburn, George M., and Sherman L. Ricards. "Unequal Opportunity on a Mining Frontier: The Role of Gender, Race, and Birthplace." *Pacific Historical Review* 62 (February 1993): 19–38.

Blassingame, John W. "The Union Army as an Educational Institution for Negroes, 1861–1865." *Journal of Negro Education* 34 (Spring 1965): 152–59.

282   Bond, Beverly G. " 'Every Duty Incumbent Upon Them': African-American
         Women in Nineteenth Century Memphis." *Tennessee Historical Quarterly* 59
         (Winter 2000): 254–73.

Boylan, Anne M. "Evangelical Womanhood in the Nineteenth Century: The Role
         of Women in Sunday Schools." *Feminist Studies* 4 (October 1978): 62–80.

Brady, Patricia. "Trials and Tribulations: American Missionary Association
         Teachers and Black Education in Occupied New Orleans, 1863–1864."
         Louisiana History 31 (Winter 1990): 5–20.

Brewer, H. Peers. "The Protestant Episcopal Freedman's Commission, 1865–
         1878." *Historical Magazine of the Protestant Episcopal Church* 26 (1957): 361–
         81.

Brophy, William J. "They Fought the Good Fight: Black Legacies of Struggle and
         Triumph in Texas." *Texas Journal of Ideas, History and Culture* 14 (Spring/
         Summer 1992): 8–11.

Browne, Joseph L. " 'The Expenses Are Borne by Parents': Freedmen's Schools in
         Southern Maryland, 1865–1870." *Maryland Historical Magazine* 86 (Winter
         1991): 407–22.

Browning, Judkin. " 'Bringing Light to Our Land . . . When She Was Dark as
         Night': Northerners, Freedpeople, and Education during Military Occupation
         in North Carolina, 1862–1865." *American Nineteenth Century History* 9
         (March 2008): 1–17.

Bryan, Charles F., Jr., and JoVita Wells. "Morristown College: Education for Blacks
         in the Southern Highlands." *East Tennessee Historical Society's Publications*
         51/52 (1980/1981): 61–77.

Bumstead, Horace. "Mrs. Lucy E. Case: A Life Devoted to Work for Atlanta
         University." In *The Atlanta University Bulletin*. Ser. 2, no. 18, 24–41. Atlanta:
         Atlanta University, 1915.

Bunkle, P. "Sentimental Womanhood and Domestic Education, 1830–1870."
         History of Education Quarterly 14 (Spring 1974): 13–30.

Burkett, H. Clark. "Jefferson College, the Freedmen's Bureau, and Union
         Occupation." *Journal of Mississippi History* 66 (Summer 2004): 201–9.

Burstyn, Joan N. "Catharine Beecher and the Education of American Women."
         New England Quarterly 47 (September 1974): 386–403.

Burton, Orville Vernon. "The Effects of the Civil War and Reconstruction on the
         Coming of Age of Southern Males, Edgefield County, South Carolina." In *The
         Web of Southern Social Relations: Women, Family, and Education*, edited by
         Walter J. Fraser Jr., R. Frank Saunders Jr., and Jon L. Wakelyn, 205–24.
         Athens: University of Georgia Press, 1985.

Butchart, Ronald E. "Caroline F. Putnam." In *Women Educators in the United
         States, 1820–1993: A Bio-Bibliographical Sourcebook*, edited by Maxine Seller,
         389–96. Westport, Conn.: Greenwood Press, 1994.

———. "Edmonia G. and Caroline V. Highgate: Black Teachers, Freed Slaves, and
         the Betrayal of Black Hearts." In *Portraits of African American Life Since 1865*,
         The Human Tradition in America, No. 16, edited by Nina Mjagkij, 1–13.
         Wilmington, Del.: Scholarly Resources, 2003.

Bibliography

——. "John C. Zachos." In *American National Biography*, edited by John A. Garraty, vol. 24, 209–10. New York: Oxford University Press, 1998.

——. "Laura Towne and Ellen Murray: Northern Expatriates and the Foundations of Black Education in South Carolina, 1862–1908." In *Women of South Carolina: Their Lives and Times*, edited by Marjorie Spruill, Valinda Littlefield, and Joan Johnson. Athens: University of Georgia Press, forthcoming.

——. "Lucelia E. Williams." In *American National Biography*, edited by John A. Garraty, vol. 23, 486. New York: Oxford University Press, 1998.

——. "Martha Schofield." In *American National Biography*, edited by John A. Garraty, vol. 19, 416–19. New York: Oxford University Press, 1998.

——. "Mission Matters: Mount Holyoke, Oberlin, and the Schooling of Southern Blacks, 1861–1917." *History of Education Quarterly* 42 (Spring 2002): 1–17.

——. " 'Outthinking and Outflanking the Owners of the World': An Historiography of the African American Struggle for Education." *History of Education Quarterly* 28 (Fall 1988): 333–66.

——. "Perspectives on Gender, Race, Calling, and Commitment in Nineteenth-Century America: A Collective Biography of the Teachers of the Freedpeople, 1862–1875." *Vitae Scholastica* 13 (Spring 1994): 15–32.

——. "Punishments, Penalties, Prizes, and Procedures: A History of Discipline in U.S. Schools." In *Classroom Discipline in American Schools: Problems and Possibilities for Democratic Education*, edited by Ronald E. Butchart and Barbara McEwan, 19–49. Albany: State University of New York Press, 1998.

——. "Recruits to the 'Army of Civilization': Gender, Race, Class, and the Freedmen's Teachers, 1862–1875." *Journal of Education* 172, no. 3 (1990): 76–87.

——. "Remapping Racial Boundaries: Teachers as Border Police and Boundary Transgressors in Post-Emancipation Black Education, USA, 1861–1876." *Paedagogica Historica* 43, no. 1 (February 2007): 61–78.

——. "Schooling for a Freed People: The Education of Adult Freedmen, 1861–1871." In *Black Adult Education in the United States: An Historical Overview*, edited by Leo McGee and Harvey Neufeldt, 45–58. Westport, Conn.: Greenwood Press, 1990.

——. " 'We Best Can Instruct Our Own People': New York African Americans in the Freedmen's Schools, 1861–1875." *Afro-Americans in New York Life and History* 12 (January 1988): 27–49.

Butchart, Ronald E., and Amy F. Rolleri. "Iowa Teachers Among the Freedpeople of the South, 1862–1875." *Annals of Iowa* 62 (Winter 2003): 1–29.

——. "Secondary Education and Emancipation: Secondary Schools for Freed Slaves in the American South, 1862–1875." *Paedagogica Historica* 40 (April 2004): 157–81.

Carroll, J. C. "The Beginnings of Public Education for Negroes in Indiana." *Journal of Negro History* 8 (October 1939): 649–58.

Chambers, Monserrat. "Annie Heacock and the Port Royal Experiment." *Journal of the West Virginia Historical Association* 12, no. 2 (1988): 26–58.

Christensen, Lawrence O. "Black Education in Civil War St. Louis." *Missouri Historical Review* 95 (April 2001): 302–16.

284   ——. "J. Milton Turner: An Appraisal." *Missouri Historical Review* 70 (October
        1975): 1–19.

——. "Schools for Blacks: J. Milton Turner in Reconstruction Missouri." *Missouri
    Historical Review* 76 (1982): 121–35.

Cimbala, Paul A. "A Black Colony in Dougherty County: The Freedmen's Bureau
    and the Failure of Reconstruction in Southwest Georgia." *Journal of Southwest
    Georgia History* 4 (Fall 1986): 72–89.

——. "Making Good Yankees: The Freedmen's Bureau and Education in
    Reconstruction Georgia, 1865–1870." *Atlanta Historical Journal* 29 (1985): 5–
    18.

——. "On the Front Line of Freedom: Freedmen's Bureau Officers and Agents in
    Reconstruction Georgia." *Georgia Historical Quarterly* 76 (Fall 1992): 577–611.

Clower, George W., ed. "Some Sidelights on Education in Georgia in the 1860s."
    Georgia Historical Quarterly 37 (1953): 249–55.

Cobb, Michael D., and Jeffery A. Jenkins. "Race and the Representation of Blacks'
    Interests During Reconstruction." *Political Research Quarterly* 54 (March
    2001): 181–204.

Cohen, William. "Black Immobility and Free Labor: The Freedmen's Bureau and
    the Relocation of Black Labor, 1865–1868." *Civil War History* 30 (September
    1984): 221–34.

Cohen-Lack, Nancy. "A Struggle for Sovereignty: National Consolidation,
    Emancipation, and Free Labor in Texas, 1865." *Journal of Southern History* 58
    (February 1992): 57–98.

Coleman, Michael. "Not Race, but Grace: Presbyterian Missionaries and
    American Indians." *Journal of American History* 67 (June 1980): 41–60.

Contee, Clarence G. "Macon B. Allen: 'First' Black in the Legal Profession." *Crisis*
    83 (February 1976): 67–69.

Cooper, Afua. "The Search for Mary Bibb, Black Woman Teacher in Nineteenth-
    Century Canada West." *Ontario History* 83 (March 1991): 39–54.

Cooper, Arnie. "A Stony Road: Black Education in Iowa, 1838–1860." *Annals of
    Iowa* 48 (Winter/Spring 1986): 113–34.

Cornelius, Janet. " 'We Slipped and Learned to Read': Slave Accounts of the
    Literacy Process, 1830–1865." *Phylon* 44 (September 1983): 171–86.

Cornish, Dudley Taylor. "The Union Army as a School for Negroes." *Journal of
    Negro History* 37 (October 1952): 368–82.

Crouch, Barry A. "Self-Determination and Local Black Leaders in Texas." *Phylon*
    39 (December 1978): 344–55.

Crumpler, Carolyn Weatherford. "The Role of Women in Baptist Missions."
    Baptist History and Heritage 27 (July 1992): 25–33.

Culpepper, Linda Parramore. "Black Charlestonians in the Mountains: African
    American Community Building in Post–Civil War Flat Rock, North Carolina."
    Journal of Appalachian Studies 8 (Fall 2002): 362–81.

Currie-McDaniel, Ruth. "Northern Women in the South, 1860–1880." *Georgia
    Historical Quarterly* 76 (Summer 1992): 284–312.

——. "The Wives of the Carpetbaggers." In *Race, Class, and Politics in Southern*

History: Essays in Honor of Robert F. Durden, edited by Jeffrey J. Crow, Paul D. Escott, and Charles L. Flynn, Jr., 35–78. Baton Rouge: Louisiana State University Press, 1989.

Dalton, Karen C. Chambers. " 'The Alphabet is an Abolitionist': Literacy and African Americans in the Emancipation Era." *Massachusetts Review* 32 (Winter 1991–92): 545–80.

Daniel, W. Harrison. "Virginia Baptists and the Negro, 1865–1902." *Virginia Magazine of History and Biography* 76 (1968): 340–63.

Davis, David Brion. "Reflections on Abolitionism and Ideological Hegemony." *American Historical Review* 92 (October 1987): 797–812.

Devens, Carol. " 'If We Get the Girls, We Get the Race': Missionary Education of Native American Girls." *Journal of World History* 3 (Fall 1992): 219–38.

Dews, Margery P. "F. H. Henderson and Howard Normal School." *Georgia Historical Quarterly* 63 (Summer 1979): 252–63.

Dilliard, Irving. "James Milton Turner, a Little Known Benefactor of His People." *Journal of Negro History* 19 (October 1934): 372–411.

Downs, Jim, Jr. "Uplift, Violence, and Service: The Experience of Black Women Teachers in the South During Reconstruction." *Southern History* 24 (Spring 2003): 29–39.

Drago, Edmund L. "Militancy and Black Women in Reconstruction Georgia." *Journal of American Culture* 1 (Winter 1978): 838–44.

Drake, Richard B. "Freedmen's Aid Societies and Sectional Compromise." *Journal of Southern History* 29 (May 1963): 175–86.

Durrill, Wayne K. "Political Legitimacy and Local Courts: 'Politicks at Such a Rage' in a Southern Community During Reconstruction." *Journal of Southern History* 70 (August 2004): 577–602.

Elliott, Mark. "Race, Color Blindness, and the Democratic Public: Albion W. Tourgée's Radical Principles in *Plessy v. Ferguson*." *Journal of Southern History* 67 (May 2001): 287–330.

Finkelstein, Barbara. "Pedagogy as Intrusion: Teaching Values in Popular Primary Schools in Nineteenth-Century America." *History of Childhood Quarterly* 2 (Winter 1975): 349–75.

Fitts, Deborah. "Una and the Lion: The Feminization of District School Teaching and Its Effects on the Roles of Students and Teachers in Nineteenth-Century Massachusetts." In *Regulated Children / Liberated Children: Education in Psychohistorical Perspective*, edited by Barbara Finklestein, 140–57. New York: Psychohistory Books, 1979.

Fitzgerald, Michael W. "Emancipation and Its Urban Consequences: Freedom Comes to Mobil." *Gulf Southern Historical Review* 18 (Fall 2002): 31–46.

———. "Radical Republicanism and the White Yeomanry During Alabama Reconstruction, 1865–1868." *Journal of Southern History* 54 (November 1988): 565–96.

Fleming, Cynthia Griggs. "The Effect of Higher Education on Black Tennesseans After the Civil War." *Phylon* 44, no. 3 (1983): 209–16.

———. "The Plight of Black Educators in Postwar Tennessee, 1865–1920." *Journal of Negro History* 64 (Fall 1979): 355–64.

Flexnor, Eleanor. "Maria W. Stewart." In vol. 3 of *Notable American Women, 1607–1950: A Biographical Dictionary*, 377–78 (Cambridge, Mass.: Belknap Press, 1971).

Foner, Philip S., ed. "Address of Frederick Douglass at the Inauguration of Douglass Institute, Baltimore, October 1, 1865." *Journal of Negro History* 54 (April 1969): 174–83.

Ford, Lacy K. "Rednecks and Merchants: Economic Development and Social Tensions in the South Carolina Upcountry, 1865–1900." *Journal of American History* 71 (September 1984): 294–318.

Foster, Sarah Whitmer, and John T. Foster Jr. "Chloe Merrick Reed: Freedom's First Lady." *Florida Historical Quarterly* 71 (January 1993): 279–99.

Fuke, Richard Paul. "The Baltimore Association for the Moral and Educational Improvement of the Colored People, 1864–1870." *Maryland Historical Magazine* 66 (Winter 1971): 369–404.

Gardner, Bettye. "Ante-Bellum Black Education in Baltimore." *Maryland Historical Magazine* 71, no. 3 (Fall 1976): 360–66.

Gatewood, Willard B., Jr. "John Francis Cook, Antebellum Black Presbyterian." *American Presbyterian* 67 (Fall 1989): 221–29.

——. " 'The Remarkable Misses Rollin': Black Women in Reconstruction South Carolina." *South Carolina Historical Magazine* 92 (July 1991): 172–88.

Glenn, Myra C. "School Discipline and Punishment in Antebellum America." *Journal of the Early Republic* (Winter 1981): 395–408.

Goldhaber, Michael. "A Mission Unfulfilled: Freedmen's Education in North Carolina, 1865–1870." *Journal of Negro History* 77 (Autumn 1992): 199–210.

Gordon, Vivian Verdell. "A History of Storer College, Harpers Ferry, West Virginia." *Journal of Negro Education* 30 (Fall 1961): 445–49.

Gravely, William B. "The Social, Political and Religious Significance of the Formation of the Colored Methodist Episcopal Church (1870)." *Methodist History* 18, no. 1 (1979): 3–25.

Green, Nancy. "Female Education and School Competition: 1820–1850." *History of Education Quarterly* 18 (Summer 1978): 129–42.

Grundman, Adolph H. "Northern Baptists and the Founding of Virginia Union University: The Perils of Paternalism." *Journal of Negro History* 63, no. 1 (1978): 26–41.

Halstead, Jacqueline J. "The Delaware Association for the Moral Improvement and Education of the Colored People: 'Practical Christianity.' " *Delaware History* 15 (1972): 19–40.

Hamand, Wendy F. "The Women's National Loyal League: Feminist Abolitionists and the Civil War." *Civil War History* 35 (March 1989): 39–58.

Hamilton, David. "Adam Smith and the Moral Economy of the Classroom System." *Journal of Curriculum Studies* 12 (1980): 281–98.

Hamilton, J. G. deRoulhac. "The Freedmen's Bureau in North Carolina." *South Atlantic Quarterly* 8 (1909): 53–67, 154–63.

Hamilton, Kenneth M. "White Wealth and Black Repression in Harrison County, Texas: 1865–1868." *Journal of Negro History* 84 (Fall 1999): 340–59.

Hargis, Peggy G. "For the Love of Place: Paternalism and Patronage in the Georgia Lowcountry, 1865–1898." *Journal of Southern History* 70, no. 4 (November 2004): 825–64.

Harlan, Louis R. "Desegregation in New Orleans Public Schools During Reconstruction." *American Historical Review* 67 (April 1962): 663–75.

Harris, Carl V. "Stability and Change in Discrimination Against Black Public Schools: Birmingham, Alabama, 1871–1931." *Journal of Southern History* 51 (August 1975): 375–416.

Harris, Theodore H. H. "Creating Windows of Opportunity: Isaac E. Black and the African American Experience in Kentucky, 1848–1914." *Register of the Kentucky Historical Society* 98 (Spring 2000): 155–77.

Harris, William C. "James Lynch: Black Leader in Southern Reconstruction." *Historian* 34 (November 1971): 40–61.

Harrison, Robert. "Welfare and Employment Policies of the Freedmen's Bureau in the District of Columbia." *Journal of Southern History* 72 (February 2006): 75–110.

Hawkins, Susan. "The African American Experience at Forts Henry, Heiman, and Donelson, 1862–1867." *Tennessee Historical Quarterly* 61 (Winter 2002): 222–41.

Haymes, Stephen Nathan. " 'Us Ain't Hogs, Us Is Human Flesh': Slave Pedagogy and the Problems of Ontology in African American Slave Culture." *Educational Studies* 32, no. 2 (Summer 2001): 129–57.

Heckman, Oliver S. "Pennsylvania Quakers in Southern Reconstruction." *Pennsylvania History* 13 (October 1946): 248–64.

———. "Presbyterian Church in the United States of America in Southern Reconstruction, 1860–1880." *North Carolina Historical Review* 20 (July 1943): 219–37.

Henle, Ellen, and Marlene Merrill. "Antebellum Black Coeds at Oberlin College." *Women's Studies Newsletter* 7 (Spring 1979): 8–11.

Herbst, Jurgen. "Teacher Preparation in the Nineteenth Century: Institutions and Purposes." In *American Teachers: Histories of a Profession at Work*, edited by Donald Warren, 213–56. New York: Macmillan Publishing, 1989.

Hickey, Damon D. "Pioneers of the New South: The Baltimore Association and North Carolina Friends in Reconstruction." *Quaker History* 74, no. 1 (1985): 1–17.

Hinshaw, Seth B. "The Miracle of Isham Cox: Leader among Friends in the Civil War Era." *Southern Friend* 17 (Spring 1995): 47–63.

Hoffert, Sylvia D. "Yankee Schoolmarms and the Domestication of the South." *Southern Studies* 24 (Summer 1985): 188–201.

Hogan, David. "Examinations, Merit, and Morals: The Market Revolution and Disciplinary Power in Philadelphia's Public Schools, 1838–1868." *Historical Studies in Education* 4, no. 1 (1992): 31–78.

———. "From Contest Mobility to Stratified Credentialing: Merit and Graded Schooling in Philadelphia, 1836–1920." *History of Education Review* 16 (1987): 21–42.

———. "The Market Revolution and Disciplinary Power: Joseph Lancaster and the Psychology of the Early Classroom System." *History of Education Quarterly* 29 (Fall 1989): 381–417.

———. "Modes of Discipline: Affective Individualism and Pedagogical Reform in New England, 1820–1850." *American Journal of Education* 99 (November 1990): 1–56.

———. "The Organization of Schooling and Organizational Theory: The Classroom System in Public Education in Philadelphia, 1818–1918." In *Research in Sociology of Education and Socialization: Historical Approaches*, edited by Ronald Corwin, 66–93. Greenwich, Conn.: JAI, 1989.

Holland, Antonio F., and Gary R. Kremer, eds. "Some Aspects of Black Education in Reconstruction Missouri: An Address by Richard B. Foster." *Missouri Historical Review* 92, no. 4 (July 1998): 407–20.

Holliday, Joseph E. "Freedmen's Aid Societies in Cincinnati, 1862–1870." *Bulletin of the Cincinnati Historical Society* 22 (July 1964): 169–85.

Hollingsworth, R. R. "Education and Reconstruction in Georgia." *Georgia Historical Quarterly* 19 (June 1935): 112–33.

Hornsby, Alton, Jr. "The Freedmen's Bureau Schools in Texas, 1865–1870." *Southwestern Historical Quarterly* 76 (April 1973): 397–417.

Horst, Samuel L. "A Life of Unfailing Toil: Jacob Eschbach Yoder." *Virginia Cavalcade* 46 (Summer 1996): 24–33.

Horton, James Oliver. "Black Education at Oberlin College: A Controversial Commitment." *Journal of Negro Education* 54 (Fall 1985): 477–99.

Hucles, Michael. "Many Voices, Similar Concerns: Traditional Methods of African-American Political Activity in Norfolk, 1865–75." *Virginia Magazine of History and Biography* 100 (October 1992): 543–66.

Huddle, Mark Andrew. "To Educate a Race: The Making of the First State Colored Normal School, Fayetteville, North Carolina, 1865–1877." *North Carolina Historical Review* 74 (April 1997): 135–60.

Huston, James L. "The Experiential Basis of the Northern Antislavery Impulse." *Journal of Southern History* 56 (November 1990): 609–40.

Jackson, Luther P. "The Educational Efforts of the Freedmen's Bureau and the Freedmen's Aid Societies in South Carolina, 1862–1872." *Journal of Negro History* 8 (January 1923): 1–40.

———. "The Origins of Hampton Institute." *Journal of Negro History* 10 (April 1925): 131–49.

Jaquette, Henrietta Stratton. "Friends' Association of Philadelphia for the Aid and Elevation of the Freedmen." *Bulletin of the Friends Historical Association* 46 (Fall 1957): 67–83.

Johnson, Howard Palmer. "New Orleans Under General Butler." *Louisiana Historical Quarterly* 24 (April 1941): 434–536.

Johnson, Whittington B. "A Black Teacher and Her School in Reconstruction Darien: The Correspondence of Hettie Sabattie and J. Murray Hoag, 1868–1869." *Georgia Historical Quarterly* 75 (Spring 1991): 90–105.

———. "Free African-American Women in Savannah, 1800–1860: Affluence and

Autonomy Amid Adversity." *Georgia Historical Quarterly* 76 (Summer 1992): 260–83.

Johnson, William R. " 'Chanting Choristers': Simultaneous Recitation in Baltimore's Nineteenth-Century Primary Schools." *History of Education Quarterly* 34 (Spring 1994): 1–23.

Jones, Jacqueline. "Encounters, Likely and Unlikely, Between Black and Poor White Women in the Rural South, 1865–1940." *Georgia Historical Quarterly* 76 (Summer 1992): 333–53.

———. "Women Who Were More than Men: Sex and Status in Freedmen's Teaching." *History of Education Quarterly* 19 (1979): 47–59.

Jones, Maxine D. "The American Missionary Association and the Beaufort, North Carolina School Controversy, 1866–67." *Phylon* 48 (Summer 1987): 103–11.

———. "Edwin Chalmers Silsby and the Talladega College." *Alabama Review* 41 (October 1988): 271–88.

———. " 'They Are My People': Black American Missionary Association Teachers in North Carolina During the Civil War and Reconstruction." *Negro Educational Review* 36 (April 1985): 78–89.

———. " 'They Too Are Jesus' Poor': The American Missionary Association and the White Community in North Carolina." *Southern Studies* 23 (Winter 1984): 386–96.

Katz, Michael B. "The Emergence of Bureaucracy in Urban Education: The Boston Case, 1850–1884 [in Two Parts]." *History of Education Quarterly* 8 (1968): 155–88, 318–47.

———. "The 'New Departure' in Quincy, 1873–1881: The Nature of Nineteenth-Century Educational Reform." *New England Quarterly* 40 (March 1967): 3–30.

Kaufman, Polly Welts. "A Wider Field of Usefulness: Pioneer Women Teachers in the West, 1848–1854." *Journal of the West* 21 (April 1982): 16–25.

Kearl, J. R., Clayne L. Pope, and Larry T. Wimmer. "Household Wealth in a Settlement Economy: Utah, 1850–1870." *Journal of Economic History* 40 (September 1980): 471–96.

Kelly, Alfred H. "The Congressional Controversy Over School Desegregation, 1867–1875." *American Historical Review* 64 (April 1959): 537–63.

Kennedy, Thomas C. "Another Kind of Emigrant: Quakers in the Arkansas Delta, 1864–1925." *Arkansas Historical Quarterly* 55 (Summer 1996): 199–220.

———. "The Rise and Decline of a Black Monthly Meeting: Southland, Arkansas, 1864–1925." *Arkansas Historical Quarterly* 50 (Summer 1991): 115–39.

———. "Southland College: The Society of Friends and Black Education in Arkansas." *Southern Friend* 7 (Spring 1985): 39–69.

Kenzer, Robert C. "The Black Businessman in the Postwar South: North Carolina, 1865–1880." *Business History Review* 63 (Spring 1989): 61–87.

Kerber, Linda K. "Separate Spheres, Female Worlds, Woman's Place: The Rhetoric of Women's History." *Journal of American History* 75 (June 1988): 9–39.

Kharif, Wali. "Black Reaction to Segregation and Discrimination in Post-Reconstruction Florida." *Florida Historical Quarterly* 64 (October 1985): 161–73.

290   Kimball, Philip Clyde. "Freedom's Harvest: Freedmen's Schools in Kentucky after the Civil War." *Filson Club Historical Quarterly* 54 (July 1980): 272–89.

King, Willis J. "The Negro Membership of the (Former) Methodist Church in the (New) United Methodist Church." *Methodist History* 7 (1969): 32–43.

Knight, Edgar W. "The 'Messianic' Invasion of the South after 1865." *School and Society* 57 (June 1943): 645–51.

——. "Reconstruction and Education in South Carolina." *South Atlantic Quarterly* 18 (1919): 350–64.

Kremer, Gary R. "Background to Apostasy: James Milton Turner and the Republican Party." *Missouri Historical Review* 71 (October 1976): 59–75.

——. "James Milton Turner and the Reconstruction Struggle for Black Education." *Gateway Heritage* 11 (Spring 1991): 66–75.

Lamon, Lester C. "Ignoring the Color Line: Maryville College, 1868–1901." In *The Adaptable South: Essays in Honor of George Brown Tindall*, edited by Elizabeth Jacoway, Dan T. Carter, Lester C. Lamon, and Robert C. McMath Jr., 64–89. Baton Rouge: Louisiana State University Press, 1991.

Lawson, Ellen N. "Sarah Woodson Early: 19th Century Black Nationalist 'Sister.'" *UMOJA* 2 (Summer 1981): 15–26.

Lawson, Ellen N., and Marlene Merrill. "The Antebellum 'Talented Thousandth': Black College Students at Oberlin Before the Civil War." *Journal of Negro Education* 52, no. 2 (Spring 1983): 142–55.

Lee, Arthur E. "The Decline of Radicalism and Its Effect on Public Education in Missouri." *Missouri Historical Review* 79 (October 1979): 1–20.

Lewis, Ronald L. "Reverend T. G. Steward and the Education of Blacks in Reconstruction Delaware." *Delaware History* 19 (Spring/Summer 1981): 156–78.

Lief, Julia Wiech. "A Woman of Purpose: Julia B. Nelson." *Minnesota History* 47 (Winter 1981): 302–14.

Lindley, Martha N. "Reminiscences." *Indiana History Bulletin* 1 (September 1924): 140–43.

Lockley, Timothy J. "Spheres of Influence: Working White and Black Women in Antebellum Savannah." In *Neither Lady Nor Slave: Working Women in the Old South*, edited by Susanna Delfino and Michele Gillespie, 102–20. Chapel Hill: University of North Carolina Press, 2002.

Logue, Larry M. "Union Veterans and Their Government: The Effects of Public Policies on Private Lives." *Journal of Interdisciplinary History* 22, no. 3 (1992): 411–34.

Lowe, W. A. "The Freedmen's Bureau and Education in Maryland." *Maryland Historical Magazine* 47 (1952): 29–39.

Lucas, Marion B. "Berea College in the 1870s and 1880s: Student Life at a Racially Integrated Kentucky College." *Register of the Kentucky Historical Society* 98 (Winter 2000): 1–22.

——. "Camp Nelson, Kentucky, During the Civil War: Cradle of Liberty or Refugee Death Camp." *Filson Club History Quarterly* 63 (October 1989): 431–52.

Mahan, Harold E. " 'We Feel to Bee a People': Historiographical Perspectives on Blacks in Emancipation and Reconstruction." *Maryland Historian* 16, no. 1 (1985): 41–56.

Mandle, Jay R. "The Re-Establishment of the Plantation Economy in the South, 1865–1910." *Review of Black Political Economy* 3 (1972–73): 68–88.

Marshall, Curtis. "Eleutherian College." *Indiana Historical Bulletin* 25 (November 1948): 201–2.

Martin, Sandy Dwayne. "The American Baptist Home Mission Society and Black Higher Education in the South, 1865–1920." *Foundations* 24 (1981): 310–27.

———. "Black Baptists, African Missions, and Racial Identity, 1800–1915: A Case Study of African American Religion." *Baptist History and Heritage* 35 (Summer/Fall 2000): 79–92.

Mattingly, Paul H. "Educational Revivals in Ante-Bellum New England." *History of Education Quarterly* 11 (February 1971): 39–71.

McAfee, Ward M. "Reconstruction Revisited: The Republican Public Education Crusade of the 1870s." *Civil War History* 42 (1966): 133–53.

McClintock, Megan J. "Civil War Pensions and the Reconstruction of Union Families." *Journal of American History* 83, no. 2 (September 1996): 456–80.

McCrorey, Henry Lawrence. "A Brief History of Johnson C. Smith University." *Quarterly Review of Higher Education Among Negroes* 1 (April 1933): 29–36.

McGehee, C. Stuart. "E. O. Tade, Freedmen's Education, and the Failure of Reconstruction in Tennessee." *Tennessee Historical Quarterly* 43, no. 4 (1984): 376–89.

McGerr, Michael. "Political Style and Women's Power, 1830–1930." *Journal of American History* 77 (December 1990): 864–85.

McKivigan, John R. "The American Baptist Free Mission Society: Abolitionist Reaction to the 1845 Baptist Schism." *Foundations* 21 (October 1978): 340–55.

McPherson, James M. "The New Puritanism: Values and Goals of Freedmen's Education in America." In vol. 2 of *The University in Society*, edited by Lawrence Stone, 611–42. Princeton, N.J.: Princeton University Press, 1974.

———. "Some Thoughts on the Civil War as a Second Revolution." *Hayes Historical Journal* 3, no. 5 (1982): 16–17.

———. "White Liberals and Black Power in Negro Education, 1865–1915." *American Historical Review* 75 (June 1970): 1357–86.

McShane, Alice. "Reading, Writing, and War: A Vermonter's Experience in the Port Royal Experiment, 1863–1871." *Vermont History* 67 (Summer/Fall 1999): 101–14.

Medford, Edna Greene. "Land and Labor: The Quest for Black Economic Independence on Virginia's Lower Peninsula, 1865–1880." *Virginia Magazine of History and Biography* 100 (October 1992): 567–82.

Melder, Keith. "Ipswich Female Seminary: An Educational Experiment." *Essex Institute Historical Collections* 120, no. 4 (October 1984): 223–40.

———. "Ladies Bountiful: Organized Women's Benevolence in Early Nineteenth Century America." *New York History* 48 (July 1967): 231–54.

Moorhead, James H. "Social Reform and the Divided Conscience of Antebellum Protestantism." *Church History* 48, no. 4 (1979): 416–30.

292   Morrow, Ralph E. "Northern Methodism in the South During Reconstruction." *Mississippi Valley Historical Review* 41 (September 1954): 197–218.

Morton, Richard L., ed. " 'Contrabands' and Quakers in the Virginia Peninsula, 1862–1869." *Virginia Magazine of History and Biography* 61 (October 1953): 564–82.

Mugleston, William F., ed. "The Freedmen's Bureau and Reconstruction in Virginia: The Diary of Marcus Sterling Hopkins, a Union Officer." *Virginia Magazine of History and Biography* 86 (January 1978): 45–102.

Naragon, Michael. "From Chattel to Citizens: The Transition from Slavery to Freedom in Richmond, Virginia." *Slavery & Abolition* 21 (August 2000): 93–116.

Nash, Margaret A. " 'Cultivating the Powers of *Human Beings*': Gendered Perspectives on Curricula and Pedagogy in Academies of the New Republic." *History of Education Quarterly* 41 (May 2001): 239–50.

Newberry, Fairar. "The Yankee Schoolmarm Who Captured Post-War Arkadelphia." *Arkansas Historical Quarterly* 17 (Autumn 1958): 265–71.

Nicholson, Elizabeth. "A Contraband Camp." *Indiana History Bulletin* 1 (September 1924): 131–40.

Ochiai, Akiko. "The Port Royal Experiment Revisited: Northern Visions of Reconstruction and the Land Question." *New England Quarterly* 74 (March 2001): 94–117.

Ogle, Natalie N. "Brother Against Brother: Baptists and Race in the Aftermath of the Civil War." *American Baptist Quarterly* 23 (June 2004): 137–54.

Oldfield, J. R. "A High and Honorable Calling: Black Lawyers in South Carolina, 1868–1915." *Journal of American Studies* 23 (December 1989): 395–406.

Pacheco, Josephine. "A Civil War Freedmen's School at Falls Church." *Northern Virginia Heritage* 3 (June 1981): 9–10.

Parker, Marjorie H. "Some Educational Activities of the Freedmen's Bureau." *Journal of Negro Education* 23 (Winter 1954): 9–21.

Parmelee, Julius H. "Freedmen's Aid Societies, 1861–1871." In *Negro Education: A Study of the Private and Higher Schools for Colored People in the U.S.*, edited by Thomas Jesse Jones. U.S. Department of the Interior, Bureau of Education Bulletin No. 3. Washington: GPO, 1917.

Paterson, Judith Hillman. "To Teach the Negro." *Alabama Heritage* 40 (Spring 1996): 6–17.

Pearce, Larry Wesley. "Enoch K. Miller and the Freedmen's Schools." *Arkansas Historical Quarterly* 31 (Winter 1977): 305–27.

Perkins, Linda M. "The Black Female American Missionary Association Teacher in the South, 1861–1870." In *Black Americans in North Carolina and the South*, edited by Jeffrey J. Crow and Flora J. Hatley, 122–36. Chapel Hill: University of North Carolina Press, 1984.

———. "The Education of Black Women in the Nineteenth Century." In *Women and Higher Education in American History: Essays from the Mount Holyoke College Sesquicentennial Symposia*, edited by John Mack Faragher and Florence Howe, 43–63. New York: W. W. Norton, 1988.

——. "The Impact of the 'Cult of True Womanhood' on the Education of Black Women." *Journal of Social Issues* 39 (1983): 17–28.

Phillips, Paul David. "Education of Blacks in Tennessee During Reconstruction, 1865–1870." *Tennessee Historical Quarterly* 46 (Summer 1987): 98–109.

Plank, David N., and Marcia E. Turner. "Contrasting Patterns in Black School Politics: Atlanta and Memphis, 1865–1985." *Journal of Negro Education* 60 (Spring 1991): 203–18.

Porter, Betty. "Negro Education in Louisiana." *Louisiana Historical Quarterly* 25 (July 1942): 778–821.

Porterfield, Amanda. "A Sister to Oneida: The Missionary Community at Mount Holyoke." *Communal Studies* 16 (1996): 1–13.

Preston, Emmett D., Jr. "The Development of Negro Education in the District of Columbia." *Journal of Negro Education* 9 (October 1940): 595–603.

Preston, Jo Anne. "Domestic Ideology, School Reformers, and Female Teachers: Schoolteaching Becomes Women's Work in Nineteenth-Century New England." *New England Quarterly* 66 (December 1993): 531–51.

Proctor, Samuel. "'Yankee Schoolmarms' in Post-War Florida." *Journal of Negro History* 44 (April 1959): 275–77.

Rabinowitz, Howard N. "Half a Loaf: The Shift from White to Black Teachers in the Negro Schools of the Urban South, 1865–1890." *Journal of Southern History* 40 (November 1974): 565–94.

Rachel, John R. "Gideonites and Freedmen: Adult Literacy Education at Port Royal, 1862–1863." *Journal of Negro History* 55, no. 4 (Autumn 1986): 453–69.

Rachleff, Peter J. "'Members in Good Standing': Richmond's Community of Former Slaves." *Virginia Cavalcade* 39 (Winter [Part 1]; Spring [Part 2] 1990): 130–43; 148–57.

Rankin, David. "The Impact of the Civil War on the Free Colored Community of New Orleans." *Perspectives in American History* 11 (1977–78): 379–416.

——. "The Origins of Black Leadership in New Orleans During Reconstruction." *Journal of Southern History* 40 (1974): 417–40.

Rapport, Sara. "The Freedmen's Bureau as a Legal Agent for Black Men and Women in Georgia: 1865–1868." *Georgia Historical Quarterly* 73 (Spring 1989): 26–53.

Reidy, Joseph P. "'Coming from the Shadow of the Past': The Transition from Slavery to Freedom at Freedmen's Village, 1863–1900." *Virginia Magazine of History and Biography* 95 (October 1987): 403–28.

Richardson, Fredrick. "American Baptists' Southern Mission." *Foundations* 18, no. 2 (1975): 136–45.

Richardson, Joe M. "The American Missionary Association and Blacks on the Gulf Coast During Reconstruction." *Gulf Coast Historical Review* 4 (Spring 1989): 152–61.

——. "Fisk University: The First Critical Years." *Tennessee Historical Quarterly* 29, no. 1 (1970): 24–41.

——. "Francis L. Cardozo: Black Educator During Reconstruction." *Journal of Negro Education* 48 (Winter 1979): 73–83.

294   ——. "The Freedmen's Bureau and Negro Education in Florida." *Journal of Negro Education* 31 (Fall 1962): 460–67.

——. "Jonathan C. Gibbs: Florida's Only Negro Cabinet Member." *Florida Historical Quarterly* 42 (April 1964): 363–68.

——. " 'Labor is Rest to Me Here in the Lord's Vineyard': Hardy Mobley, Black Missionary." *Southern Studies* 22 (Spring 1983): 5–20.

——. "To Help a Brother on: The First Decade of Talladega College." *Alabama Historical Quarterly* 37, no. 1 (1975): 19–37.

Richter, William L. " 'A Dear Little Job': Second Lieutenant Hiram F. Willis, Freedmen's Bureau Agent in Southwestern Arkansas, 1866–1868." *Arkansas Historical Quarterly* 50 (Summer 1991): 158–200.

——. " 'The Revolver Rules the Day!' Colonel DeWitt C. Brown and the Freedmen's Bureau in Paris, Texas, 1867–1868." *Southwestern Historical Quarterly* 93 (Winter 1989–90): 303–32.

Robarts, James R. "The Quest for a Science of Education in the Nineteenth Century." *History of Education Quarterly* 8 (Winter 1968): 431–46.

Robbins, Gerald. "Laura Towne: White Pioneer in Negro Education, 1862–1901." *Journal of Education* 143 (April 1961): 40–54.

——. "William F. Allen: Classical Scholar Among the Slaves." *History of Education Quarterly* 5 (December 1965): 211–23.

Rogers, George A., and R. Frank Saunders Jr. "Eliza Ann Ward: Teacher and Missionary to the Freedmen." *Bulletin of the Congregational Library* 31 (Fall 1979): 4–11.

Rothrock, Thomas. "Joseph Carter Corbin and Negro Education in the University of Arkansas." *Arkansas Historical Quarterly* 30 (Winter 1971): 277–314.

Rouse, Michael Francis. "A Study of the Development of Negro Education Under Catholic Auspices in Maryland and the District of Columbia." Edited by Florence E. Bamberger. *The Johns Hopkins University Studies in Education, No. 22.* Baltimore: Johns Hopkins Press, 1935.

Ryan, James Gilbert. "The Memphis Riots of 1866: Terror in a Black Community During Reconstruction." *Journal of Negro History* 62 (July 1977): 243–57.

Ryan, Mary P. "A Women's Awakening: Evangelical Religion and the Families of Utica, New York, 1800–1840." *American Quarterly* 30 (Winter 1978): 602–23.

St. Clair, Sadie Daniel. "Myrtilla Miner: Pioneer in Teacher Education for Negro Women." *Journal of Negro History* 34 (January 1949): 30–45.

Sansing, David G. "The Failure of Johnsonian Reconstruction in Mississippi, 1865–1866." *Journal of Mississippi History* 34, no. 4 (1972): 373–90.

Savage, W. Sherman. "Early Negro Education in the Pacific Coast States." *Journal of Negro Education* 15 (Spring 1946): 134–39.

——. "The Legal Provisions for Negro Schools in Missouri from 1865 to 1890." *Journal of Negro History* 16 (July 1931): 309–21.

Savitt, Todd L. "Straight University Medical Department: The Short Life of a Black Medical School in Reconstruction New Orleans." *Louisiana History* 41 (Spring 2000): 175–201.

Schulman, Gayle M. "The Gibbons Family: Freedmen." *Magazine of Albemarle County History* 55 (1997): 61–93.

Schweninger, Loren. "Antebellum Free Persons of Color in Postbellum Louisiana." *Louisiana History* 30 (Fall 1989): 345–64.

——. "Black-Owned Businesses in the South, 1790–1880." *Business History Review* 63 (Spring 1989): 22–60.

——. "Property Owning Free African-American Women in the South, 1800–1870." *Journal of Women's History* 1 (Winter 1990): 13–44.

Scott, Anne Firor. "The Ever Widening Circle: The Diffusion of Feminist Values from the Troy Female Seminary, 1822–1872." *History of Education Quarterly* 19 (Spring 1979): 3–25.

——. "Most Invisible of All: Black Women's Voluntary Associations." *Journal of Social History* 56 (February 1990): 3–22.

Sehat, David. "The Civilizing Mission of Booker T. Washington." *Journal of Southern History* 73 (May 2007): 323–62.

Seraile, William. "Theophilus G. Steward, Intellectual Chaplain, 25th U.S. Colored Infantry." *Nebraska History* 66, no. 3 (1985): 272–93.

Shmurak, Carole B., and Bonnie S. Handler. " 'Castle of Science': Mount Holyoke College and the Preparation of Women in Chemistry, 1837–1941." *History of Education Quarterly* 32 (Fall 1992): 315–42.

Skocpol, Theda. "America's First Social Security System: The Expansion of Benefits for Civil War Veterans." *Political Science Quarterly* 108 (Spring 1993): 85–116.

Small, Sandra E. "The Yankee Schoolmarm in Freedmen's Schools: An Analysis of Attitudes." *Journal of Southern History* 65 (August 1979): 381–402.

Smallwood, James. "Black Education in Reconstruction Texas: The Contributions of the Freedmen's Bureau and Benevolent Societies." *East Texas Historical Journal* 19 (Spring 1981): 17–40.

——. "G. T. Ruby: Galveston's Black Carpetbagger in Reconstruction Texas." *Houston Review* 5 (Winter 1983): 24–33.

Smedley, Katherine. "Martha Schofield and the Rights of Women." *South Carolina Historical Magazine* 85, no. 3 (1984): 195–210.

Smith-Rosenberg, Carroll. "The Female World of Love and Ritual: Relations Between Women in Nineteenth-Century America." *Signs* 1 (Autumn 1975): 1–29.

Soltow, Lee. "Economic Inequality in the United States in the Period from 1790 to 1860." *Journal of Economic History* 31 (December 1971): 822–39.

Sparks, Randy J. "The White People's Arms Are Longer Than Ours: Blacks, Education and the American Missionary Association in Reconstruction Mississippi." *Journal of Mississippi History* 54 (February 1992): 1–27.

Steckel, Richard H. "Poverty and Prosperity: A Longitudinal Study of Wealth Accumulation, 1850–1860." *Review of Economics and Statistics* 72 (May 1990): 275–85.

Stowell, Daniel W. "We Have Sinned and God Has Smitten Us: John H. Caldwell and the Religious Meaning of Confederate Defeat." *Georgia Historical Quarterly* 78 (Summer 1994): 1–38.

——. " 'The Negroes Cannot Navigate Alone': Religious Scalawags and the Biracial Methodist Episcopal Church in Georgia, 1866–1876." In *Georgia in Black and White*, edited by John C. Inscoe, 65–90. Athens: University of Georgia Press, 1994.

Strober, Myra H., and Audri Gordon Lanford. "The Feminization of Public School Teaching: Cross-Sectional Analysis, 1850–1880." *Signs* 11 (Winter 1986): 212–35.

Sweet, Leonard I. "The Female Seminary Movement and Woman's Mission in Antebellum America." *Church History* 54 (March 1985): 41–55.

Swint, Henry L., ed. "Reports from Educational Agents of the Freedmen's Bureau." *Tennessee Historical Quarterly* 1 (1942): 65–71.

Taylor, A. A. "The Negro in the Reconstruction of Virginia." *Journal of Negro History* 11 (April 1926): 379–94.

Taylor, Kay Ann. "Mary S. Peake and Charlotte F. Forten: Black Teachers During the Civil War and Reconstruction." *Journal of Negro Education* 74 (Spring 2005): 124–37.

Terrell, Mary Church. "History of the High School for Negroes in Washington." *Journal of Negro History* 2 (July 1917): 256–66.

TeSelle, Eugene. "The Nashville Institute and Roger Williams University: Benevolence, Paternalism, and Black Consciousness, 1867–1910." *Tennessee Historical Quarterly* 41, no. 4 (1982): 360–79.

Thompkins, Robert E. "Presbyterian Religious Education Among Negroes, 1864–1891." *Journal of the Presbyterian Historical Society* 29 (September 1951): 145–71.

Thompson, Ernest Trice. "Black Presbyterians, Education, and Evangelism After the Civil War." *Journal of Presbyterian History* 76 (Spring 1998): 55–70.

Thornbery, Jerry. "Northerners and the Atlanta Freedmen, 1865–69." *Prologue* 6 (Winter 1974): 236–51.

Thurber, Evangeline. "The 1890 Census Records of the Veterans of the Union Army." *National Genealogical Society Quarterly* 34 (March 1946): 7–9.

Towne, Laura M. "Pioneer Work on the Sea Islands." *Southern Workman* 30 (July 1901): 396–401.

Trotman, C. James. "Matthew Anderson: Black Pastor, Churchman, and Social Reformer." *American Presbyterian* 66, no. 1 (1988): 11–21.

Tyack, David, and Robert Lowe. "The Constitutional Moment: Reconstruction and Black Education in the South." *American Journal of Education* 94 (February 1986): 237–56.

Vance, Joseph C. "Freedmen's Schools in Albemarle County During Reconstruction." *Virginia Magazine of History and Biography* 61 (October 1953): 430–38.

Vaughn, William P. "Partners in Segregation: Barnas Sears and the Peabody Fund." *Civil War History* 10 (1964): 260–74.

——. "Separate and Unequal: The Civil Rights Act of 1875 and the Defeat of the

School Integration Clause." *Southwestern Social Science Quarterly* 48 (September 1967): 146–54.

———. " 'South Carolina University—1876' of Fisk Parsons Brewer." *South Carolina Historical Magazine* 76, no. 4 (1975): 225–31.

Vickers, Gregory. "Models of Womanhood and the Early Women's Missionary Union." *Baptist History and Heritage* 24 (January 1989): 41–53.

Vinovskis, Maris A. "Have Social Historians Lost the Civil War? Some Preliminary Demographic Speculations." *Journal of American History* 76, no. 1 (June 1989): 34–58.

Vinovskis, Maris A., and Richard M. Bernard. "Beyond Catharine Beecher: Female Education in the Antebellum Period." *Signs* 3 (Summer 1978): 856–69.

Washington, Delo E. "Education of Freedmen and the Role of Self-Help in a Sea Island Setting, 1862–1982." *Agricultural History* 58 (July 1984): 442–55.

Weisenfeld, Judith. " 'Who is Sufficient for These Things?' Sara G. Stanley and the American Missionary Association, 1864–1868." *Church History* 60 (December 1991): 493–507.

Wells, Jeremy. "Up from Savagery." *Southern Quarterly* 42 (Fall 2003): 53–74.

Welter, Barbara. "The Cult of True Womanhood, 1830–1860." *American Quarterly* 18 (Summer 1966): 422–61.

———. "The Feminization of American Religion." In *Clio's Consciousness Raised: New Perspectives on the History of Women*, edited by Mary S. Hartman and Lois Banner, 137–57. New York: Harper Torchbooks, 1974.

———. "She Hath Done What She Could: Protestant Women's Missionary Careers in Nineteenth-Century America." *American Quarterly* 30 (Winter 1978): 624–38.

Wertsch, Douglas. "Iowa's Daughters: The First Thirty Years of the Girls Reform School of Iowa, 1869–1899." *Annals of Iowa* 49 (Summer/Fall 1987): 77–100.

Wesley, Edgar B. "Forty Acres and a Mule and a Speller." *History of Education Journal* 8 (Summer 1957): 113–27.

West, Earle H. "The Harris Brothers: Black Northern Teachers in the Reconstruction South." *Journal of Negro Education* 48 (Spring 1979): 126–38.

———. "The Peabody Education Fund and Negro Education, 1867–1880." *History of Education Quarterly* 6 (Summer 1966): 3–21.

White, Kenneth B. "The Alabama Freedmen's Bureau and Black Education: The Myth of Opportunity." *Alabama Review* 34 (1981): 107–24.

Whitener, Daniel J. "The Republican Party and Public Education in North Carolina, 1867–1900." *North Carolina Historical Review* 37 (July 1960): 382–96.

Williams, Heather Andrea. " 'Clothing Themselves in Intelligence': The Freedpeople, Schooling, and Northern Teachers, 1861–1871." *Journal of African American History* 87 (Fall 2002): 372–89.

———. " 'Commenced to Think Like a Man': Literacy and Manhood in African American Civil War Regiments." In *Southern Manhood: Perspectives on Masculinity in the Old South*, edited by Craig Thompson Friend and Lorri Glover, 196–219. Athens: University of Georgia Press, 2004.

298   Williams, Henry Sullivan. "The Development of the Negro Public School System in Missouri." *Journal of Negro History* 5 (April 1920): 137–65.

Wilson, Keith. "Education as a Vehicle of Racial Control: Major General N. P. Banks in Louisiana, 1863–1864." *Journal of Negro Education* 50 (Spring 1981): 156–70.

Winkle, Kenneth J. "The U.S. Census as a Source in Political History." *Social Science History* 15 (Winter 1991): 565–77.

Wolf, Kurt J. "Laura M. Towne and the Freed People of South Carolina, 1862–1901." *South Carolina Historical Magazine* 98 (October 1997): 375–405.

Woodman, Harold D. "Post–Civil War Southern Agriculture and the Law." *Agricultural History* 53 (January 1979): 319–37.

Woods, Beverly Babin. "Walter H. Williams, Sr., Educator: Bureau of Refugees, Freedmen and Abandoned Land, Lafayette and Vermilion Parishes, Louisiana." *Journal of the Afro-American Historical and Genealogical Society* 6, no. 2 (1997): 86–96.

Woods, Randall B. "George T. Ruby: A Black Militant in the White Business Community." *Red River Valley Historical Review* 1 (Autumn 1974): 269–80.

Woody, R. H. "Jonathan Jasper Wright, Associate Justice of the Supreme Court of South Carolina, 1870–77." *Journal of Negro History* 18 (April 1933): 114–31.

Wyatt-Brown, Bertram. "Black Schooling during Reconstruction." In *The Web of Southern Social Relations: Women, Family, and Education*, edited by Walter J. Fraser Jr., R. Frank Saunders Jr., and Jon L. Wakelyn, 146–65. Athens: University of Georgia Press, 1985.

Yellin, Jean Fagan, "Written by Herself: Harriet Jacobs' Slave Narrative." *American Literature* 53 (November 1981): 479–86.

Yohn, Susan M. "An Education in the Validity of Pluralism: The Meeting Between Presbyterian Mission Teachers and Hispanic Catholics in New Mexico, 1870–1912." *History of Education Quarterly* 31 (Fall 1991): 343–64.

Zipf, Karin L. " 'Among These American Heathens': Congregationalist Missionaries and African American Evangelicals During Reconstruction, 1865–1878." *North Carolina Historical Review* 74, no. 2 (April 1997): 111–34.

———. " 'The whites Shall Rule the Land or Die': Gender, Race, and Class in North Carolina Reconstruction Politics." *Journal of Southern History* 55 (August 1999): 499–534.

Dissertations and Theses

Addo, Linda D. "A Historical Analysis of the Impact of Selected Teachers on Education for Blacks in Coastal South Carolina, 1862–1970." Ph.D. diss., University of North Carolina at Greensboro, 1988.

Anscombe, Francis Charles. "The Contribution of the Quakers to the Reconstruction of the Southern States." Ph.D. diss., University of North Carolina, 1926.

Asa, Robert Lynn. "The Theology and Methodology of Charles G. Finney as a Prototype for Modern Mass Revivalism." Ph.D. diss., Southern Baptist Theological Seminary, 1983.

Baker, Robert Andrew. "The American Baptist Home Mission Society and the South, 1832–1894." Ph.D. diss., Yale University, 1947.

Carson, David Melville. "A History of the Reformed Presbyterian Church in America to 1871." Ph.D. diss., University of Pennsylvania, 1964.

Cooper, Afua A. P. "Black Teachers in Canada West, 1850–1870: A History." Master's thesis, University of Toronto, 1991.

DeBoer, Clara Merritt. "The Role of Afro-Americans in the Origin and Work of the American Missionary Association, 1839–77." Ph.D. diss., Rutgers University, 1973.

Drakeman, Lisa Natale. "Seminary Sisters: Mount Holyoke's First Students, 1837–1849." Ph.D. diss., Princeton University, 1988.

Fitchet, E. Horace. "The Free Negro in Charleston, South Carolina." Ph.D. diss., University of Chicago, 1950.

Gregory, Clarence Kenneth. "The Education of Blacks in Maryland: An Historical Survey." Ph.D. diss., Teachers College, Columbia University, 1976.

Heckman, Oliver S. "Northern Church Penetration of the South, 1860–1880." Ph.D. diss., Duke University, 1939.

Herbig, Katherine Lydigsen. "Friends for Freedom: The Lives and Careers of Sallie Holley and Caroline Putnam." Ph.D. diss., Claremont Graduate School, 1977.

Johnson, Elliott McClintock. "The Influence of Blacks on the Development and Implementation of the Public Education System in South Carolina, 1863–1876." Ph.D. diss., American University, 1978.

Kimball, Philip Clyde. "Education for Negroes in Kentucky, 1865–1871: A Study in Political History, Institutional Development, and Race Relations." Master's thesis, University of North Carolina at Chapel Hill, 1969.

Littlefield, Valinda. " 'I Am Only One, But I Am One': Southern African-American Women School Teachers, 1884–1954." Ph.D. diss., University of Illinois at Urbana–Champaign, 2003.

Mansfield, Betty. "That Fateful Class: Black Teachers of Virginia's Freedmen, 1861–1882." Ph.D. diss., Catholic University of America, 1980.

Martin, Josephine Walker. "The Educational Efforts of the Major Freedmen's Aid Societies and the Freedmen's Bureau in South Carolina: 1862–1870." Ph.D. diss., University of South Carolina, 1971.

Moore, Birchill Richardson. "A History of the Negro Public Schools of Charleston, South Carolina, 1867–1942." Master's thesis, University of South Carolina, 1942.

Perry, Grace Naomi. "The Educational Work of the African Methodist Episcopal Church Prior to 1900." Master's thesis, Howard University, 1948.

Pennington, Campbell White. "Negro Labor and Education in Louisiana, 1862–1877." Master's thesis, University of Texas, 1949.

Powers, Bernard Edward, Jr. "Black Charleston: A Social History, 1822–1885." Ph.D. diss., Northwestern University, 1982.

Wilkins, Martha Huddleston. "Education for Freedom: The Noble Experiment of Sarah A. Dickey and the Mount Hermon Seminary." Ph.D. diss., University of Mississippi, 1985.

Bibliography

300   Williams, Melvin Roscoe. "Blacks in Washington D.C., 1860–1870." Ph.D. diss., Johns Hopkins University, 1975.

Wolfe, Allis. "Women Who Dared: Northern Teachers of the Southern Freedmen, 1862–1872." Ph.D. diss., City University of New York, 1982.

Wright, Stephanie. "Education and the Changing Social Identities of Black Southerners, 1865–1915." Ph.D. diss., Rutgers University, 2004.

Index

Index

Index

Index

Index

Index